Praise for House Selling For Dummies

"You won't find a better 'how-to-sell-your-home' book than this one. The authors have included practical knowledge you won't find anywhere else. . . . On my scale of one to 10, it rates a solid 10."

— Robert J. Bruss, syndicated real estate columnist

"Brown and Tyson . . . are back with a timely tome: *House Selling For Dummies*. . . . Packed with the proven punch of the Brown-Tyson combination . . . the book is destined to become a home seller's best friend."

— Broderick Perkins, *San Jose Mercury News*

"The authors cover every aspect of the home-selling process — from deciding whether you are financially able to sell, to assembling a real estate team and marketing your property, to selling it quickly for top dollar."

— Don DeBat, Crain News Service

"[Tyson and Brown] tackle the complex subject of selling a house with humor and practicality . . . the authors explain strategies that could generate or save readers thousands, perhaps even tens of thousands of dollars on the sale of their house."

— Inman News Features

"The best thing about this book [*House Selling For Dummies*] is that it doesn't recommend anything. Instead, it helps you in a far greater way. It helps you think through the relocation decision."

— Dr. David Demko, AgeVenture News

"House Selling For Dummies by Eric Tyson and Ray Brown is fun . . . and also filled with practical advice."

— Allen Norwood, *Charlotte Observer*

"Do's and Don'ts for Do-It-Yourself Home Sellers: Start by educating yourself. I recommend the book *House Selling For Dummies* by Eric Tyson and Ray Brown, which offers excellent advice on the entire process."

— Rick Wilking, Reuters News Service

"*Home Buying For Dummies* and *House Selling For Dummies*, both by Eric Tyson and Ray Brown, go into surprising depth on their topics without straying from their mission of explaining the processes simply. Perhaps the best thing is what the authors call their holistic approach. . . ."

— Maryann Haggerty, *Washington Post*

Praise for Eric Tyson and Ray Brown's best-selling Home Buying For Dummies

"This fun read for home buyers includes the essentials, laced with humor and practical advice. The new material on Internet resources updates this classic how-to-buy-a-home book. Of the many books on this topic, this is by far the best. . . ."

> — Robert J. Bruss, syndicated real estate columnist

". . . takes you step by step through the process . . . humorous insights that keep the pages turning. This is a reference you'll turn to time after time."

> — Judy Stark, *St. Petersburg Times*

". . . *Home Buying For Dummies* immediately earned a prominent spot on my reference bookshelf . . . takes a holistic approach to home buying."

> — Broderick Perkins, *San Jose Mercury News*

". . . *Home Buying For Dummies* provides a much-needed emotional stabilizer."

> — Judy Rose, Knight-Ridder News Service

"The humorous *Home Buying For Dummies* by Ray Brown and Eric Tyson is a favorite . . . because the editorial is so good. They check their facts very well. They set out to make you understand this subject and make it fun reading and informative."

> — Michelle Wong, *Minneapolis Star Tribune*

"The book *[Home Buying For Dummies]* is a primer on all the things to do and not to do when - buying a home."

> — Brian Banmiller, FOX-TV

". . . can help you buy a castle for the price of house. The authors present a balanced approach to buying a house."

> — *Times-Picayune,* New Orleans, LA

"A survival guide to buying . . . fun to read and very clearly written. . . . Whether taking over a foreclosure, determining not how much you can borrow but how much you can actually afford to spend, how to find a good broker, landing a lender . . . Tyson and Brown definitely help ease the trauma of the transaction. . . ."

> — Paula Lee Aldridge, *Homes and Real Estate Magazine*

Here's what critics have said about Eric Tyson and his previous national best-selling personal finance guides:

"*Personal Finance For Dummies* is the perfect book for people who feel guilty about inadequately managing their money but are intimidated by all of the publications out there. It's a painless way to learn how to take control. My college-aged daughters even enjoyed reading it!"

> — Karen Tofte, producer, National Public Radio's
> *Sound Money*

"Among my favorite financial guides are . . . Eric Tyson's *Personal Finance For Dummies.*"

> — Jonathan Clements, *The Wall Street Journal*

"Smart advice for dummies . . . skip the tomes . . . and buy *Personal Finance For Dummies,* which rewards your candor with advice and comfort."

> — Temma Ehrenfeld, *Newsweek*

"Eric Tyson is doing something important — namely, helping people at all income levels to take control of their financial futures. This book is a natural outgrowth of Tyson's vision that he has nurtured for years. Like Henry Ford, he wants to make something that was previously accessible only to the wealthy accessible to middle-income Americans."

> — James C. Collins, coauthor of the national bestseller *Built to Last;* Lecturer in Business, Stanford Graduate School of Business

"You don't have to be a novice to like *Mutual Funds For Dummies.* Despite the book's chatty, informal style, author Eric Tyson clearly has a mastery of his subject. He knows mutual funds, and he knows how to explain them in simple English."

> — Steven T. Goldberg, *Kiplinger's Personal Finance Magazine*

"*Personal Finance For Dummies* offers a valuable guide for common misconceptions and major pitfalls. It's a no-nonsense, straightforward, easy-to-read personal finance book. . . . With this book, you can easily learn enough about finances to start thinking for yourself."

> — Charles R. Schwab, Chairman and CEO, The Charles Schwab Corporation

"It can be overwhelming to keep up with the latest developments, which is why you might turn to the book *Mutual Funds For Dummies* by Eric Tyson. A light touch and the use of plenty of graphics help the pages fly by. This book is a primer for those who flinch when contemplating the 7,000 funds you can now buy."

> — Brian Banmiller, FOX-TV

"Best new personal finance book."

> — Michael Pellecchia, syndicated columnist

"Eric Tyson . . . seems the perfect writer for a *...For Dummies* book. He doesn't tell you what to do or consider doing without explaining the why's and how's — and the booby traps to avoid — in plain English. . . . It will lead you through the thickets of your own finances as painlessly as I can imagine."

> — Clarence Peterson, *Chicago Tribune*

"*Personal Finance For Dummies* is, by far, the best book I have read on financial planning. It is a simplified volume of information that provides tremendous insight and guidance into the world of investing and other money issues."

> — Althea Thompson, producer, PBS's *Nightly Business Report*

"This book provides easy-to-understand personal financial information and advice for those without great wealth or knowledge in this area. Practitioners like Eric Tyson, who care about the well-being of middle-income people, are rare in today's society."

> — Joel Hyatt, founder, Hyatt Legal Services, one of the nation's largest general-practice personal legal service firms

"*Personal Finance For Dummies* is a sane and useful guide that will be of benefit to anyone seeking a careful and prudent method of managing their financial world."

> — John Robbins, founder of EarthSave, author of *May All Be Fed*

More Bestselling For Dummies Titles by Eric Tyson

Investing For Dummies®

A *Wall Street Journal* bestseller, this book walks you through how to build wealth in stocks, real estate, and small business as well as other investments.

Personal Finance For Dummies®

Discover the best ways to establish and achieve your financial goals, reduce your spending and taxes, and make wise personal financial decisions. *Wall Street Journal* bestseller with more than 1 million copies sold in all editions and winner of the Benjamin Franklin best business book award.

Taxes For Dummies®

The complete, best-selling reference for completing your tax return and making tax-wise financial decisions year-round. Tyson coauthors this book with tax experts David Silverman and Margaret Munro.

Home Buying For Dummies®

America's #1 real estate book includes coverage of online resources in addition to sound financial advice from Eric Tyson and frontline real estate insights from industry veteran Ray Brown. Also available from America's best-selling real estate team of Tyson and Brown — *House Selling For Dummies* and *Mortgages For Dummies*.®

Real Estate Investing For Dummies®

Real estate is a proven wealth-building investment, but many people don't know how to go about making and managing rental property investments. Real estate and property management expert Robert Griswold and Eric Tyson cover the gamut of property investment options, strategies, and techniques.

Small Business For Dummies®

Take control of your future and make the leap from employee to entrepreneur with this enterprising guide. From drafting a business plan to managing costs, you'll profit from expert advice and real-world examples that cover every aspect of building your own business. Tyson coauthors this book with fellow entrepreneur Jim Schell.

House Selling

FOR

DUMMIES®

3RD EDITION

by Eric Tyson and Ray Brown

Authors of *Home Buying For Dummies*

BICENTENNIAL

1807

WILEY

2007

BICENTENNIAL

Wiley Publishing, Inc.

House Selling For Dummies,® 3rd Edition

Published by
Wiley Publishing, Inc.
111 River St.
Hoboken, NJ 07030-5774
www.wiley.com

Copyright © 2008 by Eric Tyson and Ray Brown

Published by Wiley Publishing, Inc., Indianapolis, Indiana

Published simultaneously in Canada

For general information on our other products and services, please contact our Customer Care Department within the U.S. at 877-762-2974, outside the U.S. at 317-572-3993, or fax 317-572-4002.

For technical support, please visit www.wiley.com/techsupport.

Wiley also publishes its books in a variety of electronic formats. Some content that appears in print may not be available in electronic books.

Library of Congress Control Number: 2007939645

ISBN: 978-0-470-17046-5

Manufactured in the United States of America

10 9 8 7 6 5 4 3 2

WILEY

About the Author

Eric Tyson, MBA, is a former financial counselor, lecturer and coauthor of the national best-seller, *Home Buying For Dummies,* as well as the author of four other best-selling books in the *For Dummies* series: *Personal Finance, Investing, Mutual Funds,* and *Taxes* (coauthor).

Eric has counseled thousands of clients on a variety of personal finance, investment, and real estate quandaries and questions. In addition to maintaining a financial counseling practice, he's a former lecturer of the San Francisco Bay Area's most highly attended financial management course at the University of California, Berkeley.

Eric is also a syndicated columnist and was an award-winning journalist for the *San Francisco Examiner.* His work has been featured and praised in hundreds of national and local publications, including *Newsweek, Kiplinger's, The Wall Street Journal, Money, The Los Angeles Times,* and the *Chicago Tribune,* and on NBC's *Today Show,* PBS's *Nightly Business Report,* CNN, *The Oprah Winfrey Show,* ABC, CNBC, Bloomberg Business Radio, CBS National Radio, and National Public Radio.

A former management consultant to Fortune 500 financial service firms, Eric is dedicated to teaching people to manage their personal finances better. Over the past two decades, he has successfully invested in securities as well as in real estate, started and managed several businesses. He earned his MBA at the Stanford Graduate School of Business and his bachelor's degree in economics at Yale.

Ray Brown, coauthor of the national best-seller *Home Buying For Dummies,* is a veteran of the real estate profession with over three decades of hands-on experience. A former manager for Coldwell Banker Residential Brokerage Company, McGuire Real Estate, Pacific Union GMAC Real Estate, and founder of his own real estate firm — the Raymond Brown Company — Ray is currently a writer, consultant, and public speaker on residential real estate topics.

Ray knows that most people are pretty darn smart. When they have problems, it's usually because they don't know the right questions to ask to get the information they need to make good decisions themselves. He always wanted to write real estate books that focused readers on what they needed to know to make sound home-buying and house-selling decisions.

On his way to becoming a real estate guru, Ray worked as the real estate analyst for KGO-TV (ABC's affiliate in San Francisco) and as a syndicated real estate columnist for *The San Francisco Examiner.* He also hosted a weekly radio program — *The Ray Brown on Real Estate,* for KNBR — for 16 years. In addition to his work for ABC, Ray has appeared as a real estate expert on CNN, NBC, and CBS and in *The Wall Street Journal* and *TIME.*

Ray's most significant achievements, however, are still Jeff and Jared, his two incomparable sons, and over 42 years of nearly always wedded bliss to the always wonderful Annie B. He's delighted to welcome Jeff's wife, Genevieve, and his grandson, Aidan Joseph Brown, to the family.

Dedication

This book is hereby and irrevocably dedicated to my family and friends, as well as to my counseling clients and customers, who ultimately have taught me everything I know about how to explain financial terms and strategies so that everyone may benefit.

— Eric Tyson

This book is lovingly dedicated to Annie B., who makes my heart sing.

— Ray Brown

Authors' Acknowledgments

Many, many people at Wiley Publishing, Inc. helped to make this book possible and (we hope in your opinion) good. These folks include Chad Sievers, Project Editor; Carrie Burchfield, Copy Editor; and all the fine folks in Production! Thanks also to everyone else at Wiley who contributed to getting this book done and done right.

Extraordinary acclamation, copious praise, and profound gratitude is due our brilliant technical reviewers for this and prior editions who toiled long hours to ensure that we didn't write something that wasn't quite right. These good folks include two extraordinary real estate professionals: Kip Oxman, McGuire Real Estate and Lynnea Key, Lynnea Key Realty; one extraordinary mortgage consultant: David Wales, Palo Alto Funding Group, Inc.; as well as Patti Wallace with ECHO Housing and Dennis Ito, Bob Taylor, and all the good folks at KPMG Peat Marwick. Thank you one and all!

We also owe an enormous debt of gratitude to Paul Bragstad, Pacific Union GMAC Real Estate, for his incredible Internet insights; Joy Alafia for helping us obtain the California Association of Realtors' exclusive listing contract and the property disclosure statement used in Chapter 8, the counter offer used in Chapter 14, and the real estate purchase contract included in Appendix A; Warren Camp, Warren Camp Inspection Services, for providing the exemplary premarketing inspection report included in Appendix B; Patty Oxman, Frank Howard Allen Realtors' super star, for her staging tips; Victoria Naidorf, VP and Brokerage Counsel for Coldwell Banker in Northern California, who developed the ten troublemakers in Chapter 12; Brian Felix, Old Republic Title Company, who provided his usual scholarly advice about title insurance and escrows; Roland Jadryev, listing-statement writer extraordinary; Barbara Pacak, who unlocked the mysteries of lockboxes; Liz Johnson, who had answers to all our questions; and last, but far from least, Esty Lawrie and Dolly Toms, for their greatly appreciated wisdom and support.

Publisher's Acknowledgments

We're proud of this book; please send us your comments through our Dummies online registration form located at www.dummies.com/register/.

Some of the people who helped bring this book to market include the following:

Acquisitions, Editorial, and Media Development

Project Editor: Chad R. Sievers

(Previous Edition: Suzanne Snyder)

Acquisitions Editor: Mike Baker

Copy Editor: Carrie Burchfield

(Previous Edition: Neil Johnson)

Editorial Program Coordinator: Erin Calligan Mooney

Technical Editor: Kip Oxman

Editorial Manager: Michelle Hacker

Editorial Assistants: Joe Niesen, Leeann Harney

Cover Photos: © Seth Joel/Getty Images

Cartoons: Rich Tennant (www.the5thwave.com)

Composition Services

Project Coordinator: Kristie Rees

Layout and Graphics: Reuben W. Davis, Alissa D. Ellet, Melissa K. Jester, Shane Johnson, Barbara Moore, Christine Williams

Anniversary Logo Design: Richard Pacifico

Proofreaders: John Greenough, Jessica Kramer, Nancy Reinhardt

Indexer: Potomac Indexing, LLC

Publishing and Editorial for Consumer Dummies

Diane Graves Steele, Vice President and Publisher, Consumer Dummies

Joyce Pepple, Acquisitions Director, Consumer Dummies

Kristin A. Cocks, Product Development Director, Consumer Dummies

Michael Spring, Vice President and Publisher, Travel

Kelly Regan, Editorial Director, Travel

Publishing for Technology Dummies

Andy Cummings, Vice President and Publisher, Dummies Technology/General User

Composition Services

Gerry Fahey, Vice President of Production Services

Debbie Stailey, Director of Composition Services

Contents at a Glance

Table of Contents

Introduction

Welcome to *House Selling For Dummies,* 3rd Edition, the completely updated companion to *Home Buying For Dummies* (also in its 3rd Edition), the #1 bestselling real estate book (that we also happened to write). If you're like most people, your biggest investment is your house. Sell your house wisely and you not only save yourself loads of time, but you also pocket thousands — if not tens of thousands — of dollars more than you would otherwise. Making a big mistake in the sale of your house, on the other hand, can easily cost you additional weeks — perhaps even months — of work and headache, as well as half a year's worth (or more) of your take-home income.

One of Ray's treasures is a well-worn fortune cookie message that says, "A wise person knows everything. A shrewd person knows everyone." We apply that same principle to house sales. Real estate is a team sport. In this book, we show you how to put together a winning team, and we alert you to key points to consider throughout your sale. Follow our advice and your house is as good as sold before the For Sale sign even goes up.

We don't care about whether you decide to sell your house or how much of the transaction you attempt to handle yourself. It's not that we're insensitive; we simply don't have a vested interest in the sale of your house. What we do care very deeply about is that you make the best possible decisions for your situation. If those decisions mean staying in your current home instead of selling, or if they mean selling through a good local real estate agent, that's terrific. We wrote this book to help you avoid making mistakes in your selling decisions and to ensure that you sell your house in the best way possible.

The Eric Tyson/Ray Brown Difference

We've received great accolades from the prior editions of this book and for *Home Buying For Dummies. House Selling For Dummies* fills a void for house sellers: It's a user-friendly book *totally* oriented to your needs as a seller.

If you've visited your local library or bought books on selling your home, you may be familiar with the shortcomings of most house-selling books. In writing this book, we attempt to avoid those shortcomings. Thus, we expect that you'll find that our book is

✔ **Holistic:** No one sells a house just for the sake of selling it. Selling a house creates tax and financial ramifications, particularly if you're selling to buy a more expensive home, relocating to a different part of the country, or retiring. Most other house-selling books, however, don't help you consider these bigger-picture issues of personal finance before you sell. In Part I, we come right out and tell you that some people who are thinking about selling their current homes *shouldn't.*

✔ **Educational:** Most house-selling books are written by real estate agents or their firms. Such books are long on singing the praises of real estate agents but short on specific advice, helpful tips, and caution signs. That's why many of those other books are less than 200 pages long. The authors aren't interested in sharing the innermost secrets of selling real estate; they're more interested in promoting their own business by convincing you to use a real estate agent. We wrote this book first and foremost to educate you. (Of course, if we end up making a few bucks for ourselves in the process, we won't complain.)

✔ **Jargon-free:** One of the hallmarks of books written more to confuse the reader than to convey information is the use of all sorts of insider terms that make things sound more mysterious and complicated than they really are. In this book, we try to keep everything in plain English. We even include a glossary, just in case you do encounter a term that appears to be Greek or Latin to you!

Conventions Used in This Book

When writing this book, we included some general conventions that all *For Dummies* books use. We use the following:

✔ **Italic:** We *italicize* any words you may not be familiar with and provide a definition.

✔ **Boldface type:** We **bold** all keywords in bulleted lists and the actual steps in numbered lists.

✔ **Monofont:** All Web sites and e-mail addresses appear in `monofont`.

Foolish Assumptions

We're not trying to scare you — quite the contrary. We just want to make it clear that, even though selling your house isn't brain surgery, you can easily make mistakes, especially if you're overconfident or do a poor job selecting people to work with in the transaction. When we wrote this book, we made a few assumptions about you.

✔ **You're humble:** You realize that you aren't a house-selling expert.

✔ **You're smart:** Even though you're not an expert, you realize the value of getting as much information as you can. This trait bodes well for your upcoming experience in selling real estate.

Although you're likely to hire some professionals to help you sell your house, you still need to educate yourself about all aspects of the transaction. Why?

✔ You're the one who ultimately must make the decision about whether or not, and when, to sell your house. No real estate agent, loan broker, or anyone else who has a vested interest in the sale can objectively advise you about whether you should sell your house or when is the best time for you to sell.

✔ You're the one (if you do decide to sell) who must interview and hire competent and affordable people who can help you with the sale. You need to know what all the people you hire do, why they do it, what to expect from them, and what they expect from you.

Oscar Wilde said, "Experience is the name everyone gives to their mistakes." We want to add a corollary to this observation: "Learning from other people's mistakes is infinitely better than learning from your own." *House Selling For Dummies* saves you money, time, and heartache — but only if you read it!

How This Book Is Organized

Perhaps you're sure that you want to sell your house. On the other hand, maybe you (like many people each year who contemplate a sale) aren't sure whether you can or should sell. If you do decide to sell your house, you must face the hard work of picking the best time to sell, preparing your house for sale, choosing the best people to help you sell, and closing the deal. And, even after the deal is done, you're sure to have questions and unresolved issues. *House Selling For Dummies* covers everything you need to know.

Part 1: The Selling Decision

Even if you think that you can or must sell, consider the big picture before you take action. This book starts with the premise that many important factors — financial and personal — should fall into place *before* you decide to sell your house. For example, how do you know if you can really afford to sell your house and buy another home if you haven't yet considered your overall financial situation and goals? Without taking stock of important financial and personal issues, you're simply guessing, or hoping, that selling is financially feasible and the right thing to do.

One element of the decision to sell hinges on the financial ramifications of selling. Amazingly, most people crunch few, if any, numbers before they decide to sell their home. Or they leave the financial analysis to a salesperson with a vested interest in the house-selling transaction. We explain that you don't need a PhD in quantum physics or even an interest in mathematics to make some simple, yet powerful, financial assessments before you sell. We also help you understand the pros and cons of lending money to the buyer of your humble abode.

Part II: Tactical Considerations

In this part, we assume that you've already made the decision to sell your house. Now you're ready to tackle important selling decisions, such as when to put your house on the market. Because most house sellers buy another home to replace the one they're leaving behind, we walk you through the logistical considerations of whether you should sell your current house before buying the next one or purchase your next home before cutting the cord to your current house.

This part also covers all the issues relating to how you're going to get your house sold. Are you going to try selling it yourself, or are you going to hire a real estate agent? We also explain the other players that you may want or need to include on your house-selling team, and we tell you how to choose the best people in their respective fields. Finally, if you've chosen to sell your house through a real estate agent, we walk you through the all-important listing contract that you complete with the agent and his or her firm, and explain the best ways to negotiate the commission for the sale of your house.

Part III: Getting Top Dollar When You Sell

Before you actually put your house on the market, read all our best tips for preparing your property to look appealing to prospective buyers (and real estate agents that many of them work with). Next comes the critical decision of determining the asking price for your house. Just as Goldilocks was looking for a bowl of porridge that was the right temperature, you don't want to over-price or under-price your home; you want to price it *just right.* In this part, we show you how.

Part IV: The Brass Tacks of Getting Your House Sold

After you price your house and put it on the market, the actual marketing of the property begins. In this part, we review different marketing methods and then explain how to choose those strategies that are best for your property. If you follow our advice up to this point in the book, you can bet that an offer or two will come rolling in before you know it.

Although you've probably never aspired to be Secretary of State, you (and your agent, if you're working with one) do need to know how to keep your composure and use proven negotiating tactics to get what you want and make the buyers of your house feel good about the deal they're getting. We also guide you through the final steps of your sale, including the escrow process and the money transfer. And, last but not least, we walk you through the unavoidable tax hoops you need to jump through when you sell your house.

Part V: The Part of Tens

This part provides counsel and advice on shorter topics that seem to stand alone well. Here, we explain ten important things to remember to do after your house sale is complete, our top ten tips for successfully selling rental real estate, and how to handle ten difficult questions you may be asked about selling your house. If you have a short attention span, or if you like the feeling you get from completing chapters, this part's for you!

Part VI: Appendixes

Appendixes are typically a tad dull and probably aren't the first thing you want to read in a book. On the other hand, the appendixes in this book include examples of important documents that can help enhance your house-selling knowledge. In this part, we provide an example of a premarketing inspection report and a real estate purchase contract and receipt for deposit. Finally, we include a handy glossary to define real estate terms that often sound like Pig Latin, unless you happen to sell real estate for a living (in which case, they probably sound very sensible).

Icons Used in This Book

Just as you use tasty seasonings in your favorite recipes, we've sprinkled helpful icons throughout this book to draw attention to key points or to denote stuff that you can skip over.

This icon flags key strategies that can improve your real estate deal and, in some cases, save you mounds of moola. Think of these icons as pointing out little words of wisdom that we would whisper in your ear if we were close enough to do so.

Numerous booby-traps await novices as well as experienced house sellers. This explosive symbol marks those mines and tells you how to sidestep them.

Occasionally, we suggest that you do more research or homework. Don't worry; we tell you exactly how to go about your investigation.

Unfortunately, as is the case in all realms of the business world, some people and companies are more interested in short-term profits than in meeting your needs and addressing your concerns. This icon highlights places in a house-selling transaction where sharks may be swimming and points to advice on avoiding such scoundrels.

To ensure that you don't forget important points, this icon serves as your little reminder, like a string tied around your finger.

This icon marks stuff that you don't really have to know, but that may come in handy at cocktail parties thrown by people in the real estate business.

This icon points out the best resources and techniques for selling your property faster, more profitably, and with less hassle.

Where to Go from Here

You don't need to read this book cover to cover. But if you're a beginner or you want to fully immerse yourself in the world of house selling, go for it! However, you may have a specific question or two today and want some other information tomorrow. No problem there, either. *House Selling For Dummies,* 3rd Edition, is lighter on its feet and easier to use than other house selling reference books. Use the Table of Contents or the Index to speed your way toward what you need to know and get on with your life.

Part I

The Selling Decision

The 5th Wave   By Rich Tennant

"Margaret would like to move to a larger house,
but I just don't see the need."

In this part . . .

*W*e help you tackle the big-picture issues that you must face before selling your house. To begin with, we ask you to consider whether you should even sell your house in the first place. Do you *need* to sell or do you just *want* to sell? Wanting to sell isn't a bad thing, but selling and moving can wreak havoc with your pocketbook if you don't first study the financial ramifications. We walk you through your options and assist you with making the selling decision.

And before you sell your house, you need to figure out how much you'll net from the transaction. Unless you're quite affluent, you're going to need to know how much money to put toward your next place, your retirement nest egg, or whatever else you envision doing with the proceeds. We tell you how to come up with an accurate estimate, not a "guesstimate." We also encourage you to think through another important issue before you put up your For Sale sign: Are you interested, willing, and able to provide financing to a prospective buyer of your house?

Chapter 1

Deciding to Sell

· ·

· ·

Selling your house and moving can be an enjoyable (not to mention profitable) experience. Unfortunately, for most people, it isn't. Selling a house not only introduces financial turmoil into most people's lives but also causes them stress.

One goal of this book is to help you make the right decision about whether to sell your house. If you do decide to sell, we want to make sure that you get as many dollars and as few upset stomachs from the sale as possible.

The reasons people want to sell their houses are almost as varied as the houses themselves. Here are some of the common, not-so common, and downright bizarre reasons:

✔ Additional debt burden because of layoff, medical expenses, disability, or overspending

✔ Bad vibes or bad luck associated with house

✔ Better job opportunities elsewhere

✔ Diminished space requirements now that children are grown

✔ House located in a flood, earthquake, or other disaster zone

✔ Increased space requirements for expanding family

✔ Lack of garage

✔ Neighborhood conditions incompatible with socioeconomic status

✔ Noisy neighborhood

✔ Noisy/messy/obnoxious family or business moved next door

✔ Recent death of spouse

✔ Recent marriage or divorce

✔ Serious house defects (such as radon or termites) that owners don't want to fix

✔ Unfriendly neighbors

✔ Unsafe neighborhood

✔ Unsatisfactory neighborhood shopping

✔ Unsatisfactory school district

✔ Unsuitable climate

As you can see from this partial list, most of the reasons why people have a desire to sell their houses are based on *wants,* not *needs.* In the United States, we sometimes take for granted how economically fortunate we are.

You don't *need* to move because your neighborhood is too noisy or because your house seems too small. You don't *need* to move because the weather in your area isn't nice enough. You don't *need* to live on quieter, tree-lined streets.

All these features are things people *want,* not things they *need.* And people who think that they can afford to pay for such things usually get more of what they *want.* Sometimes, however, people spend money moving and, ironically, still don't get what they want. The weather in the new locale may not be terrific, the neighbors may not be friendly and quiet, and the schools may not turn children into stellar students. You may move to get away from particular problems and then find yourself facing a new set of different problems.

We're certainly not going to tell you how and where to spend your money — that's your choice. However, we definitely want you to make the most of your money. Unless you're one of the few who has far more money than you can ever possibly spend, we suggest that you prioritize the demands on your money to accomplish your most important financial goals.

Nothing's wrong with spending money to trade in one house for another, but *before* you set those wheels in motion, think about the impact of that kind of spending on other aspects of your life. The more that you spend on housing, the less you'll have for your other goals, such as saving for retirement, taking annual vacations, and spending less time working and more time with your family and friends.

Figuring Out if You Really Need to Sell

Although spending your entire life in the first home you buy is an unlikely prospect, some people do end up living in the same home for 10, 20, even 30 or more years. Ray (humble coauthor of this book), for example, lived in his home nearly 30 years. Ray's no fool; staying put must have its advantages.

If, like most prospective house sellers, you have a choice between staying put and selling, *not* selling has clear advantages. Selling your house and then buying another one takes a great deal of legwork and research time on your part. Whether you sell your house yourself or hire an agent, you're going to be heavily involved in getting your house ready for sale and keeping it pristine while it's on the market.

In addition to time, selling your house and buying another one can cost serious money. Between real estate commissions, loan fees, title insurance, transfer tax, and myriad other costs of selling your house and then buying another one, you can easily spend 15 percent or more of the value of the property that you're selling (see bar on the left in Figure 1-1).

Fifteen percent sounds like a lot, doesn't it? Well, consider this: Unless you own your house free and clear of any mortgage debt, your transaction costs are going to gobble up an even larger percentage of the money you've invested in your home.

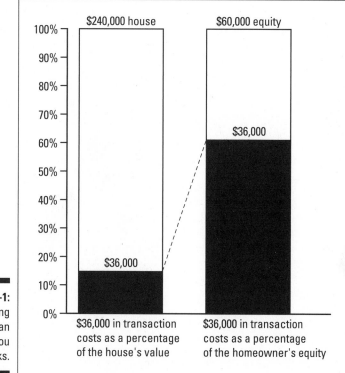

Figure 1-1:
Trading homes can cost you big bucks.

Check out this scenario: You're thinking about selling your $240,000 house. If selling your house and buying another one costs you 15 percent of the first house's value, then you're taking $36,000 out of your sale proceeds. However, if you happen to owe $180,000 on your mortgage, your *equity* in the home — the difference between the amount the house is worth ($240,000) and the amount you owe ($180,000) — is $60,000. Therefore, the $36,000 in transaction costs devours a huge 60 percent of your equity (see bar on the right in Figure 1-1). Ouch!

Before spending that much of your hard-earned money, make sure that you give careful thought and consideration to why you want to sell, the financial consequences of selling, and the alternatives to selling. In Chapters 2 and 3, we walk you through the personal financial issues that you need to weigh when contemplating the sale of your current house. But before we get to the numbers, consider the qualitative issues.

Good reasons to stay

Whereas some people have clear and compelling reasons for selling their homes, others do so for the wrong reasons. You don't want to make the financially painful mistake of selling if you don't have to or can't afford to.

The following sections offer reasons why you may be better off staying right where you are.

You're already having trouble living within your means

If you're having difficulty making ends meet, and you use high-interest consumer credit, such as credit cards or auto loans, to maintain your desired standard of living, you shouldn't spend more money on housing. Even if you're planning to trade your current house for one of comparable value, you may not be able to afford all the transaction costs of selling and buying.

Even if you aren't a consumer-debt user and you're saving a comfortable portion (10 percent or more) of your current earnings, *don't* assume that you can afford to trade up to a more expensive home. In addition to a higher mortgage payment, you may also face increased property taxes, insurance rates, and home maintenance costs.

A mortgage lender may be willing to finance a loan that enables you to trade up to a more expensive home, but qualifying for a loan doesn't mean that you can *afford* that home. Mortgage lenders use simplistic formulas, based primarily on your income, to determine the amount they're willing to lend you. Mortgage lenders don't know (or care) how far behind you are in saving for your retirement or how many children you must help with college costs or how much assistance you want or need to give to elderly parents.

Mortgage lenders are concerned about protecting their interests in the event that you default on your mortgage. As long as you meet a few minimal financial requirements (you make a sufficient down payment, and your housing expenses are less than a certain percentage of your income), the mortgage lenders can sell your loan with the backing of a government mortgage agency, effectively wiping their hands clean of you and your problems.

If you're thinking about trading in your current house for another one, especially for a more expensive one, you absolutely, positively must consider the financial repercussions of changed housing expenses in addition to the costs of buying and selling. We cover these important issues in Chapters 2 and 3.

The problems are more in your perceptions

Everybody, at some point, leaps to conclusions based on faulty assumptions or incomplete research in virtually all aspects their lives. Peter, for example, was a single parent living with his son in a nice neighborhood in an urban environment. When his son started junior high school, Peter grew increasingly concerned with the possibility that his son would become involved with drugs, which seemed to be so prevalent in their city.

Despite working in the city, Peter decided to move to an easygoing, suburban community about 45 minutes outside the city. Shortly after the move, Peter's son got mixed up with drugs anyway — perhaps, in part, because the long daily commute meant that Peter was around even less.

In addition to ignoring lifestyle issues (such as the length of his commute), Peter made a common human mistake — he assumed that things were a particular way without getting the facts. The reality was that the suburban community to which Peter moved had as many problems with teenagers on drugs as the good neighborhoods in his former city.

Crime and safety make up another common realm where people have misconceptions. Some communities often make the evening news with graphic stories and film footage of crimes. Statistically, however, most crimes committed in a given city or town occur in fairly small geographic areas. Local police departments tabulate neighborhood crime rates. If you're concerned about crime and safety, don't guess; get the facts by calling your local police department and asking them how to obtain the data.

Schools are another hot-button issue. In some areas, people make blanket statements condemning all public schools. They also insist that if you live in such-and-such town or city, you must send your children to private school if you want them to get a good education. The reality, as education experts (and good old-fashioned common sense) suggest, is that you can find good and bad public schools and good and bad private schools. You also need to evaluate if you're spending too many hours working and commuting just so you can make expensive school payments. If that's the case, you may not be able to spend adequate time with your children. The best possible teacher for your children is you.

Selling won't solve the problem(s)

Avoiding problems is another human tendency. That's what Fred and Ethel tried to do. Much to their chagrin, Fred and Ethel discovered that their home had two not-so-visible but, unfortunately, costly-to-fix problems. The new roof they needed was going to cost big bucks, because local ordinances required the removal of several layers of existing roofing material when a new roof was installed. Fred and Ethel also had recently found out that their house contained asbestos, a known carcinogen.

Rather than research and deal with these problems, Fred and Ethel decided that the easiest solution was to sell their house and buy another one in a nearby town where they thought they'd be happy. They then attempted to sell their home without disclosing these known defects — a major legal no-no, as we point out in Chapter 8 — but were tripped up by smart buyers who found out about the problems from inspectors they hired to check out the property.

Actually, the prospective buyers did Fred and Ethel two big favors:

✔ By uncovering the problems early, the buyers saved Fred and Ethel from a costly lawsuit that could easily have resulted if the flaws were discovered after the house was sold.

✔ By ultimately deciding to hold onto their home, which they otherwise were content with, Fred and Ethel saved themselves thousands of dollars in selling and buying transaction costs. Those savings more than paid for the cost of a new roof. And Fred and Ethel discovered that, because the asbestos was in good condition and properly contained, it was best left alone.

You can fix some or all the problems

When they realized that they couldn't run from their home's problems, Fred and Ethel, discussed in the preceding section, discovered how to get those problems fixed. You can address quite a number of possible shortcomings in your home less expensively than buying a new home.

If you think that home improvement projects are going to be too expensive, do some rough calculations to determine the cost of selling your current house and then buying another. Remember, you can easily spend 15 percent of the house's value on all the transaction costs of selling and then buying again.

Instead of trading houses, why not spend those transaction dollars on improving the home you currently own? Do you hate the carpeting and paint job? Get new carpets and repaint. If your home is a tad too small, consider adding on a room or two. Just be careful not to turn your home into a castle if all the surrounding houses are shacks. Overimproving your property can be an expensive mistake. By overimproving, we mean that after the improvements to your house, you'll own the most expensive house on the block, and you'll have difficulty recouping the cost of the improvements in the form of a higher house sale price.

Some people are seduced by the seeming better attributes of other houses on the market. If your house is small, larger ones seem more appealing. If you don't like your carpeting, houses that have hardwood floors may attract you. However, as is true of long-term friends or spouses, you know your current home's defects all too well because you've probably lived with them for years. Unless you're incredibly observant, you surely didn't know half your home's faults and shortcomings before you moved in. The same is true of new homes you may be lusting after.

Some problems and defects are more easily fixed and more worth fixing than others. When you're deciding whether to fix problems or move away from them, consider these important issues:

✔ **What's the payback?** Some home remodeling projects may actually pay for or come close to paying for themselves. We're not suggesting that you can have the work done for free. However, certain remodeling projects do increase your home's value by enough to make up for most or even all the cost of the improvement(s).

Generally speaking, projects that increase the cosmetic appeal or usability of living space tend to be more financially worthwhile than projects that don't. For example, consider painting and recarpeting a home versus fixing its foundation. The former projects are visible and, if done well, enhance a home's value; the latter project doesn't add to the visible appeal of the home or usability of living space. If, however, you *must* do foundation repairs or the house will collapse, spend your money on the foundation.

If you decide to stay put and renovate or improve your current home, you're going to need to find a way to pay for all that work. In Chapter 4, we discuss the way to figure out the amount you can afford to spend improving and how to actually finance your improvements. If you head down the renovation path, don't forget that contracting work often ends up costing more than you (and your contractor) originally expected.

✔ **How intrusive will the work be?** As you surely know, money isn't everything. Six months into a home remodeling project that moves you out of your bedroom, spreads sawdust all over your kitchen table, and has you wanting to flee the country, the "payback" on the project doesn't seem so important anymore. In addition to costing more than most parties expect, contracting work almost always takes longer than everyone expects.

Ask yourself and others who've endured similar projects: How much will this project disrupt my life? Your contract with the contractor should include financial penalties for not finishing on time.

Some problems or shortcomings of your current house simply can't be fixed. If you're tired of shoveling snow in the winter and dripping sweat in the summer, you're not going to be able to change your local weather. If crime is indeed a big problem, you yourself aren't going to be able to cut area crime anytime soon. Moving may be the best solution.

Reasons to consider selling

If you're in a situation where you really *need* to sell, as opposed to wanting to sell, by all means put your house on the market. And if you *want* to sell, and can *afford* to do so, you should go for it, as well. The following sections offer some solid reasons for selling.

You can afford to trade homes

Your desire to sell your current house and buy another one may be driven by a force as frivolous as sheer boredom. But if you can afford to sell and buy again, and you know what you're getting into, why not?

Now, defining *afford* is important. By *afford,* we mean that you've identified your personal and financial goals and you've calculated that the cost of trading houses won't compromise those goals.

Everyone has unique goals, but if you're like most people, you probably don't want to spend the rest of your life working full-time. To retire or semi-retire, you're going to need to save quite a bit of money during your working years. If you haven't yet crunched any numbers to see where you stand in terms of retirement saving, postpone major real estate decisions until you explore your financial future. In Chapter 2, we walk you through the important retirement planning considerations in selling your house, and in Chapter 3, we show you how to calculate the economics of selling and moving.

You need to move for your job

Some people find that at particular points in their lives they need to move to take advantage of a career opportunity. For example, if you want to be involved with technology companies, certain regions of the country offer far greater opportunities than others.

When you lack employment, paying bills is difficult, especially the costs involved in home ownership. If you've lost your job or your employer demands that you relocate to keep your job, you may feel a real need to move, especially in a sluggish economy.

Moving for a better job (or simply for *a* job) is a fine thing to do. However, some people fool themselves into believing that a higher-paying job or a move to an area with lower housing costs will put them on an easier financial street. As we discuss in Chapter 3, you must consider all the costs of living in a new area versus your current area before deciding that moving to a new community is financially wise.

And, although we don't pretend to be career counselors, we want you to consider that you may be overlooking opportunities right in your own backyard. Just because your employer offers you a better job to get you to relocate doesn't mean that you can't bargain for a promotion and stay put

---

Patience — not money — solves some problems

Some problems may solve themselves if you're patient and willing to wait things out. For example, Eric (humble coauthor of this book) once lived a block away from a busy California freeway. Although adequate fencing and safety barriers separated the speeding cars on the highway from the neighborhood, the noise was a bit of a nuisance, especially during peak commute hours.

The longer Eric, who was raised in a quiet non-urban environment, lived in the home, the more the noise bugged him. Within several years of having bought the home, however, the problem was solved. Expansion of the freeway forced the state to add sound walls, which greatly dampened the noise and enhanced home values in the area.

---

geographically. Likewise, during an economic slowdown, if your employer says you must relocate or face downsizing, explore other employment options in your area, especially if you want to stay put.

You're having (or will have) financial trouble

Sometimes, people fall on difficult financial times because of an unexpected event. Check out these two scenarios:

- After Ryan graduated from college, he landed a good marketing job and seemed financially secure. So he bought a home. After a few years in the home, Ryan discovered that he had a chronic medical problem.

  Ultimately, Ryan decided to go into a lower-stress job and work part time. As a result, his income significantly decreased while his medical expenses increased. He no longer could afford his home. It made sense for Ryan to sell his house and move into lower-cost housing that better addressed his reduced mobility.

- When Teri and her husband bought a home, they were both holding down high-paying jobs. Unfortunately, two years later, Teri discovered that her husband had an affair. After much marital counseling and many attempts to get their marriage on a better track, Teri and her husband divorced. Because neither of them alone could afford the costs of the house, Teri and her husband needed to sell.

In addition to unexpected events, some people simply live beyond their means and can't keep their heads above the financial water of large mortgage payments and associated housing costs. Sometimes, people get bogged down with additional consumer debt because they stretched themselves too much when buying their home.

Selling your house and moving to a lower-cost housing option may be just what the financial doctor ordered. On the other hand, if you can bring your spending under control and pay off those consumer debts, maybe you can afford to remain in your present home. Be sure that you're being honest with yourself and realistic about your ability to accomplish your goals given your continuing housing expenses (see Chapter 2 for more information).

You're retiring

If you decide to call it quits on the full-time working life, you may find yourself with more house than you need, or you may wish to move to a less costly area. Instead of trading up, you may consider trading down.

You can free up some of the cash you've tied up in your current house and use that money to help finance your retirement by moving to a less expensive home. If you're otherwise happy with where you're currently living, don't think that you must trade down to a less expensive home simply to tap the equity in your current property. As we discuss in Chapter 2, you can tap your home's equity through other methods, such as taking out a reverse mortgage.

Your house is associated with bad feelings

As with other financial decisions, choosing to sell or buy a home isn't only about money. Human emotions and memories can be just as powerful and just as real factors to consider.

If your spouse or child has passed away, you divorced, or your house was burglarized, the property may be a constant source of bad feelings. Although selling your house and moving won't make your troubles go away, being in a new home in a different area or neighborhood may help you get on with your life and not dwell excessively on your recent unpleasant experiences. Just be sure to temper your emotions with a realistic look at your financial situation.

Knowing the Health of Your Housing Market

Your personal financial situation clearly is an important factor in deciding whether and when to sell your house, but the state of your local housing market may also influence your decision. Check out the following sections for the lowdown on the housing market and how it affects your sale.

Selling in a depressed housing market

No one likes to lose money. If you scraped and saved for years for the down payment to buy a home, finding out that your house is worth less than the amount you paid for it can be quite a blow. Between the decline in the market value of your home and the selling costs, you may possibly even lose your entire invested down payment. And you thought the stock market was risky!

In the worst cases we've seen, some homeowners find themselves *upside down,* which simply means that the mortgage on the house exceeds the amount for which the house can be sold. In other words, upside-down homeowners literally have to pay money to sell their houses because they've lost more than their original down payment. Ouch!

When deciding whether to sell in a depressed market, consider the factors discussed in the following sections.

If you still have adequate equity

Although your local real estate market may have recently declined, if you've owned your house long enough or made a large enough down payment, you still may be able to net a good deal of cash by selling. If you can make enough money to enable yourself to buy another home, we say don't sweat the fact that your local real estate market may currently be depressed. As long as the sale fits in with your overall financial situation, sell your house and get on with your life!

All real estate markets go through up cycles and down cycles. Over the long term, however, housing prices tend to increase. So, if you sell a house or two during a down market, odds are you'll also sell a house or two during better market conditions. And if you're staying in the same area or moving to another depressed housing market, you're simply trading one reduced-price house for another. If you're moving to a more expensive market or a market currently doing better than the one you're leaving, be sure that spending more on housing doesn't compromise your long-term personal and financial goals (see Chapter 2).

If you lack enough money to buy your next home

Sometimes, homeowners find themselves in a situation where, if they sell, they won't have enough money to buy their next home. If you find yourself in such a circumstance, first clarify whether you *want* or *need* to sell:

✔ If you *want* to sell but don't *need* to and can avoid selling for a while, we say wait it out. Otherwise, if you sell and then don't have adequate money to buy your next home, you may find yourself in the unfortunate position of being a renter when the local real estate market turns the corner and starts improving again. So you'll have sold low and later be forced to buy high. You'll need to have an even greater down payment to get back into the market, or you'll be forced to buy a more modest house.

✔ If you *need* to sell, you have a tougher road ahead of you. You must hope that the real estate market where you buy won't rocket ahead while you're trying to accumulate a larger down payment. However, you may also want to look into methods for buying a home with a smaller down payment. For example, a benevolent family member may help you out, the person selling you your new home may lend you some money, or you may decide to take out one of the low-down-payment loans that some mortgage lenders offer. If prices do rise at a fast rate, you can either set your sights on a different market or lower your expectations for the kind of home you're going to buy.

If you must move or relocate and don't want to sell in a depressed market, you can rent out your home until the market turns around. Be sure that you understand the tax consequences of this arrangement, which we cover in detail in Chapter 2. Before becoming a landlord, consider your ability to deal with the hassles that come with the territory. You must also educate yourself on local rent-control ordinances and compare your property's monthly expenses with the rental income that you'll collect. (We explain how to calculate the difference between a property's income and expenses in the sidebar, "Figuring the cash flow on rental property.") If you're going to lose money each month, the constant cash drain may handicap your future ability to save, in addition to increasing your total losses on the property.

Selling during a strong market

What could be better than selling your house during a time of rising or already-elevated home prices? If you can afford the transaction costs of selling your current house and buying another home, and if the costs of the new home fit within your budget and financial goals, go for it.

Just be careful of two things:

✔ Don't get greedy and grossly overprice your house. You may end up getting less from the sale than you expected, and the sale is likely to take much longer than if you'd priced the property fairly. If you price your house too high, when you finally drop the price to the right range, you may face lower offers because your house has the stigma of being old on the market. In Chapter 11, we detail how to price your house for a quick sale that gets you top dollar.

> ✔ If you're staying in your current strong market or moving to another strong market, be careful about timing the sale of your current house and the purchase of your next one. For example, you probably don't want to sell and then spend months bidding unsuccessfully on other homes. You may get stuck renting for a while and need to make an additional move; such costs can eat up the cash from your recent sale and interfere with your ability to afford your next home. In Chapter 5, we explain how to time the sale of your house and the subsequent purchase of your new home.

INVESTIGATE

Figuring the cash flow on rental property

Cash flow is the difference between the amount of money that a property brings in and the amount you have to pay out for expenses. Some home-owners-turned-rental-property-owners can't cover all the costs associated with rental property. In the worst cases, such property owners end up in personal bankruptcy from the drain of negative cash flow (that is, expenses exceed income). In other cases, the negative cash flow hampers property owners' ability to accomplish important financial goals such as saving for retirement or helping with their children's college expenses.

Before you consider becoming a landlord, make some projections about what you expect your property's monthly income and expenses to be.

Income

On the income side, determine the amount of rent you're able to charge:

✔ Take a look at what comparable properties currently are renting for in your local market.

✔ Check out the classified ads in your local paper(s).

✔ Speak with some leasing agents at real estate rental companies.

Be sure to allow for some portion (around 5 percent per year) of the time for your property to be vacant — finding good tenants takes time.

Expenses

On the expense side, you have your monthly mortgage payment (of which we're sure that you're already painfully aware). And, of course, you have property taxes. Because you probably pay them only once or twice yearly, divide the annual amount by 12 to arrive at your monthly property tax bill.

You may end up paying some or all your renter's utility bills, such as garbage, water, or gas. Estimate from your own usage what the monthly tab will be. Expect most utility bills to increase a bit because tenants will probably waste more when you're picking up the bill.

Be sure to ask your insurance company about how your property insurance premium changes if you convert the property into a rental. As is true with your property taxes, divide the annual total by 12 to get a monthly amount.

Don't forget repairs and maintenance. Expect to spend about 1 percent of the property's value per year on maintenance, repairs, and cleaning. Again, divide by 12 to get a monthly figure.

Finding good tenants takes time and promotion. If you choose to list through them, rental brokers normally take one month's rent as their cut. If you advertise, estimate at least $100 to $200 in advertising expenses, not to mention the cost of your time in showing the property to prospective tenants. You must also plan on running credit checks on prospective tenants.

(continued)

(continued)

Estimated cash flow

Now, total all the monthly expenses and subtract that number from your estimated monthly income after allowing for some vacancy time. Voilà! You've just calculated your property's cash flow.

If you have a negative cash flow, you may actually be close to breaking even when you factor in a rental property tax write-off known as depreciation. You break down the purchase of your property between the building, which is depreciable, and land, which isn't depreciable. You can make this allocation based on the assessed value for the land and the building or on a real estate appraisal. Residential property is depreciated over 27½ years at a rate of 3.64 percent of the building value per year. For example, if you buy a residential rental property for $250,000, and $175,000 of that amount is allocated to the building, that allocation means that you can take $6,370 per year as a depreciation tax deduction ($175,000 × .0364).

After you've crunched all these numbers, if you find that you're still interested in renting your property, be sure to read Chapter 2, especially the section dealing with the tax consequences of converting your home into a rental property.

Chapter 2

Selling and Your Personal Finances

- -

In This Chapter

▶ Considering the economics of trading up

▶ Grappling with trading down, renting, or taking a reverse mortgage in retirement

▶ Understanding tax issues when selling

- -

*B*uying a home can seriously shake up your personal finances. But selling your house and then buying another one generally leads to even bigger financial shock waves. If you're considering the sale of your house, you may think, "No big deal. After all, the sale will pay off my mortgage debt and bring a big chunk of money my way. What do I have to stress over?"

In fact, the financial consequences of selling your house can be serious, especially if you're trading up to a more expensive home. You must be well prepared and alert as you sail through the often-treacherous waters of house selling. Consider this chapter your first mate, helping you make all the best moves you can.

Trading Up

Many people who still are in their prime working years and who want to sell their houses and buy others in the same general geographic areas are planning to trade up, which usually means moving into a "better" — and, therefore, more expensive — home. The desire to trade up is only natural; people usually want their next car, their next job, and their next set of living room or bedroom furniture to be better than the last. After all, you work hard for a living; you deserve "better."

A nicer neighborhood, better schools, more rooms, bigger rooms, more luxurious bathrooms, a more spacious kitchen, better shopping nearby, a bigger yard, better parking and storage space — the list of things that can be better in your life is limitless. Your budget, on the other hand, is not.

Although you may want all these extra features and amenities in the next home that you buy, those extra goodies are going to cost more money — in some cases, much more. So, unless you've recently won the lottery or earned a huge windfall from stock options or the like, you're going to have to prioritize your desires. You can't have it all — only what fits with your budget and longer-term financial and personal plans.

Examining your housing budget

Before you set out to trade in your current house for a "better" one, you need to take a good look at your overall budget and determine how much more, if any, of your monthly spending can go toward housing costs. If you haven't examined your monthly budget in a while, now is the time to do so — *before* you set the wheels in motion to trade up.

Get out your checkbook register, credit card statements, paycheck stub, most recent year's tax return, and anything else that documents where you've been spending your money during the past six to 12 months. You may also need to do some tracking or estimating of cash purchases that don't leave a paper trail. Table 2-1 can help you to organize your spending by category.

Table 2-1 Figure Your Spending, Now and After a Home Purchase

Item	Current Monthly Average Spending in Your Current Home ($)	Expected Monthly Average Spending in Your Next Home ($)
Income		
Taxes		
Social Security		
Federal		
State and local		
Housing expenses		
Mortgage		
Property taxes		
Gas/electric/oil		
Water/garbage		
Phone		
Cable TV		
Furniture/appliances		
Maintenance/repairs		
Food and eating		
Supermarket		
Restaurants and takeout		

Item	Current Monthly Average Spending in Your Current Home ($)	Expected Monthly Average Spending in Your Next Home ($)
Transportation		
Gasoline	_____	_____
Maintenance and repairs	_____	_____
State registration fees	_____	_____
Tolls and parking	_____	_____
Bus or subway fares	_____	_____
Appearance		
Clothing	_____	_____
Shoes	_____	_____
Jewelry/watches	_____	_____
Dry cleaning	_____	_____
Haircuts	_____	_____
Makeup	_____	_____
Other	_____	_____
Debt repayments		
Credit cards and charge cards	_____	_____
Auto loans	_____	_____
Student loans	_____	_____
Other	_____	_____
Fun stuff		
Entertainment (movies, concerts, and so on)	_____	_____
Vacation and travel	_____	_____
Gifts	_____	_____
Hobbies	_____	_____
Pets	_____	_____
Health club or gym	_____	_____
Other	_____	_____
Advisors		
Accountant	_____	_____
Attorney	_____	_____
Financial advisor	_____	_____
Healthcare		
Physicians and hospitals	_____	_____
Drugs	_____	_____
Dental and vision	_____	_____
Therapy	_____	_____

(continued)

Table 2-1 *(continued)*

Item	Current Monthly Average Spending in Your Current Home ($)	Expected Monthly Average Spending in Your Next Home ($)
Insurance		
Homeowners	_____	_____
Auto	_____	_____
Health	_____	_____
Life	_____	_____
Disability	_____	_____
Educational expenses		
Courses and tuition	_____	_____
Books	_____	_____
Supplies	_____	_____
Kids		
Day care	_____	_____
Toys	_____	_____
Other	_____	_____
Charitable donations	_____	_____
Other	_____	_____
_____	_____	_____
_____	_____	_____
_____	_____	_____
_____	_____	_____
_____	_____	_____
Total spending	[ ]	[ ]
Amount saved *(subtract "Total spending" line from "Income")*	[ ]	[ ]

Figuring your expected expenses after trading up

Knowing how you spend your money *now* on housing and other items is only half the picture. You also need to know how much you'll spend *after* buying your next home.

In Table 2-1, we shaded the Housing expenses category in the "Current" and "Expected" columns for a reason. These expenses probably are going to change the most when you sell your current house and buy a new home.

To help you fill in the holes in the expected costs column, check out these areas:

✔ **Mortgage payment:** Unless you've been squirreling away extra savings while living in your current house, the total amount you're borrowing through your mortgage (and, therefore, your monthly mortgage payment) will probably increase if you trade up. By using our handy-dandy mortgage payment calculator in Table 2-2, you can calculate the approximate monthly mortgage payment you'll face in your new home.

To calculate your monthly loan payment, multiply the relevant number from Table 2-2 by the total amount that you're borrowing, expressed in (that is to say, *divided by*) thousands of dollars. So, for example, if you intend to borrow $150,000 at 8 percent interest on a 30-year mortgage, you multiply 150 by 7.34 (from Table 2-2) to come up with a monthly payment of $1,101.

✔ **Property taxes:** In most communities, the annual property taxes that you pay on your next home purchase initially are set at a percentage of the property value. To find out the property tax rate in the area where you plan to purchase your new home, simply call the local tax collector, assessor, or other taxing authority (you can locate those phone numbers in the government section of your local phone directory).

Don't base your property tax estimate on the amount that the seller of the home you're interested in buying is currently paying or on the amount you're paying on your present house. When you trade up, the taxes on the home may be reassessed upward.

✔ **Utilities:** If you're trading up, some of your utility bills — such as cable TV — may stay the same, but others may change. Until you have in mind a specific home to buy, you can't request hard numbers on utility usage. In the interim, make some educated estimates.

For example, if you're planning on moving into a larger home in your area with, say, 30 percent more square footage, you can estimate that your heating and electric bills will increase by about 30 percent. However, if you're moving from an old, energy-inefficient home into a newer and more efficient one, the new home may not cost you more in utilities even if it's a bit larger.

✔ **Furniture:** If you buy a larger home, you'll have more space to fill, so you're probably going to spend more money on furnishings. Make a reasonable estimate of how much you expect to spend on new furnishings.

If and when you actually trade up, remember the amount that you budgeted for new furnishings; some trade-up buyers get carried away with redecorating and decimate their budgets after they move into their new properties.

✔ **Maintenance:** If you're buying a more expensive home, you're probably also going to spend more on maintenance, even if the home isn't a fixer-upper. A good way to estimate your annual maintenance costs is to multiply the purchase price of the home by 1 percent (use 1.25 percent of the purchase price for older and more run-down properties).

✔ **Federal and state income taxes:** If you buy a more expensive home and have larger mortgage payments and property taxes, your income tax bill will probably go down. Why? Mortgage interest and property taxes are deductible expenses on Schedule A of your federal income tax Form 1040 and on most state returns. See the sidebar "Estimating how your taxes may change if you trade up," later in this chapter.

✔ **Homeowners insurance:** If you buy a more expensive home, your homeowners insurance premiums may increase. In the absence of a specific quote for a property you're interested in buying, you can estimate that your homeowners insurance costs will increase in proportion to the increased size (square footage) of your home. Because land isn't insured, ignore the extra land that may come with your next home.

Table 2-2	Mortgage Payment Calculator	
Interest Rate (%)	**Term of Mortgage**	
	15 Years	**30 Years**
5	7.91	5.37
5⅛	7.98	5.45
5¼	8.04	5.53
5⅜	8.11	5.60
5½	8.18	5.68
5⅝	8.24	5.76
5¾	8.31	5.84
5⅞	8.38	5.92
6	8.44	6.00
6⅛	8.51	6.08
6¼	8.58	6.16
6⅜	8.65	6.24
6½	8.72	6.33
6⅝	8.78	6.41
6¾	8.85	6.49
6⅞	8.92	6.57
7	8.99	6.66
7⅛	9.06	6.74

Interest Rate (%)	Term of Mortgage 15 Years	30 Years
7¼	9.13	6.83
7⅜	9.20	6.91
7½	9.28	7.00
7⅝	9.35	7.08
7¾	9.42	7.17
7⅞	9.49	7.26
8	9.56	7.34
8⅛	9.63	7.43
8¼	9.71	7.52
8⅜	9.78	7.61
8½	9.85	7.69
8⅝	9.93	7.78
8¾	10.00	7.87
8⅞	10.07	7.96
9	10.15	8.05
9⅛	10.22	8.14
9¼	10.30	8.23
9⅜	10.37	8.32
9½	10.45	8.41
9⅝	10.52	8.50
9¾	10.60	8.60
9⅞	10.67	8.69
10	10.75	8.78
10⅛	10.83	8.87
10¼	10.90	8.97
10⅜	10.98	9.06
10½	11.06	9.15

Some lucky folks can squeeze higher housing costs into their budgets without having to cut spending in other expense categories or fall short of their savings goals. If your budget has that much padding, terrific!

But most people need to cut some fat from their budgets to afford spending more on housing. If you hope to someday retire or be able to help pay for a portion of your children's college costs, you have to be realistic about how much you need to save and how much you can afford to spend on housing and other expenses.

Determining the financial impact on your future goals

Before you trade up to a more expensive home, in addition to analyzing how the move affects your current financial picture, you also need to examine how it's going to affect your *future* financial goals.

One such goal that many people share is to enjoy a comfortable retirement. If you completed Table 2-1 earlier in this chapter, you can see that the additional monthly housing expenses from a trade up put the squeeze on — and can possibly even eliminate — your ability to save money. And, as we explain in the nearby sidebar, "Estimating how your taxes may change if you trade up," if you end up contributing less to your tax-deductible retirement savings plans, your income taxes will increase.

Before you even consider trading up to a more expensive home, do yourself a big favor and make some savings calculations for your retirement and other important financial goals. If you completed the budgeting exercise in Table 2-1 (earlier in this chapter), you have a good idea about how much you're currently saving from your monthly income and how much you may save if you trade up. Of course, you may discover that you aren't even saving enough money right now, *before trading up,* to meet your long-term goals. In this case, trading up to a more expensive home is highly inadvisable.

Exploring the other costs of trading up

If you trade up to a more expensive home, your ongoing, monthly housing expenses are sure to increase. But that isn't all the additional costs that you'll encounter.

Finding a new home to buy and selling your current one requires that you expend dozens, perhaps even hundreds, of hours of your precious free time. And if you hire real estate agents and others to help you with all the transactions, you're going to spend a good deal of money for their services.

And then there's moving — a stressful, time-consuming ordeal to get all your belongings (and family members!) to your new abode. Unless you have scads of free time and enjoy hauling heavy boxes and furniture, you're likely to end up spending thousands of dollars paying a moving company to help you.

Before you go in search of your next great home, you need to understand all the one-time fees involved in trading up and moving. Otherwise, you may run out of money and be forced to use high-interest consumer credit, or worse. In Chapter 3, we walk you through all the important considerations and calculations so that you don't have any financial surprises upsetting your proposed move.

Making Retirement Housing Decisions

If you're an older homeowner, your *home equity* — the difference between the market value of your home and the outstanding mortgage(s) on it — can be one of your largest (if not your largest) assets. Many folks nearing retirement and retirees who own their homes find that their home equity is surprisingly large. Why? First, if all goes well, the value of your property increases over the years. Second, all those years of monthly mortgage payments add up; by the time you're ready to retire, your mortgage balance should be low or even zero.

Your house's equity can help supplement the cost of your retirement . . . with or without selling. Of course, the obvious option is selling your house and buying or renting something less expensive. The less-obvious option is taking out a reverse mortgage that provides you with income based on your home's equity without selling your home. In this section, we cover these important options along with important tax and personal issues that you need to weigh before deciding what to do with your home when you retire.

Trading down

Perhaps, when you're in your living room, you hear more noise than you used to notice. Or one day, you just can't muster the desire to skim the leaves out of the pool that no one swims in anymore. And ever since your daughter went off to college, maybe you get a hollow feeling when you walk past her empty bedroom. You suddenly realize that, now that the kids have moved out of the house, you have more space than you really need or want.

Even if you don't have kids, you may find that, now that you're no longer working, you don't need to live within driving distance of the city where you spent your entire life working. You suddenly have the freedom to step out of the rat race and move to a place where life moves a bit more slowly (and costs a bit less).

If you're like most near or actual retirees, these feelings may also accompany the realization that you don't have as much money to live on during your retirement as you want. You may be "house rich and cash poor," or, to put it another way, you have "more house than you need and less cash than you want."

Don't despair! You're actually in an enviable position if you have a house with a good deal of equity in it. Now may be the time for you to *trade down* — sell your current house and either buy a less expensive home or become a renter. For some seniors, trading down is a wise move that can simultaneously meet financial and emotional needs.

TIP

Estimating how your taxes may change if you trade up

Here's a shortcut method for figuring the change in your income taxes caused by a higher mortgage payment and property taxes. Multiply the expected increase in your monthly property taxes and mortgage payment by your current federal income tax bracket which you can find at www.irs.gov or the most recent IRS Form 1040 instruction booklet you received.

In case you care — and it's okay if you don't — why this shortcut yields a pretty darn good estimate for calculating the change in your income taxes, here's an explanation: The calculation appears to overestimate your income tax savings because it assumes that your entire mortgage is tax-deductible, when in fact only mortgage interest, not the portion of your mortgage payment going to principal repayment, is tax deductible. However, in the early years of your mortgage, the interest portion of the mortgage payment represents more than 90 percent of the total payment. The state income tax savings that the residents of most states enjoy for deductibility of mortgage interest and property taxes is ignored.

If the higher housing expenses that come with trading up put a noose around your ability to save money, your income taxes may increase. If you're saving money in a tax-deductible retirement savings account, such as an employer-based 401(k) or 403(b) account or self-employed Keogh or SEP-IRA, your contributions are generally tax-deductible from your taxable income. If higher housing expenses reduce your funding of these tax-sheltered accounts, your federal and state income taxes increase. How much? Multiply your combined federal and state income tax bracket by the amount of the reduction in your retirement account contributions. (*Note:* You probably won't be able to estimate the reduction in your monthly retirement savings until you complete Table 2-1.)

Two methods may give you a better estimate of the way your income taxes may change with a house purchase. Try plugging in the estimated tax-deductible housing expenses into your most recent federal and state tax returns and see how your tax bill changes. Or you can consult with a tax advisor.

Don't ignore emotional considerations

During your working years, selling your house to move to a "better" one or to relocate to another area for a job can be an invigorating experience that you may even look forward to with pleasure. Sure, moving is a pain in the posterior, but you find some joy in the newness of things.

Retirees may look forward to change as well. But if you've lived in a home or a particular area for many years, moving someplace else may be emotionally difficult. Leaving behind happy memories is hard, and some people equate retirement with dying.

Retiring is a major life change. Take your time in assessing your options and don't be rushed into making decisions you're not ready to make. Be sure that you understand the financial ramifications of a move. At the same time, don't make the mistake of basing your retirement-housing decision entirely on a calculator, while ignoring your personal needs and emotions.

Ignoring personal considerations is what Henry did. Consider his story:

Henry was quite concerned about the cost of living in the area to which he and his wife, Lucy, would eventually retire. He did a lot of analysis and coerced his wife into moving to a rural area in a part of the country that they'd never visited before.

To make a long story short, Lucy ended up disliking the area they moved to. Few cultural activities were available in their new location, and they didn't find many people they were interested in getting to know. To add insult to injury, the area ended up not being as cheap to live in as they originally thought it would be. (In Chapter 3, we help you assess the real, total cost of living in a different area.) Henry was stubborn about wanting to stay, and he and Lucy fought a lot and eventually divorced.

(Huge) tax perk for house sellers

As we discuss in detail in Chapter 16, house sellers can shield a big portion of their house sales profits from taxation. Single taxpayers can avoid capital gains taxation on up to $250,000 and couples filing jointly up $500,000 of profit.

As long as you lived in the house as your primary residence for at least two of the previous five years, this tax exclusion is available to you without age restriction, and you can take the exclusion as many times as you want (but no more than once every two years).

This law (passed in 1997) is more expansive than the old exclusion rules, which required you to be at least 55 years old. (The old rules allowed you to take an exclusion only once per lifetime, and even then allowed an exclusion of up to only $125,000 in house sales profit from capital gains taxation.)

Presuming that you're willing to sell your primary residence, the new house sales tax law makes it easier to convert your home equity directly into liquid investments you can live off during retirement. Of course, such a strategy requires you to either trade down or become a renter. Trading to an equal cost or more expensive home won't free up more of your money (if you're thinking about simply borrowing more, please see the sidebar, "What about taking out a new mortgage or home equity loan?" later in this chapter).

Renting versus trading down

Usually, trading down is financially savvier than becoming a renter. If you're able to pay for your new home in cash, your housing costs during retirement will be next to nil.

The price range that you should consider depends on a couple of factors:

- ✔ **How much other money do you have for retirement?** If you're really pinched for money to live on during retirement, you may be willing to buy a considerably less expensive home to free up more money for living expenses. Until you run some retirement projections to see where you stand, however, you won't know how much or how little you need to carve off your home's equity. And, as we cover in the next section, you can use a reverse mortgage to tap into your property's equity while you still live there.

- ✔ **What do you want to buy?** If your retirement dream is to live on New York's Upper West Side or near the water in Hawaii, you may not be able to trade down much. However, if living in Manhattan is more your idea of a retirement nightmare than a dream, and you want to scale down and move out to the countryside, you can probably spend much less on your next home.

Some people sell their houses and simply rent in retirement. By selling, you free up all the money invested in your house and make it available to live on or do with as you desire. And when you rent, you have more flexibility to move in the future.

If you're considering the sale of your house and becoming a renter in retirement, be aware of these potential drawbacks:

- ✔ **Exposure to rental inflation:** As a renter, unless you live in a unit protected by local rental-control ordinances, your monthly rental payment is fully exposed to inflation. Today, $1,000 per month in rent may not sound like a mountain of cash, but consider that, with annual increases of only 4 percent annual increases, in 20 years, your rent will mushroom to nearly $2,200 per month. With 6 percent annual rental increases — which can happen if the United States returns to a 1970s-style period of high inflation — that $1,000 monthly rent balloons to more than $3,200. Ouch!

Getting advice (if you need it)

Sometimes, you just become overwhelmed with countless financial questions in your life — including whether to sell your home — and you may need someone to help guide and advise you. Hiring an objective, competent, and affordable advisor may be your ticket to better decision-making.

If your experience is like that of many who have come before you, finding a good advisor will be a challenge. Most financial planners work in a way that creates conflicts of interest — either because they sell financial products that pay them a commission or because they manage money for ongoing fees. So, for example, if you consider taking some of your savings and investing more in a home by trading up, most planners will rain on your idea. The reason: The home purchase depletes capital that you can invest through them and that provides them with more income. On the other hand, if you're on the verge of retiring, these same planners may just love your idea of trading down to a less costly home, if doing so frees up cash for you to invest with them.

Even if you're successful in finding a local financial advisor who has nothing to sell you but his or her time and good advice, you must be on guard for another potential problem — inexperience in dealing with the housing issues and decisions you're confronting. Most financial advisors spend the bulk of their time making investment recommendations and analyzing retirement plans, not helping people like you decide whether to sell their homes.

No matter how overwhelmed you feel by your housing quandaries, no matter how desperately you want outside help, don't abandon the process of educating yourself. No one knows your overall financial and personal situation better than you do. You've obviously demonstrated an interest in educating yourself by reading this book. Keep reading this book and consider others on financial topics of interest to you: *Personal Finance For Dummies* (Wiley), by one of us — Eric Tyson — can help you to review your overall financial situation. Besides giving you a better grasp of your personal finances, that book walks you through the process of finding and interviewing financial advisors you may consider hiring.

If you do end up hiring someone to help analyze your situation, the more educated you are, the more you can evaluate that person's competence and make efficient use of your advisor's time and, hence, your money. Always clarify what expertise you're seeking — be it tax, legal, retirement planning, investment advice, or whatever. And remember that a good advisor's job is to lay out the facts, discuss the options, and recommend what's in *your* best interests.

✔ **Obeying your landlord:** As a homeowner, you get to call the shots. You can change the interior and exterior of your home as you please. As a renter, you're largely at the mercy and whims of your landlord. If you're used to owning your own home and not having to answer to a landlord, adjusting to the realities of tenant life can be difficult. So, if you do sell and return to the ranks of renters, spend as much time inspecting and interviewing your prospective landlord as you do examining the rental unit. Remember that your landlord can sell the building, possibly forcing you to move again — with added expenses.

Researching reverse mortgages

If you're happy and content with your home but want more money to live on in retirement, a reverse mortgage may be for you. If you're house rich but cash poor, a reverse mortgage enables you to tap into the equity in your home while you still live in it.

However, if you're like most older homeowners, you've worked so hard for many years to eliminate a mortgage and get your darn home "paid for" that the thought of reversing that process and rebuilding the debt owed on your home is troubling. *Reverse mortgages* are newer loan vehicles that few people understand. And most of today's reverse mortgage borrowers are low-income, single seniors who've run out of other money for living expenses.

Thus, it isn't too surprising that people who don't fully understand reverse mortgages often have preconceived, mostly negative notions about how they work. Your first reaction may be to say, "I don't want to be forced out of my home; I could end up owing more than the house is worth."

Rid yourself of those notions. You won't be forced out of your home and you (or your heirs) won't end up owing more than your house is worth. Federal law requires that reverse mortgages be *non-recourse loans,* which simply means that the home's value is the only asset that can be tapped to pay the reverse mortgage debt balance. In the rare case when a home's value does drop below the amount owed on the reverse mortgage, the lender must absorb the loss.

Installment sale

Some house sellers don't take their proceeds in one big lump sum. Instead, they set up an installment sale — a plan that spreads out proceeds payments over future years. In addition to delaying your required income tax payments until you receive the future house-sale money (and enabling you to earn interest on that money in the meantime), an installment sale also can lower your income taxes. For example, you may save tax dollars if — because you're on the verge of retiring — you're expecting to be in a lower tax bracket in future tax years.

If you're considering an installment sale, be sure to pick up a good tax advice guidebook and/or consult a competent tax advisor who has experience with such transactions. Because you're delaying receipt of some of the sale proceeds, you're risking that the buyer may not pay you everything you're owed. In addition, the correct planning and reporting of an installment sale for tax purposes can be complicated, especially if the installment sale arrangement is unfamiliar to you.

Protecting your home's equity from nursing home expenses

Ironically, selling your house and renting in retirement has another "benefit." State governments are getting more aggressive about going after the home equity of people who enter nursing homes, deplete their assets, and then qualify for Medicaid (the state assistance program). In the past, in some states, protecting home equity from nursing home expenditures was possible. This legal protection no longer is available.

Congressional legislation passed in the mid-1990s mandated that state governments go after the home equity of Medicaid recipients. Although some states have been more aggressive than others about going after Medicaid recipient's home equity, home equity increasingly is treated as an asset available for nursing home costs, just like stocks, bonds, and mutual funds.

If you want your assets to go to your heirs rather than to your nursing home, start giving your assets to your heirs well in advance (at least five years) of your latter years of retirement when you're most likely to have more major health problems.

Current Medicaid rules include what is called *60-month lookback,* which means that, to determine whether you qualify for Medicaid coverage, Medicaid looks at assets that you held for the five years prior to your application for coverage. All assets that you disposed of during that period need to be used to pay for your nursing home expenses before Medicaid kicks in. And, if you're thinking about not disclosing the assets that you gave away, remember that it's a criminal offense to lie.

Some reverse mortgages are good, many are mediocre, and some are just plain bad. The best reverse mortgages merit your consideration. A good reverse mortgage enables you to cost-effectively tap your home's equity and enhance your retirement income. So, if you have bills to pay, want to buy some new carpeting, need to paint your home, or simply feel like eating out and traveling more, a good reverse mortgage can be your salvation.

Reverse mortgage basics

So what exactly is a *reverse mortgage,* and how does it work? Well, as the name suggests, a reverse mortgage *reverses* the traditional mortgage process. Think back to when you bought your first home. Unless you had generous and affluent relatives, you probably had to scrape together the money for the down payment and seeming never-ending closing costs. And then you were likely saddled with what seemed like a mountain of mortgage debt.

Every month, thereafter, you dutifully mailed to the mortgage lender a check for the monthly mortgage payment. In the early years of your mortgage, a major portion of those monthly mortgage payments went to pay interest on your outstanding loan balance, but a small amount of each of payment went toward lowering the principal, or in other words, reducing the loan balance. (As the years roll by, the loan balance should pay down at a faster and faster rate until, eventually, your mortgage is paid off.)

A reverse mortgage reverses that process. When you take out a reverse mortgage, the mortgage lender typically sends you a monthly check. Imagine that! You can spend the check any way your heart desires. And, because the check represents a loan, the payment to you isn't taxable.

As the reverse mortgage lender gives you more payments, you accumulate an outstanding loan balance. You typically don't have to pay back your reverse mortgage loan until the home is sold (and then the loan and the accrued interest is paid back from the sale proceeds) or, with some reverse mortgage programs, when you move out of the property.

Reverse mortgage payment options

The whole point of taking out a reverse mortgage on your home is to receive money that is drawn from the equity you have in your home. How much can you tap? That amount depends mostly on how much your home is worth, how old you are, and the interest and other fees that a given lender charges. The more your home is worth, the older you are, and the lower the interest rate and other fees a lender charges, the more you should realize from a reverse mortgage.

You can decide how you want to receive your reverse mortgage money:

- **Monthly:** Most people need monthly income to live on. Thus, a commonly selected reverse mortgage payment option is monthly. However, not all monthly payment options are created equal. Some reverse mortgage programs commit to a particular monthly payment for a preset number of years, and other programs make payments as long as you continue living in your home or for life. Not surprisingly, if you select a reverse mortgage program that pays you for the rest of your life, you're going to receive less monthly, probably a good deal less, than from a program that pays you for a fixed number of years.

- **Line of credit:** Rather than receiving a monthly check, you can simply create a line of credit from which you draw money by writing a check, whenever you need income. Because interest doesn't start accumulating on a loan until you actually borrow money, the advantage of a credit line is that you pay for only what you need and use. If you have fluctuating and irregular needs for additional money, a line of credit may be for you. Because you have to take the initiative to draw on a line of credit, some thrifty seniors have a hard time tapping and spending the money. The size of the line of credit is either set at the time you close on your reverse mortgage loan or may increase over time.

What about taking out a new mortgage or home equity loan?

You may be wondering, "Why do I want to get involved with this complicated reverse mortgage business when I could just take out a home equity loan or a new mortgage on my home?" The problem with traditional "non-reverse" mortgage loan options is that you have to begin paying them back soon after taking them out.

The following example illustrates the problem: Suppose that you're the proud owner of a home worth $225,000, and you have no mortgage on the home. You want to stay in the home and have no desire to sell it and move. You speak with some lenders and discover that they're willing to lend you $100,000 through a 15-year mortgage at 8 percent.

Getting $100,000 in your hands right now sounds appealing. However — and this is a big however — you need to begin making payments of $956 per month on your traditional mortgage loan.

Now, if you invested the $100,000 that you borrowed in some high-quality bonds, you'd discover that you may get only about a 7 percent return, which bring in only $583 of monthly income, not nearly enough to cover your monthly mortgage payments. If you invest in stocks and earn the market average return of 10 percent per year, which is by no means guaranteed, that return translates into only $833 per month — still less than the monthly payment required by the mortgage.

Now, if you're thinking that you can simply live on the $100,000 principal to supplement the money from the investment returns, don't forget that you're going to have to keep making payments, and the longer you live in the house, the more likely you are to run out of money and begin missing loan payments. If that happens, unlike with a reverse mortgage, the lending institution may foreclose on your loan, and you can lose your property.

- ✔ **Lump sum:** The least beneficial type of reverse mortgage is the lump sum option. When you close on this type of reverse mortgage, you receive a check for the entire amount that you were approved to borrow. Lump sum payouts usually only make sense if you have an immediate need for a substantial amount of cash for some purpose, such as wanting to gift money to family or to make a major purchase.

- ✔ **Mix and match:** Perhaps you need a large chunk of money soon for some purchases you've been putting off, but you also want the security of a regular monthly income. You can usually put together combinations of the preceding three programs. Some reverse mortgage lenders even allow you to alter the payment structure as time goes on. Not all reverse mortgage lenders offer all the combinations, so shop around even more if you're interested in mixing and matching your payment options.

The costs of reverse mortgages

Reverse mortgage lenders, of course, aren't charities; they make money on reverse mortgages by charging an interest rate on the amount borrowed and by collecting other fees. Although many of the costs of a reverse mortgage are similar to those charged on a traditional mortgage loan, some are unique. On a reverse mortgage, you typically see these types of fees:

- ✓ **Interest:** As with a traditional mortgage, the interest rate on a reverse mortgage can either be fixed or adjustable. Fixed-rate loans offer peace of mind because you know upfront what your loan's interest rate will be. However, you typically end up paying more interest over the life of the loan for the security of a stable interest rate.

  With adjustable-rate reverse mortgages, the overall level of market interest rates determines your loan's future interest rate. If you get an adjustable-rate mortgage and rates significantly increase, your outstanding loan balance increases faster, thus leaving less equity for the day when your home is finally sold. Odds are better, though, that an adjustable-rate loan will save you on interest costs over the long run, because interest rates rarely skyrocket and remain elevated. Because you're taking on additional risks with an adjustable loan, you'll probably owe less total interest on your reverse mortgage with more equity remaining for you and your heirs after your house is sold.

  Fixed-rate reverse mortgages make the most sense for seniors who anticipate using their loans over a number of years — preferably seven or more. Fixed-rate loans also help you sleep better at night if you're the type who frets over fluctuating interest rates.

- ✓ **Upfront fees:** Most reverse mortgage lenders charge you fees for processing your application, fees for pulling a copy of your credit report, and other fees for originating your loan.

- ✓ **Closing costs:** Your reverse mortgage lender will want to appraise your home to determine its worth. This appraisal helps determine how much you can borrow on your home. The more your home is worth, the more money a reverse mortgage lender lets you tap from your home's equity. Other common closing costs include title insurance, local recording fees, and inspections.

- ✓ **Insurance costs:** When a reverse mortgage lender commits to giving you a reverse mortgage, the institution is taking a risk. If you live much longer than the lender expects, and your home's future value falls far short of the expected worth, the reverse mortgage lender can actually lose money if the amount of your outstanding loan balance exceeds the value of your home. To reduce the risk, mortgage lenders buy insurance. And guess what? You get to pay for the insurance, either as a yearly fee (sometimes called a *risk pooling fee*) or as a percentage of your home's value when you take out your reverse mortgage.

> ✔ **A portion of your home's value or future appreciation:** Some reverse mortgages include an additional cost. On some loans, this cost is based on a portion of the appreciation in your home's value from when your reverse mortgage began. On other loans, this added cost is a portion of the value of your home when your reverse mortgage is ultimately paid off from the sale of your home.

Understanding and shopping for reverse mortgages takes time and patience. Don't rush the process. A number of nonprofit counseling agencies, supported through government funding, stand ready to assist you with sorting through the reverse mortgage options in your area. Start with the AARP (202-434-6044; www.aarp.org/revmort). At the state level, check with the Department of Aging; at the local level, check with the Area Agency on Aging (call the Eldercare Locator Service at 800-677-1116 for the agency nearest you). We also encourage you to pick up a copy of the latest edition of *Mortgages For Dummies* (which we also co-wrote) for its wealth of useful material about all types of mortgages including reverse mortgages.

Tax Facts Sellers and Landlords Ought to Know

You can exclude from taxation a large amount of profits on the sale of a house: up to $250,000 for single taxpayers and $500,000 for couples filing jointly. Conditions are relatively lax: The seller must have used the property as his or her principal residence for at least two of the previous five years. The exclusion is allowed as many times as a taxpayer sells a principal residence but no more than once every two years.

If you're considering renting your home, even for just a short time, after you move out of it and before you sell it, tread carefully! *After you've converted your house into rental property, you can't avoid taxation on the profits from that property simply by purchasing another primary residence.* See Chapter 18 for more details.

We don't mean to frighten you out of turning your house into a rental property. You don't lose all your tax breaks; you get different ones. If you decide to turn a property into a rental, and then later sell it, you can roll over your capital gain into another "like kind" investment real estate property. Currently, the IRS broadly defines what a "like kind" property is. They allow you, for example, to exchange undeveloped land for a multi-unit rental building. Just remember that the IRS draws a sharp line between a primary residence and a rental property, and they won't let you roll profits over that line.

The rules for rolling over a gain from one rental property to another (called a *1031* or *Starker exchange*) are strict. To begin with, you're allowed little time to complete the rollover — only six months — and you must also identify a replacement property within 45 days of the sale of the first property. You aren't allowed to handle the proceeds: They must pass through an escrow account. Because of the complexity of the transaction, please do yourself a favor and find an attorney and/or tax advisor who can guide you through the process and ensure that you do it right.

Before you consider converting your home into a rental property, in addition to understanding the tax issues that we just discussed, also weigh the following:

✔ **How do you feel about being a landlord?** Managing a rental property takes time, patience, and knowledge of local rent-control laws. Some tenants are a pain, and premises occasionally need repairs. You can hire a property manager, but this service costs money, and finding a good one can be a challenge.

✔ **What about wear and tear?** If you've gone to great lengths to make your house immaculate, realize that renters aren't going to treat your home with the same loving care that you gave it. Although you can protect your interests somewhat by securing from your tenants a large security deposit (*at least* one month's rent), you can't expect them to pay for the inevitable and gradual wear and tear.

For documentation purposes, you may also videotape the interior of the rental, including the condition of floors, walls, and so on. Beware, though; you may find that, at the end of the lease, your tenants disagree with you over what you think is unreasonable wear and tear.

✔ **What's the cash flow?** Tally up all the monthly property expenses that you anticipate and compare that amount with the expected rental income. If you've recently bought your property or have little equity in it, you may be unable turn a profit. The worst-case scenario is that the additional monthly cash drain cramps your budget and causes you to accumulate consumer debt or underfund your tax-deductible retirement accounts.

See Chapter 18 for more information about selling rental property.

Chapter 3

Exploring the Economics of Selling

As Forrest Gump would've said if he'd been a real estate agent, "House selling is like a box of chocolates . . . you never know what you're gonna get." You never know how much your house is really worth until you reach an agreement with a prospective buyer. And even after you decide to accept an offer, you never know what surprise costs may crop up before your deal actually closes.

We don't mean to introduce uncertainty here. Although it's an inexact science, there's no reason you can't reasonably *estimate* your expected proceeds of sale. This chapter can show you how.

If money isn't a constraint for you and you can comfortably make the move that you're proposing, feel free to skip this chapter. Spend the free time reflecting on how fortunate you are!

Estimating Proceeds of Sale

You may need to get a certain amount of money from the sale of your house, or at least know before you can close on a deal how much you'll receive. Take the time to understand the particular probable proceeds of sale under the following scenarios:

✔ **You're strapped for cash because you want to buy a more expensive home.** You need to know *before* you sell if you'll have enough money to complete your next purchase. If you don't know this amount, the worst-case scenario is that the sale of your current house doesn't leave you enough money to buy your next one. Although you probably won't end up homeless, you may end up renting for a while and having to make an extra move, or having to scrounge around at the last minute for money.

✔ **You're trading down because you need more money for retirement.** Perhaps you want to receive a certain amount of money from your house sale to afford a particular retirement standard of living. If you're not realistic about how much cash you'll net from the sale, you may end up wasting a great deal of time and money on a house sale that yields less cash than you need or expect.

✔ **You're relocating, in part, because of finances.** If you have a choice about taking a job in some other part of the country, you may be tempted to relocate if you think that you'll be more comfortable financially. However, if you're simply assuming or guessing that you'll be better off in the new area, you may be wrong. You need to gather and review some facts before you move.

Note: Throughout this discussion of estimating house sale proceeds, we assume that you don't have an employer who's willing to pay for some of your house selling and moving costs. If you're relocating because of a new job, by all means negotiate to have your new employer pay for some or even all the expenses related to your house sale. You'll have that much more money to plow into your next home.

Estimated sale price

Clearly, the price at which you can sell your house is the biggest factor in determining how much money you'll be able to put into your pocket from selling your house. The estimated sale price, unfortunately, is also the hardest number to pin down.

You shouldn't allow your *needs* to dictate the price at which you list your house for sale (see Chapter 10). Prospective buyers of your house don't care about your needs, wants, or desires — such as, "I need $250,000 from the sale of my house to retire." Your house's asking price should be based on the house's worth — which sometimes may not be to your liking. Your house's worth is best determined by examining the recent sale prices of comparable houses. A good real estate agent can put together a comparable market analysis for you. If you're selling your house yourself, we explain in Chapter 10 how to prepare a comparable market analysis yourself.

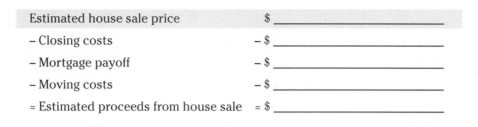

Estimated house sale price	$ _____
– Closing costs	– $ _____
– Mortgage payoff	– $ _____
– Moving costs	– $ _____
= Estimated proceeds from house sale	= $ _____

Closing costs

Selling a house costs a good deal of money. Generally, expect to pay about 7 to 10 percent of the house's sale price in various closing costs for which you, as the seller, may be responsible. A *closing cost* is an expense that you incur in the sale of your house and that reduces the total money you receive from the sale. The typical closing costs include

- ✔ **Real estate agent commissions:** If you're selling your house through real estate agents, they typically take a commission of 5 to 6 percent of the selling price. As we discuss in Chapter 6, you may choose to work with agents. If you do work with agents, the commission percentage you pay is negotiable and may be somewhat lower on higher-priced properties.

- ✔ **Repairs:** Unless you've taken really good care of your house over the years, or you're selling in a strong local real estate market, you can also expect to shell out some money for corrective work. For example, in some communities, you may need a pest-control and dry-rot clearance to sell your property. Inspections of your property may uncover building-code violations, such as faulty electrical wiring or plumbing problems, that you must repair. You need to consider having your house inspected before listing it for sale (see Chapter 7 for more info).

- ✔ **Transfer tax:** Taxes, taxes, taxes — the three sure things in life. Some cities and towns whack you with a transfer tax when you sell your house. Such taxes typically are based on the sale price of the property. Check with your friendly local real estate agent or your local tax collector's office to get an idea about your community's transfer tax rates.

- ✔ **Prorated property taxes:** Depending on the date you close on the sale of your house, you may owe money to bring your property tax payments up-to-date. In most towns and cities, unless you're delinquent with your payments, you probably won't owe more than six months of property taxes. In fact, because many communities require that you pay your property taxes in advance of the period that the payments cover, you may find that you're owed a refund of taxes from the buyer of your property.

Because you can't predict the date your house will sell, estimating the amount that you may owe in property taxes at closing is a tad difficult. You do know, however, whether you have to pay your taxes well in advance. If your local community has such a pay-in-advance payment system or you wait until the last minute to pay your taxes or make delinquent payments, you may want to budget three months or so of property taxes as a closing cost.

✔ **Possible credits:** If you've paid ahead on your property taxes, you may be getting a "refund" from the buyer of your house. You may also get a refund from your homeowners insurance company for the unused portion of your homeowners policy. And, finally, if you put less than 20 percent down when you originally purchased the house, your lender may have required that you pay a portion of your property taxes and homeowners insurance in advance each month and then held these payments in an impound account. (An *impound account* refers to money held in a trust account established by the lender which is used to pay property taxes and insurance premiums on your behalf when they're due). The lender refunds the unused funds from your impound account money when the sale is complete.

Do the necessary research for the above expenses if you want to more closely estimate expenditures on closing costs. Otherwise, for a safe, ballpark estimate, assume that 10 percent of the expected sale price of your house will go toward paying closing costs.

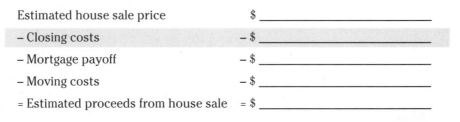

Estimated house sale price	$ _____
– Closing costs	– $ _____
– Mortgage payoff	– $ _____
– Moving costs	– $ _____
= Estimated proceeds from house sale	= $ _____

Mortgage payoff

For most people, the need to payoff an outstanding mortgage (or two) greatly depletes the expected proceeds from a house sale. Figuring out your mortgage payoff balance usually is a snap.

Simply whip out the most recent monthly statement you've received from your mortgage lender to find out the amount you still owe as of the date of the statement. You may need to make a couple of adjustments to this amount to make it more accurate.

First, on most mortgages, your outstanding balance should decline each month as you make additional payments. Because you can't sell your house immediately, your balance should decline between now and the date that you actually close on the sale. If your loan has negative *amortization* (the monthly payment falls short of paying the monthly interest that's accruing), your loan balance may be growing rather than shrinking.

Subtract from your outstanding balance the sum of the principal payments you'll be making between now and the proposed sale date. For example, if your most recent monthly mortgage statement shows that $200 of your payment went toward principal reduction, and you expect to hold onto the house for at least six more months, you can subtract $1,200 from your current outstanding balance.

Add to your balance any penalties that your mortgage lender may charge you for prepaying. Of course, if you bought *Home Buying For Dummies* (Wiley) when you bought your home, you avoided mortgages with a prepayment penalty.

If you have *any* doubts at all about whether your mortgage has a prepayment penalty, find out. You can either check your loan agreement (issued to you at the time you originally closed on your mortgage) or ask your mortgage lender (check your statement for a phone number). Write down the information you're given, the name of the person you spoke with, and the date. You may also ask that person to send you something in writing to confirm the information you were provided by phone.

You can try negotiating with the lender to reduce or remove the prepayment penalty. A good bank may offer to cut you a deal if they realize that you may do more of your future banking with them if they keep you happy. Your lender may also waive or greatly reduce a mortgage prepayment penalty if the buyers of your house use your lender to finance their purchase. If it's a large prepayment penalty, you can ask that the buyers obtain their mortgage from your lender, presuming the lender has competitive loan terms.

Most mortgage lenders assess a nominal fee for sending you a payoff statement detailing, to the penny, the cost of paying off your loan balance on a specific day, as well as for other paperwork fees. These fees usually don't amount to more than $100 or so, but if you want to know exactly how much to expect, simply call your lender. If the fee seems excessive or you're willing to haggle, ask the lender to reduce these fees; some will comply with your request.

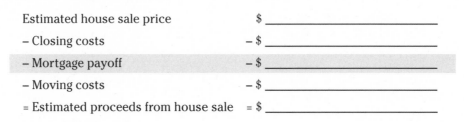

Estimated house sale price $ _____

– Closing costs   – $ _____

– Mortgage payoff   – $ _____

– Moving costs   – $ _____

= Estimated proceeds from house sale   = $ _____

Moving expenses

Over the years, you've probably accumulated more stuff than you realize. Whether you've piled knickknacks in your closets, filled your attic with boxes of gadgets, lined your garage with old bikes, or decorated every room with the finest furnishings, you're going to have to pack up all your stuff and have someone haul it away.

Most people don't have the equipment, experience, and muscle power to move all their stuff themselves. If you're like most folks on the move, you call a moving service. As with any other service business, prices and quality of service vary.

The farther you move and the more weight you're moving, the more the costs escalate. Move the contents of a typical one-bedroom house about one-third of the way across the United States, and you can easily spend several thousands of dollars. Move the same items all the way across the country, and the cost may double. Moving the contents of a spacious four-bedroom house halfway across the country can run you about $15,000 to $20,000.

Be sure to research moving costs, especially if you're selling a big house filled with furniture and other personal possessions or if you're moving a great distance. Get bids from several reputable movers and check references. Price and quality of service vary greatly.

Estimated house sale price $ _____

– Closing costs   – $ _____

– Mortgage payoff   – $ _____

– Moving costs   – $ _____

= Estimated proceeds from house sale   = $ _____

Putting it all together

After you understand the important elements of determining your proceeds from the expected sale of your house, you can work through the numbers to figure how much moola you hope to have coming your way.

Estimated house sale price	$ _____
– Closing costs	– $ _____
– Mortgage payoff	– $ _____
– Moving costs	– $ _____
= Estimated proceeds from house sale	= $ _____

Now that you know what proceeds you can expect from your house sale, what can and should you do with this information? As we discuss earlier in the chapter, this estimate is necessary if you're at all cash constrained in buying your next home or if you're selling to finance some important financial goal, such as retirement. (Be sure to review Chapter 2 to see if you can really afford to trade up and to make sure that you understand the important financial and tax issues involved in selling your home, particularly in retirement.)

Tax deductions for moving costs

If you're moving to a new job location, you can deduct from your taxable income many of the incurred moving costs that aren't paid for by your employer. These deductions include the cost of moving your household goods and personal effects and the cost of transporting yourself and your family from your old homestead to your new one. However, you can't deduct the costs of house-hunting trips, transaction fees for selling and buying the old and new residences, temporary living expenses, or the cost of meals during relocation travel.

To qualify for the IRS moving tax deduction (which is claimed on IRS Form 3903), you must pass two tests. First, the distance between your former house and your new job must be at least 50 miles greater than the distance between your former house and your old job. For example, suppose that you currently work 20 miles from your house. You get transferred to a new office that is 71 miles from your house. Because the difference between the two distances is greater than or equal to 50 miles, you pass the first test.

You must also pass the second test. During the 12-month period following your relocation, you must work at your new job on a full-time basis for at least 39 weeks. If you get fired after 38 weeks, you can't take any deductions.

These rules are even stricter for the self-employed. Refer to a good tax book (we're partial to *Taxes For Dummies* by Eric Tyson, Peggy Munro, and David Silverman) to get more information on these deduction details.

Assessing the Financial Feasibility of a Move

In the event that you're staying in the same neighborhood or community, estimating the cost of living in another home should be fairly easy. See Chapter 2 to help you organize and analyze potential changes in your budget.

If, on the other hand, you're relocating to a new area, don't make the common mistake of neglecting to consider possible changes in your overall expenses. Many people simply assume that their finances "will work out" while others fall prey to wishful thinking: "Because housing costs are lower in the area we're moving to, I'm sure we'll be financially better off."

We wish life was that simple, but unfortunately it isn't.

Researching living costs and employment opportunities

Before you commit to listing your house for sale and actually selling it, understand what your cost of living will be in the new area (check out Chapter 2). Your property taxes, utilities, food, commuting costs, and many other important items in your personal budget will change when you move into a new home in a different area.

If you don't consider the cost of living in the new location, you may end up facing unpleasant surprises. That's what happened to **Joanne** and **Andy:**

> Weary of working long hours to afford the seemingly high cost of living in Northern California, the couple viewed Andy's Midwest job offer as their ticket to financial freedom. Although the pay was about what Andy was receiving in his present job, Joanne and Andy figured they'd be on easy street, given how much cheaper home prices were in the town where they expected to live.

> So Andy happily accepted his new job offer, and he and Joanne quit their current jobs. They sold their house and decided to rent for a while after they moved so that they could better assess exactly where they wanted to live.

> After moving, Joanne and Andy spent the next several months in their new Midwest community looking for a home. Although they'd thought that housing was far less costly in their new area, they discovered that replicating what they had in Northern California — a community with parks, cultural amenities, and a good school system — cost more than they expected.

And then they discovered that some of the other things that they spend money on each month were even more costly in their new area. For example, Joanne and Andy found that their first winter's heating bill eclipsed the total annual utility bill that they paid out West! Food was more expensive, as were property taxes. And Joanne had great difficulty replicating her previous job because her profession was less in demand in the new area. When all was said and done, Joanne and Andy's new home in the Midwest put them in the same financial boat as they were in out in California.

Now, if Joanne and Andy had moved for nonfinancial reasons, then the fact that they didn't end up being better off financially may not have mattered. But, except for the seemingly high cost of living, Joanne and Andy had liked their location in Northern California. As they found, however, high home prices are only a piece of the local financial puzzle. You must also consider the other items in your budget and figure out how your income and expenses may change if you move.

Five years after their move, Joanne and Andy moved back to the San Francisco Bay Area. They made some adjustments to their spending so that they could accomplish their goals and live in the community of their choice.

Using a bridge loan to take equity out of a current house before a sale

Some people put themselves in a housing pickle that causes them to incur additional house-selling costs. The pickle results from buying a new home before their current one is sold.

Most people can't afford to own two homes at the same time; they need to get the cash out of their current home to buy a new one. Not surprisingly, the friendly lenders invented a way for people to get around this little inconvenience. It's called a bridge loan, and if you qualify, this loan enables you to borrow against the equity in your current property, giving you the cash to buy your new home before your current house sells.

Bridge loans are a bad idea for a number of reasons. First, if you get stuck holding both houses for many months, you face a continuing cash drain from making two mortgage payments, two property tax payments, and two insurance payments, as well as maintaining two houses. Second, the interest rate and fees on a bridge loan are quite high compared with a conventional mortgage. Finally, if housing prices head south, you may end up in deep financial trouble if you're unable to sell your current house for enough money to pay the outstanding loans against it.

As we advise in Chapter 5, you should sell your current house before buying a new one.

Numerous resources are available for estimating the cost of living in a particular area:

- ✔ The American Chamber of Commerce Research Association (ACCRA) publishes a quarterly cost-of-living index (online at ACCRA's Cost of Living Index Web site www.coli.org or by calling ACCRA at 703-522-4980). They charge $7.95 for a two-city comparison.

- ✔ The U.S. Department of Labor, Bureau of Labor Statistics calculates the cost of living for major metropolitan areas, and you can access this free information online at www.bls.gov/cpi/home.htm.

- ✔ Homefair.com offers a free salary calculator that easily enables you to compare salaries between two different towns or cities. Visit the Web address www.homefair.com and click "The Salary Calculator" link on the home page.

Cost-of-living indexes and surveys should be used only as a starting point and as general guidelines. They shouldn't replace a thorough budgetary breakdown that addresses the specifics of your situation. Sure, the indexes may tell you that Louisville generally is cheaper than Boston, but they ignore the fact that, for example, you never needed a car in Boston, because you could walk to work and take the subway almost everywhere else. Your job in Louisville may require you to buy a car, auto insurance, and fuel for commuting, in addition to more airplane trips to visit your family in the Northeast.

Avoiding relocation traps

As Joanne and Andy found in the preceding section, you shouldn't act first (move and buy a new home) and ask questions later (see the section "Researching living costs and employment opportunities" earlier in this chapter). Don't base such a critical decision on assumptions and wishful thinking.

Here are the common pitfalls that ensnare those making relocation decisions so you can avoid falling into them yourself:

- ✔ **Equating lower housing costs with a lower cost of living:** This was one of the big mistakes Joanne and Andy made. The cost of housing probably accounts for no more than a third of your spending. So if you don't consider the other goods and services you spend money on, you neglect the lion's share of your budget. *Research all the major costs of living in an area before you commit to relocating to the area.*

✔ **Not doing an apples-to-apples comparison of housing costs:** Again, Joanne and Andy made this mistake. To a certain extent, you get what you pay for. Housing costs are lower in communities with fewer amenities, inferior schools, poor commuting access, and so on. So if you're looking at relocating to an area with much lower housing costs, you need to be skeptical instead of thinking that you've found the deal of the century. Ask yourself, "What does that area lack that my current area offers?"

✔ **Ignoring the overall opportunities in the local job market:** Your next job is just that — your next job. You're probably not going to stay in this job for decades on end. So, when you're contemplating moving to a new area, think bigger than just this "next" job. Unless you enjoy the cost and hassle of relocating frequently, consider your chances for finding your next couple of jobs in a given area. Although it's impossible for some people to know what they're going to want to do several years down the road, considering the job market for more than your current job can save you from relocating more than you need to or leaving behind an area you otherwise like.

If you're married, you also need to consider your spouse's job prospects in your new community. In the case of Joanne and Andy, they learned the hard way about the pitfalls of focusing on only one person's job.

✔ **Taking the place where you live for granted:** All too often you appreciate what you liked about a place only after you move away. Maybe, for example, you're tired of the urban congestion and dream of the relaxed pace of a more rural community. After you make the move, however, you really start missing going to the theater and eating out at cosmopolitan restaurants. Pretty soon, you find yourself spending a great deal of money to escape the "boondocks," traveling back into the city to see musicals and eat Indian food.

Chapter 4

Confronting Financing Issues

In This Chapter

▶ Analyzing mortgage options when you trade up

▶ Understanding the ins and outs of lending money to buyers

"Financing issues?" you're wondering to yourself. "What does that have to do with selling my house? I'll worry about financing my next home when the time comes." It would be nice if sellers could ignore financing issues . . . one less thing to worry about. Unfortunately, sellers aren't off the hook on that one.

You definitely should pay attention to financing issues when trading up. If you sell your house to buy another and take on too much debt and a risky mortgage, you can end up strapped for cash or, worse, losing your new home and the equity in it. The more that you borrow, the more money you can save through the wise shopping and selection of the best mortgage for your situation. You may decide to improve your current home and will face the challenge of paying for those expenditures.

Or perhaps the prospective buyers of your current house want you to lend them money to make their purchase a reality. If you agree, you have to think about financing issues but from the other side of the fence — that of the lender. Lend money to a non-creditworthy buyer who can't afford to make mortgage payments and you may have to play Mr. or Ms. Banker with the unpleasant duty of foreclosing your old property. This chapter helps you to deal with these important borrowing considerations.

Financing Decisions When Trading Up

You need to examine your overall financial situation *before* you commit to trading up to a more costly property. Make that assessment now if you haven't already done so (see Chapters 1 and 2 for more info). This section highlights a few important decisions you need to make.

Choosing your mortgage

Because this book is about selling a house rather than buying one, we won't cover in detail how to choose a mortgage when you're buying a home. However, if you're thinking about trading up, you'll ultimately buy as well as sell, so we highlight the important considerations in selecting a mortgage. Keep these issues in mind as you begin thinking about selling your house, particularly if you're stretching your finances for the trade up.

Because you already own a home, this section may just be a refresher course. But the following are some brief definitions for the major types of mortgage options:

- **Fixed-rate loan:** As the name implies, this loan is one with a permanent interest rate that never changes. You take out the loan at a certain interest rate, and that rate is locked in for the life of the loan, which, in most cases, is a term of 15 or 30 years. Obviously, with an interest rate that is constant, your monthly mortgage payment is also constant.

- **Adjustable-rate mortgage (ARM):** The interest rate of an ARM varies over time, typically adjusting every 6 to 12 months, but sometimes as frequently as every month. These adjustments reflect the fluctuations in the interest rates of the overall economy. The monthly mortgage payment usually changes as often as the loan's interest rate does.

- **Hybrid loans:** Mortgage lenders weren't content to leave you with only two options, so they did some grafting and came up with another one, sometimes called *intermediate ARMs*. A hybrid loan starts out like a fixed-rate loan and then, after a certain number of years — three, five, seven, or even ten years — converts into an ARM, usually adjusting every 6 to 12 months thereafter.

  A newer twist on this type of mortgage, which we generally don't recommend, is interest-only loans that have lowered payments in their early years because you're only paying interest. When you begin paying back principal, the mortgage payment jumps significantly.

When choosing among the three mortgage options, ask yourself two questions:

- **How able and willing are you to take on financial risk?** Getting an ARM is a bit of a gamble. Although its initial interest rate usually is lower than that of a fixed-rate loan, if market interest rates go up, so does your monthly mortgage payment. If your cash flow doesn't have much breathing room, you may get into trouble. Before you take out an ARM, check out its *periodic adjustment cap* (the amount that the loan's interest rate can change at each adjustment) and *life of loan adjustment cap* (the highest interest rate allowed on the loan) so that you know how fast your monthly payments can increase and how high the allowable interest rate and your payment can go. If the ARM's maximum monthly payment would break your budget, don't get the loan.

✔ **How long do you plan to keep the mortgage?** If you don't intend to stick around in your new home for longer than five to seven years, then a hybrid loan makes more sense. Because the initial interest rates are lower than the rates on fixed loans, a hybrid loan definitely saves you money on interest charges in the early years of your mortgage. If, however, you intend to keep your mortgage more than seven years, you may be better off with a fixed loan.

If, after analyzing your financial situation as we discuss in Chapter 2, you see that you're stretching yourself financially, but you nevertheless want to trade up, be extra careful in going with an ARM. Although a fixed-rate loan starts off at a higher interest rate than an adjustable-rate loan, at least you know that your payment on a fixed-rate loan can't increase. If an ARM's potentially higher future payments would destroy your budget, stick with a fixed-rate loan.

Financing improvements

After reading our discussion in the earlier chapters of this book, you may decide to stay in your current home because you can improve it and make it more to your liking. Instead of having to go through all the time, trouble, and expense of selling your home and buying another, you can "trade up" by upgrading your current property.

Although improving your current home may enable you to get the home you want at less total cost than selling and buying another, you still need to make sure that you can afford the costs of the improvements. The more you spend on housing, the less you have for other important future expenditures, such as retirement, college educations for your little gremlins, and vacations.

Just be careful not to overimprove your home. For example, suppose that you want to add a second story and put in a pool. If those additions give you the most expensive house on the block, you may have a problem recouping the renovation costs when you attempt to sell your house. If that situation is okay with you or you can rationalize by saying, "Heck, it'll cost me big bucks to sell this house and buy another," then improve to your heart's content.

You have several options for financing the work to be done on your home. If you can afford it, the simplest route is to pay cash for the improvements. Unless you have some investment in mind that you think can provide a high enough rate of return to justify borrowing to finance the project, you're better off using your available cash.

Here's why. Suppose that you have the choice of using available cash or borrowing money at 7 percent interest to finance your home improvements. If you borrow to pay for the project and keep your cash to invest, you're going to lose out financially if you don't earn at least 7 percent, before state and federal income taxes, on your investments. (Note that, although your mortgage interest may be tax-deductible, your investment profits are generally taxable.)

For example, if you invest your cash in a boring old bank savings account that pays just 3 percent interest, you'd have been better off using your cash to pay for your home improvements instead of borrowing. Unless you invest in growth investments, such as stocks or rental real estate, you're unlikely to earn an average of more than 7 percent annually over the long-term. "Safer" investments, such as Treasury bonds or certificates of deposit (CDs), simply won't provide returns that high.

What if you don't have tens of thousands of dollars burning a hole in your wallet, crying out for you to spend them on remodeling your kitchen? If you have equity in your home — that is, the market value of your home exceeds the mortgage balance you owe on it — you may be able to borrow against that equity.

Generally, you can most cost effectively borrow on your home's equity up to the point where the total mortgage(s) outstanding on the property is equal to or less than 80 percent of the market value of your home. For example, suppose that your home is currently worth $250,000 (as determined by a lender's appraisal), and you have an outstanding mortgage of $150,000. As long as your financial situation enables you to qualify, you can borrow up to a total of $200,000 (that is, 80 percent of $250,000) — $50,000 more than you currently owe — under reasonably favorable terms. If you borrow more than 80 percent of the current market value of your home, you generally must pay a higher interest rate and more upfront loan fees. You may also get stuck paying private mortgage insurance, which protects the lender financially in the event you default.

You can tap the equity in your home in two ways. You can pay off your current mortgage and get a new first mortgage for enough additional money to cover the remodeling job, or you can take out a separate home-equity loan. The best option for you depends mainly on how good the deal is on your current mortgage compared to the current level of mortgage interest rates.

For example, suppose that your existing fixed-rate mortgage was taken out at an interest rate of 6 percent and fixed-rate mortgages currently are going for 7 percent. You probably don't want to give up your existing loan because the interest rate is lower than current loan rates. Under this scenario, taking out a home-equity loan (second mortgage) probably makes more sense. (***Note:*** Because home-equity loans are riskier from a lender's perspective — they make the lender a secondary creditor to the first mortgage lender — the interest rate on a home-equity loan generally is a little higher than the rate on a comparable first mortgage.)

Now reverse the scenario. Suppose that you took your fixed-rate mortgage out years ago at a higher interest rate, say 8 percent. Now, you can obtain a loan at a lower rate, 7 percent. In this case, you may as well go ahead and refinance to benefit from the current, lower interest rates.

One final consideration in choosing between a home-equity loan and a refinanced mortgage: If you don't need to borrow much money to pay for the improvements and you think that you can pay the money back within a few years, you may want to go with a home-equity loan. The reason: Refinancing a large first mortgage is probably going to run you much more in upfront fees than taking out a smaller home-equity loan.

The Trials and Tribulations of Seller Financing

In an episode of the popular television series *Seinfeld,* Newman, a mailman and a buffoon, appeals a speeding ticket in court. Newman's defense: He was rushing to the aid of his friend, Kramer, who was on the verge of killing himself because he had failed to achieve his lifelong dream of becoming a banker. In that episode, Newman loses the case not only because he's a terrible liar, but also because Kramer's failed career aspirations seemed, well, so preposterous!

Have you ever dreamed of being a banker? Unless you're in the business, probably not. As a child, your career aspirations were probably more along the lines of being an astronaut, athlete, doctor, or police officer. However, when selling your house, you may need to know a bit about lending and financing. This section has you covered.

Asking yourself why you'd ever want to be a lender

So, why all this talk about bankers and why in the world would you want to be one? You may want to take on the role to lend money to the buyer of your house, that's why. And what would possibly motivate you to do such a thing? Usually one of the following:

> ✔ **Desperation:** Some houses are difficult to sell because of major warts and some won't sell because they're overpriced.
>
> ✔ **A high interest rate on your money:** We can see those dollar signs in your eyes. You can earn a higher rate of interest lending money to the buyer of your house than you can investing through bank accounts and most bonds.

If your local real estate market is slow or you're having difficulty selling your property, you may sweeten the appeal of your house by offering to be the mortgage lender. Prospective buyers of your property may realize that they can save thousands of dollars in loan application fees and points (upfront interest). After all, you're not a big bank with costly branches to operate and countless personnel to pay.

By offering seller financing, you broaden the pool of potential buyers for your house. Traditional mortgage lenders are subject to many rules and regulations that force them to deny quite a number of mortgage applications. But, as we discuss in upcoming sections, making loans to borrowers rejected by banks can be risky business.

So you absolutely, positively must thoroughly review a prospective borrower's creditworthiness *before* you agree to lend him money as a condition of selling him your house. We explain how to make this evaluation later in this chapter in "Finding creditworthy buyers."

In addition to helping sell a house, some sellers are motivated to play banker and lend money to the buyer of their property because the mortgage usually carries an attractive interest rate, at least when compared to the typical returns on conservative investments, such as bank savings accounts (currently 3 percent) or CDs and Treasury bonds (currently around 5 percent). If you have money to invest but investing in stocks terrifies you, lending money to the buyer of your house may interest you. You may be able to earn 8+ percent in interest by lending your money to a borrower.

Agreeing to offer a mortgage to the buyer of your house can clearly be advantageous; the loan may help sell your house faster and at a higher price and, at the same time, provide a better return on your investment dollars. However, nothing that sounds this good ever comes without some real risks. If you lend your money to someone who falls on difficult financial times or simply chooses to stop making mortgage payments, you can lose money, perhaps even a great deal of money. And you may have to take legal action and foreclose if the buyer defaults on the loan. And if all that isn't bad enough, you'll again be the owner of a house that you thought you'd sold, with all the associated expenses of home ownership, including higher loan payments for the buyer's new first mortgage and, most likely, a higher property tax bill. Foreclosed homes also tend to deteriorate under the care of the prior owners so you can also expect fix-up costs.

The dangers of relying on faith and hope

Ron was interested in selling his house, and Mark, an old college buddy, happened to be renting nearby and was looking to buy. Ron and Mark thought it was a real estate match made in heaven. "I can sell without paying those exorbitant real estate agent commissions," said Ron. "I can buy a house now without having a large down payment," said Mark.

Mark, in fact, had only 5 percent of the purchase price for his down payment. Ron had another friend, an attorney, draw up a loan agreement that didn't require any down payment. Ron didn't want his good friend, Mark, to deplete what little cash he had, so Ron agreed to a no-money-down loan.

Within in a few short weeks, Mark moved into his new home and Ron moved out of the area. Mark mailed his monthly mortgage checks to Ron and all seemed well.

Two years after the purchase, the proverbial horse manure hit the fan. Mark, who was already up to his eyeballs in consumer debt (credit cards and an auto loan), lost his job. Mark was already a couple of months behind in his mortgage payments, and he obviously didn't start catching up after he lost his job.

Ron, being a good friend, was extremely understanding, but his patience evaporated when Mark stopped calling him and filed for bankruptcy. To make a long, ugly story short, in addition to losing what appeared to be a good friend, Ron also lost a good deal of money. Home prices had dropped about 20 percent since Mark bought the house, which Ron foreclosed and became the proud owner of once again.

What are the lessons of this story?

✔ Never make a loan without thoroughly and completely reviewing the financial situation of the borrower. Neither assume, nor guess, nor act on faith, nor hope.

✔ Be careful in doing business with friends. If the deal goes sour, you can lose more than money.

Deciding if seller financing is for you

Most house sellers aren't in a position, financially or otherwise, to provide financing to the buyer of their home. So, before you waste too much of your time reviewing and reading the rest of this chapter, make sure that you're in a position to seriously consider providing financing.

To consider making a loan against the house that you're selling, you should be able to answer yes to all the following questions:

✔ **Will you be able to purchase the next home you desire without the cash you're lending to the buyer of your current house?** This issue keeps most sellers out of the financing business. If you need all the cash that you have as a down payment to qualify for the mortgage on your next home, seller financing is out of the question. And, if you can lend some of your money to the buyer of your house, don't make the loan if you then need to borrow more yourself for your next home purchase. Even if you can charge the buyer of your current house a percent or two more in interest on the money you lend than you'll pay for the money you're borrowing to buy your next home, such an arrangement generally isn't worth the hassle and financial pitfalls.

✔ **Do you desire income-oriented investments?** Understand that mortgages are a type of bond. When you invest in a bond, your return comes from interest if you hold the bond to maturity. Unlike investing in stocks, real estate, or a small business, you have no potential for making money from appreciation when investing in bonds held to maturity. So if you're looking for growth as well as income, seller financing isn't for you.

✔ **Are you in a low enough tax bracket to benefit from the taxable interest income on the mortgage loan?** If you're in the federal 28 percent or higher tax bracket, consider investing in tax-free bonds, such as municipal bonds, and *not* mortgages, the interest on which is fully taxable. The reason: The interest income from municipal bonds is free of federal taxation and sometimes state income taxation. By contrast, the interest income from a mortgage is taxable as ordinary income at the federal and state levels.

✔ **Are you willing to do the necessary and time-consuming homework to determine the creditworthiness of a borrower?** As we discuss in the next section, unless you secure a large down payment (25 percent or more of the value of the property) from the buyer of your house, you need to be darn sure that the borrower can pay you back. So if you're looking for a simple, non-time-consuming investment, look elsewhere. Try mutual funds.

✔ **Can you weather a default?** Even if you do all the homework we suggest in this chapter before agreeing to lend money, the buyer/borrower still can default on you just as he can on a banker. Bad and unforeseen events can happen to borrowers. Accept this reality. Ask yourself if you can financially tolerate going without the borrower's payments for many months during the costly and time-consuming process of foreclosure.

Finding creditworthy buyers

After you determine that you have spare cash to invest or lend, and you're looking for taxable interest income, the hard work comes: putting on your detective hat and assessing the merits of lending your money to a prospective buyer who's more than likely a complete stranger.

Doing second mortgages

A prospective buyer of your house may ask you to provide 10 percent of the financing in the form of a second mortgage while a traditional mortgage lender provides an 80 percent first mortgage and the buyer makes a down payment of 10 percent of the purchase price of your house. A second mortgage means that if the borrower defaults, you're second in line behind the first mortgage lender who has first rights to the value of the property after foreclosure. You're entitled to the amount left over.

Consider such a loan if, *and only if,* you do all the homework we suggest in this chapter to check out the creditworthiness of a borrower, and if you can accept the risk that you can lose your entire investment (the loan) if property prices

fall and the borrower defaults. Be sure that you also meet the criteria we laid out earlier in this chapter in the section entitled, "Deciding if seller financing is for you."

As an alternative to making a risky second mortgage loan yourself, some lenders make loans when the borrower makes less than a 20-percent down payment. Such low-down-payment loans keep you, the house seller, out of the financing business and enable you to sell your house to a prospective buyer with a 10-percent or less down payment. Tell your cash-short prospective home buyers to ask mortgage lenders and brokers about low-down-payment loans.

So how do you, someone who isn't a mortgage lender by profession, become a savvy credit analyst? Perhaps you've heard the expression, "Imitation is the sincerest form of flattery." Well, do what bankers do when deciding whether to lend someone money.

The first thing that a lender does in her evaluation of the creditworthiness of a prospective borrower is to bury him in paperwork. As a lender, you absolutely, positively must gather financial facts from the borrower. You can't accurately assess the risk of lending money to a buyer, even one whom you've known personally for a number of years, without going through the information-gathering exercise in this section.

 Only agree to make a loan to the buyer of the property when he's able to make at least a 20 percent down payment. Bankers normally require a down payment of that size for good reason: If the borrower defaults and the banker is forced to hold a foreclosure sale, the down payment provides a cushion against the expenses of sale and possible losses in property value if real estate prices have declined since the loan was made. If the buyer falls on hard times at the same time real estate prices go into the tank, you may find yourself in the unfortunate position of repossessing a house that's worth less than the amount the borrower owes on it.

So, what documents should you request and what information should you look for? We're glad you asked; we tackle that topic in the following sections.

The loan application

The best way we know to get data from a prospective borrower is to have him complete the Uniform Residential Loan Application (see Figure 4-1), also known as Form 1003, which mortgage lenders almost always use. You can obtain one of these forms through mortgage lenders or mortgage brokers. (If, because no profit is in it for them, they're unwilling to send you a form for your personal use, you can pose as a prospective borrower and have them mail you their standard application package. You can also find the forms online for free at www.efanniemae.com/sf/formsdocs/forms/1003.jsp.

Be sure to review the sample real estate purchase contract (for California) in Appendix A. Pay particular attention to Paragraph 2, which covers financing terms and conditions. Even if you don't live in California, the provisions and precautions in this excellent contract are useful.

After you receive the completed application from the borrower, be sure that it's completely filled out. Ask for explanations for unanswered questions. The following list explains how to evaluate the information in various parts of the form:

- **Type of mortgage and terms of loan:** Asking the borrower to fill in these sections isn't vital; the legal loan document that you both sign later contains information on the terms of the loan — the loan amount, interest rate, length of the loan, and the loan type (fixed-rate or adjustable-rate). Later in this chapter, we walk you through the steps for setting the terms of your loan and having a loan agreement prepared.

- **Property information and purpose of loan:** You can also skip most of this section of the application. The address of the property and its legal description (the block and lot number that come from the title report) are specified in the loan agreement. Although you know that the borrower is obviously buying, you may not know whether he's going to use the property as a primary or secondary residence or as an investment property. If the buyer intends to rent the property for investment purposes, your loan is riskier, and you should charge a higher interest rate than you'd charge an "owner-occupied" buyer (see "Deciding what to charge" later in this chapter).

Verify the source of the buyer's down payment and closing costs to ensure that this money isn't yet another loan that may handicap the buyer's ability to repay the money that you're lending him. The down payment and closing costs should come from the buyer's personal savings. Ask to see the last several months of the buyer's bank and investment account statements to verify that the funds have been in the accounts during that time and didn't arrive there recently as a loan, for example, from a relative.

Uniform Residential Loan Application

This application is designed to be completed by the applicant(s) with the Lender's assistance. Applicants should complete this form as "Borrower" or "Co-Borrower," as applicable. Co-Borrower information must also be provided (and the appropriate box checked) when ☐ the income or assets of a person other than the Borrower (including the Borrower's spouse) will be used as a basis for loan qualification or ☐ the income or assets of the Borrower's spouse or other person who has community property rights pursuant to state law will not be used as a basis for loan qualification, but his or her liabilities must be considered because the spouse or other person has community property rights pursuant to applicable law and Borrower resides in a community property state, the security property is located in a community property state, or the Borrower is relying on other property located in a community property state as a basis for repayment of the loan.

If this is an application for joint credit, Borrower and Co-Borrower each agree that we intend to apply for joint credit (sign below):

Borrower _____   Co-Borrower _____

I. TYPE OF MORTGAGE AND TERMS OF LOAN

Mortgage Applied for:	☐ VA ☐ FHA	☐ Conventional ☐ USDA/Rural Housing Service	☐ Other (explain):		Agency Case Number	Lender Case Number
Amount $	Interest Rate %	No. of Months	**Amortization Type:**	☐ Fixed Rate ☐ GPM	☐ Other (explain): ☐ ARM (type):	

II. PROPERTY INFORMATION AND PURPOSE OF LOAN

Subject Property Address (street, city, state & ZIP)	No. of Units
Legal Description of Subject Property (attach description if necessary)	Year Built

Purpose of Loan	☐ Purchase ☐ Construction ☐ Other (explain): ☐ Refinance ☐ Construction-Permanent	Property will be: ☐ Primary Residence ☐ Secondary Residence ☐ Investment

Complete this line if construction or construction-permanent loan.

Year Lot Acquired	Original Cost $	Amount Existing Liens $	(a) Present Value of Lot $	(b) Cost of Improvements $	Total (a + b) $

Complete this line if this is a refinance loan.

Year Acquired	Original Cost $	Amount Existing Liens $	Purpose of Refinance	Describe Improvements ☐ made ☐ to be made Cost: $	

Title will be held in what Name(s)	Manner in which Title will be held	Estate will be held in: ☐ Fee Simple ☐ Leasehold (show expiration date)
Source of Down Payment, Settlement Charges, and/or Subordinate Financing (explain)		

III. BORROWER INFORMATION

Borrower	Co-Borrower
Borrower's Name (include Jr. or Sr. if applicable)	Co-Borrower's Name (include Jr. or Sr. if applicable)

Social Security Number	Home Phone (incl. area code)	DOB (mm/dd/yyyy)	Yrs. School	Social Security Number	Home Phone (incl. area code)	DOB (mm/dd/yyyy)	Yrs. School

☐ Married ☐ Unmarried (include ☐ Separated single, divorced, widowed)	Dependents (not listed by Co-Borrower) no. ages	☐ Married ☐ Unmarried (include ☐ Separated single, divorced, widowed)	Dependents (not listed by Borrower) no. ages
Present Address (street, city, state, ZIP) ☐ Own ☐ Rent ___No. Yrs.		Present Address (street, city, state, ZIP) ☐ Own ☐ Rent ___No. Yrs.	
Mailing Address, if different from Present Address		Mailing Address, if different from Present Address	

If residing at present address for less than two years, complete the following:

Former Address (street, city, state, ZIP) ☐ Own ☐ Rent ___No. Yrs.		Former Address (street, city, state, ZIP) ☐ Own ☐ Rent ___No. Yrs.	

IV. EMPLOYMENT INFORMATION

Borrower	Co-Borrower
Name & Address of Employer ☐ Self Employed	Yrs. on this job	Name & Address of Employer ☐ Self Employed	Yrs. on this job
	Yrs. employed in this line of work/profession		Yrs. employed in this line of work/profession
Position/Title/Type of Business	Business Phone (incl. area code)	Position/Title/Type of Business	Business Phone (incl. area code)

If employed in current position for less than two years or if currently employed in more than one position, complete the following:

Freddie Mac Form 65   7/05   Page 1 of 5   Fannie Mae Form 1003   7/05

Figure 4-1:
The first page of the Uniform Residential Loan Application.

✔ **Borrower information:** In this section, the borrower tells you about himself/herself, or themselves, with regard to educational background and housing history. More schooling typically translates into greater job stability for a borrower.

If the borrower hasn't lived in his most recent housing situation for at least two years, be sure that he also lists two prior residences. If the borrower was renting in his recent housing situation(s), request a letter from the buyer's landlord to verify that rent was paid on time. Alternatively, ask for both sides of canceled checks or checking account statements covering the most recent 12-month period evidencing timely rental payments. If the person moved frequently in recent years, check with more than the most recent landlord. Borrowers who've had trouble paying rent on time may well have trouble making regular mortgage payments. Ask for explanations of any red flags you find.

✔ **Employment information:** Even more important than a borrower's recent housing record is the employment record. Here, you're again looking for stability as well as an adequate income to make housing payments. If the borrower hasn't been in the most recent position for at least two years, ask the person to list prior employment to cover the past two years. (*Note:* The borrower actually lists the monthly income from the current job in the next section of the application.)

✔ **Monthly income and housing expense projections:** In this important section, the borrower details monthly employment income as well as income from bank, brokerage, and mutual fund investments. In addition to income from bank accounts, stocks, bonds, or mutual funds, a borrower may have income from real estate rental properties. For most people, obviously, employment provides the lion's share of their income.

The buyer's expected monthly housing expenses (which include the mortgage payment, property taxes, and insurance) should be compared against (divided by) the borrower's gross (before-tax) monthly income. Most mortgage lenders require that a homebuyer's monthly expenses do not exceed about 33 percent of the homebuyer's monthly income; we think that's a good ratio for you to work with as well.

However, like a good banker, you don't want to be rigid. If someone's proposed monthly housing expenses come in at 34 percent or 35 percent of her monthly income and the borrower has a good job, large down payment, solid references, and so on, then you may decide to go ahead and make the loan, especially if the deal gets your house sold.

✔ **Assets and liabilities:** The borrower should also tell you about her personal assets and liabilities. The mortgage application form divides the buyer's assets between those that are liquid and therefore available for a down payment or closing costs (for example, savings and money market account balances outside retirement accounts), and those that aren't so liquid (retirement account investments or real estate).

In the liabilities section, the borrower should detail any and all outstanding loans or debts. Be wary of lending to someone who carries a great deal of high-interest consumer debt (such as credit cards or auto loans). If the borrower has the cash available to pay off consumer debts before closing, have her pay those balances.

✔ **Details of transaction:** The purpose of this section is for you and the borrower to make sure that the borrower has enough money to close the purchase. The first part of this section tallies the cost of the house, including closing costs. Subtract the expected loan amount from this total. The result is how much money the borrower needs to come up with to close the purchase.

✔ **Declarations:** In this section, the borrower should disclose any past financial or legal problems: foreclosures, bankruptcies, and so on. If the borrower answers any of these questions in the affirmative, ask for a detailed written explanation.

Documentation, documentation, documentation

If you borrow from a lender, the staff asks that you provide a raft of financial documents. If you're the lender, you need to ask for the pile of papers, too. You may rightfully wonder why you need more paperwork after the buyer completes a detailed loan application.

Unfortunately, some people lie. Even though you may think that you have the most financially stable, honest, and creditworthy buyers nibbling on your "house for sale" fishing line, don't start reeling them in yet. You need to get the additional paperwork to prove and substantiate the borrower's financial status. Pay stubs, tax returns, and bank and investment-account statements document the borrower's income and assets. Just because someone tells you on an application form that he's earning $5,000 per month doesn't prove that he really is.

When verifying the information supplied on the mortgage application, ask the prospective borrower for the following documents:

✔ Federal income tax returns and W-2s for the past two years

✔ Original pay stubs for the past month or two (if the borrower is self-employed, request a year-to-date income statement and balance sheet)

✔ Award letter and copy of the most recent check if the borrower receives pension, Social Security, or disability income

✔ Past three months of account statements for money to be used for down payment, as well as copies of all other investment accounts (including retirement accounts)

✔ Most recent statement for all outstanding loans

✔ Divorce or separation papers if the borrower pays or receives alimony or child support

You also should obtain, at the borrower's expense, a copy of his or her credit report(s) to check credit history and to ensure that you're aware of all outstanding debts. Check your local yellow pages under "Credit Reporting Agencies" for such providers. The larger consumer credit reporting agencies include Experian, Trans Union, and Equifax.

Even when you request and receive all this documentation, some buyers still can falsify information, which is committing perjury and fraud. For example, some people, particularly those who are self-employed, may make up phony income tax returns with inflated incomes.

Borrower problems

As you may know from your own personal experience, some people don't have perfect financial and credit histories. In some cases, a prospective borrower may have enough problems for you to reject the application. In other situations, however, the problems may be minor, and can be overcome by taking some simple steps and precautions.

Here are common problems likely to crop up with prospective borrowers, and our best advice on how to deal with each situation:

✔ **Income appears too low to support monthly housing costs:** The best way to protect your interests if you're considering lending to someone who's stretching (in terms of monthly income) to afford your house is to ask for a larger down payment. As we discuss in the next section, you can charge a higher rate of interest for lending to someone who's a greater credit risk. Another strategy is having the borrower get a cosigner, such as a parent.

✔ **Past credit problems:** Just because someone has nicks on her credit report doesn't mean that you should immediately reject the loan application. Credit reporting agencies and creditors who report information to the agencies sometimes make mistakes. Someone who has a small number of infrequent late payments shouldn't be as big a concern as someone who has reneged on a loan. Ask the borrower for a detailed explanation of any problems you see on the report and use your common sense to determine whether that person is simply human or irresponsible with credit. In the latter case, you may suggest that the borrower enlist a cosigner.

> ✔ **Outstanding consumer debt:** If the borrower has the cash available to pay off the debt, have him or her do so as a condition of making the loan. If the borrower lacks the cash to pay off consumer debt and lacks a 20-percent down payment, you're probably better off not making the loan, unless the buyer's income provides a great deal of breathing room. If you're on the fence, consider having the borrower get a cosigner.

Deciding what to charge

After determining that a buyer is creditworthy, you can get down to the brass tacks of setting the terms — interest rate and fees — on the mortgage. As with collecting the financial data on a borrower, you don't need to reinvent the wheel.

Because agreeing to terms and administering an adjustable-rate loan are complicated, you're far more likely to make a fixed-rate mortgage. Call several local lenders to find out the rates they're charging for the size and type loan that you're contemplating (for example, 15- or 30-year fixed-rate mortgage, first or second mortgage, owner-occupied or rental property). Be sure to ask about all the fees — application, appraisal, credit report, points, and so on. Although you may not charge all these same fees, you nevertheless need to understand what the competition is charging.

Some states have usury laws that forbid unregulated lenders (that is, private individuals like you) to charge loan origination fees, prepayment penalties, and so on. These laws also put a ceiling on mortgage interest rates that unregulated lenders can charge. You should consult a local, competent real estate lawyer about local usury laws.

All else being equal, you should charge a higher interest rate for jumbo loans (loans in excess of $417,000 for a single-family dwelling as of 2007), longer-term loans, loans with less than 20 percent as a down payment, rental property loans, and second mortgages.

If the borrower is in good financial health and can easily qualify to borrow from a traditional lender, offer better terms than the commercial competition. You may decide to charge the same interest rate but not upfront fees. Most buyers are short on cash, so a reduction in closing costs usually is well received. Besides, unless the buyer sells or refinances within a few years, a mortgage's ongoing interest rate is the greatest determinant of how much you make anyway.

Charge a premium to borrowers to whom you're willing to lend but who are unable to get a good loan — or any loan — from traditional lenders. Remember, you need to be compensated for the extra risk you're taking. You may add as

Getting permission to request tax and financial documents and to verify employment

As an extra precaution in verifying the authenticity of a borrower's income tax return, have the borrower complete and sign IRS Form 4506 *(Request for Copy of Tax Return)*. This measure enables you to request and obtain, directly from the IRS, a copy of the actual tax return(s) the borrower filed with the IRS.

To verify bank and other investment account balances, as well as current employment, mortgage lenders usually have borrowers sign a simple one-page permission form authorizing them to contact organizations that can confirm the borrower's financial information.

Copies of statements can be falsified and so can pay stubs. And, even if a prospective borrower produces a recent pay stub, that doesn't mean that he's still employed. If you want to maximize your chances of making a successful and profitable loan, get authorization to verify account balances and employment. On the other hand, if the borrower is making a substantial down payment (20 percent or more) and you otherwise feel confident in his ability to repay the loan that you're extending, you may simply rely on copies the borrower provides for you.

The figure shows a sample form that you can use to obtain the borrower's permission for you to request account balances and verify employment.

Authorization Release

I/we authorize (insert your name) to verify any necessary information in connection with evaluating my/our mortgage application, including but not limited to the following:
1. Credit history
2. Employment records
3. Bank/investment account histories
4. Loan histories
Authorization is further granted to (insert your name) to use a photostatic copy of my/our signature(s) below, to obtain information regarding any of the aforementioned items.

_____	_____
Applicant/Borrower	Social Security Number
_____	_____
Applicant/Borrower	Social Security Number

much as 1 percent or 2 percent to the ongoing interest rate on the loan and charge fees comparable to a lender. Be absolutely sure about the reasons why the borrower got turned down for a loan from a traditional lender and make certain that you're comfortable with taking on a risk that an experienced mortgage lender wouldn't.

Protecting yourself legally

Unless you've made mortgage loans before, you may not have a clue as to how to go about drawing up a loan agreement, so hire a real estate attorney to draw one up for you. Expect the cost to be several hundred dollars — that amount is money well spent. See Chapter 7 for how to find a good real estate attorney.

One final piece of advice: If you sell the house and make an owner-occupied loan to the buyer, you may afterward want to ask for proof that the borrower is living in the property rather than renting it out. You can ask for utility and other household bills to see if the bills are in the buyer's name. Or you may just stop by and knock on the front door of your old house to see who's living there.

Part II
Tactical Considerations

The 5th Wave   By Rich Tennant

"I just don't get it. The Robinson's next door
sold their house in 5 days and it was the exact
same model 3-room ranch house that I have."

In this part . . .

If you've decided to part company with your humble abode, this part is where you tackle some challenging questions: Should you sell your current house before or after you buy your next home? When during the year is the best time to sell your house? Should you sell your house yourself or use a real estate agent? How do you go about assembling an all-star team of professionals to help you sell your house? Last, but not least, we explain the all-important listing contract you negotiate and sign if you hire a real estate broker.

Chapter 5

Timing Is Everything

. . . .

In This Chapter

▶ Knowing how to time the sale of your house

▶ Figuring out when to purchase your new home

▶ Closing both transactions simultaneously

. . . .

Thomas Edison, one of our country's foremost inventors, was often called a genius. He modestly said that genius was 1 percent inspiration and 99 percent perspiration. He should know. It took him years of hard work to invent the phonograph. And Edison tested more than 4,000 different filaments before discovering the one he ultimately used in the first practical electric light bulb. Insight helps, but there's no substitute for hard work and planning.

You don't have to be a genius to get top dollar for your house when you sell it. Nor do you have to be lucky, although a little luck here and there never hurts. To paraphrase Edison, lucky sales are 1 percent good fortune and 99 percent planning and perspiration.

If you follow the right steps *before* you put your house on the market, good fortune may come your way throughout the transaction. You can control the selling process instead of reacting to it on a crisis-by-crisis basis. You can create your own luck. This chapter shows you how to make time your best pal.

Timing the Sale of Your House

Time is your most precious gift. When it's gone, you can never get it back. Some people spend their time wisely; others foolishly fritter it away. Depending on how well or how poorly you use it, time can either be an ally or a terrible enemy during the sale.

In most communities, choosing the date that you put your house on the market is an important decision. Certain periods of each year are predictably advantageous for sellers. Others are just as predictably less than stellar.

Real estate marketing activity isn't flat throughout the year. No matter where you live in the United States, the real estate marketing calendar generally has two distinct peaks and valleys created by ebbs and flows of activity in your local real estate market (see Figure 5-1).

The sales peaks are higher and longer in good years, and the valleys are deeper and longer in bad years, but the marketing calendar's relentless rhythm never changes. These seasonal cycles are heartless. They don't care about birth, death, divorce, job loss, or any other life changes that force you to sell. You can't alter the rise and fall of market cycles any more than you can stop the tides. You can, however, use the predictability of these cycles to your advantage. This section helps you identify when the best times are to put your house on the market and which are the worst.

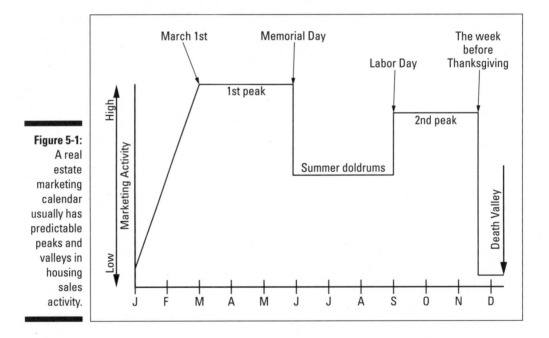

Figure 5-1: A real estate marketing calendar usually has predictable peaks and valleys in housing sales activity.

First peak season: Spring flowers and For Sale signs bloom

Calendar years begin January 1, but real estate years don't. Depending where you live, the longer and stronger of two annual peak seasons begins somewhere between late January and early March. If you live in a temperate area, such as Florida or California, the market kicks into gear a little sooner. If you're still digging out from under ten feet of snow on March 1, your market may take a little longer to heat up.

Weather aside, most folks don't bound out of bed on New Year's Day to buy a house. They need several weeks to adjust to the daily grind after that happy whirl of holiday parties and vacations. The buy-now, pay-later monster also rears its ugly head; people need time to recover from the trauma of paying all their holiday bills. As a result, many January buyers are extremely price conscious.

February through May normally is the most active selling time for residential real estate. Families with children want to get their purchase or sale out of the way by late spring so moving (which typically occurs 30 to 60 days after the ink dries on the contract of sale) won't disrupt the kids' schooling for the next academic year. Other people buy or sell early in the year for tax purposes or to avoid interference with their summer vacations. The annual outpouring of new listings pulls buyers out of the woodwork. Sellers are drawn into the market by all the buying activity.

The first peak season is usually the best time to put your house on the market. High sale prices result from spirited buyer competition. Because more buyers are in the market now than at any other time of the year, your best chance of getting a fast, top-dollar sale is during the first season. If you intend to buy another home after yours is sold, this time period offers the best selection of homes to purchase.

First valley: Summer doldrums

Memorial Day usually marks the beginning of the first valley. Sales activity usually slows during June, July, and August. People who bought or sold in the spring move in the summer. Buyers, sellers, and agents often take summer vacations, which reduces market activity. Many folks spend their weekends having fun in the sun instead of looking at houses. Who wants to be cooped up inside on a sumptuous summer day?

Houses ordinarily take somewhat longer to sell in the summer because of a lower level of buyer activity. Unless you have to sell now (or if property values are declining), wait until the fall to put your house on the market. You're likely to get a higher price after people return from vacation.

If you're selling your house to buy another one, keep in mind that summer is your first opportunity to go bargain shopping. Summer is a good time to find motivated sellers who bought a new home and *must* sell their old one fast before the ownership expenses of two properties put them in the poorhouse. Less property is available to choose from in the summer than in the spring, but plenty is still on the market.

Second peak season: Autumn leaves and houses of every color

Labor Day usually starts the second peak season. This peak normally rolls through September, October, and into November. Don't let the beautiful autumn leaves fool you, however. Just as fall brings a chill to the air, an icy edge of desperation develops in the second season for some sellers.

People who sell during late autumn tend to be *strongly* motivated. Some bought new homes in the spring before selling their old ones. Now they're slashing their asking prices — finally getting realistic after wasting months marketing overpriced turkeys.

Others are calendar-year taxpayers who sold houses earlier in the year and want to buy their new home before December 31. Why? So they can pay tax-deductible expenses (such as the loan origination fee, mortgage interest, and property taxes) prior to the end of the year to reduce the impact of federal and state income tax. Either way, these folks are under pressure to sell.

If you're a bit of a gambler, the second peak season may be the most reward-ing time to sell. Given that you correctly apply the pricing techniques we describe in Chapters 10 and 11, your house should sell quickly and profitably. Unless prices are rapidly increasing in your area, wait until activity slows in mid-November and then buy your next home at a discount price. You get the best of both worlds — "sell high and buy low."

Deciding to sell during the second peak season can be a risky gambit. If you inadvertently overprice your house, it won't sell. If you need to sell, carefully monitor buyer response to your property. Be prepared to drop your asking price as soon as you identify the danger signs (noted in Chapter 11). Don't wait until Thanksgiving to reduce your price. You may end up attempting to sell your house during the dreaded dead season (see the next section).

Another problem with waiting until the second valley in the real estate marketing calendar to sell your house and buy your next home is that you'll probably have a very small selection of houses to choose from. What good is a fantastically low price on a house you hate?

"Never try to catch a falling safe"

"Never try to catch a falling safe" is a common expression that describes the crushing financial burden of folks who compound their losses because they refuse to accept the reality of falling house prices in a declining market.

One of those safes smashed into Carlos and Jody, who bought a new home before selling their old one. Their tale began one Sunday about six months *after* prices peaked in one of San Francisco's real estate booms. A Victorian house they'd always admired had just come on the market. They decided to attend the open house and have a peek. The Victorian had high ceilings, great architectural details, and a gourmet kitchen. The master bedroom contained a working fireplace, and the extra bedroom would make a perfect home office. It was love at first peek.

"Can you believe our luck, Carlos? It's a steal at $895,000. They're practically *giving* it away. If we don't buy it today, someone else will."

"I like it, too, Jody. But how can we buy it? Our money is tied up in our house."

"Don't worry. Our house will sell fast. It's worth enough for us to afford this one. We'll get a long close of escrow so we have plenty of time to sell our house. What can go wrong?" Fortified by those comforting thoughts, they made a full-asking-price offer, which the sellers accepted.

Jody and Carlos then spent three weeks selecting an agent and spiffing up their house before putting it on the market. They asked $799,500, a price wishfully based on what they needed to net from the sale to buy their dream home.

Carlos and Jody were underwhelmed with offers. After five frustrating weeks with not even a nibble, they cut their asking price to $749,500 and pulled money out of their old house with a home equity loan to increase the deposit on their dream home. That "long" escrow was quickly nearing an end.

Jody and Carlos had a few showings after the price cut, but no offers. They finally got another home equity loan to close escrow. To their dismay, they'd inadvertently joined the elite ranks of people who own two homes. Their agent advised them to cut their asking price to $699,500 to prove that they were serious about selling.

At that price, they wouldn't clear enough from the sale to pay off the mortgage and home equity loans, but they had no alternative. They now had two mortgage payments, two insurance payments, two property tax payments, and two utility bills each month. They unhappily lowered the asking price and covered the shortfall by selling some bonds that they'd been saving for their kids' college expenses. (That swooshing sound you hear is a falling safe.)

Knowing that the longer they kept the house, the more bonds they'd ultimately have to sell to make ends meet, Jody and Carlos sold their house for $675,000 six weeks after their final price reduction. This financial debacle wouldn't have happened if Jody and Carlos had used the techniques described in this chapter.

Death Valley: Real estate activity hibernates until spring

The second peak season usually drops dead a week or two before Thanksgiving. With the exception of a few, mostly desperate, sellers and bargain-hunting or relocating buyers who stay in the market until the bitter end of December, residential real estate sales activity ordinarily slows significantly by mid-November. Folks stop buying property and start buying gifts. Would-be sellers take their houses off the market while their kids are out of school and their guests are visiting for the holidays. Ski slopes and sunny beaches beckon.

This real estate Death Valley is generally the worst time of year to sell a house. Even the brilliant pricing techniques in this book may not be able to save you from getting your financial bones picked clean by bargain-hunting vultures if you're forced to sell at this time of the year. The weather is miserable, and very few buyers are in the market. Time will show you no mercy if you wait until this point to get realistic about pricing your house to sell. Don't put your house on the market during Death Valley days unless you have absolutely no other alternative.

The Seller's Quandary: Timing the Purchase of Your Home

So which comes first, selling your house before buying a new one, or buying first and then selling? Neither course of action is risk free. The adverse consequences of buying a new home before selling your present house, however, can be far more dire. At worst, buying your dream house before selling your present house may put you in the poorhouse.

If you read the sad tale of Carlos and Jody in the "Never try to catch a falling safe" sidebar, you may think that selling first is the only correct answer. Believe it or not, you can make a compelling case for either course of action:

  ✔ **Selling before you buy eliminates financial risk.** When you sell first, you know precisely how much money you have from your sale to put toward your next home. No sleepless nights worrying about how you'll come up with the cash you need for a down payment on your new home or how much longer you'll have to make mortgage, property tax, and insurance payments on two houses. Your fiscal future is clear.

✔ **Selling first, however, introduces uncertainties and problems.** If you sell first, you may be forced out of your old house before you have somewhere else to go. Where will you live? Where will your kids go to school? Where will you store your grand piano and your bowling-ball collection if you're forced to rent an apartment while looking for another home? Do you really want to move twice? What if you can't find a home you like as much as the one you just sold? Putting your life on hold indefinitely while searching for a new home is emotionally draining and insomnia-producing.

Given a choice between either selling your present house first *or* buying your next home first, we strongly recommend that you sell your present house before purchasing a new home. Even in good real estate markets, sales frequently drag on much longer than you expect. Selling in a weak market usually compounds the problem. Homeowners tend to overestimate their house's resale value and underestimate the length of the selling process — a fiscally deadly one-two punch.

Consolidating Your Sale and Purchase

Suppose you don't want to sell your house first and then buy a new one. Nor do you wish to buy a new home before selling the old one. What then? You can use a third option to sell your old house and buy your dream home without terror, chaos, pain, or privation. Your best alternative is to consolidate the sale and purchase into a seamless whole. The following sections describe how.

Determine your house's current value

The ultimate success or failure of your transaction depends on *accurately* determining your house's present fair market value. Don't kid yourself. This isn't a place for wishful thinking. Overpricing is bad in any real estate market — in a weak market, overpricing is a sure prescription for disaster. You must be realistic when pricing your house, or the sale of your present property and the purchase of your new home may flounder.

In a nutshell, you can either pay to have your house appraised or get a written opinion of its fair market value (called a *comparable market analysis*) from several real estate agents who fervently want to represent you during your sale. Chapter 10 covers everything you need to know about establishing your house's value.

Check your buying power

Buying power is a function of the amount of cash you put down on your new home and the size of the mortgage you get. Both numbers are easy to figure out. Here's how:

- ✔ **Calculate your cash position by subtracting the probable expenses of sale from your house's estimated resale value.** Chapter 3 goes into probable expenses of sale, such as mortgage payoffs, corrective work credits, real estate agent's commissions, and property tax prorations. We also cover relocation traps, such as higher housing costs associated with buying a more expensive home than the one you own now. You see how to figure your proceeds of sale *before* putting your house on the market.

- ✔ **Have a lender evaluate your creditworthiness.** Find out the size of the mortgage you can get based on current interest rates, your income, and the probable down payment you can make on a new home if your present house sells at its estimated resale value. If you're nearly ready to sell your current house and buy another, now is a perfect time to get prequalified or, better yet, preapproved for a loan. Read Chapter 14 to see why preapproval can give you a negotiating advantage.

Lenders can't tell you how much money *you can afford to borrow* — just how much money *they're willing to loan you* based on their assessment of your ability to repay the mortgage. Lenders don't know or care about your other financial goals and objectives, such as providing for your retirement or socking away money to help your kids through college.

We, however, care a great deal about your financial well-being. That's why we devote Chapter 2 to helping you determine how the next home you buy fits into your overall financial picture.

Familiarize yourself with the market

Harry S. Truman, our country's 33rd president, was a renowned skeptic. He was fond of saying, "I'm from Missouri. You'll have to show me." Folks from the "show me" state don't value silver-tongued talkers. They live by the doctrine that seeing is believing.

When buying or selling houses, everyone needs to adopt Missouri's principle. Reading Chapter 10 to explore the *theory* of pricing property is all fine and good. However, merely reading about valuing houses can't turn you into an educated buyer or seller.

To properly educate yourself about property values, you must tour comparable houses. No amount of book smarts beats good old shoe leather and eyeballing.

You have to wear two different hats during your property tours:

✔ **Seller's hat:** A good comparable market analysis (CMA) prepared by a real estate agent to determine your house's current value contains two lists. One documents houses comparable to yours in condition, size, age, and location (called *comps*) that have sold within the past six months. The other shows comps that are currently on the market. You probably won't be able to get into properties that have already sold, but you should make a point of touring each comp currently on the market to verify your house's resale value.

If you're working with an agent, have him or her tag along when you tour property. As you walk through a house, ask the agent to point out similarities and differences between it and recently sold properties that you haven't seen. This "show and tell" greatly speeds up your discovery process. After visiting a few comps, you start to *see* which houses are priced to sell and which houses are overpriced turkeys.

✔ **Buyer's hat:** The house that you intend to sell and the home you want to buy may be different — different neighborhoods, styles, sizes, ages, conditions, and prices. Your new home may not even be in the same city or state. You won't, however, have to reinvent the wheel as a buyer because most principles of valuing property apply whether you're a buyer or a seller. Smart buyers also use CMAs. Seeing is still believing, and nothing beats touring property currently on the market so you know what's available when the time is right.

We also wrote a book to help buyers find their way through the purchasing maze. It's called — surprise, surprise — *Home Buying For Dummies* (Wiley).

Take action

Now you're ready to start the action phase — selling your old house and buying a new one. Timing is critical. If you structure your transactions properly from inception, you'll be in firm control of the process instead of the process controlling you.

Putting your house on the market

First things first. Let the world know that your house is for sale. You must, however, continue looking at any new comps that come on the market after yours *as well as* other new homes being offered for sale. The market constantly changes. New property becomes available. Houses currently on the market sell. A good real estate agent can keep you posted regarding important changes that may affect your situation.

Push your hands deeply into your pockets whenever you tour prospective dream homes. Untimely dreams have a way of turning into nightmares. As long as your hands are safely out of harm's way, you can't sign any purchase offers.

Don't make an offer to purchase your next home yet, for the following reasons:

- **Your asking price may be too high.** Even though you try your best to price your property to sell, you may inadvertently overprice it. You know that you've overpriced your property if purchase offers fail to appear. Because the amount you can afford to spend for your next home probably depends on the amount you net from the sale of your current house, knowing how much money you'll have available may be critical. If your budget provides little wiggle room and you're forced to reduce your asking price, you can simply make a commensurate adjustment in the amount you eventually pay for your new home.

- **You aren't a real buyer until you have a solid contract on the house you're selling.** Read Chapter 14 to understand why this statement is true. For now, trust us; any offer you make on a new home that depends on first selling your present house (if your house isn't in contract yet) won't be taken seriously. Real sellers refuse to tie up their property indefinitely while you attempt to sell your house.

Structuring your terms of sale

Chapter 14 gets into information you must know when offers for your house begin pouring in from potential buyers. For now, concentrate on one extremely important aspect of the deal you make — structuring your terms of sale to provide enough time to purchase your new home. You shouldn't need a ton of time because you're already familiar with prospective new homes currently on the market, and you're probably either preapproved or, at least, prequalified for a mortgage.

Here's how you can give yourself the time that you need to make a well-planned and executed purchase:

- **Schedule close of escrow on your old house to occur 30 days after the buyers remove all their conditions of purchase and increase their deposit.** Buyers may take three or four weeks to remove the two most common conditions of nearly all house purchases — mortgage approval and property inspections. Getting loan approval usually takes somewhat longer than completing the various property inspections. Thirty days is your magic number, because lenders normally won't hold their loan commitment more than 30 days after they approve a mortgage.

  Some lenders may be willing to hold mortgage commitments more than 30 days. One quick call to the buyers' loan officer is necessary to determine the lender's policy on this issue. If, for example, the buyers' lender guarantees a loan commitment 45 days after the loan is approved, schedule your close of escrow accordingly. The more time you give yourself to close your other transaction, the better.

✔ **You can get even more time by putting a "rent-back" clause in your counter offer to the buyers' purchase offer.** This clause lets you rent your house back from the buyers after escrow closes. It can buy you an extra month or two (or more) *if* the buyers agree to a rent-back. Sellers usually pay rent equal to their buyers' actual cost for principle, interest, taxes, and insurance. For example, if the buyers pay $1,500 a month for mortgage payments plus their prorated property tax and insurance payments, that amount is your rent. Although the rent may be more than you currently pay to live in your house, the amount is probably less than it would cost you to move into a motel for a month or two and much more convenient. As we note in Chapter 14, sellers are wise to prepare a formal lease agreement that covers the rent-back.

No standard rent-back clause exists. Check with your real estate agent or a lawyer to determine how rent-backs are best handled where you live.

Timing the offer to buy your new home

You may be tempted to rush out and make an offer on your dream home while the ink still is drying on the contract you just signed to sell your present house. Don't. Give yourself time to shake out deal-killing glitches in your sale before you make any offers on a new home.

✔ **Don't present an offer to buy your next home until the contract on your present house resembles the Rock of Gibraltar.** If you want the sellers of your new home to treat your offer with respect, delay making an offer until your buyers remove all their conditions of purchase and increase their deposit on the house you're selling. Until you know the buyers' mortgage is approved, and you resolve questions related to handling corrective work discovered during the property inspections, your contract is as solid as a bowl of pudding.

You may think that we're overly cautious when we urge you to wait until the contract for the sale of your house is rock solid before making an offer to buy your new home. We've seen seemingly solid deals blown apart out of the blue. The real estate gods can be cruel and fickle.

✔ **Make the offer to purchase your new home subject to the sale of your present house.** This step protects you from being forced to buy a second home. Your offer should specify that if the escrow for the sale of your house doesn't close within the time specified in your contract of sale, you have the right to cancel the contract to purchase the new property. If for some utterly unforeseen reason the sale of your house falls apart, at least you can get out of the contract to buy the new home.

Combining a 30-day close of escrow with a two-month rent-back clause gives you a three-month comfort zone in which to close the purchase of your new home. Ideally, you can simultaneously close the sale of your present house and the purchase of your new home. If you can't, however, then sell before you buy. You'll sleep better.

Chapter 6

For Sale By Owner

In This Chapter

▶ Selling without using a real estate agent — the pros and cons

▶ Hiring advisors to help with your sale

Approximately 20 percent of the houses sold in the United States each year are sales made directly by property owners without using a real estate agent. Selling your house yourself, without having an agent represent you, is commonly referred to as a *For Sale By Owner* or FSBO ("fizz-bo").

We know some people who've successfully sold their houses by themselves and others who've made a major mess of their transactions. Whether you opt to sell your house without an agent or conclude that hiring an agent is a better way to go, our paramount concern is simple: that your sale is as profitable and painless as possible. To that end, this chapter contains an objective look at the pros and cons of FSBOs.

Eyeing the Potential FSBO Advantages

After conversations with people who've actually gone through a FSBO, we've concluded that each seller's personal situation and motivation for selling is unique. The following sections describe the most common reasons why sellers choose to sell without using an agent.

You want to save money on commissions

People who've gone through a FSBO often do so to avoid having to pay real estate agent commissions. As we discuss in Chapter 1, the lion's share of the expenses related to selling your house are typically real estate agent commissions, which can gobble a large portion of your house's *equity* (that is, the difference between the market value of your house and outstanding mortgages). In most areas of the country, a 5 to 6 percent real estate brokerage commission is common. Thus, on a $250,000 house, the commission typically sets you back $12,500 to $15,000.

You may already have a ready, willing, and able buyer

If you spread the word that you're planning to sell your house, you may turn up someone who's financially able to buy and willing to pay you the amount that you feel your house is worth. Good for you. Why pay a full commission if you've already found a buyer? As we note in Chapter 8, you're in a good position to either negotiate a reduced commission with a real estate broker or hire an attorney to help you complete your transaction.

Whether you're contemplating selling your house with an agent or doing a FSBO, tell as many prospective buyers as possible that you're interested in selling. Although most people don't find a buyer for their house simply by getting the word out through their own network of friends and contacts, you won't know whether you'll be one of the fortunate few who successfully sell their houses this way unless you try.

Before you start getting the word out, take these tips to heart:

✔ Follow our advice in Chapter 1 to make sure that selling your house is the correct course of action for you.

✔ Read Chapter 10 to discover how to determine the fair market value of your property.

✔ Follow the tips in Chapter 9 to ensure that your house looks its absolute best.

✔ Hire a good real estate lawyer to review your house sale contract and other documents.

You may know the house and neighborhood well

You may know more about the strengths of your house and neighborhood than local real estate agents, especially if you've lived in an area for many years. You may be able to speak from personal experience about how child-friendly the neighborhood is and how terrific the local schools are. You can praise the virtues of nearby shopping, transportation, and entertainment. You can gush about your wonderful neighbors. And you can point with pride to all the improvements you've made to your house over the years.

Be careful in praising your house and neighborhood. As Chapter 12 explains, even the most interested prospective buyer can get turned off if you're overbearing or sound like a used car salesman. And, as we discuss in Chapter 8, what you say about your property may cause you legal problems down the road. If you're going to sell without a real estate agent, be sure to have a good real estate lawyer on your team to assist you with mandatory property transfer disclosures and to provide advice about what you should *avoid* saying about your house.

How much can you really save by doing a FSBO?

Maybe a friend, neighbor, relative, or business associate is interested in buying your house. If you know a ready, willing, and financially qualified buyer who wants to work with you directly, you may save the full standard real estate brokerage commission for your area, less a nominal fee paid to a real estate attorney.

In the best-case scenario, given that you make all the right moves and are an astute negotiator, you may save yourself a good deal of money. You're more likely, however, not to save the typical 5 percent to 6 percent real estate brokerage commission. Here's why:

- Unless you already have a buyer in hand or you find one quickly, you have to spend money advertising and marketing your house, as we describe in Chapter 12. Advertising costs money; the longer your house is for sale, the more you spend.

- You may have to pay a real estate commission if a cooperating real estate agent brings you a buyer. Most homebuyers work with agents, and these agents must be paid for bringing you a bona fide buyer. This expense alone can cut your expected commission savings in half.

- Last, but not least, most buyers expect to share the commission savings you're enjoying by not using an agent. They may expect to split the savings with you. If you're a strong negotiator and the prospective buyers aren't, you may be able to keep most of the savings for yourself.

Unless you can find a buyer without having to advertise your house for sale, or you sell your house to a buyer who isn't working with an agent, you can realistically expect to save about 1 percent to 2 percent of the sale price in a typical FSBO. Ultimately, of course, the amount you do or don't save depends on how much the buyers pay for your house. If you end up selling for a lower price than a good real estate agent could've fetched for you, the lower sale price may wipe out any commission savings.

Also, don't forget the value of your time — especially if you're self-employed or in a profession where your income suffers if you work less. Handling buyer and agent phone calls, showing the property, holding open houses, meeting property inspectors and appraisers, and handling escrow details take time.

You may be more motivated than an agent

Your house and the money you have tied up in it are important to you. Some real estate agents, despite having dollar signs in their eyes in anticipation of the commissions they'll earn if they sell your house, may be less than eager to invest sufficient time in promoting and showing your property.

If you decide to use an agent to help you with your sale, as we discuss in Chapter 7, exercise great care in choosing the right agent. Avoid overextended agents who juggle too many listings and clients to give your house sale the attention it deserves.

You like challenges

Some people don't select the easier path. For example, instead of working for a corporation, you may be the type who starts your own business. Many small business owners say that the desire for a potentially higher income wasn't the primary reason they started their own business. Some small business owners pursue this career path as a means of self-expression, to make a contribution to a particular field, or for the pleasure of working with and satisfying customers.

For the same reasons, some people try to sell their houses by themselves. Although most FSBO sellers are eager to save commission dollars, a few do it for the challenge or because they want to apply skills they possess to selling their own house.

You want to be in control

Some folks just don't like giving up control. If you're the type of person who wants to be in charge, you may be unwilling to relinquish control to an agent.

If you sell your house yourself, you can decide when and where to place ads for your house and exactly what features to emphasize. You may want to say when it is and *isn't* okay to have strangers (interested buyers and their agents) strolling through your house. Perhaps you want to ensure that your cat or the family dog isn't let out of the house by an agent who fails to notice your special showing instructions. Whatever the reason, for better or worse, you're the boss with a FSBO.

Your house may sell itself

If the local real estate market is strong, and good houses get multiple offers as soon as the For Sale sign goes up, you may feel that selling your wonderful house will be a snap. All things considered, FSBOs usually are more successful in a sellers' market than a buyers' market.

Focusing on Potential FSBO Disadvantages

Although selling a house isn't rocket science or heart surgery, it nevertheless requires some important skills as we discuss throughout this book. Even the smartest of FSBO sellers can get into trouble. This section points out a few cons to going the FSBO route.

You may not know how to price property

Grossly overpriced property isn't going to sell. Buyers and agents who know property values will, in fact, avoid it like the plague. In the end, you may not get as much for your house as you could have by pricing it realistically to begin with.

If you under price your house, you may sell it below its market value — shortchanging yourself thousands of dollars — perhaps even tens of thousands. Say goodbye to the commission you "saved." Chapter 10 deals with using a comparable market analysis (CMA) to determine your house's fair market value. Chapter 11 is filled with tips about how to fine-tune your asking price.

You may not know how to prepare your house for sale

Your familiarity with your house can be a liability if it blinds you to your house's flaws. You may like your house's clutter and quirks, but their dubious charms may turn off prospective buyers. One important benefit that a good agent brings to the table is a fresh pair of eyes and a desire to whip your house into get-it-sold shape. Chapter 9 spells out, in detail, what you should — *and shouldn't* — do to your property prior to putting your house on the market.

You may not know how to market your property

Did you know that a humble, low-tech For Sale sign and a classified ad are two of the most potent forms of advertising available to people who sell their houses without using an agent? Do you know how to use the Internet to market your house? Unless you have a background in real estate or marketing, you probably have some research to do. And, by undertaking a FSBO, you miss out on two powerful promotional tools only available to agents: the Multiple Listing Service (MLS) and brokers' tours of newly listed properties.

If you're undertaking a FSBO, be sure to read Chapter 12, which details the best advertising and marketing techniques to get the word out about your house. Chapter 8 delves into how, if you're selling without an agent, you can gain access to the MLS and brokers' open house tours on a fee basis from discount brokers. Scrutinize Chapter 13 to see what role computers can play in selling your house.

You may not know how to separate real buyers from fakes

Serious buyers make good offers. Bogus buyers waste your time and money. In the worst of all possible scenarios, you may unintentionally allow someone with criminal intentions into your house. Chapter 14 points out the three qualities that all good offers have in common. You can also find a section in Chapter 14 to help you distinguish real buyers from time-wasting fake ones.

You may not have enough experience as a negotiator

If you know that you're a weak negotiator, you have to be especially careful about selling your house without an agent. Not knowing smart negotiating tactics can cost you big bucks. Even if you *are* a good negotiator, your financial and emotional involvement in the sale may cause you to lose your cool when bargaining with a buyer, or you may undermine the deal by appearing greedy. Chapter 14 is brimming with techniques and tips for negotiating your price and terms of sale. Secure the services of a good real estate lawyer who, in addition to keeping you out of legal hot water, can also act as your negotiating agent.

You may get yourself into legal trouble

Selling your house yourself to save on real estate brokerage commissions is a hollow victory if the buyers sue you after close of escrow. Perhaps you didn't give them the mandatory federal, state, and local property disclosures about problems such as lead-based paints or work you did on the property without a building permit.

House selling is a team sport. Chapter 7 describes players you may need on your team, one of whom is a real estate lawyer who can help you put together a proper disclosure statement and sales contract if you're selling your house yourself. Also, be sure to read the section about property disclosures in Chapter 8.

Trying to save money by avoiding legal fees is a false economy. If you're not using an agent, you need to have a lawyer review the sales contract before you sign it. If that's not possible, at least put a clause in the contract to say your acceptance is subject to review and approval of the contract by an attorney of your choice within five business days after you sign it.

Don't discriminate! Disqualifying prospective buyers on the basis of race, color, religion, sex, handicap, familial status, or national origin is illegal. Discrimination can get you into a heap of legal trouble and can cost you big bucks. If in doubt, check with the Equal Housing Opportunity agency in your area.

You may not know how to close the sale

You won't save on commissions if your deal falls apart in escrow. As a FSBO seller, you have to make arrangements that a good listing agent normally handles. Do you, for example, know how to open an escrow, get a preliminary title report, order property inspections, handle contingency removals, and order a payoff demand for your mortgage? Chapter 15 guides you through the blocking and tackling necessary to complete your house sale after you have a signed purchase contract in hand.

Increasing Your Chances of Success

Selling a house without an agent is doable, but it's considerably more challenging than it looks. If, after weighing the pros and cons of doing a FSBO, you decide to attempt to sell your house yourself, be sure to read our final words of wisdom.

Educate yourself

The things you don't know generally are what get you into trouble. This book is crammed with tips and advice to help you sell your house for top dollar and steer clear of problems, whether you do a FSBO or use an agent. Unread, this book won't do you a darn bit of good — unless you're looking for a yellow paperweight.

We strongly urge you to read this *entire* book if you're going to sell your house yourself. Then again, if you decide to hire an agent, you may still want to read this entire book! Why? Because you can manage the transaction better and feel much more comfortable if you're knowledgeable about what's going on.

Even if you're certain about selling your house *sans* agent, interview several good agents (using the criteria we outline in Chapter 7). Interviewing agents may reaffirm that you can handle the sale yourself, or the interviewing process may convince you that you're better off hiring the best agent you contacted. You'll probably pick up some helpful advice and information you can implement if you do decide to sell yourself. And, if your FSBO isn't successful, you can always hire the best candidate after you've given FSBOing a shot. Either way, interviewing agents is well worth your time.

Ensure that other team members are especially strong

Without a real estate broker or agent on your team, making sure that your other players are the best they can be is all the more critical. Be especially careful to hire an excellent real estate lawyer. Chapter 7 details criteria you can use to select the members of your team.

Cooperate with agents

Because the vast majority of buyers work with agents, be sure to mention in your classified ads and listing statement that you "will cooperate with agents." This statement tells local agents that you're willing to pay them a commission if they procure the buyer who ultimately purchases your house.

Financially qualify prospective buyers

When someone makes an offer on your house, don't take your property off the market until you're sure that the buyer is going to be able to swing the deal financially. Few buyers are wealthy enough to pay all cash for your house. Most folks need to qualify for a mortgage.

Ideally, the buyers are *preapproved* for a loan with a conventional lender. As opposed to merely being *prequalified* — a quick financial once-over — preapproval means that they've gone through a rigorous financial examination. If, however, the buyers are just starting to shop for a mortgage, inquire about their occupations, incomes, and the source of their down payment for the purchase. When the buyers apply for a mortgage, get their permission to contact the lender to find out the likelihood of loan approval. (Even though you probably aren't going to be financing their purchase of your house, check out Chapter 4 to see what smart lenders look for on a mortgage application.)

Watch out for buyers who make their offer to purchase your house subject to the sale of their own house first. As we note in Chapter 14, this tactic, if handled improperly, can tie up your property and scare away other prospective buyers who are ready, willing, and able to buy immediately.

Chapter 7

Your Real Estate Team

A dentist Ray knows once compared what he'd just gone through during a protracted house sale to having root-canal work done on every tooth in his head . . . without Novocain. Don't take the dentist literally; he's a master of understatement.

Unless you're a masochist, you never willingly seek out intense pain. Yet we've seen smart people blunder into painful situations while selling their houses. The key word is *blunder*. What usually gets people into trouble is something that they (or the professionals they hire to handle the transaction) should've known, but didn't. No need to worry, though. This chapter takes a closer look at who you need on your real estate team and how to select them.

Teaming Up — a Winning Concept

Knowing everything about everything is impossible. What *is* possible, however (and much more important, to boot), is putting good people on your team — people who know the things you need to know to solve the problems that invariably arise during your sale.

You don't have to become an expert in property values, mortgages, tax and real estate law, title insurance, escrow, pest-control work, and construction techniques to play the house-selling game well. Instead, you can hire people who've already mastered the skills that you lack.

House selling is a team sport. Your job is to lead and coach the team, not play every position. After you assemble a winning team, your players should give you solid advice so you can make brilliant decisions.

If cost were no object, you'd hire every competent expert you could get your hands on. However, because you probably don't have an unlimited budget, you need to determine which experts are absolutely necessary and which tasks you can handle yourself. In this section, we explain which experts generally are worth hiring and which ones you can pass on. Ultimately, of course, you're the one who must determine how competent or challenged you feel with the various aspects of the house-selling process.

Here's an overview of the possible players on your team:

- ✔ **Your favorite person:** *You* are the most important player on your team. Sooner or later, another player is bound to drop the ball or fail to satisfy your needs. You have every right to politely, yet forcefully, insist that this person make things right. Remember that you hire the players on your team; they work for you. Bad players may see things the other way around — they want to believe that they're in charge. They may attempt to manipulate you into acting in their best interests rather than yours. Don't tolerate this behavior. You're the boss — you can fire and hire.

- ✔ **Real estate agent:** Because the house that you're getting ready to sell is probably one of your largest investments, you want to protect your interests by having someone on your team who knows property values. Your agent's primary mission is to *accurately* tell you what your house is worth and then negotiate on your behalf to sell it for top dollar.

- ✔ **Real estate broker:** All states issue two different real estate licenses: one for salespeople (agents) and one for brokers. Real estate brokers must satisfy more stringent educational and experience standards than agents do. If your real estate agent isn't an independent broker or the broker for a real estate office, a broker must supervise the agent. The broker is responsible for everything that your agent does or fails to do within the course and scope of the duties of real estate sales professionals. In a crisis, your transaction's success may depend on backup support from your agent's broker.

- ✔ **Property inspectors:** Your house's physical condition greatly affects its value. Smart buyers will insist on having your house thoroughly inspected from roof to foundation as a condition of the purchase. Don't passively wait for buyers to give you a copy of their report. Get your house thoroughly inspected *before* putting it on the market so that you know what to expect during any subsequent corrective-work negotiations with the buyer.

- ✔ **Escrow officer:** Mutual distrust is the underlying rule of many real estate deals. You and the buyer need a neutral third party, an *escrow officer,* to handle funds and paperwork related to the transaction without playing favorites. The escrow officer is the referee in the game of house selling.

✔ **Financial and tax advisors:** Before selling your house, make sure that you understand how the sale (and the purchase of another home, if applicable) fits into your overall financial situation. In Part I of this book, we explain how financial and tax advisors can help you evaluate these considerations.

✔ **Lawyer:** Whether you need a lawyer on your team depends on three things: the complexity of your contract, the location of your house, and your personal comfort level. As we discuss in Chapter 6, if you decide to sell your house without an agent, you definitely need a lawyer who specializes in real estate law on your team.

The purchase agreement you sign to sell your house is a legally binding contract. If you have any questions about your contract's legality, put a real estate lawyer on your team.

Each player brings a different skill into the game. Assemble members of a great team, and they guide you through any situation that may arise during your transaction.

Keep in mind that good players serve as *advisors* — not decision makers. Decision making is your job. After all, it's *your* money on the line.

Landing the Perfect Listing Agent

The real estate agent that you hire to sell your house, known as the *listing agent,* must be able to accurately answer your most important question: "What's it worth?" Houses sell for *fair market value,* which is whatever buyers are willing to offer and sellers are willing to accept. Fair market value isn't a specific number; it's a price range.

For example, suppose that an agent says that your property is worth $300,000, more or less. If your agent is a better negotiator than the buyer's agent, and the buyer desperately wants your house, you may sell it for $315,000. On the other hand, if you have to sell your house immediately, and the buyer has a better agent than you do, you may only get $285,000.

Sale prices often are directly related to a listing agent's knowledge of the price that comparable houses sell for and negotiating skills. Of course, other factors (such as the buyer's and seller's motivation, needs, and market knowledge) also are important.

A good agent can be the foundation of your real estate team. An agent helps you price your property, orchestrates the marketing and showing activities, negotiates with buyers on your behalf, supervises property inspections, and coordinates the closing. A good agent's negotiating skills and knowledge of property values can add 5 percent to 10 percent to your house's sale price.

Bad agents may pressure you to accept a low offer to make a quick sale. The real estate world is full of many well-intentioned-but-inept agents. In this section, we show you how to avoid the bad agents and how to sift through the hordes of mediocre agents to narrow the field down to good agents who are worthy of their commissions.

Understanding agent relationships

Sellers and buyers can have two types of relationships with real estate agents:

✔ **Single agency:** In this form of representation, an agent represents only one of the two parties (the seller or the buyer) in the transaction. In single agency, an agent may play one of two roles:

• **Seller's agent:** In this type of single agency, an agent works solely for the seller.

• **Buyer's agent:** In this type of single agency, the agent works only for the buyer. A buyer's agent isn't an agent of the seller even if the buyer's agent gets a portion of the commission paid by the seller.

✔ **Dual agency:** In this form of representation, the same agent represents the seller and the buyer. Dual agency is the most confusing and least understood form of agency. See the nearby sidebar, "Dual agency problems" for more info.

Ideally, you want a single agency relationship. However, given the ever-expanding market presence of large regional and nationwide brokerage firms, it's increasingly likely that you'll find yourself in a dual agency situation where the same estate brokerage *firm* represents both you and the buyer. Should that happen, we *strongly* recommend that you and the buyer at least work with different individual agents within the firm. If humanly possible, avoid having the same agent represent you and the buyer.

Recognizing the best listing agents

Good agents come in a variety of races, colors, creeds, and ages and may be male or female. All the best listing agents, however, have certain important qualities in common. They do the following:

✔ **Educate you:** Your agent knows the selling process and carefully explains each step so that you understand exactly what's happening *at all times*. Agents should be patient, not pushy. A good agent *never* uses your inexperience to manipulate you.

✔ **Enable you to make good decisions:** Your agent *always* explains what your options are so *you* can make wise decisions regarding your best course of action.

Dual agency problems

Most people think that *dual agency* means that one person represents the buyer and the seller. Although such arrangements are possible, that type of dual agency is highly inadvisable. Logically, one agent can't represent your best interests as a seller (getting the *highest* possible price) and the buyer's best interests (getting the *lowest* possible price) at the same time.

A more common kind of dual agency involves two different agents who work for the same real estate broker. For example, you list your house for sale with Sarah, an Acme Realty agent, who agrees to be your exclusive agent. Unknown to you and Sarah, Betty Buyer met Bob, who's also an Acme Realty agent. Betty liked Bob's style and asked him to represent her exclusively as a buyer's agent. Bob enthusiastically accepted. So far, so good. You have Sarah, your exclusive agent. Betty has Bob, her exclusive agent. Everything is fine, until Bob shows Betty your house. Betty loves it and instructs Bob to write up an offer on it immediately.

At the moment Betty decides to make an offer on your house, the agency relationships that you and Betty have with your respective agents change. Like it or not, Sarah suddenly represents you and Betty. Similarly, Bob becomes your agent as well as Betty's agent.

Why? Even though two different agents are involved in the transaction, both agents work for the same real estate broker — Acme Realty. As soon as Bob starts to work on Betty's offer, Acme Realty represents the seller and the buyer of the same property. *That's dual agency.*

You probably won't have to worry about dual agency if your agent works in a small office that has only a few agents. The odds that one of the other agents in your agent's office will have a buyer for your house are quite small. However, if the agent that you select works for a large brokerage operation with multiple offices and thousands of agents (such as Coldwell Banker, Century 21, and the like), your odds of having to deal with dual agency increase.

Most states permit dual agency relationships as long as the agency status is disclosed to the sellers and the buyers in advance, and both parties agree to it. Undisclosed dual agency, which occurs if the buyer and seller haven't been advised about or consented to dual agency, can be used as grounds for having a purchase agreement revoked and usually permits the injured parties to seek recovery against (that is, *sue*) the real estate agents.

✔ **Advise you if they think that you should add other experts (property inspectors, lawyers, and so on) to your team:** Experts don't threaten a good agent. The agent's ego should always be secondary to the primary mission of serving you well.

✔ **Voluntarily limit themselves geographically and by property type:** Good agents know that trying to be all things to all people invariably results in mediocre service. Even though real estate laws are the same throughout your state, different areas within the state generally have radically different market conditions, local zoning ordinances, and building code restrictions.

Agents go out of their area of geographical or property expertise for one of two reasons: because they're greedy or because they're too darn inept to know better. Whatever the reason, avoid such agents like the plague.

✔ **Are full-time professionals:** To reduce the financial impact of changing jobs, many people begin their real estate careers as part-timers, working as agents after normal business hours and on weekends. Such an arrangement is fine for the agents but not for you.

One of the first questions to ask any agent who you're considering working with is "Are you a full-time agent?" Just as you wouldn't risk letting a part-time lawyer defend you, don't let a part-time agent represent you.

✔ **Have contacts:** Folks prefer doing business with people they know, respect, and trust. You can make use of your agent's working relationships with local lenders, property inspectors, lawyers, title officers, insurance agents, government officials, and other real estate agents.

✔ **Have time for you:** Success is a two-edged sword. An agent who's already working with several other sellers and buyers probably doesn't have enough surplus time to serve you properly. Occasional scheduling conflicts are unavoidable. If, however, you often find your needs being neglected because your agent's time is overcommitted, get a new agent.

✔ **Are technologically savvy:** Good agents know how to use technology to get the job done. They (or their staff) know how to use the Internet to make property searches, can put listing information about your house on a variety of Web sites, and routinely utilize digital cameras and desktop publishing software as marketing tools. They understand the importance of staying in close touch with you and their other important contacts via cell phone, e-mail, or some other yet-to-be invented high-tech tool that works immediately if not sooner.

Some agents think technology has replaced human interaction. They're wrong. A geek who spends all his time in the office hiding behind a computer is the wrong agent for you. A good real estate agent harnesses technology to make more efficient use of her time, maximize your property's exposure, and stay in closer touch with clients and others involved in real estate transactions. Personal relationships still are critically important.

Choosing your listing agent

When you're ready to get down to the nitty-gritty specifics of selecting your own agent, we recommend that you interview at least three agents before selecting the lucky winner. (Chapter 6 deals with the pros and cons of selling your house without using an agent.)

To help you find three good agents to interview, tap into the following referral sources:

✔ **Friends, business associates, and members of professional, social, and religious organizations to which you belong:** In short, anyone you know who recently sold a house or is in the process of selling a house *in your neighborhood* is a source of agent referrals. Don't just ask for names; find out *why* they liked the agent.

✔ **Your employer:** The company you work for may have a relocation service that you can consult.

✔ **Professionals in related fields:** Financial, tax, and legal advisors can be good sources of agent referrals.

✔ **Sunday open houses:** Visit houses currently on the market in your neighborhood to check out the competition and to see how well the agents hosting the open houses handle the process. Here's your chance to "audition" agents without their knowledge. Listen to the agent answer questions from prospective buyers. Observe the way people respond to the agent.

Seeing is believing. Chapter 9 covers preparing property to optimize its favorable impression on prospective buyers. When you tour an open house, note whether the house makes a good impression on you. If not, drop the agent from further consideration as your listing agent.

In the next few sections, we outline the process of choosing your listing agent.

Step 1: Showing off your house

After you identify at least three prospective agents, start the selection process by inviting these agents to tour your house — individually, of course — so each can prepare a *comparable market analysis* (CMA) for your property. The CMA establishes your house's value by comparing it to other houses in your neighborhood that are approximately the same size, age, and condition as your house. Chapter 10 goes into detail about how to use sale prices and asking prices of comparable houses *(comps)* to determine the probable value of your house.

During that first meeting, tell each agent that you intend to interview several agents before selecting the one to work with to sell your house (the *listing* agent). Schedule second meetings with each agent a few days later to review their CMAs, their marketing plans for your property (a topic we cover in Chapter 12), and their activity lists (see the nearby sidebar, "The proof is in the activity list").

Before the second meeting with your prospective listing agents, you have to do a little homework (pun intended) yourself. Be sure to read Chapters 10 and 12 *before* the second meeting so you know the difference between good and bad CMAs and marketing plans. Read Chapter 8, as well, to find out about the different types of listing agreements and ideal length of the listing period. Chapter 8 also explains real estate commissions, a subject that should be of great interest to you because sellers usually pay the commission.

Step 2: Conducting agent interviews

Begin each interview by analyzing the agent's CMA, marketing proposal, and activity list. After you review the written material, get answers to the following questions:

- **Are you a full-time agent?** You should've asked this question before inviting the agent to be interviewed. If you didn't, do so now. *Don't work with part-time agents.*

- **Whom do you represent?** This question gets back to the fundamental concept of agency. Be sure that you know whom your agent represents at all times.

- **What can you tell me about your office?** Office size is a matter of personal preference. Some folks feel that they need the depth and scope of services a large office provides. Others think that they'll get more personal attention in a small office. No matter whether you prefer large or small offices, check on staff support, market specialization, and reputation. Determine whether the agent's broker is knowledgeable, is available to you if necessary, and is a good problem solver. In a crunch, the success of your transaction may depend on the quality of backup support that you and the agent receive.

The proof is in the activity list

The *activity list* is exactly that — a list of every property the agent either listed or sold during the preceding 12 months. This list is a powerful analytical tool. Here's what the activity list should include and how you can use it during the interview:

- **Property addresses:** Addresses help you zero in on the agent's geographical focus. See how many properties the agent listed and sold in your neighborhood. Eliminate agents who are focused outside your area or who have no geographical focus.

- **Property types (house, condo, duplex, and the like):** This information indicates whether the agent works on property similar to yours. If, for example, an agent specializes in condos, and you want to sell a house, you may have a problem.

- **Sale prices:** Does the agent handle property in your price range? An agent who

deals in *much* more or *much* less expensive property than yours may not be the right agent for you. If, for example, your house is worth about $300,000, and the most expensive property the agent sold in the past year was $150,000, you likely have a mismatch. Such agents probably don't know how to value and market higher-priced property like yours.

- **Days on market (DOM):** Ask agents you interview to specify how long property they listed was on the market before it sold. Compare that to the average DOM for your neighborhood according to statistics developed by a reliable independent source such as the local Multiple Listing Service (MLS). Eliminate agents whose listings habitually take far longer to sell than the average DOM in your area.

✔ **Dates of sale:** Sales should be fairly evenly distributed throughout the year. If they aren't, find out why. A lack of recent sales activity may be caused by illness or marital problems that could reduce the agent's effectiveness. Be understanding of resolved problems. Remember, however, that your house and money are on the line when considering agents who are in the midst of ongoing problems that may affect their ability to do a good job for you.

✔ **Who the agent represented — sellers or buyers:** Seasoned agents work about half the time with sellers and the other half with buyers. Avoid agents who focus primarily on buyers; such agents tend to lack the qualities you need as a seller. When discussing transactions in which the agent represented sellers, see which offices represented the buyers. Eliminate agents who either personally sell all their own listings or who sell listings only through other agents in their office. You want an agent who cooperates with other good agents throughout the brokerage community to sell your house as quickly as possible and for top dollar.

✔ **Total dollar value of property sold during the preceding 12 months:** Comparing the three agents' grand total property sales is a quick way to measure individual activity and success. However, you don't necessarily want a "top producer" representing you. These agents may not have the time or patience to provide the level of personal service and education you may need.

✔ **Names and current phone numbers of sellers/buyers:** Later, you can spot-check these references. Although a few people may request that their names or phone numbers be kept confidential, be suspicious of any agent who claims that *all* his or her clients made this request. Such a claim is most likely a pathetic attempt to get out of giving you references.

Actions speak louder than words. Activity lists transform cheap chatter into firm facts. Good agents willingly give you their lists and encourage you to check references. Eliminate from consideration any agent who won't provide an activity list.

Don't select an agent based *solely* on the size of the agent's office. Office size, or lack thereof, doesn't affect how quickly property sells. Some excellent agents operate as sole practitioners; other excellent agents prefer the synergism and support services of a huge office. Although larger offices tend to have more listings, no one office ever has a monopoly on the good listings. Quality of service is more important than quantity of agents or listings.

✔ **How long have you been an agent?** You want an agent who keeps learning and growing. After five years in real estate, a good agent has five years' experience, whereas a mediocre agent has one year's experience five times. Time in the saddle is one factor to consider when selecting an agent, but, by itself, it's no guarantee of competence. Even with a time-tested agent, you still have to review activity lists and ask all the other questions (see the sidebar, "The proof is in the activity list" for more info).

✔ **Do you have a salesperson's license or a broker's license?** An agent must satisfy rigorous educational and field sales experience requirements to get a broker's license. Many fine agents have a salesperson's license throughout their entire career. Although a broker's license isn't a guarantee of excellence, good agents often get a broker's license to improve their professional skills and to give themselves an advantage in agent-selection situations.

✔ **Do you hold any professional designations? Have you recently taken any real estate classes? What do you read to keep current in your field?** Taking continuing education courses and reading to stay informed about changes in real estate brokerage is a good characteristic in an agent. So is obtaining professional designations, such as the GRI (Graduate Realtor Institute) and CRS (Certified Residential Specialist) designations through the National Association of Realtors' study programs. Credentials in and of themselves are no guarantee of competence or ethics, but they usually indicate that the agent has a desire for self-improvement.

✔ **What do you think of the other two agents (name them) that I'm interviewing?** To encourage frankness, assure the agents that you won't repeat their comments. Good agents never build themselves up by tearing down other agents. If all three agents are good ones, you won't hear derogatory comments about any of them. If, however, one of the agents (or the agent's firm) has a bad reputation in the community, the other two agents' silence will speak volumes. *Remember:* Good or bad, the reputations of your agent and the agent's office rub off on you.

✔ **How many other sellers and buyers do you currently represent?** If, for example, the agent holds four listings open every weekend and is working with six buyers, *where will you fit in?* Don't contort your life to fit the agent's schedule. The agent who's right for you has time to accommodate your schedule.

✔ **Do you work in partnership with another agent or use assistants?** Sometimes an agent teams up with another agent to handle sellers and buyers jointly. In such cases, you must interview both agents. Other agents delegate time-consuming detail work to their assistants so that they can focus on critical points in the transaction. If an agent relies on such assistants, be sure that you understand exactly how and when during the buying process the agent plans to work directly with you. You don't want to hire an agent only to find that you end up working most of the time with an assistant whom you can't stand.

✔ **Is there anything I haven't asked about you or your firm that you think I should know?** Perhaps the agent is planning to change firms or is leaving next week for an extended vacation. Maybe the agent's broker is going out of business. Always ask this "make sure I find out everything that I need to know to make a good decision" question.

Step 3: Checking the all-important agent references

By checking up on agent references, you can gain experience the easy way — by learning from other people's mistakes. Be sure to get activity lists with names and phone numbers of *every* seller and buyer the agent represented during the past 12 months. With a complete activity list, you can pick and choose whomever you want to call, instead of permitting the agent to limit you to a highly selective list of references who are primed to tell anyone who calls that this agent is God's gift to real estate.

What's to prevent agents from culling their worst transactions from the activity list? Nothing. However, the more deals they delete, the less activity they have to show you — and the worse they look when you compare the agents' overall sales activity.

Any agent who refuses to give you an activity list is trying to hide either a lack of sales or unhappy clients. *Dump the agent.*

Suppose that each agent gives you a list containing 50 transactions. Assuming one seller or buyer for each transaction, 50 clients per agent times 3 agents interviewed equals 150 phone calls. No way. Your doctor would have to surgically remove the phone from your ear by the time you finished checking references.

Good news. You don't have to call every client to check references — that is, unless you want to. You can get a pretty darn accurate picture of the agents you're considering by making just six calls per agent. Here's how:

1. **Because you're a seller, ignore buyer references.**

   That restriction probably cuts the list in half.

2. **Next, look for people who sold property comparable to yours in price, location, and property type.**

   Because their property is like yours, their experiences also are likely to be similar to yours.

3. **Of these sellers, call two who sold a house about 12 months ago, two who sold approximately 6 months ago, and two whose sales just closed.**

   By spreading references evenly over the past year, you can see whether the agent's service has been consistently good.

After you identify which sellers to call, ask the following questions while you have them on the phone:

✔ **Is the agent trustworthy and honest? Did the agent follow through on promises?** Your agent can't be even slightly untrustworthy, dishonest, or unreliable. Consider a "no" answer to either of these questions to be the kiss of death.

✔ **Did the agent have enough time to properly serve you? Was the agent available to fit your schedule?** An occasional scheduling conflict is okay. Frequent conflicts are absolutely, flat-out unacceptable.

✔ **Did the agent clearly and satisfactorily explain in sufficient detail everything that happened during the selling process?** What one person thinks is ample detail may not be nearly enough for another. For example, some folks are content just to know what time it is. Others aren't happy until they know exactly how to make a clock. You know which type you are; question agent references accordingly.

✔ **Did the agent set realistic contract deadlines and then meet or beat them?** "Time is of the essence" is a condition of every real estate contract. Contract deadlines for obtaining financing, completing property inspections, and so forth are extremely important and must be met, or your sale will fall apart. A good agent makes sure that you *and the buyer* meet all contract deadlines.

✔ **Do the words *self-starter*, *committed*, and *motivated* describe the agent?** No one likes pushy people. But if you need to sell quickly, the last thing you want is a lethargic agent. You shouldn't have to jab your agent periodically with an electric prod to make sure that he's still breathing. Find out how energetically your prospective agent is prepared to work for you.

✔ **Did the agent get a good sale price for your house?** See whether the agent's clients still think that they did well on their sale.

✔ **Would you use the agent again?** *This question is the ultimate test of customer satisfaction.* If someone answers "No," find out why. The negative answer may be the result of a personality conflict between client and agent that won't bother you. On the other hand, the negative answer may reveal a horrendous agent flaw that you haven't yet uncovered.

✔ **Is there anything I haven't asked you about the agent or the agent's office that you think I should know?** You never know what you may find out when you ask this open-ended question.

Step 4: Picking the best of the lot

By analyzing all three agents' CMAs, marketing plans, and activity lists; interviewing the agents; and talking to their clients, you can gather facts that you need to make an intelligent decision. Here are three final considerations to help you select the paragon of virtue that you need on your real estate team:

✔ **Will you be proud having the agent represent you?** People who deal with your agent will form opinions of you based on their impressions of your agent. You can't afford to have anyone on your team who isn't a competent professional.

✔ **Do you communicate well with the agent?** Good agents make sure that you completely understand everything they say. If you can't understand your agent, don't blame yourself; the agent is probably a poor communicator.

✔ **Do you enjoy the agent's personality?** Don't kid yourself. House selling is stressful. You share extremely intense situations with your agent. Working with an agent you like may transform the selling process from a horrible experience into an exciting adventure — or, at least, a tolerable transaction.

Achieving top performance from the winner

After working so hard to find a great agent, the last thing you want to do is inadvertently ruin the relationship. Good seller-agent relationships aren't accidental. On the contrary, these relationships are based on pillars of mutual loyalty and trust that develop over time.

You obviously don't want to tell your innermost secrets to an agent who's going to blab them to a buyer or the buyer's agent. To that end, some sellers view their agent as an adversary. These sellers think that the less their agent knows about them, the better. Such sellers believe that, if their agent finds out what their bottom line is and why they want to sell, the agent will manipulate them into selling their house for less than it's worth just to make a quick commission.

Good agents don't betray your trust. They know that if they take care of you, their commission will take care of itself. If you can't trust your agent, don't play cat-and-mouse games; *get a new agent.* Smart agents know that you have the power to make or break their careers. If they please you, you'll be a geyser of glowing referrals for them. If your agent upsets you, you'll be like a festering thorn in her paw.

Use the immense power of potential referrals to control your relationship with the agent. If your agent does a lousy job, don't get mad — get even. Tell the world every gory detail of your rotten experience. Nothing ruins an agent's career faster than dissatisfied clients.

Bringing in the Broker

When you select an agent, your agent's broker is part of the package. If your purchase rolls merrily along, you may never meet the broker. But if a truly nasty problem rears its ugly head, guess who you can turn to for a quick fix? Brokers are the invisible grease in problematic transactions.

All states issue two markedly different types of real estate licenses: one for salespeople (agents) and one for brokers. Agents who have broker's licenses must satisfy much more stringent educational and experience standards than agents with only a salesperson's license.

Your agent may have either type of license. Broker's licensees have the option either to operate independently or to work for another broker. An agent who has a salesperson's license, on the other hand, *must* work under a broker's direct supervision, ensuring that you have access to the broker's higher lever of expertise if you need it.

The broker's image, good or bad, will be obvious from comments that you hear while checking agent references. You want the buyer, lender, and all other people involved in your transaction working with you *because* of your broker's reputation, not *in spite* of it. You shouldn't have to overcome guilt by association. If an agent's references disparage the agent's broker, dump the agent.

Good brokers develop and maintain relationships with the people with whom their offices deal — other brokers, lenders, title officers, city officials, and the like. This reservoir of good will is yours to use if the going gets rough. Brokers with strong business relationships can work near-miracles for you in a crisis.

House sales sometimes become highly emotional. If your life savings are on the line, you may lash out at other players. Someone must handle the resulting quarrels and misunderstandings. That someone is the broker. Because the broker participates directly or indirectly in every deal the office handles, your broker's practical experience is directly related to the number of agents in the office. A broker who manages a 25-agent office, for example, gets 25 years of real estate experience per calendar year. Any broker who can survive five years of handling all the office's gut-wrenching messes becomes a superb problem solver out of sheer necessity.

Call your broker into the game if your agent is stymied by a tough problem or if you're having problems with the agent. Everything an agent does or fails to do is ultimately the broker's responsibility. After all, the broker's job is to help make your problems go away.

Handling House Inspectors

Houses in good physical condition sell for top dollar. Fixer-uppers sell at greatly reduced prices because whoever buys them must spend money on repairs to get them back into pristine condition.

Even if you've lived in your house for the past 20 years, it may have hidden problems you know nothing about. You probably can't see, for example, whether your house's electrical system is shot or whether dry rot is turning the woodwork into sawdust or whether the roof is one rainstorm away from springing a Niagara of leaks.

Invisible defects can be deal breakers because they cost major money to repair. The more you know about your house's hidden problems, the better you can effectively deal with those problems. For that reason, we recommend that you have your property thoroughly inspected *before* putting it on the market.

Arranging premarketing property inspections

Count on it. Prudent purchasers will have your property *thoroughly* inspected before they buy it. Expect inspectors to poke into everything — your house's roof, chimney, gutters, plumbing, electrical wiring, heating and cooling systems, insulation, smoke detectors, all the permanent appliances and fixtures in your kitchen and bathrooms, and the foundation. They'll also check for health, safety, and environmental hazards. If you live in a temperate climate, you can bet that they'll have a structural pest control inspector look for damage from wood-destroying insects (carpenter ants, termites, and powderpost beetles) as well as dry rot and fungus infections. Whew!

Flowers, fragrances, and all that other staging stuff aside, smart buyers know that a house's physical condition greatly affects its value. No matter how beautifully your property is staged, buyers won't pay top dollar for a house that needs extensive and expensive repairs.

Exploring the advantages of inspecting before marketing

The best defense is a good offense. Beat buyers to the punch — get your inspections before they get theirs. Discover everything wrong with your house before putting it on the market. Defusing a crisis begins by discovering that a problem exists.

Some real estate agents argue against getting a house inspected before putting it on the market. As we explain in Chapter 8, many states now require that sellers disclose any *known* property defects to prospective buyers. These agents point out that you can't tell buyers about problems if you don't know that the problems exist. Handing buyers a long list of repair problems as they enter your house will turn many of them off. They recommend getting buyers emotionally committed to the property first, before their own inspectors drop the bomb. That line of reasoning is based on an ostrich-like logic: What you don't know can't get you in trouble — for a while, anyway.

Agents may use a second argument to convince sellers not to get their own property inspections: Buyers generally won't believe anything in reports paid for by sellers. According to these agents, buyers suspect that you'll hire a go-easy inspector to falsely report that your house is as solid as the Rock of Gibraltar. Why spend several hundred dollars on an inspection report that buyers won't believe? Again, you can find a nugget of truth in this argument. Only a suicidal chicken would ask the fox about how things are in the hen house. More than one unscrupulous seller has paid an equally unscrupulous inspector to write a false inspection report.

What you don't know CAN get you in trouble

One of San Francisco's more infamous real estate horror stories involves a man trying to sell his house. He didn't get his property inspected before putting it on the market because he was *absolutely* certain his house was in perfect condition. He should know. He had never experienced one single problem with it during nearly 25 years of ownership. The house showed beautifully and was priced to sell. He got a full asking price offer just two days after the house went up for sale — so far, so wonderful.

About a week later, the seller was stunned to receive a copy of the buyer's property inspection report stating that his house had a crumbling foundation and needed a new roof. According to three contractor estimates the buyers had obtained, repairs would cost about $45,000 for the indicated corrective work. The seller was convinced that the buyer's inspector was an incompetent boob. He insisted on getting a second inspection by an inspector of *his* choice to debunk the buyer's report.

The seller's inspector confirmed everything in the buyer's report and, worse yet for the seller, found additional damage that the first inspector had missed. The seller's contractor estimated repairs would total nearly $60,000. Armed with the second report, the seller offered the buyers a $45,000 credit per their request. Too late. For some strange reason, the buyers now wanted a $60,000 corrective-work credit. The seller offered to split the difference between the two estimates, the buyers held out for $60,000, and the deal fell apart.

The property sold nearly three months later, shortly after the seller reduced his asking price by $60,000 to compensate for the necessary repairs. By that time, the seller had learned a bitter truth: Killing the messenger doesn't get rid of a corrective work problem.

On the other hand, consider these four reasons to have your property thoroughly inspected before putting it on the market:

✔ **Damage control:** Suppose that your house needs a new roof. The problem is there whether you know about it or not. Why wait passively for an ultimatum to fix the roof at a cost established by the buyer's inspection or kiss the deal goodbye? If you discover the problem before marketing the house, you can either disclose it to prospective buyers with a repair estimate or, *although — as noted in Chapter 9 — we don't recommend this*, you can do the work before putting your house up for sale. Your negotiating position is much stronger if you know about problems in advance — and accurately know the cost to correct them.

You can't lose what you never had. Some buyers won't want to tour your house if they know that it needs a great deal of repair work. Those buyers don't want a fixer-upper. Even if you paid for all the repairs, they still wouldn't buy your house. Forget them. Concentrate on buyers who are willing to do corrective work after the close of escrow if your price and terms are fair.

✔ **Financial planning:** Chapter 3 explains that it's very important to have a realistic estimate of your present house's *net* proceeds of sale before committing to buy a new home. *Asking prices aren't sale prices.* If your house needs major repairs, you'll pay for them one way or another — either by doing the repairs yourself, by reducing your asking price to reflect the cost of repairs, or by giving buyers a credit in escrow to do the work.

Latent defects — flaws hidden out of sight behind walls or concealed in inaccessible areas, such as under your house or up in the attic where you can't see them — are time bombs. Defects you can't see and don't know about (such as faulty wiring, a cracked heat-exchanger in your furnace, asbestos insulation, lead in your water pipes, and so on) are potential deal killers. A good premarketing inspection can reveal all these problems.

✔ **Fine tuning:** Professional property inspectors can help you spot minor defects, such as dirty filters in the heating system; ventilation problems in the basement, garage, or crawl space; blocked gutters; loose doorknobs; stuck windows; a missing chimney hood or spark arrester, and so on. Eliminating small maintenance problems like these gives prospective buyers who tour the property a favorable — and correct — impression that your house is extremely well-maintained.

✔ **Peace of mind:** The inspector alerts you to health and safety precautions you should take. Installing smoke detectors, grounding electrical outlets, clearing a clogged sewer line, and keeping flammable products away from furnaces, heaters, and fireplaces, for example, make your house safer for the next owner *and* safer for you as long as you continue living in it.

Investigating inspectors

Quite a few so-called house inspectors have neither the background nor the special training required to do premarketing house inspections. Compounding your problem of finding a qualified inspector, few states certify, license, or regulate house inspectors. And, as we all know from personal experience with government regulation, states that do regulate house inspectors don't always do a good job. Anyone with a clipboard, a pickup truck, and a decent houseside manner can instantly anoint himself or herself a house inspector nearly anywhere in the country.

Avoid contractors who graciously offer to inspect your house and then do repairs that *they* discover during *their* inspection. If, like us, you're mechanically challenged, unscrupulous contractors can use your ignorance to fatten their wallets by billing you for phony corrective work they create themselves.

The best way around this conflict of interest is to hire someone who *only* performs property inspections — a professional property inspector, not a contractor wearing two hats. Doing property inspections requires special expertise that not all contractors, engineers, and architects have. Good professional property inspectors earn their living solely from inspection fees and don't do corrective work. This restriction removes any temptation to find unnecessary corrective work during inspections.

Finding property inspectors

Locating house inspectors is usually quite easy. One good source of property inspectors is the Yellow Pages of your local phone book under "Building Inspection Services" or "Home Inspection Services." You can also ask friends and business associates who've either bought or sold a house recently for the names of their property inspectors. If you're working with an agent, ask the agent to recommend several highly regarded inspectors. Using a well-known inspector with an excellent reputation increases your report's credibility.

In the interest of full disclosure, allow prospective buyers to review your inspection report prior to making an offer if they want. However, encourage buyers to get their own inspections. Even the best inspector occasionally misses defects. If the buyers rely solely on your report and find repair problems after the sale is complete, you don't want them claiming that you intentionally gave them a faulty inspection report to mislead them about your house's condition.

The American Society of Home Inspectors (ASHI) is a professional association of independent property inspectors. ASHI membership doesn't guarantee that the inspector is competent, but hiring a member of this organization increases the likelihood that you'll be working with a qualified professional. You can't buy your way into the ASHI by paying a fee. All ASHI-certified members must have performed at least 250 property inspections and must pass two written proficiency exams as a prerequisite of membership. ASHI members must also adhere to the ASHI standards of practice, continuing education requirements, and code of ethics. To find members in your area, call ASHI at (800) 743-ASHI (2744) or visit its Web site at www.ashi.com.

Selecting your inspector

Choosing the right inspector takes a little effort. We recommend that you interview several property inspectors before hiring one. The following questions can help you select the best inspector:

- ✔ **Are you a full-time, professional property inspector?** The only satisfactory answer is *yes*.

- ✔ **How many houses do you personally inspect annually?** Although the number of inspections varies from area to area, active inspectors usually average from 100 to 300 inspections per year. Be sure that the inspector works primarily in the vicinity of your house and is familiar with local building regulations and codes as well as local problems (such as mud slides, earthquakes, floods, or tornadoes).

- ✔ **Do you have any special certifications or licenses?** Property inspectors generally have experience in some related field (such as construction, architecture, or engineering) or have worked as an electrician, plumber, or insurance-claim adjuster. This diversity brings extra depth to their inspections. Membership in ASHI or other trade associations indicates at least a minimal knowledge of house-inspection procedures. Ask about the size of the inspector's company and how long the company has been in business.

- ✔ **What's the scope of your premarketing inspection?** Be certain that the inspection covers all your house's major structural and mechanical systems, inside and out, from foundation to roof. Anything less is unacceptable. *Thoroughly* inspecting a house or condo of average size usually takes three to four hours.

You probably won't be invited to join the buyers when their property inspector goes through your property. That's why it's critically important that you (and your agent, if possible) tag along when your inspector does the premarketing inspection. Reading the best report ever written is no substitute for seeing defects with your own eyes and hearing your inspector's commentary on the significant findings. Use this opportunity to question the inspector about a defect's ramifications and explore corrective work alternatives. After completing the inspection, you understand why some defects cost megabucks to fix, and others are no big deal.

- ✔ **Will your report include a cost estimate for you to do necessary corrective work?** Trick question. If the inspector says *yes*, don't use the inspector. Good property inspectors *only* do inspections. They don't do repair work themselves or generate referral fees for themselves by sending work to their pals. A good inspector can, however, help you determine repair costs by giving you a list of reputable contractors, roofers, electricians, plumbers, and other tradespeople who can give you corrective work quotes. Generally, more than one way is possible to fix a defect. You must decide the best way to deal with a problem after you consult the appropriate repair people.

✔ **What type of report will I receive?** Verbal reports and boilerplate, checklist reports are usually worthless. You need a written, narrative-type report that provides a detailed description of your house's mechanical and structural condition and clearly explains the implications of the findings *in plain English.*

Get a sample report from each inspector you interview. The best way to find out if an inspector writes good reports is to read one and draw your own conclusion. We thoughtfully include a premarketing inspection report in Appendix B so you know exactly what a good report looks like.

✔ **Do you have errors-and-omissions (E & O) insurance?** To err, unfortunately, is all too human. Even the best inspector misses a defect or two every now an then, which is why good property inspectors carry E & O insurance. If your inspector accidentally makes a boo-boo that costs you big bucks, E & O insurance can help ease your pain.

✔ **May I call your recent customers for references?** Good inspectors happily give you names and phone numbers for all the satisfied customers you want. Bad inspectors, by definition, don't have satisfied customers. Check at least three references per inspector. Ask references if, after the transaction was completed, major defects were discovered that the inspector missed. Also see if they'd hire the inspector again.

✔ **How much will your inspection cost?** A good inspection can cost anywhere from $350 to $800 depending on the property's size, the inspection's scope and degree of detail, and where the property is located — inspections cost least in the Midwest and South; they're much more expensive in urban areas of New York and California. Beware of unrealistically low, "this week only" promotional fees offered by new inspectors just starting in the business. Don't let inexperienced inspectors practice on you.

See if the premarketing inspection includes an additional consultation at a later date to discuss the report's findings with buyers who make an offer to purchase your house. Because time is money, the inspector probably adds an extra charge for this service. The fee is worth every penny, though, if the property inspector's explanation helps you negotiate a lower corrective work credit.

The Officiating Escrow Officer

Even the simplest house sale involves many details that must be resolved to everyone's satisfaction before the sale can be completed. Without someone to bridge the gulf between mutual buyer and seller distrust that exists in most transactions, deals would grind to a halt.

Bridging that gulf of distrust, real estate (like other team sports) engages the escrow officer, a referee who keeps the game civilized. Escrow officers aren't on anyone's team; they're neutral. They act as a disinterested third party for buyers and sellers without showing favoritism to either party.

After you and the buyer have a signed contract, all the documents, funds, and instructions related to your transaction usually are given to the escrow holder specified in your purchase agreement by the buyer's agent. We cover this process, known as *opening an escrow,* in detail in Chapter 15.

Buyers and sellers often select an escrow holder based on the recommenda-tions of their real estate agents. Depending on the location of your property, local custom dictates whether your escrow is handled by a lawyer, bank, real estate broker, or the firm that issues the title insurance.

Escrow fees range from a few hundred dollars to several thousand dollars and are based on your property's sale price. Once again, local custom nearly always determines whether the buyer or seller pays for escrow, or whether escrow fees are split 50/50. However, as Chapter 15 explains, this item often is negotiable.

Finding Financial and Tax Advisors

If you need the services of another advisor, such as a tax or financial advisor, find one who works by the hour and doesn't have a vested interest — because they sell investments or manage money for an ongoing fee — in your house-selling decision. Few financial advisors work on this basis. Although tax advisors are more likely than financial advisors to work for an hourly fee, they tend to have a narrower-than-needed financial perspective. A competent tax advisor may be able to help you structure the sale to maximize your tax benefits. For most transactions, however, a tax advisor is unnecessary.

If you want to hire a financial or tax advisor, interview several before you select one. Check with your agent, banker, lawyer, business associates, and friends for referrals. As is the case with selecting your agent, you should get client references from each tax advisor and call the references.

A good financial or tax advisor should possess the following qualities:

✔ **Does the advisor work full time in this occupation?** The realm of personal finances and taxes is too vast for you to trust a part-timer. You need the services of a full-time professional.

✔ **Does the advisor speak your language?** Good advisors can explain your options in simple terms. If you don't understand exactly what the tax advisor is saying, ask for clarification. If you still don't understand, get another tax advisor.

✔ **Is the advisor objective?** Hire someone who works solely by the hour and doesn't have a vested interest in the advice that they give you. Never blindly follow the advice of experts because you're in awe of their expertise. Experts can be just as wrong as ordinary mortals.

✔ **What is the advisor's fee schedule?** Hourly fees vary widely. Don't pick someone strictly on a cost-per-hour basis. An advisor who's just beginning to practice, for example, may only charge half as much as one with 20 years of experience. If the rookie takes four hours to do what the old pro does in an hour, which advisor is more expensive in the long run? Furthermore, the quality of the seasoned veteran's advice may be superior to the quality of the novice's advice.

✔ **Is the tax advisor a Certified Public Accountant (CPA) or Enrolled Agent (EA)?** These professional designations indicate that the tax advisor has satisfied special education and experience requirements and has passed a rigorous licensing exam. A CPA does general accounting and prepares tax returns. An EA focuses specifically on taxation. Only CPAs, Enrolled Agents, and attorneys are authorized to represent you before the IRS in the event of an audit.

✔ **Does the tax advisor have experience with real estate transactions?** Tax practice, like law or medicine, is an extremely broad field. The tax advisors that big corporations use may be wonderful, but they aren't necessarily best for you. You need a tax advisor whose clients have tax problems like yours.

The best advisors in the world can't do much to change the financial and tax consequences of a transaction *after* the deal is done. If you're going to consult advisors, do so *before* you make significant financial decisions.

Locating a Good Lawyer

Lawyers are like seat belts. You never know when you may need one. Your deal is rolling merrily along when out of nowhere — slam, bam, wham — you hit a legal pothole and end up in Sue City.

The real estate purchase agreement you sign is a legally binding contract between you and the buyer. If you have *any* questions about the legality of your contract, get a lawyer on your team *immediately.* No one else on the team is qualified to give you legal advice.

Suppose the buyer's contract is presented to you at night or on a weekend when a lawyer isn't readily available. Put a clause in the contract to stipulate that your acceptance is contingent upon review and approval of the contract by an attorney of your choice within five business days after you sign it.

To determine whether you need a lawyer on your team, check out the following factors:

- **If no agent is involved:** For example, suppose that you're selling your house by yourself. If neither you nor the buyer has an agent, get a lawyer to prepare the contract, and have the lawyer do the work that an agent would normally handle. As Chapter 6 explains, eliminating the real estate agent doesn't eliminate the disclosures, inspections, contingency removals, and other details involved in the house-selling process.

- **The location of your property:** In states such as California, lawyers rarely work on deals that only involve filling in the blanks on a standard, preprinted purchase agreement that's been previously reviewed and approved by members of the state bar association. In other states, however, lawyers routinely do everything from preparing purchase contracts to closing the escrow. Your agent, if you're working with one, knows the role that lawyers play in your locale.

- **The complexity of your transaction:** You need a lawyer if you get into a complex financial or legal situation that can't be covered by a standardized contract. For example, suppose that you hold title as a tenant-in-common and are selling a partial interest in the property, or that you want to structure the transaction as an intricate installment sale. Whatever. Unless your agent also is a lawyer, the agent isn't qualified to do creative legal writing.

- **If consulting an attorney helps you sleep at night:** You may have the world's easiest deal. Still, if you feel more comfortable having a lawyer review the contract, your peace of mind certainly is worth the cost of an hour or two of legal time.

Choosing among lawyers

If, for whatever reason, you decide that you need a lawyer, interview several before making your selection. Real estate law, like medicine, is highly specialized. A corporate attorney or the lawyer who handled your neighbor's divorce isn't necessarily the best choice for your real estate team. Get a lawyer who specializes in residential real estate transactions. Good agents and brokers usually are excellent referral sources because they work with real estate lawyers all the time in their transactions.

A lawyer working for you needs to have the following qualities in her favor:

- ✔ **Is a full-time lawyer and licensed to practice law in your state:** Of course.

- ✔ **Is local talent:** Real estate law, like real estate brokerage, not only varies from state to state, it also changes from area to area within the same state. Rent control laws, condominium conversion statutes, and zoning codes, for example, usually are formulated and adopted by city or county governing agencies. A good *local* lawyer knows these laws and has working relationships with people who administer them in your area.

- ✔ **Has a realistic fee schedule:** Lawyers' fees vary widely. A good lawyer gives you an estimate of how much it costs to handle your situation. As with financial and tax advisors, the experience factor comes into play. Seasoned lawyers generally charge more than novice lawyers, but seasoned lawyers also may get more done in an hour than inexperienced lawyers can. A low fee is no bargain if the novice is learning on your nickel. And you may pay the consequences if the novice fails to handle your case properly.

- ✔ **Has a good track record:** If the lawyer you consult thinks that your case may go to trial, find out whether that lawyer has courtroom experience or intends to refer you to another lawyer. (Some lawyers don't do trial work.) Always ask about the lawyer's track record of wins versus losses. What good is a lawyer with a great deal of trial experience if that lawyer never wins a case?

- ✔ **Is a deal maker or a deal breaker (whichever is appropriate):** Some lawyers are great at putting deals together. Others specialize in blowing them out of the water. Each skill is important. Depending on whether you want the lawyer to get you out of a deal so you can accept a better offer or need legal assistance to keep your deal together, be sure that you have the right type of lawyer for your situation.

  If your lawyer's *only* solution to every problem is a lawsuit, you may be in the clutches of a deal breaker who wants to run up big legal fees. Find another lawyer!

- ✔ **Speaks your language:** A good lawyer explains your options clearly and concisely without resorting to incomprehensible legalese. Then she gives you a *risk assessment* of your options to help you make a sound decision. For example, the lawyer may say that one course of action will take longer but will give you a 90 percent chance of success, whereas the faster option only gives you a 50/50 chance of prevailing.

Working well with your lawyer

Whoever said that an ounce of prevention is worth a pound of cure must've been thinking of lawyers. A two-hour preventative consultation with your lawyer is infinitely less expensive than a two-month trial.

Good lawyers are excellent strategists. Given adequate lead time, they can structure nearly any deal to your advantage. Conversely, if you bring wonderful lawyers into the game after the deal is done, all they can do is damage control. *The best defense is a good offense.*

Beware of the *awe factor.* People tend to hold lawyers in awe because their word is law. Disobey lawyers and you go to jail. Baloney. Don't blindly follow your lawyer's advice. If you don't understand the advice or if you disagree with it, question it. You may be correct and the lawyer may be wrong. Lawyers are every bit as fallible as everyone else.

Chapter 8

Listing Contracts and Commissions

*T*he single most important contract that you sign throughout the entire process of selling your house is the one between you and the person who ultimately buys your property. Without that contract, you'd never be anything more than a property owner who wants to be a seller.

What's the second most important contract? If you guessed the listing contract that you sign with the agent you hire to help sell your house, you win an all-expenses-paid trip to the next paragraph.

You've probably heard of listings, but most folks don't really understand what listings are or how they operate. We're not talking about a listing of names in a phone book. Nor does this listing have anything to do with transferring ownership of your property to buyers. This chapter spells out everything you need to know about listing contracts and tips on how you can negotiate commissions with agents.

Understanding Listing Contracts

In the context of selling property, a *listing contract* is a personal service contract between you and a licensed real estate broker. This contract authorizes the broker to act as your agent by finding someone to buy your house. The listing contract contains two basic promises: The broker promises to do his or her best to find a buyer for your property, and you promise to pay the broker a commission.

Sounds simple, doesn't it? Legally speaking (because listings *are* meant to be legally binding agreements), the definition of a listing contract is a bit more complex:

- **An employment contract:** A listing contract specifies the exact terms and conditions of your employment contract with a licensed real estate broker. It also authorizes the broker to represent you during the sale of your property. As Chapter 7 explains, if the real estate agent you select to work with doesn't have a broker's license or isn't the broker of record for the office, a licensed broker must supervise the agent and be responsible for everything he does or fails to do.

- **A compensation agreement:** Although the listing broker's pay is almost always a commission based on a specified percentage of the sale price, compensation doesn't have to be a commission. Other possible options include paying your broker a set fee for selling the property or compensating the broker on an hourly fee basis.

Regardless of how the broker is paid, compensation is a *negotiable* item decided by mutual agreement between you and the broker.

Although the listing contract doesn't obligate you to sell your house, it may obligate you to pay the broker a commission *even if you don't sell.* The key is whether the broker gets you an "acceptable" offer.

You may think that an acceptable offer is any offer a buyer makes to purchase your house that you'd be willing to sign. If an offer isn't acceptable to you, you won't sign it. But suppose that your broker brings you a valid, written offer made by a ready, willing, and able buyer who wants to purchase your house *for the exact price and terms specified in your listing contract.* You reject the offer solely because you don't like the buyer's red tennis shoes.

In this example, you probably owe the broker a commission, even though you didn't accept the offer. Technically speaking, whether you ultimately sell the house to the buyer who submitted the offer doesn't matter if the buyer met your price and terms.

"That's not fair," you say. "If I decide not to sell, why should I pay a commission?" The answer: Because you agreed to those terms when you signed the listing. The broker found a buyer who was *ready* to accept your terms, *willing* to enter into a contract of sale with you, and financially *able* to buy your property. The listing agreement doesn't specify that you actually have to *sell* your property. If your broker fulfills his end of the contract by procuring an acceptable buyer, you must honor your promise and pay the broker.

Buyers and agents almost always cooperate with sellers who are forced to cancel a transaction because of the sudden occurrence of some dire unforeseen situation beyond their control, such as job loss or a death in the family. They may get upset, though, if a seller suddenly decides not to go through with a deal *for no good reason.*

Breaking any contract may have serious legal consequences. A listing contract is a legal contract. Don't list your property on a lark just to test the water — the water could get boiling hot quickly.

Considering the Types of Listings

Some brokers are *so* desperate for listings that they take oral listings. A broker may, for example, introduce himself to you at a party, tell you he has always admired your house, and ask if you're interested in selling it. To brush him off, you say that you may sell "at the right price." He responds that he'll see what he can do for you.

The next thing you know, you're besieged day and night by eager buyers waving lowball offers in your face. Take one guess about who told these vultures your house was for sale.

Oral listings are a no-no. Samuel Goldwyn, the famous movie producer, once said, "A verbal agreement isn't worth the paper it's written on." Heed his advice. If you want an enforceable contract, get the contract in writing and *always* get a file copy of anything you sign (listing contract, purchase contract, and so on) as soon as you sign it. 'Nuf said.

At first glance, you may think that you can choose from many different kinds of listings. Appearances are, as usual, deceiving. All your various listing options boil down to variations on two types of listings: exclusive listings and open listings. This section gives you the lowdown.

Exclusive listings

An *exclusive listing* is exactly that — an exclusive authorization giving only one broker the right to find a buyer for your house. As simple as it sounds, an exclusive listing contract can take two different forms.

Exclusive agency listings

The broker designated in an exclusive agency listing is the one and only *agent* authorized to sell your house during the term of the listing. If any other licensed real estate broker or agent finds a buyer, your broker gets paid. Even so, brokers think that this form of exclusive listing is just barely better than no listing at all.

About now you may be wondering about the downside from the broker's perspective? After all, you authorize the broker to be your sole agent. You're not playing the field with 50 or 100 other brokers on a winner-take-all basis. So what's the problem? You, dear house seller.

Because you aren't a licensed real estate agent, the listing contract excludes you. Under the terms of an exclusive agency listing, owners specifically reserve the right to sell their own house directly and ace the broker out of a commission. Your broker — who should be your strongest ally — is your competitor. The adversarial relationship isn't good for you or your broker. Exclusive agency listings discourage brokers from spending time or money marketing property because the arrangement offers no assurance of a reward for their efforts. Keeping listed property a secret isn't the best way to sell it quickly for top dollar.

Exclusive right to sell listings

An *exclusive right to sell* listing is also referred to as an *exclusive authorization and right to sell* or just a plain, old *exclusive.* The exclusive is the most widely used form of listing contract in the United States. It's popular with sellers and brokers because it provides the following:

- **Maximum incentive for brokers:** Under this form of exclusive listing, the listing broker gets paid if anyone — *even the owner* — finds a ready, willing, and able buyer for the property during the life of the contract. Owner and broker are allies, not adversaries, with a mutually beneficial goal of getting the listed property sold as quickly as possible for as much money as possible. (See the nearby sidebar, "Listing exclusions: Avoiding a commission by selling to friends," for information about listing exclusions, the one way you can sell your property without paying a commission.)

- **Maximum effort for seller:** An exclusive right to sell listing gives your listing broker a strong monetary incentive to focus his or her time, energy, and advertising dollars on one priority — a fast, top-dollar sale of your house. To that end, the listing broker should *immediately* cooperate with any and all other brokers who may have buyers for your property by offering to split the compensation 50/50 (or whatever split is customary in your area) with the broker who generates a ready, willing, and able buyer.

You know that you're dealing with a bad broker if she wants to keep your listing quiet for several weeks before advertising it and opening it up to cooperating brokers. Greedy brokers sit on listings to give themselves and the agents in their offices time to sell your house to buyers with whom they're working. They want someone in their office to generate an offer for your property so the listing office can get the entire commission. Brokers call this tactic "getting both ends of a deal." From your perspective, a more apt description would be "getting the shaft."

Chapter 11 reveals that the secret of getting a top-dollar price when you sell is to generate spirited buyer competition for your house by getting broad, *immediate* market exposure. Nothing is terribly wrong with giving your listing broker a day or two head start on other brokers, if you approve. A broker who wants to keep your listing in-house more than 48 hours, however, is unworthy of being your listing agent.

Listing exclusions: Avoiding a commission by selling to friends

Suppose that you invited your best friends over to your house last year for Thanksgiving dinner. After a magnificent feast, you're all sitting by the fireplace eating scrumptious slices of pumpkin pie. Basking contentedly in the fire's rosy glow, your pal Martin says, "You know Faye (his wife) and I have always admired your home. If you ever decide you want to sell it, let us know. We would buy your place in a nanosecond."

You may have heard something like that from friends or business associates. When push comes to shove, however, nothing usually comes of these conversations. Talk is cheap.

But what if Martin and Faye really meant it? If there's even one chance in a thousand that they were serious, why pay a broker to find buyers until you give your pals a chance to put up or shut up? You can use a perfectly acceptable method to avoid paying a commission for people you identify as potential buyers of your house. This method is called a listing exclusion.

You can amend your listing agreement so that if Faye and Martin — or anyone else you specifically exclude from the listing — actually purchases your house during the exclusion period, you won't have to pay the broker a commission.

Always put a time limit on listing exclusions. A couple of weeks usually is enough time for serious buyers to explore their financial options and get back to you with a decision. For example, tell your broker that you want a two-week exclusion for Martin and Faye. Don't sign the listing unless the broker agrees to the exclusion and further agrees not to market your house at all during those two weeks. If the broker agrees to these stipulations, sign the listing.

By listing your house with a broker, your actions prove to Faye and Martin that you're a serious seller. By putting a fuse on the listing exclusion, you establish a time frame within which they must act or be treated like any other buyers. Without a deadline, folks tend to stall by asking for more time to think it over.

Don't make the mistake of giving any buyers you exclude additional time. How long can you put your life on hold while they think it over? What's to think over? Either they want to buy your house, or they don't want to buy it. Real buyers will tie up your property with a contract of sale as fast as possible.

During the two-week exclusion period, you don't have to worry about paying a commission to the broker. If Martin and Faye make an offer you can't refuse, you simply cancel the listing and sell the house to your friends. The broker won't be upset because she didn't waste any time or money marketing your house.

If, however, the two weeks pass without an offer from your pals, your house goes on the market without the stigma of any exclusions. And you have the comfort of knowing that you explored the possibility of avoiding a commission by selling directly to your friends.

Exclusive right to sell listing contracts vary widely in length, wording, and complexity from one state to another and from city to city within any given state. Under these circumstances, the listing contract you ultimately sign probably won't look exactly like the California Association of Realtors (C.A.R.) exclusive listing contract shown in Figures 8-1a, 8-1b, and 8-1c. The C.A.R. listing is, nonetheless, a fine example of a well-written, comprehensive listing agreement.

Regardless of the wording in your contract, here are a few fundamental facts to keep in mind about all exclusive listings:

- ✔ **Listings are intended to be legal contracts.** Real estate agents hate the word *contract* because it scares people and puts them on guard. They prefer to call contracts *agreements* because agreements sound less threatening. Whatever your listing is called, the intent is to create a legally binding contract between you and the listing broker. *Read it carefully.* Consult a real estate lawyer if you have questions or concerns about the listing's fine points. Agents aren't qualified to answer legal questions.

- ✔ **An exclusive listing must have a definite termination date.** Note that paragraph 1 of the form in Figure 8-1a provides a "Listing Period" commencing on a specific date and expiring at 11:59 p.m. on an equally specific date. Don't sign any exclusive listing that starts when the contract is prepared and runs "until sold" or "until canceled in writing" or any other type of indefinite duration.

- ✔ **A broker protection clause keeps everyone honest.** Just as a few real estate agents are dishonest, some sellers and buyers also behave unethically. For example, a seller may tell an interested buyer that the listing contract with the broker is about to expire. Without a broker, the seller won't have to pay a commission. The seller offers to pass on a portion of the savings to the buyer by lowering the asking price, *if* they sign the deal after the listing contract's expiration date. Paragraph 4.A. (2) of the sample listing contract shown in Figure 8-1a is known as the *broker protection clause.* This clause prohibits (for a specified period of time) the homeowner from selling directly to a buyer. If a broker finds a suitable buyer for a property, the clause requires that the seller pay the broker's commission according to the listing contract.

Brokers generally ask for at least a 90-day buffer period. The time frame is, however, negotiable. In most cases, 30 to 60 days gives the broker sufficient protection. Regardless of the buffer period you agree to, be sure that the broker protection clause in your listing contract includes this statement: *This section shall not apply if Seller enters into a valid listing agreement with another licensed real estate broker after the final termination of this agreement.* This clause protects you from the possibility of paying two commissions if you relist your house with a second broker and a dispute develops after the first broker's listing expires.

- ✔ **Title verification is critically important.** Paragraph 5 of the sample listing contract in Figure 8-1b asks who has title to the property, because anyone who signs a listing contract obligates himself to pay a commission, even if that person ultimately can only convey a partial interest in the property.

RESIDENTIAL LISTING AGREEMENT
(Exclusive Authorization and Right to Sell)
(C.A.R. Form RLA, Revised 4/07)

a1. EXCLUSIVE RIGHT TO SELL: _____ ("Seller")
hereby employs and grants _____ ("Broker")
beginning (date) _____ and ending at 11:59 P.M. on (date) _____ ("Listing Period")
the exclusive and irrevocable right to sell or exchange the real property in the City of _____,
County of_____, Assessor's Parcel No. _____
California, described as: _____ ("Property").

2.   **ITEMS EXCLUDED AND INCLUDED:** Unless otherwise specified in a real estate purchase agreement, all fixtures and fittings that
are attached to the Property are included, and personal property items are excluded, from the purchase price.
ADDITIONAL ITEMS EXCLUDED: _____.
ADDITIONAL ITEMS INCLUDED: _____.
Seller intends that the above items be excluded or included in offering the Property for sale, but understands that: **(i)** the purchase
agreement supersedes any intention expressed above and will ultimately determine which items are excluded and included in the sale;
and **(ii)** Broker is not responsible for and does not guarantee that the above exclusions and/or inclusions will be in the purchase
agreement.

3.   **LISTING PRICE AND TERMS:**
A.   The listing price shall be: _____
_____ Dollars ($ _____).
B.   Additional Terms: _____
_____

4.   **COMPENSATION TO BROKER:**
**Notice: The amount or rate of real estate commissions is not fixed by law. They are set by each Broker
individually and may be negotiable between Seller and Broker (real estate commissions include all
compensation and fees to Broker).**
A.   Seller agrees to pay to Broker as compensation for services irrespective of agency relationship(s), either ☐ _____ percent
of the listing price (or if a purchase agreement is entered into, of the purchase price), or ☐ $ _____,
AND _____, as follows:
(1) If during the Listing Period, or any extension, Broker, Seller, cooperating broker, or any other person procures a buyer(s)
who offers to purchase the Property on the above price and terms, or on any price and terms acceptable to Seller. (Broker
is entitled to compensation whether any escrow resulting from such offer closes during or after the expiration of the Listing
Period.)
OR (2) If within _____ calendar days **(a)** after the end of the Listing Period or any extension; or **(b)** after any cancellation of this
Agreement, unless otherwise agreed, Seller enters into a contract to sell, convey, lease or otherwise transfer the Property to
anyone ("Prospective Buyer") or that person's related entity: **(i)** who physically entered and was shown the Property during
the Listing Period or any extension by Broker or a cooperating broker; or **(ii)** for whom Broker or any cooperating broker
submitted to Seller a signed, written offer to acquire, lease, exchange or obtain an option on the Property. Seller, however,
shall have no obligation to Broker under paragraph 4A(2) unless, not later than **3 calendar days** after the end of the Listing
Period or any extension or cancellation, Broker has given Seller a written notice of the names of such Prospective Buyers.
OR (3) If, without Broker's prior written consent, the Property is withdrawn from sale, conveyed, leased, rented, otherwise transferred,
or made unmarketable by a voluntary act of Seller during the Listing Period, or any extension.
B.   If completion of the sale is prevented by a party to the transaction other than Seller, then compensation due under paragraph
4A shall be payable only if and when Seller collects damages by suit, arbitration, settlement or otherwise, and then in an amount
equal to the lesser of one-half of the damages recovered or the above compensation, after first deducting title and escrow
expenses and the expenses of collection, if any.
C.   In addition, Seller agrees to pay Broker: _____
D.   Seller has been advised of Broker's policy regarding cooperation with, and the amount of compensation offered to, other brokers.
(1) Broker is authorized to cooperate with and compensate brokers participating through the multiple listing service(s)
("MLS") by offering MLS brokers either ☐ _____ percent of the purchase price, or ☐ $ _____.
(2) Broker is authorized to cooperate with and compensate brokers operating outside the MLS as per Broker's policy.
E.   Seller hereby irrevocably assigns to Broker the above compensation from Seller's funds and proceeds in escrow. Broker may
submit this Agreement, as instructions to compensate Broker pursuant to paragraph 4A, to any escrow regarding the Property
involving Seller and a buyer, Prospective Buyer or other transferee.
F.   **(1)** Seller represents that Seller has not previously entered into a listing agreement with another broker regarding the Property,
unless specified as follows: _____
(2) Seller warrants that Seller has no obligation to pay compensation to any other broker regarding the Property unless the
Property is transferred to any of the following individuals or entities: _____
(3) If the Property is sold to anyone listed above during the time Seller is obligated to compensate another broker: **(i)** Broker is
not entitled to compensation under this Agreement; and **(ii)** Broker is not obligated to represent Seller in such transaction.

Seller acknowledges receipt of a copy of this page.
Seller's Initials (_____)(_____)

RLA REVISED 4/07 (PAGE 1 OF 3)   Print Date

Reviewed by _____ Date _____

EQUAL HOUSING
OPPORTUNITY

RESIDENTIAL LISTING AGREEMENT - EXCLUSIVE (RLA PAGE 1 OF 3)

Reprinted with permission, CALIFORNIA ASSOCIATION OF REALTORS™. Endorsement not implied.

Figure 8-1a:
Your
exclusive
listing
contract
may look
something
like this.

Property Address: _____ Date: _____

5. **OWNERSHIP, TITLE AND AUTHORITY:** Seller warrants that: **(i)** Seller is the owner of the Property; **(ii)** no other persons or entities have title to the Property; and **(iii)** Seller has the authority to both execute this Agreement and sell the Property. Exceptions to ownership, title and authority are as follows: _____.

6. **MULTIPLE LISTING SERVICE:** All terms of the transaction, including financing, if applicable, will be provided to the selected MLS for publication, dissemination and use by persons and entities on terms approved by the MLS. Seller authorizes Broker to comply with all applicable MLS rules. MLS rules allow MLS data to be made available by the MLS to additional Internet sites unless Broker gives the MLS instructions to the contrary. MLS rules generally provide that residential real property and vacant lot listings be submitted to the MLS within 48 hours or some other period of time after all necessary signatures have been obtained on the listing agreement. However, Broker will not have to submit this listing to the MLS if, within that time, Broker submits to the MLS a form signed by Seller (C.A.R. Form SEL or the locally required form) instructing Broker to withhold the listing from the MLS. Information about this listing will be provided to the MLS of Broker's selection unless a form instructing Broker to withhold the listing from the MLS is attached to this listing Agreement.

7. **SELLER REPRESENTATIONS:** Seller represents that, unless otherwise specified in writing, Seller is unaware of: **(i)** any Notice of Default recorded against the Property; **(ii)** any delinquent amounts due under any loan secured by, or other obligation affecting, the Property; **(iii)** any bankruptcy, insolvency or similar proceeding affecting the Property; **(iv)** any litigation, arbitration, administrative action, government investigation or other pending or threatened action that affects or may affect the Property or Seller's ability to transfer it; and **(v)** any current, pending or proposed special assessments affecting the Property. Seller shall promptly notify Broker in writing if Seller becomes aware of any of these items during the Listing Period or any extension thereof.

8. **BROKER'S AND SELLER'S DUTIES:** Broker agrees to exercise reasonable effort and due diligence to achieve the purposes of this Agreement. Unless Seller gives Broker written instructions to the contrary, Broker is authorized to order reports and disclosures as appropriate or necessary and advertise and market the Property by any method and in any medium selected by Broker, including MLS and the Internet, and, to the extent permitted by these media, control the dissemination of the information submitted to any medium. Seller agrees to consider offers presented by Broker, and to act in good faith to accomplish the sale of the Property by, among other things, making the Property available for showing at reasonable times and referring to Broker all inquiries of any party interested in the Property. Seller is responsible for determining at what price to list and sell the Property. **Seller further agrees to indemnify, defend and hold Broker harmless from all claims, disputes, litigation, judgments and attorney fees arising from any incorrect information supplied by Seller, or from any material facts that Seller knows but fails to disclose.**

9. **DEPOSIT:** Broker is authorized to accept and hold on Seller's behalf any deposits to be applied toward the purchase price.

10. **AGENCY RELATIONSHIPS:**
    A. **Disclosure:** If the Property includes residential property with one-to-four dwelling units, Seller shall receive a "Disclosure Regarding Agency Relationships" form prior to entering into this Agreement.
    B. **Seller Representation:** Broker shall represent Seller in any resulting transaction, except as specified in paragraph 4F.
    C. **Possible Dual Agency With Buyer:** Depending upon the circumstances, it may be necessary or appropriate for Broker to act as an agent for both Seller and buyer, exchange party, or one or more additional parties ("Buyer"). Broker shall, as soon as practicable, disclose to Seller any election to act as a dual agent representing both Seller and Buyer. If a Buyer is procured directly by Broker or an associate-licensee in Broker's firm, Seller hereby consents to Broker acting as a dual agent for Seller and such Buyer. In the event of an exchange, Seller hereby consents to Broker collecting compensation from additional parties for services rendered, provided there is disclosure to all parties of such agency and compensation. Seller understands and agrees that: **(i)** Broker, without the prior written consent of Seller, will not disclose to Buyer that Seller is willing to sell the Property at a price less than the listing price; **(ii)** Broker, without the prior written consent of Buyer, will not disclose to Seller that Buyer is willing to pay a price greater than the offered price; and **(iii)** except for (i) and (ii) above, a dual agent is obligated to disclose known facts materially affecting the value or desirability of the Property to both parties.
    D. **Other Sellers:** Seller understands that Broker may have or obtain listings on other properties, and that potential buyers may consider, make offers on, or purchase through Broker, property the same as or similar to Seller's Property. Seller consents to Broker's representation of sellers and buyers of other properties before, during and after the end of this Agreement.
    E. **Confirmation:** If the Property includes residential property with one-to-four dwelling units, Broker shall confirm the agency relationship described above, or as modified, in writing, prior to or concurrent with Seller's execution of a purchase agreement.

11. **SECURITY AND INSURANCE:** Broker is not responsible for loss of or damage to personal or real property, or person, whether attributable to use of a keysafe/lockbox, a showing of the Property, or otherwise. Third parties, including, but not limited to, appraisers, inspectors, brokers and prospective buyers, may have access to, and take videos and photographs of, the interior of the Property. Seller agrees: **(i)** to take reasonable precautions to safeguard and protect valuables that might be accessible during showings of the Property; and **(ii)** to obtain insurance to protect against these risks. Broker does not maintain insurance to protect Seller.

12. **KEYSAFE/LOCKBOX:** A keysafe/lockbox is designed to hold a key to the Property to permit access to the Property by Broker, cooperating brokers, MLS participants, their authorized licensees and representatives, authorized inspectors, and accompanied prospective buyers. Broker, cooperating brokers, MLS and Associations/Boards of REALTORS® are **not** insurers against injury, theft, loss, vandalism or damage attributed to the use of a keysafe/lockbox. Seller does (or if checked ☐ does not) authorize Broker to install a keysafe/lockbox. If Seller does not occupy the Property, Seller shall be responsible for obtaining occupant(s)' written permission for use of a keysafe/lockbox.

13. **SIGN:** Seller does (or if checked ☐ does not) authorize Broker to install a FOR SALE/SOLD sign on the Property.

14. **EQUAL HOUSING OPPORTUNITY:** The Property is offered in compliance with federal, state and local anti-discrimination laws.

15. **ATTORNEY FEES:** In any action, proceeding or arbitration between Seller and Broker regarding the obligation to pay compensation under this Agreement, the prevailing Seller or Broker shall be entitled to reasonable attorney fees and costs from the non-prevailing Seller or Broker, except as provided in paragraph 19A.

16. **ADDITIONAL TERMS:** _____
_____
_____

Figure 8-1b: Sample exclusive listing contract, continued.

Seller acknowledges receipt of a copy of this page.
Seller's Initials (_____)(_____)

Reviewed by _____ Date _____

RESIDENTIAL LISTING AGREEMENT - EXCLUSIVE (RLA PAGE 2 OF 3)

Property Address: _____ Date: _____

17. MANAGEMENT APPROVAL: If an associate-licensee in Broker's office (salesperson or broker-associate) enters into this Agreement on Broker's behalf, and Broker or Manager does not approve of its terms, Broker or Manager has the right to cancel this Agreement, in writing, within **5 Days** After its execution.

18. SUCCESSORS AND ASSIGNS: This Agreement shall be binding upon Seller and Seller's successors and assigns.

19. DISPUTE RESOLUTION:

A. MEDIATION: Seller and Broker agree to mediate any dispute or claim arising between them out of this Agreement, or any resulting transaction, before resorting to arbitration or court action, subject to paragraph 19B(2) below. Paragraph 19B(2) below applies whether or not the arbitration provision is initialed. Mediation fees, if any, shall be divided equally among the parties involved. If, for any dispute or claim to which this paragraph applies, any party commences an action without first attempting to resolve the matter through mediation, or refuses to mediate after a request has been made, then that party shall not be entitled to recover attorney fees, even if they would otherwise be available to that party in any such action. THIS MEDIATION PROVISION APPLIES WHETHER OR NOT THE ARBITRATION PROVISION IS INITIALED.

B. ARBITRATION OF DISPUTES: (1) Seller and Broker agree that any dispute or claim in law or equity arising between them regarding the obligation to pay compensation under this Agreement, which is not settled through mediation, shall be decided by neutral, binding arbitration, including and subject to paragraph 19B(2) below. The arbitrator shall be a retired judge or justice, or an attorney with at least 5 years of residential real estate law experience, unless the parties mutually agree to a different arbitrator, who shall render an award in accordance with substantive California law. The parties shall have the right to discovery in accordance with California Code of Civil Procedure §1283.05. In all other respects, the arbitration shall be conducted in accordance with Title 9 of Part III of the California Code of Civil Procedure. Judgment upon the award of the arbitrator(s) may be entered in any court having jurisdiction. Interpretation of this agreement to arbitrate shall be governed by the Federal Arbitration Act.

(2) EXCLUSIONS FROM MEDIATION AND ARBITRATION: The following matters are excluded from mediation and arbitration: (i) a judicial or non-judicial foreclosure or other action or proceeding to enforce a deed of trust, mortgage, or installment land sale contract as defined in California Civil Code §2985; (ii) an unlawful detainer action; (iii) the filing or enforcement of a mechanic's lien; and (iv) any matter that is within the jurisdiction of a probate, small claims, or bankruptcy court. The filing of a court action to enable the recording of a notice of pending action, for order of attachment, receivership, injunction, or other provisional remedies, shall not constitute a waiver of the mediation and arbitration provisions.

"**NOTICE: BY INITIALING IN THE SPACE BELOW YOU ARE AGREEING TO HAVE ANY DISPUTE ARISING OUT OF THE MATTERS INCLUDED IN THE 'ARBITRATION OF DISPUTES' PROVISION DECIDED BY NEUTRAL ARBITRATION AS PROVIDED BY CALIFORNIA LAW AND YOU ARE GIVING UP ANY RIGHTS YOU MIGHT POSSESS TO HAVE THE DISPUTE LITIGATED IN A COURT OR JURY TRIAL. BY INITIALING IN THE SPACE BELOW YOU ARE GIVING UP YOUR JUDICIAL RIGHTS TO DISCOVERY AND APPEAL, UNLESS THOSE RIGHTS ARE SPECIFICALLY INCLUDED IN THE 'ARBITRATION OF DISPUTES' PROVISION. IF YOU REFUSE TO SUBMIT TO ARBITRATION AFTER AGREEING TO THIS PROVISION, YOU MAY BE COMPELLED TO ARBITRATE UNDER THE AUTHORITY OF THE CALIFORNIA CODE OF CIVIL PROCEDURE. YOUR AGREEMENT TO THIS ARBITRATION PROVISION IS VOLUNTARY.**"

"**WE HAVE READ AND UNDERSTAND THE FOREGOING AND AGREE TO SUBMIT DISPUTES ARISING OUT OF THE MATTERS INCLUDED IN THE 'ARBITRATION OF DISPUTES' PROVISION TO NEUTRAL ARBITRATION.**"

Seller's Initials _____ / _____   Broker's Initials _____ / _____

20. ENTIRE AGREEMENT: All prior discussions, negotiations and agreements between the parties concerning the subject matter of this Agreement are superseded by this Agreement, which constitutes the entire contract and a complete and exclusive expression of their agreement, and may not be contradicted by evidence of any prior agreement or contemporaneous oral agreement. If any provision of this Agreement is held to be ineffective or invalid, the remaining provisions will nevertheless be given full force and effect. This Agreement and any supplement, addendum or modification, including any photocopy or facsimile, may be executed in counterparts.

By signing below, Seller acknowledges that Seller has read, understands, received a copy of and agrees to the terms of this Agreement.

Seller _____ Date _____
Address _____ City _____ State _____ Zip _____
Telephone _____ Fax _____ E-mail _____

Seller _____ Date _____
Address _____ City _____ State _____ Zip _____
Telephone _____ Fax _____ E-mail _____

Real Estate Broker (Firm) _____ DRE Lic. # _____
By (Agent) _____ DRE Lic. # _____ Date _____
Address _____ City _____ State _____ Zip _____
Telephone _____ Fax _____ E-mail _____

THIS FORM HAS BEEN APPROVED BY THE CALIFORNIA ASSOCIATION OF REALTORS® (C.A.R.). NO REPRESENTATION IS MADE AS TO THE LEGAL VALIDITY OR ADEQUACY OF ANY PROVISION IN ANY SPECIFIC TRANSACTION. A REAL ESTATE BROKER IS THE PERSON QUALIFIED TO ADVISE ON REAL ESTATE TRANSACTIONS. IF YOU DESIRE LEGAL OR TAX ADVICE, CONSULT AN APPROPRIATE PROFESSIONAL.

This form is available for use by the entire real estate industry. It is not intended to identify the user as a REALTOR®. REALTOR® is a registered collective membership mark which may be used only by members of the NATIONAL ASSOCIATION OF REALTORS® who subscribe to its Code of Ethics.

Published and Distributed by:
REAL ESTATE BUSINESS SERVICES, INC.
a subsidiary of the California Association of REALTORS®
525 South Virgil Avenue, Los Angeles, California 90020

Reviewed by _____ Date _____

Figure 8-1c:
Sample exclusive listing contract, continued.

RLA REVISED 4/07 (PAGE 3 OF 3)

RESIDENTIAL LISTING AGREEMENT - EXCLUSIVE (RLA PAGE 3 OF 3)

Unless all the parties who hold title in a property join in the sale, a full interest in the property can't be sold. To avoid future problems, the listing broker wants to be sure that all property owners sign the listing contract.

Just as death is nature's way of warning you to slow down, a co-owner's refusal to sign a listing is real estate's way of warning you about a potential deal killer. If your spouse (or a co-owner in a tenancy-in-common partnership) won't sign the listing, that person probably will also refuse to sign a sale contract. Don't sign a listing until you resolve the co-owner's problem, and *all* owners are willing to sign it.

✔ **A Multiple Listing Service (MLS) option offers benefits.** Paragraph 6 of the form in Figure 8-1b gives sellers the option of having information about their listing put into the local MLS. Chapter 12 provides reasons why listing information about your property in the MLS is a good idea.

In some areas, brokers use the MLS contract to sign up their listings. If that's the case in your area, signing your contract automatically places your property in the MLS database. In all other respects, a multiple listing contract operates the same way as any other exclusive right to sell listing contract.

✔ **Alternative dispute resolution options can save you time and money.** Lawsuits are time consuming and darned expensive, to boot. Most real estate contracts — listing contracts *and* purchase contracts — now have provisions for *alternative dispute resolution,* a phrase that describes using either mediation or arbitration (see paragraph 19 of Figure 8-1c) to resolve contract disputes faster and generally in less expensive ways than litigation in a court of law. This provision makes sense. No one, including a good lawyer, wants you to needlessly waste time and money in court.

How long is long enough?

We can offer no one correct answer to the question of how long your listing's duration should be. Unless you have good reason to believe that extra time will be necessary to find a buyer for your house (because either the property is unusual or because the local real estate market is in the dumps), we strongly recommend a 90-day listing period.

Why 90 days? Dr. Samuel Johnson, the famous 18th-century writer, once said, "When a man knows he is to be hanged in a fortnight, it concentrates his mind wonderfully." Three months are, under normal circumstances, long enough to give the listing broker a good chance to sell your house, yet short enough to keep the broker's mind concentrated on the job at hand — finding a buyer for your property before the listing expires.

If your house hasn't sold after 90 days but you were pleased with the listing broker's efforts on your behalf, you can simply renew the listing. But, on the other hand, if you were unhappy with the listing broker's service, 90 days isn't forever. After the listing expires, find yourself a different and, hopefully, a better broker.

Open listings

An open listing is a *nonexclusive* authorization for brokers to find a buyer for your property. You can give as many brokers as you want an open listing on your house. It's the real estate version of a winner-take-all horse race.

You're obligated to pay a commission to the first broker who fulfills either of the following conditions:

- ✔ Finds a buyer ready, willing, and able to enter into a contract that meets the exact terms of your listing
- ✔ Procures the buyer whose offer you ultimately accept

If you find the buyer by yourself, you don't have to pay any of the brokers. And you can cancel an open listing any time you want without penalty.

If this arrangement sounds wonderful, think again. Smart sellers won't give brokers an open listing and good brokers won't accept them. Here's why:

- ✔ **Limited advertising and marketing of your property:** In many places, depending on the local rules, brokers can't put open listings into the MLS. This restriction is a big disadvantage. As we note in Chapter 12, the MLS is a highly effective tool that brokers use to internally advertise listings to other MLS members who may have buyers for their listings. Nor do brokers produce fancy brochures or put big classified ads in the newspaper to tell the world about an open listing. Why should they? Potential buyers may end up going to another broker or directly to the seller to write up an offer. The seller may also suddenly decide to cancel the listing.

  Brokers only advertise or market open listings as a last resort if they have nothing more promising to do. They disdainfully refer to open listings as *pocket listings* because brokers tuck them away "in their pocket" passively waiting for a buyer to come along. If you want a quick sale, an open listing isn't the way to get one.

- ✔ **No control:** If you give 10 brokers an open listing on your house, you end up doing work that a listing agent normally handles. All the agents call *you* to coordinate showings of your property. You must prepare the house for showings. You also have to debrief agents after showings to find out whether you're getting an offer and, if not, find out why not. You have no neck to wring if you come home after work and find that someone left the front door unlocked and let the cat out after a showing. If you like chaos, you'll like an open listing.

✔ **Your broker is your competitor:** Because you don't have to pay any broker if you sell the house yourself, brokers see you as a competitor. This adversarial relationship encourages brokers to work for buyers, not you. Brokers know that if they take care of their buyers, they'll get a commission sooner or later. No such loyalty exists in their relationship with you.

An open listing is barely better than no listing at all. Unless you have an *extremely* compelling reason that you absolutely, positively *must* list your house with a bevy of brokers, you'll be better served with an exclusive listing.

Examining Broker Compensation

When most people hear the term *broker compensation,* they immediately think of a commission based on a percentage of the property's sale price. Commissions are the most common method of broker compensation so that's a logical place to start. However, commissions aren't the only way to pay brokers. Keep reading this section for a rundown on commissions.

Commissions

In the following list, we try to answer questions you've had about commissions but may have been too embarrassed to ask. Don't worry. Questions are good. If you didn't have any questions, we wouldn't get to write a book! Check out the following important questions:

✔ **Who pays the commission?** Usually sellers pay the commission, although in rare cases, buyers pay their agents directly. After all, sellers get money when property sells. Buyers generally don't have funds left for anything more expensive than a Big Mac after making a cash down payment to buy the house, plus paying loan charges, property inspections fees, homeowners insurance premiums, moving costs, and other miscellaneous expenses of purchase.

✔ **Are commissions set by law?** There's no such thing as a legal minimum commission or a mandatory percentage. Commissions vary from one area to the next. The price and type of property being sold also affect the percentage. Commissions on houses, for example, usually range from 4 to 7 percent of the sale price, and commissions on vacant land can go as high as 10 percent.

✔ **Are commissions negotiable?** Absolutely! If a real estate broker or agent tells you otherwise, dump 'em. In fact, most listing contracts contain language similar to the following notice contained in paragraph 4 of the C.A.R. listing: "Notice: The amount or rate of real estate commissions is not fixed by law. They are set by each Broker individually and may be negotiable between Seller and Broker (real estate commissions include all compensation and fees to Broker)."

Unbelievably, the vast majority of people who use the services of real estate agents erroneously believe that commissions aren't negotiable. In an Opinion Research Corporation survey for AARP, only 26 percent of respondents correctly chose the answer that commissions can be negotiated.

Bartering over commissions

Knowing that commissions are negotiable is fine. By itself, however, that information is worthless. This section deals with ways to translate your knowledge into a lower commission.

Be sure to read Chapter 13 before beginning your negotiations. Good negotiators replace emotions with facts. People can get their feelings hurt. Facts don't have any feelings to hurt. Don't try to outargue agents; out*fact* them.

Mediation and arbitration

Mediation generally is the fastest, least expensive way to resolve simple problems. You and the broker (if the dispute is over a listing contract) or you and the buyer (if the problem arises from a dispute related to the purchase contract) present your differences to a neutral third party called a *mediator.* The mediator can't impose a settlement on either of the quarreling parties. Instead, the mediator attempts to help both parties work together to reach an agreement regarding a mutually satisfactory solution to their problem.

If mediation fails to resolve the dispute, or if your problem is too complex to handle by mediation, arbitration also is generally less costly and faster than going to court. During arbitration, the parties present their differences to a neutral arbitrator who listens to all the evidence and then makes a binding decision that resolves the dispute. The arbitrator's decision is final and is as enforceable as a judgment handed down in court. If you're ever a party in a mediation or arbitration, consult a good real estate lawyer.

Commission splits

Suppose that your house sells for $300,000. With a 6 percent commission, the sale generates an $18,000 commission. If your listing broker receives the entire $18,000, she'll be one happy camper. Unfortunately for her, that isn't what happens.

Brokerage commissions almost always are split 50/50 at the close of escrow. In your transaction, for example, your listing broker gets half $9,000 in our example) of the commission. The other $9,000 goes to a cooperating agent from another firm who represents the buyer.

Because your broker is a licensed independent broker, she doesn't split her $9,000 with anyone. The buyer's agent holds a salesperson's license, however, so the selling-side commission is paid

to the agent's broker, who then splits the $9,000 50/50 with the agent so each end up with $4,500. (Top-notch agents can receive 80 percent or more of the total commission.)

If you want to be effective during commission negotiations, understanding internal commission splits among agents and brokers is important. Most agents don't have the authority to cut a commission without getting their broker's approval. By the same token, brokers can't unilaterally agree to commission cuts that affect their agents. As a rule, brokers and agents have to agree to a commission reduction because a cut reduces both of their commissions.

Before entering into commission negotiations, you *must* know these important facts:

- ✔ **What's the going rate for commissions in your area?** Straight 6 percent commissions on the sale price may be the norm in your neighborhood. A tiered commission schedule is possible, such as 6 percent on the first $100,000 of sale price, 5 percent on the next $50,000, and 4 percent on the balance. Or, to provide more incentive to agents, commissions may increase from 5 percent on the first $100,000 to 6 percent on the balance. Check local commission rates by questioning several real estate agents as well as friends and business associates who've sold property recently.

    Note: In some areas, high-end houses are listed at a reduced commission rate. If, for example, you're the proud owner of a $500,000 house, the standard commission rate on property in that price range may be 5 percent rather than the 6 percent commission for less expensive houses.

- ✔ **How's the real estate market?** Market competition is the number one reason commissions are *or aren't* cut. In a buyers' market when listings are a dime a dozen, agents have little incentive to cut commissions. They need buyers, not more listings. In a sellers' market, however, when listings are extremely scarce and buyers are plentiful, agents are more willing to shave commissions.

✔ **How badly does the broker or agent need listings?** Brokerage firms love listings because they make phones ring for agents in the office. Buyers who read about your house in the broker's classified ad call the office to get more details. If your house isn't right for them, the agent who got the call can, at least, make a contact and may end up selling the caller another property. The listing agent uses your listing to develop more business by mailing prospecting letters about the listing to other property owners in your neighborhood and by holding open houses to generate buyers and listings. If a prospective listing broker's weekly ad seems short of listings compared to other offices, you probably have a good chance of cutting a deal on the commission.

✔ **Is your house in good condition and will it be priced to sell?** The faster that your house sells, the less time, money, and effort a broker must spend advertising and marketing it. Houses in good condition usually sell faster than fixer-uppers. If your house is not only in great shape but also is priced realistically, some brokers share their savings with you by reducing the commission. However, commission cuts are hard to negotiate when you want a record-high sale price for your neighborhood, expect the broker to do a great deal of expensive advertising, and want your house held open every Saturday and Sunday until it sells.

✔ **Are you a package deal?** If you intend to sell your house *and* purchase a new home through the same broker, you're twice as valuable to the broker because you represent two deals: a listing and a sale. Brokers may take that fact into account and offer you a "volume discount" by reducing the listing commission.

As we discuss in Chapter 7, you need to select an agent who has the skills and experience required for your particular transaction. Unless you're moving within the same geographical area, you're buying a similar type of property, and your listing agent has the requisite skills to work as a buyer's agent, you may need a different agent to represent you in the purchase of your new home.

Recognizing good versus bad commission cuts

Handled properly, a good commission reduction saves money without adversely affecting the length of time the house is on the market or the sale price. Bad commission cuts are false economies, because they end up extending the selling process and reducing your ultimate sale price by cutting the incentive of cooperating brokers to show and sell your property.

Assume that the prevailing commission rate in your area is 6 percent for houses like yours. During the agent selection interviews, you point out to the prospective listing agents that your house is in excellent condition. You tell each of them that you want to price your house realistically for a fast sale because you want to buy a larger house in the immediate vicinity before your baby is born three months from now. By determining how the listing broker proposes to split the commission with selling brokers, you can know when a commission cut is good or bad. For example:

- ✔ **Deep discount special:** "I'll list your house for 4 percent," the first broker says, "but only if I sell it myself. I want the whole commission. I won't cooperate with other agents." A 4 percent commission sounds great. In fact, it's awful. If your listing agent won't work with other agents to find a buyer, your house's market exposure is severely reduced. As a result, your house takes longer to sell and ultimately sells for less money. On top of all that, you'll have months of extra payments on your mortgage, property taxes, and homeowners insurance. This "deal" costs you far more than you can save.

- ✔ **Selling broker absorbs cut:** The second broker offers you a 5 percent commission. He proposes to give cooperating agents 2 percent and keep 3 percent (half of a full 6 percent commission) for himself. Picking the pockets of agents who represent buyers is stupid. This split makes the greedy listing broker happy, but turns off cooperating agents. Why? Because, under this arrangement, your house is advertised in the Multiple Listing Service with a 2 percent commission, putting it at a competitive disadvantage to other houses advertised paying a 3 percent commission to cooperating agents. If agents can find another house as nice as yours in the same price range but offering a full 3 percent commission, guess which house they'll try harder to sell?

- ✔ **Even split:** The third broker offers to list your house for a 5 percent commission, which she'll split 50/50 if a cooperating agent obtains the buyer for your house. Both listing and selling agents get 2.5 percent, which isn't too much off the going rate of 3 percent. That deal seems fair, you think. Fair, yes. Smart, no. A reduction in the cooperating agent's commission from the norm for a property like yours acts as a disincentive for commission-motivated real estate agents to show and sell your house.

- ✔ **Listing broker absorbs cut:** The last broker suggests a 5.5 percent commission, but says that he'll take 2.5 percent for the listing side and give cooperating agents 3 percent. Offering selling agents a full 3 percent commission ensures that you'll have their enthusiastic cooperation. This commission split is the best way for you to go.

Suppose that your house sells for $300,000. Each 1 percent of the sale price equals $3,000, which is significant money for you and the agents. If the listing agent volunteers to shave the listing-side commission by $1,500 (0.5 percent), that's swell. But don't mess with the selling side. Taking another 0.5 percent out of the selling-side commission may cost you more than $1,500 in reduced activity by cooperating agents.

The amount of commission that you pay ultimately is less important than the value you receive for the money you spend. Some top-notch agents won't cut commissions. Compared to mediocre agents, the best agents pay their own commissions because they're able to get more money for a house.

Consider this premise when you're trying to negotiate a lower commission with a prospective listing agent: If the agent can't defend *her* money (the commission) by persuading you that she's worth the commission she charges, how effectively will she defend *your* money from buyers who want to cut your asking price or get a bigger credit for corrective work? The agent who ultimately convinces you that she's *worth* every penny of a full commission may be the best agent for your team — given that the agent satisfies all the other listing agent selection criteria in Chapter 7.

Net listings

Unlike an open listing or an exclusive listing, a net listing isn't a type of listing. Rather, a *net listing* is a way to pay brokers. Under the terms of a net listing, the seller and broker make this agreement: When property sells, the broker is paid all money received over and above a predetermined net amount that goes to the seller. Because the net listing is a payment method, it can be used with either open or exclusive listing contracts.

For example, you tell the listing broker that you want to net $200,000 from the sale of your house after paying off the existing $70,000 mortgage and all other expenses of sale except, of course, the brokerage fee. According to the broker, your house is worth around $300,000, and expenses of sale in your area typically run about $10,000.

If everything goes according to plan and your house actually sells for $300,000, the broker earns $20,000 — $300,000 less $70,000 to pay off the loan, $10,000 for expenses of sale, and $200,000 to you. As far as you're concerned, you're happy to pay a $20,000 brokerage fee if you can clear $200,000 for yourself.

Unfortunately, sales rarely go according to plan in the real world. For example, consider the following possibilities:

- ✔ **The broker overestimated your house's value.** What if no one will pay more than $280,000 for your property? That's fine with you. You can pay off the loan, pay the $10,000 for expenses of sale, and still walk away with $200,000. Because no money is left, however, all your broker gets is a pat on the back.

  Under the circumstances, a bad listing broker may discourage prospective buyers from offering $280,000 by falsely telling them that you absolutely won't accept a penny less than $300,000. If a cooperating broker brings in a $280,000 offer, a bad listing agent may advise you not to accept the "lowball" offer and tell you to hold out for more money. Or worse yet, the broker may not even tell you about the offer in the first place. In either case, the broker is putting the commission (or lack thereof) ahead of your best interests as a seller.

- ✔ **The broker underestimated your house's value.** What if your house sells for $320,000? As Chapter 10 explains, pricing property is an imprecise art. If the listing broker says that your house is "worth around $300,000," a $20,000 variation in its value one way or the other is an acceptable margin of error. Even so, how will you feel paying the broker $40,000 (a whopping 12.5 percent commission!) because your house sold at the high end of its fair market value? Worse yet, what if the listing broker purposely understated your house's value to get a bigger fee? That's fraud.

Net listings are illegal in some states because of their high level of risk for broker fraud or misrepresentation. Even if using a net listing is perfectly legal in your area, that still doesn't make it a good way to compensate brokers. *Don't use a net listing.*

Discount brokers

So-called full-service real estate brokers, as their title indicates, handle many tasks and details related to your property's sale and charge a full commission for their services. A good listing broker does the following:

- ✔ Determines your house's fair market value
- ✔ Helps you prepare the property for marketing
- ✔ Handles all its advertising
- ✔ Holds Sunday open houses as well as open houses for cooperating brokers

✔ Schedules private showings for buyers

✔ Negotiates with buyers or their agents to get you the best possible price and terms of sale

✔ Makes sure that all the contract details are handled properly right up to the close of escrow

Your job is to serve as supervisor and decision maker.

At the opposite end of the service spectrum is the *For Sale By Owner (FSBO) option.* As Chapter 6 discusses, FSBO sellers don't have a listing broker. If you choose the FSBO option, you handle all the listing broker's chores yourself and thus avoid paying the listing agent's portion of a brokerage fee when your house sells. (As we note in Chapter 6, you may have to pay the buyer's agent a brokerage fee to put your deal together.)

Discount brokers occupy the middle range of the real estate brokerage service spectrum. If you use a discount broker, you pick and choose the tasks you want to do yourself to market your house. The more work you're willing to handle yourself, the less you typically pay the broker.

Your savings, although not as great as those offered by the FSBO option, may be better than simply cutting the commission on your house's sale price from 6 to 5.5 percent. Discount brokers utilize different pricing programs:

✔ **Flat fee:** With some discount brokers, you pay a flat fee for services rendered. For example, services can include providing a For Sale sign to put in your front yard, putting a write-up about your house in sales brochures published by the firm and distributed in free newsstands located around town, and training you in fundamentals (such as how to write a classified ad, how to hold an open house, and how to negotiate). For an extra fee, discount brokers may put a house's listing in the local MLS. (You're obligated to pay an additional commission if an MLS cooperating broker procures the buyer.)

✔ **Percentage commission:** Instead of charging 5 or 6 percent, which traditional real estate firms charge, some discount brokers charge 3 or 4 percent.

✔ **Hourly:** If you prefer, some discount brokers also provide assistance on an hourly fee basis. For example, you want a firm to handle all your Sunday open houses, negotiate contract terms whenever you receive written offers, and help you fill out sale-related paperwork. The drawback to this approach is that if you don't end up selling, you're out all the fees you've already paid.

Some full-service/full-commission brokers aren't keen about working on discount broker listings. For one thing, their listings often offer lower fees for cooperating brokers. Even if the fee is equal to the prevailing local rate, however, full-service agents know that they'll probably have to do extra work because you don't have a full-service broker handling your end of the deal. For these reasons, discount broker listings get less than enthusiastic showings by most full-service brokers.

Using discount brokers makes the most sense if your local real estate market is strong, pricing your house is relatively simple, and you're willing to handle some of the work. However, if your property will be difficult to sell (because of the amount of corrective work it needs or its unusual floor plan, for example), you may have to use a full-service broker to make a sale.

Flat fees and hourly charges vary from one discount broker to the next. If you decide to use a discount broker, do some comparison shopping. Look for a discount broker who'll give you a bundle of services that best meets your needs for the lowest flat fee or hourly charge. Larger discount real estate brokerage firms include

✔ **Help-U-Sell:** (800) 366-1177; www.helpusell.com

✔ **ZipRealty.com:** (800) 225-5947; www.ziprealty.com

Preparing Seller Disclosure Statements

The days of *caveat emptor* — let the buyer beware — are gone forever. In fact, given the flood of federal, state, and local consumer protection laws enacted during the last couple of decades, this is the era of *caveat vendor* — let the seller beware. Prudent house sellers and agents must now follow two simple guidelines:

✔ Beware of belligerent buyers.

✔ All buyers become belligerent if not given full disclosure.

As a seller, you may think that some of the disclosure requirements are overly protective of buyers. Because, however, you probably intend to purchase a new home to replace the one you're selling, you can benefit from disclosures as a buyer. All things considered, it's a fair trade.

What information should you disclose?

Disclosure statements aren't identical throughout the United States. Like other real estate contracts and forms, disclosure statements vary enormously in scope and intricacy because the disclosures themselves differ widely from state to state and from one area to another within any given state.

The documents you give prospective buyers probably won't look like the California Association of Realtors' Real Estate Transfer Disclosure Statement, shown in Figure 8-2. The C.A.R. form, however, gives you an idea of the kind of disclosures you may have to make.

CALIFORNIA ASSOCIATION OF REALTORS®

REAL ESTATE TRANSFER DISCLOSURE STATEMENT
(CALIFORNIA CIVIL CODE §1102, ET SEQ.)
(C.A.R. Form TDS, Revised 10/03)

THIS DISCLOSURE STATEMENT CONCERNS THE REAL PROPERTY SITUATED IN THE CITY OF _____, COUNTY OF _____, STATE OF CALIFORNIA, DESCRIBED AS _____.

THIS STATEMENT IS A DISCLOSURE OF THE CONDITION OF THE ABOVE DESCRIBED PROPERTY IN COMPLIANCE WITH SECTION 1102 OF THE CIVIL CODE AS OF (date) _____. IT IS NOT A WARRANTY OF ANY KIND BY THE SELLER(S) OR ANY AGENT(S) REPRESENTING ANY PRINCIPAL(S) IN THIS TRANSACTION, AND IS NOT A SUBSTITUTE FOR ANY INSPECTIONS OR WARRANTIES THE PRINCIPAL(S) MAY WISH TO OBTAIN.

I. COORDINATION WITH OTHER DISCLOSURE FORMS

This Real Estate Transfer Disclosure Statement is made pursuant to Section 1102 of the Civil Code. Other statutes require disclosures, depending upon the details of the particular real estate transaction (for example: special study zone and purchase-money liens on residential property).

Substituted Disclosures: The following disclosures and other disclosures required by law, including the Natural Hazard Disclosure Report/Statement that may include airport annoyances, earthquake, fire, flood, or special assessment information, have or will be made in connection with this real estate transfer, and are intended to satisfy the disclosure obligations on this form, where the subject matter is the same:

☐ Inspection reports completed pursuant to the contract of sale or receipt for deposit.
☐ Additional inspection reports or disclosures: _____

II. SELLER'S INFORMATION

The Seller discloses the following information with the knowledge that even though this is not a warranty, prospective Buyers may rely on this information in deciding whether and on what terms to purchase the subject property. Seller hereby authorizes any agent(s) representing any principal(s) in this transaction to provide a copy of this statement to any person or entity in connection with any actual or anticipated sale of the property.

THE FOLLOWING ARE REPRESENTATIONS MADE BY THE SELLER(S) AND ARE NOT THE REPRESENTATIONS OF THE AGENT(S), IF ANY. THIS INFORMATION IS A DISCLOSURE AND IS NOT INTENDED TO BE PART OF ANY CONTRACT BETWEEN THE BUYER AND SELLER.

Seller ☐ is ☐ is not occupying the property.

A. The subject property has the items checked below (read across):

☐ Range	☐ Oven	☐ Microwave
☐ Dishwasher	☐ Trash Compactor	☐ Garbage Disposal
☐ Washer/Dryer Hookups		☐ Rain Gutters
☐ Burglar Alarms	☐ Smoke Detector(s)	☐ Fire Alarm
☐ TV Antenna	☐ Satellite Dish	☐ Intercom
☐ Central Heating	☐ Central Air Conditioning	☐ Evaporator Cooler(s)
☐ Wall/Window Air Conditioning	☐ Sprinklers	☐ Public Sewer System
☐ Septic Tank	☐ Sump Pump	☐ Water Softener
☐ Patio/Decking	☐ Built-in Barbecue	☐ Gazebo
☐ Sauna		
☐ Hot Tub	☐ Pool	☐ Spa
☐ Locking Safety Cover*	☐ Child Resistant Barrier*	☐ Locking Safety Cover*
☐ Security Gate(s)	☐ Automatic Garage Door Opener(s)*	☐ Number Remote Controls ____
Garage: ☐ Attached	☐ Not Attached	☐ Carport
Pool/Spa Heater: ☐ Gas	☐ Solar	☐ Electric
Water Heater: ☐ Gas	☐ Water Heater Anchored, Braced, or Strapped*	
Water Supply: ☐ City	☐ Well	☐ Private Utility or
Gas Supply: ☐ Utility	☐ Bottled	☐ Other _____
☐ Window Screens	☐ Window Security Bars ☐ Quick Release Mechanism on Bedroom Windows*	

Exhaust Fan(s) in _____ 220 Volt Wiring in _____ Fireplace(s) in _____
☐ Gas Starter _____ ☐ Roof(s): Type: _____ Age: _____ (approx.)
☐ Other: _____

Are there, to the best of your (Seller's) knowledge, any of the above that are not in operating condition? ☐ Yes ☐ No. If yes, then describe. (Attach additional sheets if necessary): _____

(*see footnote on page 2)

TDS REVISED 10/03 (PAGE 1 OF 3) Print Date

Buyer's Initials (_____)(_____)
Seller's Initials (_____)(_____)

Reviewed by _____ Date _____

EQUAL HOUSING OPPORTUNITY

REAL ESTATE TRANSFER DISCLOSURE STATEMENT (TDS PAGE 1 OF 3)

Reprinted with permission, CALIFORNIA ASSOCIATION OF REALTORS™. Endorsement not implied.

Figure 8-2a: A disclosure statement looks something like this.

Property Address: _____ Date: _____

B. Are you (Seller) aware of any significant defects/malfunctions in any of the following? ☐ Yes ☐ No. If yes, check appropriate space(s) below.

☐ Interior Walls ☐ Ceilings ☐ Floors ☐ Exterior Walls ☐ Insulation ☐ Roof(s) ☐ Windows ☐ Doors ☐ Foundation ☐ Slab(s) ☐ Driveways ☐ Sidewalks ☐ Walls/Fences ☐ Electrical Systems ☐ Plumbing/Sewers/Septics ☐ Other Structural Components

(Describe: _____
_____
_____)

If any of the above is checked, explain. (Attach additional sheets if necessary.): _____
_____
_____
_____

*This garage door opener or child resistant pool barrier may not be in compliance with the safety standards relating to automatic reversing devices as set forth in Chapter 12.5 (commencing with Section 19890) of Part 3 of Division 13 of, or with the pool safety standards of Article 2.5 (commencing with Section 115920) of Chapter 5 of Part 10 of Division 104 of, the Health and Safety Code. The water heater may not be anchored, braced, or strapped in accordance with Section 19211 of the Health and Safety Code. Window security bars may not have quick release mechanisms in compliance with the 1995 edition of the California Building Standards Code.

C. Are you (Seller) aware of any of the following:

1. Substances, materials, or products which may be an environmental hazard such as, but not limited to, asbestos, formaldehyde, radon gas, lead-based paint, mold, fuel or chemical storage tanks, and contaminated soil or water on the subject property . . . . ☐ Yes ☐ No
2. Features of the property shared in common with adjoining landowners, such as walls, fences, and driveways, whose use or responsibility for maintenance may have an effect on the subject property . . . . ☐ Yes ☐ No
3. Any encroachments, easements or similar matters that may affect your interest in the subject property . . . . ☐ Yes ☐ No
4. Room additions, structural modifications, or other alterations or repairs made without necessary permits . . . . ☐ Yes ☐ No
5. Room additions, structural modifications, or other alterations or repairs not in compliance with building codes . . . . ☐ Yes ☐ No
6. Fill (compacted or otherwise) on the property or any portion thereof . . . . ☐ Yes ☐ No
7. Any settling from any cause, or slippage, sliding, or other soil problems . . . . ☐ Yes ☐ No
8. Flooding, drainage or grading problems . . . . ☐ Yes ☐ No
9. Major damage to the property or any of the structures from fire, earthquake, floods, or landslides . . . . ☐ Yes ☐ No
10. Any zoning violations, nonconforming uses, violations of "setback" requirements . . . . ☐ Yes ☐ No
11. Neighborhood noise problems or other nuisances . . . . ☐ Yes ☐ No
12. CC&R's or other deed restrictions or obligations . . . . ☐ Yes ☐ No
13. Homeowners' Association which has any authority over the subject property . . . . ☐ Yes ☐ No
14. Any "common area" (facilities such as pools, tennis courts, walkways, or other areas co-owned in undivided interest with others) . . . . ☐ Yes ☐ No
15. Any notices of abatement or citations against the property . . . . ☐ Yes ☐ No
16. Any lawsuits by or against the Seller threatening to or affecting this real property, including any lawsuits alleging a defect or deficiency in this real property or "common areas" (facilities such as pools, tennis courts, walkways, or other areas co-owned in undivided interest with others) . . . . ☐ Yes ☐ No

If the answer to any of these is yes, explain. (Attach additional sheets if necessary.): _____
_____
_____
_____

Seller certifies that the information herein is true and correct to the best of the Seller's knowledge as of the date signed by the Seller.

Seller_____ Date _____

Seller_____ Date _____

Buyer's Initials (_____)(_____)
Seller's Initials (_____)(_____)

Copyright © 1991-2003, CALIFORNIA ASSOCIATION OF REALTORS®, INC.
TDS REVISED 10/03 (PAGE 2 OF 3)

Reviewed by _____ Date _____

Figure 8-2b: A disclosure statement continued.

REAL ESTATE TRANSFER DISCLOSURE STATEMENT (TDS PAGE 2 OF 3)

Property Address: _____ Date: _____

III. AGENT'S INSPECTION DISCLOSURE
(To be completed only if the Seller is represented by an agent in this transaction.)

THE UNDERSIGNED, BASED ON THE ABOVE INQUIRY OF THE SELLER(S) AS TO THE CONDITION OF THE PROPERTY AND BASED ON A REASONABLY COMPETENT AND DILIGENT VISUAL INSPECTION OF THE ACCESSIBLE AREAS OF THE PROPERTY IN CONJUNCTION WITH THAT INQUIRY, STATES THE FOLLOWING:

☐ Agent notes no items for disclosure.

☐ Agent notes the following items: _____
_____
_____
_____

Agent (Broker Representing Seller) _____ By _____ Date _____
(Please Print)   (Associate Licensee or Broker Signature)

IV. AGENT'S INSPECTION DISCLOSURE
(To be completed only if the agent who has obtained the offer is other than the agent above.)

THE UNDERSIGNED, BASED ON A REASONABLY COMPETENT AND DILIGENT VISUAL INSPECTION OF THE ACCESSIBLE AREAS OF THE PROPERTY, STATES THE FOLLOWING:

☐ Agent notes no items for disclosure.

☐ Agent notes the following items: _____
_____
_____
_____

Agent (Broker Obtaining the Offer) _____ By _____ Date _____
(Please Print)   (Associate Licensee or Broker Signature)

V. BUYER(S) AND SELLER(S) MAY WISH TO OBTAIN PROFESSIONAL ADVICE AND/OR INSPECTIONS OF THE PROPERTY AND TO PROVIDE FOR APPROPRIATE PROVISIONS IN A CONTRACT BETWEEN BUYER AND SELLER(S) WITH RESPECT TO ANY ADVICE/INSPECTIONS/DEFECTS.

I/WE ACKNOWLEDGE RECEIPT OF A COPY OF THIS STATEMENT.

Seller _____ Date _____ Buyer _____ Date _____
Seller _____ Date _____ Buyer _____ Date _____

Agent (Broker Representing Seller) _____ By _____ Date _____
(Please Print)   (Associate Licensee or Broker Signature)

Agent (Broker Obtaining the Offer) _____ By _____ Date _____
(Please Print)   (Associate Licensee or Broker Signature)

SECTION 1102.3 OF THE CIVIL CODE PROVIDES A BUYER WITH THE RIGHT TO RESCIND A PURCHASE CONTRACT FOR AT LEAST THREE DAYS AFTER THE DELIVERY OF THIS DISCLOSURE IF DELIVERY OCCURS AFTER THE SIGNING OF AN OFFER TO PURCHASE. IF YOU WISH TO RESCIND THE CONTRACT, YOU MUST ACT WITHIN THE PRESCRIBED PERIOD.

A REAL ESTATE BROKER IS QUALIFIED TO ADVISE ON REAL ESTATE. IF YOU DESIRE LEGAL ADVICE, CONSULT YOUR ATTORNEY.

Figure 8-2c:
A disclosure statement continued.

Reviewed by _____ Date _____

TDS REVISED 10/03 (PAGE 3 OF 3)

REAL ESTATE TRANSFER DISCLOSURE STATEMENT (TDS PAGE 3 OF 3)

Generally speaking, the law requires that you disclose to prospective buyers any information you have that materially affects your property's value or desirability. A *material fact* is anything that reasonably affects either a buyer's decision to purchase your house or the price he'd pay. This disclosure must cover facts that you, as an owner, are expected to know about your property and the neighborhood that couldn't be known by (or wouldn't be apparent to) the buyer. For example:

- **Physical condition:** Are your built-in appliances in good working order? Do you know about any hidden defects or malfunctions in your house's major components (roof, foundation, electrical system, plumbing, sewer, insulation, windows, doors, walls, and so on)?

   Although you certainly ought to know whether your air conditioner works properly, no one expects you to be a professional property inspector. Disclosure laws are just one more reason why, as we note in Chapter 7, getting a premarketing inspection of your house is wise. You (and your agent, if you're using one) should also encourage buyers to conduct *their own* investigations and obtain inspections from *their own* experts instead of relying solely on your inspections or the information you provide about the property's physical condition.

- **Health, safety, and environmental hazards:** You must comply with federal, state, and local disclosure laws regarding property problems related to asbestos, formaldehyde, lead-based paints, underground fuel or chemical storage tanks, radon gas, contaminated soil or water, and other health hazards. Is your property in harm's way from earthquakes, floods, hurricanes, or other natural disasters? Does your property comply with local energy or water conservation ordinances?

   Don't worry about running all over town to stock up on the various booklets, pamphlets, and forms the law requires you to give to prospective buyers. Your listing agent or real estate lawyer (if you're selling without an agent) should provide all necessary disclosure information prior to marketing your property.

- **Legal condition:** Are any lawsuits pending that affect your property? Did you make any modifications or alterations to your property without getting the necessary building permits? Do these modifications or alterations comply with state and local building codes? If you're selling a condominium, you must give the buyer copies of the Covenants, Conditions, and Restrictions (CC&Rs), the Homeowners Association bylaws, and the budget.

If you have any legal problems related to the property, clear them up *before* marketing your property if possible. Nobody wants to buy a lawsuit. Legal problems are deal killers. Buyers generally don't want to inherit legal problems, which tend to take a long time to resolve and are expensive, to boot.

✔ **Subjective areas:** Until now, you could provide objective answers to the various disclosure questions. Your roof either leaks or it doesn't. You either have lead-based paint in your house or you don't. Either you're being sued or you aren't. Now things get fuzzy. Is your neighborhood quiet? Can you find parking spaces easily near your house? Is car traffic excessive in the neighborhood? Would you call the morning commute horrendous? Are schools in the area overcrowded?

Subjective questions can't be answered with a simple yes or no. The environment that you think is extremely quiet, the buyer may consider a boiler factory. Parking a block from your house may be close in your opinion, but a long walk to your buyer. How much traffic is excessive? And so it goes. Answer all subjective questions to the best of your ability, and then encourage buyers to familiarize themselves with the area so they can draw their own subjective conclusions about these issues.

Some state courts have ruled that certain unpleasant facts materially affect the desirability and value of property and insist that sellers disclose these facts. One such fact is a death on the property within several years of the sale — especially if the death was gruesome or violent. For example, the difference between an elderly man dying peacefully in his sleep and a homicide is obvious. Other examples of unpleasant material facts are high crime rates in the immediate area or the presence of known child molesters or rapists who've been released from prison and now live in the neighborhood.

If you're not sure whether you have to make this type of disclosure about your property, consult your listing agent or a real estate lawyer.

An ounce of prevention is worth a pound of cure

Sometimes, lawsuits are unavoidable. Certain litigious lads and lasses will take you to court at the drop of a summons whether they have a case or not. Other than identifying them in advance as troublemakers and refusing to

Disclose work done without permits

This cautionary note is for do-it-yourselfers who've done carpentry, plumbing, and electrical work around the house without bothering to get a permit for the work or having it inspected by their friendly local building department. We, your friendly authors, are keenly aware that building permits can be expensive, are sometimes difficult to get, and may trigger property tax increases. We also know that, for these reasons, many folks do work without a permit.

That's all fine and good. But when you sell, 'fess up in writing about work performed without a building permit.

Your written disclosure, for example, that you built that magnificent deck without a permit (and that the deck may not meet local building codes) serves to protect you if the buyer sues you about it after the deal closes.

Remember: The key to avoiding lawsuits is complete, timely, written disclosure of all problems so your buyer can make an informed purchasing decision.

accept an offer from them, you can't protect yourself from people who believe that a lawsuit is their only solution for real or imagined problems. If you have the misfortune of selling your house to one of these misguided souls, your best recourse is to get a good lawyer to defend you.

The best defense is a good offense. Here are four suggestions you can enact to reduce the possibility of a legitimate lawsuit:

- ✔ **If in doubt, disclose.** If you have to ask whether to disclose something about your property or the neighborhood, you've answered your own question. Overdisclosure is better than running the risk of being sued for damages or having the sale rescinded because you failed to reveal a fact that materially affects your property's desirability or value. Remember the golden rule. "Do unto others as you would have them do unto you" may sound hokey, but it's mighty fine real estate advice.

- ✔ **Don't guess.** Not sure about the square footage of your house, the roof's age, the life expectancy of your water heater, or any other material fact? It's better by far to answer "unknown" than to guess. If prospective buyers are concerned about any of your "unknowns," they can hire their own experts to render opinions.

- ✔ **Put your disclosure in writing.** Have the buyers affirm receipt of your disclosure statement by signing and dating it. Be sure to keep a copy for your file.

- ✔ **Hire a professional to inspect your house prior to putting it on the market.** After seeing the results, you have the option of fixing defects you want to repair and disclosing the others.

Don't fight the problem. Like it or not, disclosure statements are a fact of real estate life. They're here to stay. Handled properly, mandatory disclosures speed up the sale of your house and ensure that, when your house sells, it stays sold.

Part III

Getting Top Dollar When You Sell

The 5th Wave   By Rich Tennant

"Most of the gingerbread is still in good shape and I had the roof re-frosted just last year."

In this part . . .

Before the For Sale sign goes up, you must prepare your property for sale. Fear not, we detail all the work you do and don't need to do, including staging, to make your house look its best. We also explain how you (and your agent, if you're using one) can analyze the sales of comparable houses in your neighborhood to determine your house's fair market value. Finally, using time-tested and proven techniques, we show you how to hone in on the perfect asking price for your castle.

Chapter 9

Preparing Your House for Sale

A magical metamorphosis occurs the moment you decide to sell your property. The "home" you love so dearly turns into a "house." This shift in vocabulary is an important part of letting go — the emotional detachment process all sellers experience sooner or later. Home is where your heart is. Houses, like TV sets, toasters, and tangerines, are commodities sold on the open market. You're getting ready to sell a *house*.

Most folks don't *really* see their houses after they've lived in them for a while. Things that buyers may find objectionable, owners accept as charming quirks. The bathroom door, for example, that sticks whenever it rains. That weird noise the refrigerator makes every so often in the middle of the night. The dirty spot on the hall carpet near the front door where the family dog always takes his afternoon nap. Little stuff.

Nor do homeowners tend to notice the insidious effects of gradual physical deterioration and equally gradual junk accumulation. Homeowners fail to see how badly the house needs a new paint job, how big that "little" stain from the leaky roof has grown, and how many clothes they've jammed into the once-spacious closets over the years. Not so little stuff.

A "lived-in" look is fine — until you want to sell. You may not see this decline, but buyers who tour your property definitely will. To be a successful seller, you must have your house looking its best. This chapter highlights what you can do to your house, outside and inside, to make it stand out above the other houses on the market and what common mistakes to avoid so you can get the best offer.

Handling Presale Preparation

Getting your house ready to put on the market takes time. Exposing your property to the market before it looks its best gives buyers and agents who tour the house a bad initial impression. It's nearly impossible to get them back for a second look after you correct the showing flaws. After you read this section, you'll know why you probably need at least two weeks to prepare your property for marketing.

If you make the right improvements when fixing up your property, you increase the odds of selling it quickly for top dollar. If, conversely, you make the wrong changes to your property, you waste the time and money you spent, prolong the sale, and possibly even reduce the ultimate sale price.

Start the presale fix-up process by getting outside opinions of your house's strengths and weaknesses. Don't ask your best friends or the next-door neighbors. They may have the same blind spots you do. Worse yet, they may sugarcoat the truth in a misguided attempt to spare your feelings.

Good real estate agents are an excellent source of advice about readying your house for sale. Because agents see your house with fresh eyes, they can spot flaws you no longer notice. Furthermore, agents look at your house the way buyers do. They know how to prepare houses so they're appealing for marketing — a process sometimes referred to as *staging.* And, last but not least, because agents work on commission, good agents don't want to waste your time or theirs trying to sell a house that isn't up to snuff. The more you get for your house, the bigger their commission. This section focuses on how to prepare your house for sale, starting from the curb and working your way inside.

Creating curb appeal

Most buyers make snap judgments about your house. Their first impressions, good or bad, generally are lasting impressions. Buyers begin forming their opinion of your house long before they go inside. *Curb appeal,* the external attractiveness of your property when viewed from the street, is critically important. If you want to see how your house looks to strangers, go across the street and take a good, hard look at it.

No matter how magnificent your house is on the inside, many buyers will drive by your house without stopping if the property lacks curb appeal. Your house's exterior appearance and landscaping either attract buyers or repulse them. You can enhance your house's curb appeal through some tried-and-true ways:

✔ **Painting:** Painting your house's exterior before you put it on the market can be expensive (unless you do it yourself), but it gives the biggest bang for your fix-up buck — *if* you use colors that conform with your neighborhood's decorating norm. Now isn't the time to make a fashion statement! White, light grays, or soft tans are safe choices for exterior walls. If your house doesn't need a new paint job, at least touch up window frames, front shutters, gutters, and down spouts and have your house gently power washed by people who know what they're doing. Also, be sure to give your mailbox and front door a fresh coat of paint. Greet prospective buyers by dressing up your freshly-painted entrance with a new welcome mat.

In addition to spending big bucks on a paint job, house painting is a time-consuming project. Because exterior painting is seasonal work, professional painters are busy folks after the snow melts and during the dry season. Don't wait until a week before you want to put your house on the market to call several painters for bids to do the job. Schedule your painting contractor well in advance of the crunch or you may end up with two nasty choices: either painting the house yourself or putting it on the market with peeling, faded paint.

✔ **Lawn:** A freshly mowed, neatly trimmed lawn gives your house a well-maintained appearance. Don't leave toys, lawn equipment, or garden hoses scattered around the yard. You can make your grass look extra lush and green by fertilizing it in the appropriate season. However, if your pet, or your neighbor's pet, tries to help out with the fertilizing, use your pooper-scooper daily to clean up.

✔ **Sidewalks:** Sweep your sidewalks daily. Keep your walks free of snow and ice in the winter. Nothing puts buyers in a foul mood faster than falling flat on their faces while trying to navigate your icy sidewalk.

A badly cracked, crumbling sidewalk is a lawsuit waiting to happen if someone trips and injures himself due to the sidewalk's poor state of repair. In addition, a poorly maintained sidewalk creates a terrible first impression of your property. Compounding the problem, buyers know that if you don't fix the sidewalk, they'll have to do it. Patching cracks or replacing damaged portions of a sidewalk prior to putting your house on the market is money well spent. Keep cost to a minimum by getting bids to do the corrective work from several reputable contractors.

✔ **Shrubbery:** Remove or replace any dead or dying trees, hedges, or shrubs, and prune anything that looks scraggly or overgrown. Cut back overgrown shrubs that block windows and keep light from entering your house.

✔ **Flowers:** Filling flowerbeds with seasonal flowers is an inexpensive way to add color and charm to property. Choose bright, fresh colors that draw buyers' eyes to otherwise ignored areas of your yard. Don't forget to keep flowerbeds watered and weeded throughout the marketing process until your sale closes. If you're among the flower-growing impaired, allow us to recommend *Perennials For Dummies* by Marcia Tatroe and the National Gardening Association (Wiley).

✔ **Repairs:** Be sure that all gutters and downspouts are in place and clean. Replace missing roof shingles and broken or cracked windows. Repair cracks in your driveway and remove large oil stains. Replace or repair broken stairs, torn window screens, broken or missing fence slats, and defective doorknobs. Make sure that your front and back doors, garage doors, and all windows open easily. Check exterior lights to be certain that they're working properly.

✔ **Windows:** Keep your windows spotless inside and out throughout the marketing period. When you're not home, curious buyers attracted by the For Sale sign *will* peek through the windows to size up your house. Don't let their first impression be windows covered with cobwebs and smeared with fingerprints. Don't forget that interior window treatments can be seen from the outside. Worn or faded drapes or lopsided window shades need to be replaced or removed.

✔ **Eliminate or hide clutter:** Clear everything you don't need out of the garage. Friends and family who live nearby can be a great source of temporary places to stash your excess stuff. If you can't clean your garage out, at least keep the door closed to conceal the mess from prying eyes. Store recycling bins in an out-of-the-way spot in back of your house. Don't have a fleet of cars, trucks, boats, and campers cluttering up your driveway or parked in front of your house. You're selling a house, not a parking lot.

If just reading this list makes you tired, you're not alone. You probably lack the time and the desire to do all this prep work yourself. If you can afford it, make your life easier by hiring competent folks to help you with these chores. Your real estate agent, if you're working with one, should be brought into the spiffing process as soon as possible. The agent should help prioritize the various projects and can probably refer you to people who specialize in this kind of work.

Exteriors attract, but interiors sell

Curb appeal draws buyers into your house. Appealing interiors make the sale. But you don't have to spend tens of thousands of dollars on your house prior to putting up the For Sale sign. On the contrary, the little things you do generally give the biggest increase in value. Concentrate on the three Cs.

Clean up

Clean, scrub, and polish your house. Your stove, oven, refrigerator, microwave oven, and other appliances must be spotlessly clean inside and out. Scour walls, floors, bathtubs, showers, sinks, and faucets until they sparkle. Clean or repair tub and shower grout. Don't forget to clean the ventilating hood in your kitchen as well as the dusty heating and air conditioning vents throughout your house.

Buyers *will* notice strong smells as soon as they walk through your front door, so eliminate smoke, mildew, and pet odors. Cleaning drapes and carpets helps get rid of odors. So does cleaning your cat's litter box *daily.* Remove ashes from the fireplace. If you're a smoker, clean all ashtrays daily and take your smoking breaks in the great outdoors until you sell your house. Use air fresheners or citrus-scented potpourri to keep your house odor free. Open windows at least ten minutes every day to let in fresh air (unless you live near something emitting an undesirable odor). Whether you do the work or hire someone, make sure that your house is spotless and smell-less.

Fix drippy faucets. If any of your sinks or bathtubs drain slowly, unclog them. Just as car buyers love to kick tires, some property buyers test houses by flushing toilets and running water in sinks and bathtubs to check drains. Buyers consider leaky faucets and clogged drains a sign of poor maintenance and, more often than not, they're right!

Clear out

Get rid of clutter. Be ruthless. Removing clutter increases the perceived size of your house. Eliminating clutter and excess furniture makes rooms appear larger. Try this simple test: take shoes, sweater boxes, and so on off your closet floor and look again. Small rooms such as closets and bathrooms seem larger without a ton of stuff all over the floor.

Where furniture is concerned, less is more. Go through your house room by room with your real estate agent or a friend who isn't a packrat. Get their opinion on what to eliminate. Set a goal of getting rid of at least a quarter of the furniture in each room — half would probably be better. Big furniture such as large sofas or grand pianos make a room look smaller. A glass table, for example, seems smaller than a solid wood table of the same size. Think visually. If you want a better idea of what your room looks like, take pictures of each room.

Remember the rule of three: No more than three items should be on your kitchen and bathroom counters, tabletops, and mantels. Keep dirty dishes out of the kitchen sink. Store, sell, or give away surplus or bulky furniture. Recycle those stacks of old magazines and newspapers you've been saving for no good reason. Don't just move stuff into the attic or garage. On the contrary, dump all that junk from your attic, basement, and garage that you've accumulated over the years.

Closet space sells houses. Create additional space in your closet by weeding out all those old clothes you never wear anymore. Clean and organize closets, bookcases, and drawers. Like it or not, serious buyers inspect your closets and open built-in drawers. Be sure that they're neat and roomy. Closets look more organized if you replace wire hangers with matching wood or plastic hangers.

Ironically, the clutter that reduces your house's value is far from worthless. On the contrary, your junk is someone else's treasure. Make a donation to your favorite charity and earn a tax deduction (be sure to ask for a donation receipt). Have a garage sale. Who knows? You may make enough from a garage sale to pay for your move.

Cosmetic improvements

Make cosmetic improvements. Painting isn't expensive if you do it yourself, but be careful when selecting interior colors. Lighter colors make rooms look larger. Avoid cherry red, canary yellow, cobalt blue, emerald green, and other bold colors with strong visual impact. You may love the effect, but you aren't the buyer. Stick to conventional whites, soft pastels, warm tans, honey, taupe, and other neutral colors that won't clash with most prospective buyers' tastes. If, like most basements, yours is dark and gloomy, paint the walls and ceiling a light color and put the highest wattage light bulbs that you can safely use in your light fixtures to brighten up the space. Repair cracks in the floor.

Just because we recommend using neutral colors doesn't mean that you should turn your house into a bland, boring blob of mush. You have our permission to give it visual spice. Use fabric — area rugs, tablecloths, napkins, sofa cushions, window curtains or drapes, bedspreads and quilts, bath and hand towels, shower curtains, and so on — to create *temporary* color accents in rooms. Unlike other more permanent improvements, you can take these items with you for use in your next home. You can also use flower arrangements to add bright splashes of color to rooms.

Staging

Staging a house goes way beyond your efforts to make it look nifty before having friends over for a dinner party. After all, your pals are there to eat your food and drink your wine — not buy your house. Just as stagehands set the stage for Broadway productions, you can stage your house to create a production designed to wow prospective purchasers. Good stagers know how to emphasize the best features of a house and minimize the worst.

Staging became even more important with the advent of Internet marketing, which we cover in Chapter 13. Today it's no longer a simple matter of how your house looks to people who walk through it. Many buyers shop online prior to actually seeing a house, so be sure your house looks good online too.

If you've ever visited a new home development and walked through the builder's model home, you've seen staging. Builders usually do extremely elaborate staging jobs. They use professional decorators who take care of everything: placing furniture, choosing soothing colors for carpets and drapes, hanging artwork, having a bowl of fruit on the kitchen counter, putting flower arrangements in the living room, and leaving an open book on a table by the bed in the master bedroom.

All cabinets, closets, and drawers are empty, of course, so buyers can easily see that the house appears to have plenty of room for their stuff. That unnaturally clean, utterly bare garage looks huge. The patio is furnished with nice lawn furniture and one of those tables with an umbrella in the center. Staging the property this way helps prospective buyers visualize themselves living in the home.

The message a bright, cheerful, immaculately clean model home in perfect working condition sends to buyers is, "What are you waiting for? Go ahead. Buy me. You won't regret it. Living here will be easy. You can relax and enjoy life."

Staging finishes the process you started with the three Cs (see the preceding section). You don't have to spend wads of cash to stage your property. Small bucks spent staging can bring big rewards. If you're looking to increase your house's emotional appeal, check out the following areas of improvement:

- **Kitchen:** Aromas from fragrant goodies like freshly baked gingerbread or just-brewed coffee bring back wonderful memories of home. Conversely, many people find odors from pungent foods such as liver, fish, and cabbage a turnoff. Be careful about the foods you cook throughout the marketing process; you never know when prospective buyers may tour your house.

- **Bathrooms:** Always have fresh towels and potpourri in bathrooms. Buy new shower curtains; old ones may have water spots or mildew on them. Put new soap in the soap dishes. Take toothbrushes, toothpaste, combs, prescription bottles, and rubber duckies off the bathroom counter. Clear out the medicine cabinet, make sure the toilets are flushed and cleaned, and remove the tub mat and rug in front of the toilet.

✔ **Collections:** Everyone has collections — family photos on the wall, autographed baseballs, dolls, CDs and DVDs, sports and school trophies, model airplanes, whatever. Unfortunately, now isn't the time to have prospective buyers thinking about your family living in the house. You want them to focus on *their* family living in it. *Depersonalize your property.* Put away your collections so people focus on the task at hand — buying your house.

Most folks use magnets or tape to stick everything from vacation snapshots and finger-painting masterpieces to notes for the kids and "to do" lists on the surface of their refrigerator. That's a mighty distracting collection. Clear *everything* off the top and sides of your refrigerator.

✔ **Comfort:** Keep your house warm in winter and cool in summer. A house that's too hot or too cold isn't inviting. Remember Goldilocks.

✔ **Fireplace:** Functioning fireplaces are utilitarian (another heat source) and romantic (candlelit dinners by the fire). If you have a fireplace, spotlight it. Polish your fireplace tools. Pile logs neatly in the fireplace. When your house is shown on cold fall or winter days, nothing says "Welcome" like the warmth, glow, crackle, and smell of a blazing fire in the fireplace.

✔ **Flowers:** Vases of colorful, fresh flowers spotted throughout the house make a wonderful impression on prospective buyers. You don't have to spend a fortune on hothouse orchids. Bouquets of daisies, tulips, or other seasonal flowers from your local supermarket are fine.

✔ **Furniture:** Rearrange furniture to create a warm, inviting feeling. If you're selling a vacant house, consider renting furniture to create a homey atmosphere.

✔ **Light:** Bright, well-lit houses seem more spacious and cheerful. Wash all your windows. Clean the window screens. During the day, open all your curtains and drapes (unless you overlook the city dump or your view is a brick wall). If the view is unattractive, get sheer window coverings that let light through but mask the view. Don't force buyers and agents to grope around in the dark looking for light switches. When you show your house, brighten up rooms by turning on *all* your lamps, even during the day. Be sure hallways and stairways are brightly lit. Don't forget to turn on closet lights, oven lights, and the lights over your stove and kitchen counter.

Prospective buyers often drop in or drive by in the evening to see how your house looks at night. Interior lights that can be seen from the street make a house look cozy and inviting. From sunset until you go to bed, keep at least one light on in each room that faces the street.

As you may know, some folks earn their living (either part-time or full-time) as home stagers. If you're working with a real estate agent to sell your house and you've done a thorough job interviewing agents, as we explain in Chapter 7, your agent can probably recommend several stagers. In the event your agent is unable to suggest anyone, she should ask fellow agents in her office and her office manager for advice.

Think Again: Avoiding Major Improvements

You're about ready to sell your home, and you realize (or perhaps already know because you had the premarketing inspection we recommend in Chapter 7) that your house needs a new roof, a new foundation, new copper plumbing, kitchen remodeling, or bathroom upgrades. What's the best way to handle major expenses like these?

At this stage in the marketing process, you shouldn't bite off more than you can chew. If you only have a few weeks before you want to put your house on the market, you simply don't have the time to manage a huge project. Rehabs, larger and small, have two things in common:

- ✔ **No surprise number one:** All rehabs take longer than you though they would.

- ✔ **No surprise number two:** All rehabs cost more than you thought they would.

If you have to ask how much longer or how much more, you've never done a rehab. If your house is in need of a major improvement, heed the two following points:

- ✔ **Don't spend big bucks on major improvements.** For example, don't install a new roof just before putting your house on the market. As we note in Chapter 14, a wiser plan is to give buyers a credit in escrow to cover the repair cost. Prepare for negotiations regarding the credit by getting several competitive bids for the corrective work from reputable local contractors, and then base your credit on the lowest realistic bid.

    Why offer to give the buyer a credit in escrow? For one thing, you can avoid a huge out-of-pocket expense by handling the repairs this way. Furthermore, this arrangement allows the new owners to have the work done by their own contractor whenever they want after the sale is completed. Last, but not least by a long shot, if the buyers have problems with their new roof after the sale, the repair is their problem — not yours. You aren't liable for *their* contractor's work.

- ✔ **Don't do a major rehab of the kitchen or bathroom.** You generally can't increase your sale price enough to fully compensate you for all the work and money you put into these projects. Furthermore, you can't guess the next owner's preferences in toilets, tile, and tubs. Don't even try. Odds are that you'll make the wrong decisions on appliances, cabinets, colors, finishes, and other design choices. A much better plan is to reduce your asking price so it reflects that your house has an old kitchen or bathroom instead of squandering your time and money on a major remodeling job that people may dislike.

Chapter 10

Determining Your House's Value

· ·

In This Chapter

▶ Knowing the difference between cost, price, and value

▶ Determining your house's resale value

▶ Understanding a comparable market analysis

▶ Finding out how real estate agent bidding wars ruin the pricing process

· ·

Step into our handy-dandy time machine, please. Be careful. Don't bump your head. These darn economy models have such low ceilings. We're about to transport you back to the day you began looking for your current home — the house hunt that culminated in the purchase of the home you now own. Ah. There you are, hesitantly wandering from one Sunday open house to the next with the classified ads in your hand and a puzzled look on your face.

When you first started your search, you didn't have a clue about how much any of the houses you toured were worth. Do you remember how the asking prices were merely meaningless sequences of numbers to you? If, for example, you saw a house being offered at $274,950, you didn't know whether it was a steal at that price or grossly overpriced. Your experience is common. Everyone goes through that phase during the initial stage of the home-buying process.

Hold on while we make a short leap forward in time. What a difference a couple of months make. Now look at you, confidently zipping in and out of open houses. You figured out property values by personally eyeballing as many houses as you could. Then you kept checking the status of the properties to see whether they'd sold and, if they had, at what price. You discovered that sale prices, not asking prices, establish a house's value. Your hard work paid off. You became a market-savvy, educated buyer.

Okay, buckle up for your return to the present. How do you think that things will change when you become a seller? Surprise. Where property values are concerned, the rules of the game are identical for buyers and sellers. Being an educated seller is just as important as being an educated buyer. You get educated exactly the same way — by touring houses comparable to yours that are currently for sale in your neighborhood.

Good news. You don't have to spend every weekend between now and the sale of your house touring property. If you choose to use the services of a good real estate agent, he can accelerate your learning curve by screening which houses you visit. After seeing no more than a dozen houses comparable to yours in size, age, condition, and location, you'll be an educated seller. (You can spend the time you save gussying up your house for sale!) After you've made these tours, you can start to set a value on your own house. This chapter helps you determine that price.

Defining Cost, Price, and Value

Winston Churchill sagely observed that England and the United States were countries separated by a common language. Citizens of the two countries use the same words, but the words may have entirely different meanings in each country. For example, folks in Merry Old England buy bangers with pounds. "What an odd country," Americans think, "they purchase hot dogs with weights?"

You don't have to go all the way to England for a verbal joust. A similar breakdown in communication occurs here in the good old USA whenever Americans use *cost, price,* and *value* interchangeably. This linguistic imprecision creates big problems during negotiations between homebuyers and house sellers.

The fact is: Neither *cost* nor *price* is the same as *value.* After you understand the meanings of these words and how they differ, you can say exactly what you mean and replace emotion with objectivity during price negotiations. Out*fact*ing buyers is always better than attempting to out*argue* them.

Value is elusive

Value is your opinion of your house's worth to you based on the way you use it now and plan to use it in the future. Note that, in the preceding sentence, the words "your" and "you" each appear twice. Because *your* opinion is subjective, the features *you* value may not be the universal standard for all of humanity.

You may, for example, be of the strongly held opinion that the one and only acceptable house color is beet red. We, your humble authors, may feel just as resolutely that only sky blue houses are gorgeous and all other colors are major ugly. No harm done, as long as everyone realizes that a big difference exists between opinions and facts.

Two factors greatly affect value:

- ✔ **Internal factors:** Your personal (internal) situation has a fascinating way of changing over time. Suppose that 30 years ago, when you bought your present house, you put great value on a four-bedroom home with a fenced-in backyard. The house had to be located in a town with a terrific school system. Why? Because 30 years ago, you were the proud parent of two adorable little rug rats.

  Now your children are grown and have their own homes. They left you rattling around in your house like a tiny pea in a gigantic pod. Without kids, you don't need the big house, huge yard, or terrific school system. The house didn't change — what changed were the internal factors regarding your use for the house and, thus, its value to you. Divorce and retirement are other internal factors that compel folks to buy or sell houses.

- ✔ **External factors:** Circumstances outside your control that affect property values also change for better or worse. If, for example, commute time to the big city where you work is cut from 1 hour to 30 minutes when mass transit rail service is extended into your area, your house's value increases. If, on the other hand, a toxic waste dump is discovered next to your house, the house's value takes a hit.

  The law of supply and demand is another external factor that affects value. If more people want to buy houses than sell them, buyer competition drives up house prices. If, on the other hand, more people want to sell than buy, reduced demand results in lower property prices.

Cost is history

Cost measures past expenditures — for example, the amount you originally paid for your house. But that was then, and this is now. The amount you paid long ago, or the amount you spent fixing up the house after you bought it, doesn't mean diddlypoo as far as your house's present or future value is concerned.

For example, when home prices began skyrocketing in many areas of the country during the late 1980s, some buyers accused sellers of being greedy. "You paid $75,000 fifteen years ago. Now you're asking $250,000," they said. "That's a huge profit."

"So what?" sellers replied compassionately. "If you don't want to pay our modest asking price, move out of the way so the nice buyers standing behind you can present their offers." In a hot sellers' market, people who base their offering prices on the original price paid for a property waste everyone's time.

The market changed radically in a few short years. By the early 1990s, prices had declined dramatically in many areas. Sellers would've been ecstatic to find buyers willing to pay them the amount they'd paid five years earlier when home prices peaked. In those areas, sellers who priced their houses based on the inflated purchase prices they'd paid years earlier learned a painful lesson: Your potential profit *or loss* as a seller doesn't enter into the equation when determining your house's present value.

Price is the here and now

You put an *asking* price on your house. Buyers put an *offering* price in their contract. You and the buyers negotiate back and forth to establish your house's *purchase* price. Today's purchase price becomes tomorrow's cost, and so it goes.

Cost is the past, price is the present, and value (like beauty) is in the eyes of the beholder. Neither the price you paid for your house eons ago when you bought it, nor the amount you want to get for it today matters to buyers. Don't waste valuable time on fantasy pricing.

Determining Fair Market Value (FMV)

Every house sells at the right price. That price is defined as its *fair market value* (FMV) — the price a buyer will pay and a seller will accept for the house — given that neither buyer nor seller is under duress. Duress comes from life changes, such as divorce or sudden job transfer, which put either the buyers or sellers under pressure to perform quickly. If appraisers know that a sale was made under duress, they raise or lower the sale price accordingly to more accurately reflect the house's true FMV.

FMV is a zillion times more powerful than plain old *value*. As a seller, you have an opinion about the amount your house is worth. Buyers have a separate, not necessarily equal, and probably lower, opinion of your house's value. Values are opinions, not facts.

FMV, conversely, is fact. It becomes fact the moment you and the buyer agree on a mutually acceptable price. Just as it takes two to tango, it takes you and a buyer to make FMV. Facts are bankable.

Need-based pricing isn't FMV

Whenever the residential real estate market gets soft and squishy like a rotten tomato, many would-be sellers feel that FMV isn't fair at all. "Why doesn't our house sell?" they ask. "Why can't we get our asking price? It's not fair."

Don't confuse "fair" with equitable or favorable. Despite its amiable name, FMV is brutally impartial and sometimes even cruel. Need is not an integral component of FMV. FMV doesn't give a hoot about any of the following:

- ✔ How much money you *need* because you overpaid for your house when you bought it
- ✔ How much money you *need* to replace the money you spent fixing up your house after you bought it
- ✔ How much money you *need* to pay off your mortgage or home-equity loan
- ✔ How much money you *need* from the sale to buy your next home

Here's why *need* doesn't determine FMV. Suppose that two identical houses located right next door to one another are listed for sale at the same time. One house was purchased by Marcia for $30,000 in 1970. You made a $60,000 cash down payment when you bought the other house for $300,000 two years ago. As luck would have it, property values declined a year after you bought your house.

You clearly *need* more money from the sale than Marcia. After all, you paid ten times as much for your house. What's more, Marcia paid off her loan five years ago. You, on the other hand, owe the bank big bucks on your mortgage.

Because the houses are identical in size, age, condition, and location, they have the same FMV. Under the circumstances, the fact that they both sold for $285,000 isn't surprising. Marcia got a nice nest egg for her retirement. You barely cleared enough from the deal to pay off your mortgage and other expenses of sale. Fair? Marcia thinks so. You don't.

FMV is utterly unbiased. It's the amount your house is worth in the market today — not the amount you or the buyers would like it to be.

Median prices aren't FMV

Organizations such as the National Association of Realtors, the Chamber of Commerce, and private research firms gather data on house sales activity in a specific geographic region, such as a city, county, or state. They use this information to prepare reports on housing topics, such as the average cost of houses in an area and the increase or decline in regional house sales on a yearly or monthly basis.

One of the most widely quoted housing statistics is the *median sale price,* which is simply the midpoint in a range of all house sales in an area during a specified reporting period, such as a month or a year. Half the sales during the reporting period are above the median, and half fall below it.

The median-priced house, in other words, is the one exactly in the middle of the prices of all the houses that sold during the specified reporting period. Figure 10-1 demonstrates what we mean.

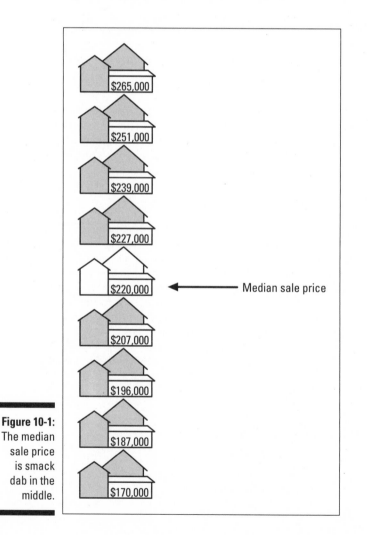

Figure 10-1: The median sale price is smack dab in the middle.

$265,000

$251,000

$239,000

$227,000

$220,000 ◄──────── Median sale price

$207,000

$196,000

$187,000

$170,000

For example, the median sale price of an existing single-family house in the United States was about $220,000 in 2007 — meaning that half the houses in the U.S. sold for more than $220,000 and the other half sold for less than $220,000. (In case you're interested, the median sale price was just $118,000 in 1996 when the first edition of this wonderful book went to press.) Unfortunately, all you know about this hypothetical median-priced American house is its price.

You don't know how many bedrooms or baths the mythical median-priced house contains. Nor do you know how many square feet of interior living space the house offers, how old it is, whether it has a garage or a yard, or how well maintained it is. You don't even know where in the U.S. this elusive median-priced house is located.

As a homeowner, you can use median sale price statistics to measure *general* property value trends. For example, suppose that your local Chamber of Commerce says that the median sale price of a house in your area was $200,000 five years ago when you bought your house, and it's $240,000 today. Based on that information, you can safely say that median sale prices have increased 20 percent over the past five years.

Just because the median sale price of a house in your area went up 20 percent doesn't mean that the house you paid $250,000 for five years ago is worth $300,000 today. Median sale price statistics aren't any more accurate for determining your house's value than median income statistics are for calculating your paycheck. You need much more precise information to establish the FMV of the house you're about to sell.

Using a Comparable Market Analysis

The best way to accurately determine your house's FMV is by using a written *comparable market analysis* (CMA) to see how your house compares to other houses like yours that have either sold recently or currently are on the market. If you hire a real estate agent to sell your house and use the techniques we cover in Chapter 7 to select your agent, you get several CMAs during the selection process. You can use these CMAs to fine-tune your asking price.

The "Recent Sales" section of the CMA helps establish the FMV of *your house* by comparing it to all other houses that

✔ Are located in the same neighborhood as your house

✔ Are of approximately the same age, size, and condition as your house

✔ Have sold in the past six months

Houses meeting these criteria are called *comps,* which is short for *comparables.* Depending on the date you started looking at houses for sale in your neighborhood, you may not have visited all the sold comps. No problem. A good real estate agent can show you listing statements for the houses you haven't seen, take you on a verbal tour of every house, and explain how each one compares with your house.

Every residential real estate office develops its own CMA format. Regardless of the way your agent's office presents its CMA information, Tables 10-1 and 10-2 illustrate the elements that all good CMAs contain. Suppose that you live at 220 Oak Street. These tables provide CMA information for your house (abbreviated as YH).

Table 10-1			Sample CMA — "Recent Sales" Section			
Address	Date Sold	Sale Price	Bedrm/ Bath	Parking	Condition	Remarks
210 Oak	04/30	$290,000	3/3	2 car	Very good	**Best comp!** Approx. the same location, size, and condition as *your house (YH)* with a slightly smaller lot. 1,867 square feet. $155 per square foot.
335 Elm	02/14	$268,500	3/2	2 car	Fair	Busy street. Older baths. 1,805 square feet. $149 per square foot.
307 Ash	03/15	$285,000	3/3	2 car	Good	Slightly larger than YH, but nearly the same condition. Good comp. 1,850 square feet. $154 per square foot.

Address	Date Sold	Sale Price	Bedrm/ Bath	Parking	Condition	Remarks
555 Ash	01/12	$282,500	3/2.5	2 car	Excellent	Smaller than YH, but knockout renovation. 1,740 square feet. $162 per square foot.
75 Birch	04/20	$293,000	3/3	3 car	Very good	Larger than YH, but location isn't as good. Superb landscaping. 1,910 square feet. $153 per square foot.

When you analyze the sales in Table 10-1, you find that houses comparable to your house are selling in the range of $149 to $162 per square foot. Putting the sale prices into a *price-per-square-foot format* makes property comparisons much easier. As Table 10-2 shows, any price that's way above or below the norm really leaps out at you.

The "Currently For Sale" section of the CMA compares your house to neighborhood comps that are *currently on the market.* These comps are included in the analysis to check price trends. If prices are falling, asking prices of houses on the market today will be lower than sale prices of comparable houses. If prices are rising, you'll see higher asking prices today than sale prices for comps that sold three to six months ago.

Table 10-2	Sample CMA — "Currently For Sale" Section					
Address	Date on Market	Asking Price	Bedrm/ Bath	Parking	Condition	Remarks
220 Oak (Your House)	Not on market	To be determined	3/3	2 car	Very good	Quieter location than 123 Oak, good detailing, older kitchen. 1,880 square feet.

(continued)

Table 10-2 *(continued)*

Address	Date on Market	Asking Price	Bedrm/ Bath	Parking	Condition	Remarks
123 Oak	05/01	$299,500	3/2	2 car	Excellent	High-end rehabilitated and priced accordingly. 1,855 square feet. $161 per square foot.
360 Oak	02/10	$275,000	3/2	1 car	Fair	Kitchen & baths need work, no fireplace. 1,695 square feet. $162 per square foot.
140 Elm	04/01	$279,500	3/3	2 car	Good	Busy street, small rooms, small yard. 1,725 square feet. $162 per square foot.
505 Elm	1/15	$325,000	2/2	1 car	Fair	Delusions of grandeur. Grossly overpriced! 1,580 square feet. $206 per square foot.
104 Ash	04/17	$294,500	3/2.5	2 car	Very good	Best comp! Good floor plan, large rooms. Surprised it hasn't sold. 1,860 square feet. $158 per square foot.

Address	Date on Market	Asking Price	Bedrm/ Bath	Parking	Condition	Remarks
222 Ash	02/01	$319,500	3/2	1 car	Fair	Must have used 505 Elm as comp. Will never sell at this price. 1,610 square feet. $198 per square foot.
47 Birch	03/15	$319,000	4/3.5	2 car	Good	Nice house, but overimproved for neighborhood. 2,005 square feet. $159 per square foot.
111 Birch	04/25	$289,500	3/3	2 car	Very good	Gorgeous kitchen, no fireplace. 1,870 square feet. $155 per square foot.

Playing with the numbers

Suppose today's date is May 15th. You and your agent are sitting at the kitchen table looking at two sheets of paper. One page shows all the recent sales of comps in your neighborhood. The other lists houses comparable to yours that currently are on the market in your area. Each set of comps tells you something important.

"Sold" comps indicate probable FMV

Your agent says that 210 Oak is an ideal "sold" comp because it's two doors away from your house, is roughly the same size as your house, and is in about the same condition as your house. Furthermore, no major changes have occurred in your local real estate market since 210 Oak sold two weeks ago for $155 per square foot. The only other recent sale at a higher price per square foot was 555 Ash, but that comp isn't as good because the house is in better condition than your house (no offense).

Factually establishing your house's probable sale price based on its square footage is easy after you know how. Multiply your house's square footage by estimated FMV expressed in a price per square foot. In this case, because your house (220 Oak) has 1,880 square feet multiplied by $155 per square foot, it should sell for about $291,400. Simple.

"Currently For Sale" comps define asking price

You've toured every one of the comparable properties listed in the "Currently For Sale" section of your agent's CMA. Having seen 104 Ash with your own eyes, you agree that it's more like your house than any other property now on the market in your area. Even so, it isn't a perfect comp because 104 Ash is smaller than your house and has only two and a half baths versus three full baths in your house. You know enough about property values to realize that the house is priced to sell at $158 per square foot.

Even though 123 Oak and 360 Oak are closer to your house than 104 Ash, neither house is as good a comp as the Ash Street property. The house at 123 Oak is totally renovated, has a wonderful kitchen, and should sell for a higher price per square foot than your house. Whether they can get $161 per square foot remains to be seen. The house at 360 Oak, on the other hand, is smaller than your house, doesn't show well, and has one less bath and a smaller garage. No way will 360 Oak sell for $162 per square foot.

All things considered, you decide to base your asking price on $158 per square foot. For one thing, that amount is the upper limit of comparable houses' asking prices. The extra $3 per square foot over your house's probable FMV gives you a little room to negotiate with buyers. Multiplying 1,880 square feet times $158 per square foot equals $297,040, which is an odd asking price. To make the asking price more exciting for prospective buyers, you round it down to an even $295,000.

This example is rather straightforward. Pricing in the real world, however, is usually somewhat complicated. That's why we devote Chapter 11 to more sophisticated pricing considerations.

Give sale prices more weight than asking prices when determining your house's asking price. Don't guess about your house's worth. Analyze the sale prices of comparable houses. Your CMA should note any price reductions made while the comps were on the market as well as the credits sellers gave buyers for corrective work repairs.

Interpreting CMA adjustments and flaws

CMAs beat the heck out of median price statistics for establishing FMV, but keep in mind that CMAs aren't perfect. We've seen buyers and sellers use exactly the same comps and arrive at stunningly different opinions of FMV. Here's where discrepancies can creep into your CMA:

✔ **Incomplete comps:** Your CMA must be comprehensive. It should include *all* comp sales in the past six months and *all* comps currently on the market. Be sure that the comp sales data reflects price reductions during the marketing period and credits given for corrective work repairs. Getting an accurate picture of FMV may be difficult if parts of the puzzle are missing.

✔ **Old comps:** Like milk in your refrigerator, comps have expiration dates. Lenders rarely accept as comps houses that sold more than six months ago, because their sale prices don't reflect current consumer confidence, business conditions, or mortgage rates. As a rule, the older the comp, the less likely that it represents today's FMV.

Why six months? Because six months generally is accepted as long enough to represent a good cross section of comparable sales, but short enough to have fairly consistent market conditions. This time period, however, isn't carved in stone. If, for example, the biggest employer in your area had a massive layoff three months ago, six months is too long for a valid comparison. Conversely, if houses in your area rarely sell, you'll probably have to use comparable sales that occurred more than six months ago.

✔ **House condition:** No two homes are the same after they've been lived in. Suppose that two identical tract homes are located next door to one another. One, owned by an older couple with no children or pets, is in pristine condition. The other, owned by a family with five small kids and three large dogs, resembles a federal disaster area. It's Guesstimate City when trying to determine the cost to repair the wear-and-tear damage in the second house. A good CMA, however, makes adjustments for this type of difference between houses.

✔ **Site differences within your neighborhood:** Even though all the comps are in the same neighborhood, they aren't located on precisely the same plot of ground. How much is being located next to the beautiful park worth to a buyer? How much will a buyer pay to be seven blocks closer to the bus stop during the rainy season? These value adjustments are subjective and, thus, imprecise.

✔ **Out-of-neighborhood comps:** Suppose that, in the past six months, no houses sold in your neighborhood. Going into other areas to find comps forces you and your agent to make value adjustments between two different neighborhoods' amenities (schools, shopping, transportation, and so on). Comparing different neighborhoods is a lot more difficult than making value adjustments within your neighborhood.

✔ **Noncomp house sales:** What if five houses sold in your neighborhood in the past six months but not one was remotely comparable to yours in age, size, style, or condition? You and your agent must estimate value differences for three-bedroom versus four-bedroom houses, old versus new kitchens, small versus large yards, garages versus carports, and so on. If your house offers a panoramic view and none of the other houses have any view at all, how much does the view increase your house's value? Guesstimates like these are highly subjective.

A valid comparison of your house to the other houses is impossible if you and your agent have only read about the comps in listing statements. Seeing is believing. Most listing statements (those one-page property descriptions we cover in Chapter 12) are exaggerated to greater or lesser degrees. You don't know how overstated if you haven't seen the house for yourself. You may discover that a "large" master bedroom is tiny. A "gourmet" kitchen's only distinction may be an especially fancy hot plate. That "sweeping" view from the living room may be visible only if you're as tall as Michael Jordan. Of course, you won't know any of these things if you only read the houses' puff sheets instead of visiting each house in person.

Floor plans also greatly affect a house's value. Two houses, for example, may be approximately the same size, age, and condition, yet vary wildly in value. One house's floor plan flows beautifully from room to room; the rooms themselves are well proportioned with high ceilings. The other house doesn't work well because its floor plan is choppy and the ceilings are low. You can't tell which is which just by reading the two listing statements.

Eyeballing — touring houses and noting important details inside and out — is the *best* way to decide which houses are true comps for your house and which differences you must adjust for in your comparable analysis. (When you read Chapter 13, you'll see for yourself why online CMA providers such as Zillow may be wildly inaccurate.)

Considering appraisals versus CMAs

If you're the suspicious type, you may want to double-check your agent's opinion of value before putting your house on the market. You can do so by paying several hundred dollars for a professional appraisal of your house.

Getting an *unbiased* second opinion of value is always reassuring. Appraisers, unlike agents, have no reason to tell you what you want to hear to get a listing. Whether your house sells or not, an appraiser gets paid. On the other hand, if you think that a professional appraisal is vastly superior to your agent's opinion of value, think again. A good agent's CMA usually is as good as an appraisal for purposes of marketing your house. Conversely, if a professional appraisal is vastly superior because your agent is a lousy judge of property values, get a better agent.

In any given area, appraisers don't usually see as many houses as do agents who focus on that area. Appraisers aren't lazy; they use their time in other ways. Formal appraisals are time consuming. An appraiser inspects a property from foundation to attic, measures its square footage, makes detailed notes regarding everything from the quality of construction to the amount of wear and tear, photographs the house inside and out, photographs comps for the house being appraised, writes up the appraisal, and so on. Agents can tour 15 to 20 houses in the same amount of time an appraiser requires to do one appraisal.

As a result, appraisers frequently call agents to find out about houses the agents listed or sold that may be comps. Regardless of how good an agent's description of the house, eyeballing property is better. Any appraisal's accuracy suffers if the appraisal is based on comps the appraiser hasn't seen.

Agents also call each other about houses they haven't seen, so don't jump to the conclusion that appraisers are the only ones who do such things. Reading listing statements and picking other agents' brains to find out about property is no substitute for first-hand eyeballing. If your agent hasn't seen most of the comps used in your CMA, get an agent who knows your local market.

Unless you're pretty darn uncertain about your house's worth or are considering selling your house yourself (a topic we cover in Chapter 6), don't waste money on an appraisal.

Bidding Wars

In a perfect world, buyers and sellers would only use facts to establish property values, and sales would be fast and easy. Unfortunately, the world is far from perfect. The following sections provide two reasons.

How buyers and sellers get to FMV

Buyers and sellers zero in on a house's FMV from utterly different directions (see Figure 10-2). Buyers bring their offering price *up* to FMV because they don't want to overpay. Sellers, conversely, ratchet their asking price *down* to FMV because they don't want to leave any of their profit on the table.

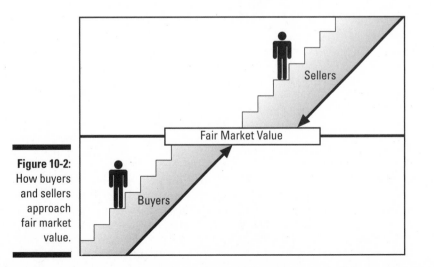

Figure 10-2:
How buyers and sellers approach fair market value.

Even though sellers and buyers approach FMV from opposite directions, note that they end up at exactly the same place. That result is no surprise. If you and the buyers rely on the same data — the asking prices and sale prices of comparable houses — to determine FMV, you're bound to reach the same conclusion sooner or later.

Why "buying a listing" ruins property pricing

One crucial aspect of selling a house is correctly establishing its initial asking price. If a seller prices a house near its FMV, the house usually sells quickly for top dollar. If, on the other hand, a seller grossly overprices a property, it tends to linger on the market month after month until the owner corrects the problem.

Why would you be tempted to overprice your house? Because an unprincipled real estate agent takes advantage of your legitimate concern about underpricing your property, or, perhaps, the agent just wants to exploit your greed. A bidding war develops among the agents who're competing to list your house for sale. The first victim of this bidding war is, unfortunately, the concept of FMV. Here's what happens:

> "Thanks for giving me a chance to represent you during the sale of your handsome house," says Tommy Truthful, an agent from Honest Realty. "As you can see from the CMA I prepared today, 142 houses sold in your neighborhood during the past six months. Two are considerably larger than yours, so they aren't good comps. The 140 properties comparable to your house in size, age, location, and condition sold in a price range of $225,000 to $227,500. Based on this astonishing abundance of undeniable, irrefutable, incontestable, indisputable, incontrovertible, unquestionable facts, I recommend an initial asking price of not more than $229,500."

> "Wait just a second," cautions Sally Slick from Aim To Please Realty. "You may be leaving money on the table if your asking price is $229,500. Comps aren't everything. Your chimney is made of better quality bricks than any of those other 140 houses' chimneys. Even more importantly, not one of the 140 houses has an ostrich-sized birdbath in its front yard. These special features, in my humble opinion, are easily worth an additional $20,000. I recommend that you ask $249,500."

> "Facts, schmacts," oozes Otto Outrageous from Sky High Realty, who figures he won't get your listing unless he outbids the other two agents. "I think that $249,500 isn't even close to what you should ask. We'll feature your house on our Internet page and include it in the glossy, full-color brochures we mail every week to our affiliate offices in Paris, London,

Rome, and Nome. Massive exposure is the key to maximizing your sale price. I'm sure that if we look long enough and hard enough we can find a buyer in some secret nook of this vast planet who'll pay $275,000 for your wonderful house."

This deceptive approach — when several agents give a seller increasingly outrageous opinions of a house's value — is called *buying a listing*. Agents who use this ploy think that the best way to get listings is to tell sellers what they want to hear — that their house is unique and is worth way, way, waaaaaaaaaaay more than any comparable house. Greed conquers reason.

This ruse may be a successful tactic for getting listings, but it's a rotten way to sell them. Property owners who succumb to fantasy pricing are condemned to waste their time until they finally return to real-world economics. These misguided homeowners confuse the act of listing a house with the act of selling it. Unless their listing agent intends to buy the house, the owners and agent are playing an expensive game of let's pretend.

The price you and your listing agent agree on doesn't really matter. Until you find a buyer who agrees with you, your house won't sell. Resist the temptation to base your asking price on:

- ✓ The amount that you want your house to be worth

- ✓ The amount you need to receive from the sale to be able to buy your dream home

Let the comps tell you the price your house is worth. Unlike unscrupulous agents, comps don't lie.

Chapter 11

Price It Right and Buyers Will Come

. . . .

In This Chapter

▶ Understanding house-pricing methods

▶ Using buyer enticements to help you sell and avoiding gimmicks

▶ Figuring out why your house is still on the market

. . . .

*I*f you *really* want to be a successful seller, think like a buyer. You probably didn't buy the first house you looked at. Few folks do. On the contrary, most people spend months industriously inspecting many houses on the market. To avoid overpaying for the home they ultimately purchase, buyers are forced to become experts on property values.

It's a free country. You can ask any price you want for your house. But your house won't sell until you find a buyer who agrees that it's worth the price you're willing to accept. Smart sellers know that although only *one* person sets a price, *two* people — a seller and a buyer — make a sale.

Adverse factors outside your control (such as a flood of houses on the market, high mortgage interest rates, or dismal consumer confidence) may negatively affect your sale price. Even so, you don't have to passively let the real estate gods crush you. This chapter offers proven ideas that you can use to create demand for your house no matter how poor prevailing market conditions are.

Getting a Grasp on Pricing Methods

Chapter 10 explains how to use the asking prices and sale prices of *comps* (houses comparable to your house) to *factually* determine your house's value. This information puts you light years ahead of sellers who either don't know about using comps or, worse yet, choose to ignore comps when pricing property.

You can pick a price for your house in a hundred different ways — visit an astrologer, poll your friends for their guesses about its worth, roll dice, pay for a professional appraisal, grab a number out of your hat, interview dozens of real estate agents until you find one with a suitably elevated opinion of your house's value, and so on. In the final analysis, however, they're all variations of the two pricing methods we discuss in the following sections.

Four-phase pricing: Prevalent but ineffective

The consequences of pulling an unsubstantiated asking price out of the air are unacceptable for a smart seller. You may undervalue your house and risk leaving money on the table when you sell. Or, more likely, you may overprice your house, which results in an exhaustingly slow marketing process that ultimately lowers your sale price. Houses marketed by unrealistic sellers usually go through the following four distinct pricing phases prior to sale:

- ✔ **Phase one:** Sellers start by blithely disregarding any factual pricing method, such as checking comparable property sales. Why? Some sellers don't know any better or get lousy advice from their real estate agents. Other sellers think that their house is infinitely superior to those ticky-tacky comps. They're sure that their house's inherent superiority will quickly attract a buyer with more money than good sense. Either way, this misguided method generally results in grotesque overpricing.

- ✔ **Phase two:** After several months of total market rejection, the sellers grudgingly make a tiny price reduction, which brings their asking price down from the grotesque level to merely absurdly overpriced. Fantasy moderated is, however, still abject fantasy.

- ✔ **Phase three:** More lonely months pass, and then two things happen. First, the sellers typically get a new agent — poetic justice for an agent who either didn't know property values or who intentionally misled the sellers about pricing to get the listing. Second, the sellers reduce their asking price to one that "leaves room to negotiate." Even though the revised price still is moderately higher than the house's probable sale price based on sales of comparable property, at least the new asking price has some basis in market reality.

- ✔ **Phase four:** The sellers ultimately accept the validity of comps and reduce their asking price accordingly to a "let's sell it" level. After the sellers establish a good correlation between asking price and fair market value (FMV), their house *finally* sells.

Ironically, instead of getting more money with this method, four-phase pricing usually stigmatizes a property and reduces the eventual sale price to *less* than it would've been with more realistic pricing. Here's why:

✔ **The listing agent can't justify an indefensible asking price.** If the asking price has no factual basis, the agent can't provide a good answer to buyers who ask, "Why hasn't the house sold after all this time on the market? What's *wrong* with it?" In degree of difficulty, this situation ranks right up there with, "Just what do you think you're doing?" when your mom caught you with your hand deeply buried in the cookie jar.

✔ **The property is slowly but surely buried by new listings that come on the market.** After several months, most buyers and agents either forget that your house still is on the market or belittle the house by saying, "That old thing. It'll never sell." In desperation, sellers are forced to slash their asking price to the bone to attract buyers.

Four-phase pricing creates a self-fulfilling prophecy. Folks who use this pricing method expect it will take a long time to sell their house. In a strong market, they're correct because the market will ultimately rise to their price level. In a weak market, they're disastrously correct as they chase the market ever lower.

Pleasure-pleasure-panic pricing: Fast, top-dollar sales

If the four-phase pricing plan is a flop, what's your alternative? We're glad you asked. The smart way to sell your property is the pleasure-pleasure-panic pricing method. You can sell your house quickly *and* get the highest possible price by using this method. The secret of success is establishing a realistic asking price for your house when you first place it on the market.

As we note in Chapter 10, the correct way to establish an asking price is to analyze houses comparable to yours in size, age, condition, and location — houses that currently are on the market and those that have sold within the past six months. Don't be misled by asking prices; many sellers use four-phase pricing. *Sale prices,* not asking prices, determine FMV.

Here's how the pleasure-pleasure-panic pricing method works — Milt and Judy have spent the last three months looking at houses on the market in their price range. They're educated buyers; they know how to distinguish between a well-priced house and an *OPT (overpriced turkey).*

Judy and Milt nearly bought a great house a couple of months ago. It had all the features they wanted and was fairly priced, to boot. However, Milt didn't realize how well priced it was because he'd just started the education process. While Milt was haggling over the price and terms of sale, the seller accepted a better offer. Judy still blames Milt for losing their dream house.

They're spending today the same way they've spent the previous 11 Sundays, touring what seems like an endless series of newly listed OPTs with their agent. Then Judy and Milt trudge into your *first* open house and pleasure-pleasure-panic kicks into gear.

- ✔ **Pleasure Number 1:** Judy and Milt love your property. It's the best place they've seen in the past three months. They could live in your house happily ever after. Their eyes start to sparkle.

- ✔ **Pleasure Number 2:** Milt and Judy can't believe their eyes when they look at the asking price on your listing statement. By now, they know property values every bit as well as their agent. Your house is definitely priced to sell. Their hands start to tremble.

- ✔ **Panic:** Judy and Milt see another couple entering your house. They've seen these folks at many other open houses during the past couple of months. That familiarity isn't a coincidence. The other couple obviously wants to buy a house in the same neighborhood and price range.

  Judy and Milt stare at each other in horror. If they love your house and know that it's well priced, so will the other couple. Their deodorants fail when they realize that if they don't act quickly, the other couple will snap up the house. Milt tells their agent to write up a full-asking-price offer. Judy kicks Milt in the shin and instructs the agent to go $1,000 above your asking price just to be safe. Milt agrees. He doesn't want to be a two-time loser.

That scenario explains how pleasure-pleasure-panic pricing creates a seller's market even in the midst of a ﹍﹍er's market. This approach puts intense pressure on buyers to perform quickly.

Don't be surprised if you get several purchase offers, including some that are equal to or more than full asking price, as soon as your house hits the market — if your house is priced right. After your property has been given broad, immediate market exposure, spirited competition forces buyers to pay top dollar for your house. This method works almost every time. (And, by the way, we cover exactly how to handle multiple purchase offers in Chapter 14.)

Quantum pricing: An effective technique

Put yourself in the buyer's shoes for a moment and imagine that you're buying, not selling, your house. If you're like most people, one of the first things you do is decide how much you want to spend. For example, you set your upper limit of affordability at $250,000. If you're working with a real estate agent, you probably tell the agent, "I don't want to spend more than $250,000," or "Don't show me anything that costs more than $250,000." Why waste time looking at property you can't afford to buy?

Buyers use price limits, called *quantums,* to simplify house hunting. Pricing quantums are initially expressed in nice, round, easy-to-work-with numbers, such as $100,000 and $50,000, and then fine-tuned to $25,000 and $10,000 quantums.

Think of buyers as fish swimming in an ocean of houses for sale. At any given time, huge schools of buyer-fish usually are swimming in this sea. However, the buyer-fish swim at many different levels; one school swims at the $150,000-to-$200,000 price quantum level, another swims at the $200,000-to-$250,000 price quantum level, and so on.

Buyer-fish from higher-price quantums occasionally swim down to a lower quantum in their searches for a house. However, buyer-fish rarely swim up to a higher quantum (if they establish realistic affordability limits). When a buyer-fish can't afford to swim *up,* the price must drop *down* to the buyer-fish's price quantum for the house to sell.

Establishing price quantums

Follow these steps to use price quantums to hone your initial asking price to razor sharp, pleasure-pleasure-panic perfection:

1. **Determine your house's market value within the appropriate $100,000 quantum, unless you happen to live in an area where no house ever has sold for more than $99,999.99.**

   Use the comparable market analysis (CMA) method described in Chapter 10 to define a general price range for your property. For example, if a CMA shows that five houses similar to yours in size, age, condition, and location sold within the past six months for $310,000 to $335,000, your house clearly belongs in the $300,000 to $400,000 quantum. So far, so easy.

2. **Adjust the price within the correct $50,000 quantum.**

   Continuing with the same example, decide whether your asking price should be over or under $350,000. Because not one of the comps sold for more than $335,000, your price belongs in the $300,000 to $350,000 quantum. As problems go, still no head-scratcher.

3. **Fine-tune your price to the closest $25,000 quantum.**

   The more accurate your pricing, the more exacting your scrutiny. Deciding whether the price should be in the $300,000 to $325,000 quantum or the $325,000 to $350,000 quantum requires careful analysis. If, for example, four of the five comps sold between $310,000 and $325,000 and the fifth went for $335,000, you'd be wise keeping the asking price under $325,000.

4. **Ultrafine-tune your price to the nearest $10,000 quantum.**

   This is the moment of truth. Now you must decide on the *precise* point between $310,000 and $325,000 to put your price. If the actual prices of comparable houses that sold under $325,000 were $310,000, $317,500, $319,500, and $322,000, three out of four sales point toward an asking price under $320,000.

Recognizing quantum-pricing finesse points

If you seriously want to sell quickly for top dollar, don't put your asking price in the next higher quantum to give yourself "room to negotiate." Here's why:

First offers are worth a second look

No law guarantees that the first purchase offer you get will be the best one. However, as the following example illustrates, it often is.

Elaine decided to sell her house shortly after her husband died. The house was tough to price. It was in mint condition, had a great view, and was located on a large lot. It was far-and-away the best house on the block. No homes of equal quality had sold in her neighborhood in well over a year. Elaine's agent analyzed recent sales of similar properties that sold in comparable neighborhoods to determine an approximate value per square foot for Elaine's house. Based on these sales, her agent recommended asking $499,500. Neither Elaine nor the agent expected a fast sale because the highest previous sale in the neighborhood was $425,000.

Fortune smiled on Elaine. She got a $450,000 offer only two days after the For Sale sign went up. The people who made the offer were educated buyers who'd been looking at houses in her neighborhood for several months and were primed to pounce on any new listing that fit their needs. When their agent presented the offer, he told Elaine that the contract's terms and conditions of sale were flexible, but that the buyers were at their absolute upper limit financially.

Elaine's lawyer reviewed the offer. He found no legal flaws, but told Elaine he thought she was giving the house away. He reasoned that if she could get a $450,000 offer so quickly, she'd probably get a full-price offer soon.

Based on her lawyer's gratuitous advice, Elaine made a full-price counteroffer to the buyers.

They rejected the counteroffer and moved on. Elaine's house had many showings the first month, but no other offers. After six weeks, her agent called the agent of the couple who'd offered $450,000 to see if they would submit another offer. No such luck. They had bought another house.

The real estate market went down the drain a couple of months later because of a severe economic slowdown. Elaine's house finally sold for $435,000 almost a year later. Had she taken the first offer she received, she would've made $15,000 more and spared herself a year of aggravation.

With 20/20 hindsight, blaming the lawyer for this fiasco is easy. However, blaming the lawyer is unfair. His advice was logical and compelling. When he gave it, no one could've said with certainty that a full-asking-price offer wouldn't be forthcoming.

That's the problem — uncertainty. Whether your house is the most expensive one on the block or the cheapest, no one knows what it's worth until it sells. FMV is established by the amount buyers pay and sellers accept.

When a house hits the market, uncertainty about FMV favors sellers. Therefore, the first offer is often the best one. If the property is priced close to the amount it's worth, educated buyers take their best shot at it. They want to get the house before someone else does. The fear of losing the house to another buyer works to the seller's advantage.

The longer a house sits on the market unsold, however, the more uncertainty about FMV favors buyers. Prospective buyers logically reason that the house can't be worth the asking price because, if it were, it would already have already sold. The more buyers who see the property and don't make an offer, the more discredited the asking price becomes.

Fast first offers frighten sellers and buyers. Neither has the benefit of lengthy market exposure to confirm FMV. Sellers who reject a speedy first offer because it isn't full asking price take a calculated risk. A better offer may come along — but, then again, maybe not.

- ✓ **Excitement:** It takes courage to price your house a hair *below* the nearest price quantum (rather than above the quantum, so that you have room to negotiate downward). For example, suppose that the comps indicate a probable sale near $250,000. A $249,500 asking price may create enough buyer excitement to generate multiple purchase offers that push your sale price higher than the asking price. Price your property at $269,500 to give yourself a $20,000 negotiating cushion, and your house is just another yawner.

- ✓ **Computers:** All agents now use computers tied to their multiple listing service's (MLS) database to perform property searches. For example, a buyer decides on a neighborhood and asks the agent for a list of homes with the following features: three bedrooms, two-and-a-half baths, a two-car garage, and an asking price of $250,000 or less. Per the agent's request, the MLS computer spews out listings that meet these conditions. The computer isn't smart enough to make allowances for properties with negotiating room in their prices. If your house is listed at $269,500 or even $251,500, it won't be on the printout, and buyers won't know it exists.

True, some agents show buyers higher-priced houses they think will sell in the buyers' price range, because the asking prices are "soft." Smart agents, however, know that buyers are deeply concerned about being manipulated into purchasing a more costly house. These agents won't show buyers property over the stated price limit until the buyers have seen every house on the market in their specified price range and requested to see more expensive homes.

Less buyer exposure to your house means less buyer competition for it. Less competition translates into a longer time on the market — and usually a lower sale price, to boot. High sale prices come from spirited buyer competition.

- ✓ **Conditioning:** Whether people are buying houses or blouses, everyone loves a bargain. Believe it or not, *$9.95 advertising* is mighty effective. A nickel ain't much, but most folks are well-conditioned to think that $9.95 is much cheaper than $10. Subconsciously, $249,500 is more exciting than $250,000, and $299,950 sounds like a much better deal than $300,000. Don't try to buck a lifetime of Pavlovian conditioning; smart pricing makes buyers drool.

Don't price your property to dazzle your pals. You may impress people at a party by telling them that you're asking $300,000 for your house, but that's a foolish price compared to $299,950. Price your house to sell, not to feed your ego.

Identifying Incentives and Gimmicks

In strong real estate markets with many ready, willing, and able buyers clamoring to purchase good houses, property priced near its market value typically sells quickly. You don't need additional inducements in a red-hot market.

But when the tables are turned, and sellers far outnumber buyers, even pleasure-pleasure-panic pricing may not do the trick (see "Pleasure-pleasure-panic pricing: Fast, top-dollar sales" earlier in this chapter). If that's the case, you may have to offer buyers additional enticements to make a deal. In a buyers' market, the key to success is using incentives that help put a sale together instead of fancy gimmicks that tarnish your property and make it harder to sell. This section highlights a few incentives and gimmicks you may encounter when selling your house.

Deal-making incentives

In a really rotten market, you can sweeten the deal by offering buyers money in the form of special financial concessions. One or more of the following incentives may be the key to putting a deal together:

- **Credits in escrow:** One effective financial inducement is offering to pay a portion of your buyer's nonrecurring closing costs for such expenses as loan origination fees, title insurance, and property inspections. You may also graciously offer to pay for some or all of the repairs found by the property inspections. As we explain in Chapter 14, these payments usually are made as a credit in escrow from sellers to buyers.

- **Seller financing:** Chapter 4 explains the risks and rewards of seller financing. On the plus side, financing some or all of the buyer's mortgage may get you a higher sale price, a faster sale, an attractive return on your money, and possibly some tax savings. Doing seller financing, however, ties up money you may need for the down payment on your new home. Worse yet, if the buyer defaults on your loan, you must foreclose on the mortgage to protect your money.

Deceptive gimmicks

Smart financial incentives make deals happen. Improper inducements (which we call *gimmicks,* because that's what they are) waste time and usually result in lower sale prices. Impractical sellers sometimes resort to subterfuge in a futile attempt to disguise how ridiculously overpriced their property actually is. Instead of reducing the asking price to a realistic level, they try in vain to enhance their house's value with gimmicks that fall into one of the following three categories:

- ✔ **Buyer baubles:** "Buy our house, and we'll give you a free week in Paris for two (or a diamond ring, a brand new motorcycle, whatever) to sweeten the deal." Occasionally, sellers make this type of offer in phases one or two of four-phase pricing (explained earlier in this chapter in the section "Pleasure-pleasure-panic pricing: Fast, top-dollar sales"). Sellers erroneously assume that buyers will be so dazzled by the "free" goodies that they won't notice that the house's asking price is outrageously high.

Buyers usually know that the asking price includes a gimmick's cost. They aren't about to add the price of a trip to Paris, for example, into their 30-year mortgage. Opportunities to fly now and pay forever won't sell a house. Neither will drive-now-and-pay-forever deals, or wear-now-and-pay forever gimmicks. *Buyers aren't stupid.*

- ✔ **Agent payola:** Some sellers offer special inducements, such as trips or double commissions, to the agent who sells their property. These gimmicks are nothing more than blatant bribes for agents to sell their buyers down the river. Good agents categorically reject this kind of sleazy offer.

- ✔ **Contests:** As the California real estate market hit bottom in the mid 1990s, a few desperate sellers decided that, if they couldn't sell their houses, they would give them away in contests. Owners of a $150,000 house, for example, put an ad in the local paper inviting folks who wanted to enter their contest to write a 250-word essay explaining why they wanted to live in the house. Each contestant had to submit a $100 money-order entry fee with the essay. If 1,500 people entered the contest at $100 a pop, the property owners got their asking price. If, however, not enough people entered to make the contest worthwhile, owners reserved the right to cancel the contest and return all entry fees.

At least a dozen different California property owners tried variations of the contest gimmick. The ploy was a resounding flop. These contests uniformly drew far too little attention from contestants and far too much attention from state law enforcement personnel concerned about possible violation of California's antigambling statutes. The name of the game is *selling your house,* not *going to jail!*

Even if you can find buyers gullible enough to overpay for your house, lenders can't consider the value of gimmicks when appraising property; the mortgage won't be approved if the property is overpriced. Our advice: Don't waste time and money on gimmicks.

Overpricing Your House

In a perfect world, your house will sell quickly for top dollar if you faithfully follow our sage advice. By now, however, you've probably discovered that the world is frequently far from perfect, and things don't always go according to plan.

What if you can't sell your house even though you've done everything we recommend? Did you waste the money you paid for this book? Should you abandon all hope of making a sale? Is it the end of the world as we know it? No. This section can help you understand why no one may have made an acceptable offer for your house.

Can't sell versus won't sell

The *San Francisco Chronicle* ran a front-page story about a Bay Area house that was sliding down a muddy ridge that had been weakened by torrential rains. Battered by a series of severe storms, the house was slowly cracking in half. Mother Nature was putting the finishing touches on a remodeling job the ill-fated homeowner had started only a few months earlier.

"Can't," used in the context of selling a house, means that the property is impossible to sell. Unlike most people who claim that they *can't* sell their houses, the poor guy who owned this property really *couldn't* sell it. There's no market for unintentional mobile homes.

Fortunately, the vast majority of homeowners who claim that they "can't" sell their houses are exaggerating. They aren't disaster victims whose property values have been abruptly reduced to zero. Usually, plenty of purchasers are willing to buy their houses, and many lenders are ready to make loans to those buyers.

If nothing is physically wrong with their properties, what's the problem? Most of the time, the predicament is because of overpricing camouflaged by denial. A more accurate statement of the situation, for most would-be house sellers, is "We are unwilling to accept the price the market tells us our house is currently worth."

These homeowners *can* sell. They simply *won't* sell. As long as you *choose* not to take the amount that buyers will pay for your house, it will continue to languish unsold on the market. Saying that you can't sell your house is a self-fulfilling prophecy.

If your house is under 6 feet of water, has been carried away by a tornado, is now a pile of rubble because of an earthquake, or was ravaged by some other natural disaster, you have a valid reason for saying that you can't sell. If not, don't let denial blind you to the truth. You control your fate. You *can* sell your house after you correct the problem that's driving away prospective buyers. Perhaps you didn't follow our advice elsewhere in this book; you may have overimproved your property for the neighborhood, done a poor job of selecting an agent, or failed to properly prepare your house for sale. More often than not, however, the problem is overpricing.

Three factors all buyers consider

Sooner or later, all buyers hear that the three most important things to consider when buying a home are *location, location, location.* Because you've been through the purchasing process, you know that this cliché is a gross oversimplification. Here are the three factors buyers actually consider when selecting a home:

- ✓ **Where the property is:** Okay. The old "location, location, location" myth is one-third true. Urban, suburban, or rural; high in the mountains, smack in the middle of the Great Plains, or by a shining sea; you can't get around the fact that a house's location greatly affects its value. People pay dearly to buy into "good" neighborhoods. Folks buy location every bit as much as houses.

- ✓ **What the property is:** A house's cost depends on many factors such as its size, age, condition, and architectural style. The quality of construction materials and interior appointments also enter into property valuation.

- ✓ **How much the property costs:** Whether they're buying the most expensive house on the block or the cheapest, smart buyers try to get the biggest possible bang for their bucks. Furthermore, most people do a heck of a lot of comparison-shopping before they buy just to make sure that they don't overpay.

If you're having trouble selling your house, look at it in the same way buyers do. What can you change to bring your house's price in line with a buyer's perception of its value? Analyze your property with these three crucial factors in mind:

- ✔ **Can you change *where* the property is?** Nope. Even if you *could* move the house, the land under it stays put.

- ✔ **Can you change *what* the property is?** Possibly. For example, if a rusted-out car is the focal point of your front yard, hauling the car away will probably improve your prospects for making a sale. Reinspect your property inside and out. Make sure that everything is in tip-top condition. Be sure to read Chapter 9 to find out the best ways to prepare your property for sale.

- ✔ **Can you change *how much* the property costs?** Bingo. If you can't change the property's location, and you've done everything you can to prepare your house for sale, what's left to change? The price! Don't feel bad if you unintentionally overprice the property. Anyone can make that mistake. As we explain in Chapter 10, pricing isn't an exact science.

Danger signs of overpricing

When you price property correctly, it sells. Conversely, even if your property is in exquisite condition and actively marketed (open houses, classified ads, MLS, Internet Web site, and so on, as we describe in Chapters 12 and 13), a dearth of offers indicates that it's overpriced. The warning signs of overpricing may include any or all of the following:

- ✔ **No second showings:** Well priced or not, agents and buyers rush to see new listings. Watch out for a precipitous decline in showings after the initial flurry of activity when your house first hits the market. If nobody returns for a second look, you have a problem.

- ✔ **Many showings, but no offers:** Switch hats — suppose that you're a buyer. Your agent shows you a three-bedroom, two-bath house for $249,500. Then the agent takes you to a newer four-bedroom, three-bath home just two blocks away — *with the same asking price.* The agent doesn't have to say anything; the difference between price and value is starkly obvious. The first house helps sell the second one.

Your listing agent (if you're selling through a real estate agent) should help other agents route house tours by pointing out overpriced properties the agents can show their buyers *before* bringing them to your well-priced house. Successful agents show buyers OPTs (overpriced turkeys) to sell well-priced houses.

The foolproof way to correct overpricing

During Ray's 20 years as an active real estate broker, he managed hundreds of real estate agents and participated directly or indirectly in thousands of sales. Having studied the correlation between asking prices and sale prices through all those years, he made an amazing discovery: Good market or bad, more than 97 percent of all property sells within 10 percent of its final asking price.

Ray's observation doesn't mean that every house starts out with the correct asking price — quite the contrary. Many properties go through a needless series of ineffective price reductions before ultimately arriving at the correct asking price. However, after owners finally reduce their houses' asking prices to within 10 percent of FMV, their properties sell.

If your house hasn't generated any offers, even though it shows wonderfully and is aggressively marketed, update your CMA. You may discover that your house is overpriced by 5 percent, or by 20 percent, or, gasp, by even more. When you update your CMA, consider the following:

- ✔ **As we note in Chapter 10, it's tough to precisely establish the value of attributes such as proximity to bus lines, wonderful landscaping, and views.** Your listing agent, if you're using one, or you may have given your house's amenities a much higher value than buyers do.

- ✔ **You (or your listing agent) may have put too much emphasis on asking prices or used inaccurate sales data.** Perhaps houses that were on the market when you prepared the CMA ultimately sold for much less than their asking prices. Maybe some sale prices of comparable houses didn't reflect big credits in escrow from sellers to buyers for corrective work or nonrecurring closing costs.

- ✔ **The local real estate market may have gone down the drain.** Did mortgage interest rates skyrocket, or did consumer confidence plummet since the CMA was prepared? Adverse market conditions drag prices down. Find out how many properties similar to yours have sold since your house came on the market. Maybe *nothing* is selling. On the other hand, if comparable houses are selling and yours isn't, put on your hard hat — falling price zone ahead.

- ✔ **You may have missed the prime selling time.** As we discuss in Chapter 5, every real estate market has peaks and valleys of sales activity. For example, suppose that you base your price on sales made during September and October, when more buyers were active in your area. However, your house actually went on the market the day after Thanksgiving, after most buyers had vanished. Your timing is awful. To make a sale, you either have to cut your price to the bone or take your house off the market until buyers return in the spring.

Whatever the problem, don't compound it with excessive tenacity. If you haven't gotten any offers after approximately six weeks on the market, and other houses similar to yours are selling all around you, the odds are high that your asking price is *at least* 10 percent more than your house's FMV. Under these circumstances, correct the problem by cutting the price 10 percent. Here's how to maximize the impact of your price reduction:

- ✔ **Bite the bullet and make a full 10-percent cut.** Making a series of smaller price reductions only prolongs the agony. Your property will be forgotten as more and more new listings come on the market. Don't turn your house into "That old thing? Something must be terribly wrong with it. It's been on the market forever."

- ✔ **Use quantum pricing to fine-tune the new price.** Suppose that your asking price is $279,500. A 10-percent reduction ($27,950) cuts the price to $251,550, which isn't a smart price. Never leave your asking price dangling just *above* the next quantum. You lose exposure to all the buyers who, for instance, instruct their agents not to show them anything over $250,000. As we explain in the section "Quantum pricing: An effective technique," a smarter price is $249,950.

- ✔ **If you still haven't gotten an offer after another six weeks or so of active marketing at the new price, make another 10-percent reduction.** You may have been 20 percent or more over FMV when you put your house on the market. Perhaps you're in a market where prices are declining. If that's the case, the longer you delay a price cut, the greater the gap between your asking price and actual market value.

Six weeks isn't carved in stone. In a hot market, three or four weeks may be more than enough time to give your house maximum buyer exposure. In a slower market (such as the long, hot summer when kids are out of school and many buyers and agents take vacations), you may be wise to wait seven or eight weeks before a price cut. Let local market activity be your guide when you time price reductions.

Placing the blame where it belongs

Telling sellers that they must cut their asking price if they want to sell is extremely difficult for agents. Many agents can't do it. They're afraid sellers will respond by saying, "This mess is all your fault. We relied on your advice to set the price. A halfway competent agent could've sold our magnificent house months ago. We don't need a price cut; we need a new agent. Get out of our house. Never darken our doorway again. We rue the day we ever met you. Curse you and all your offspring forevermore." Or words to that effect.

Firing the agent may be the correct thing to do. An agent who intentionally overstates your house's value to get the listing deserves to be dumped. By the same token, a likable but inept agent is utterly worthless. You need a good agent, not a fraud or a friendly fool.

Sometimes, however, dumping your agent is like throwing the baby out with the bath water. Perhaps your house is tough to price because it's unique or because no recent comparable sales have occurred in the neighborhood. Maybe the local economy took a nose dive right after your house went on the market. Venting your frustration on the agent for telling the truth won't get your house sold.

Concentrate on real money

Ray had lunch a while ago at Perry's (his favorite San Francisco restaurant) with a friend who was trying to sell her house. Jeannine had a good agent, her house showed well, and the property was being aggressively marketed. But, after more than three months on the market, she had nary a nibble.

"Why hasn't my house sold, Ray? Is my problem the lousy real estate market?"

"Lousy is a matter of opinion, Jeannine. Compared to the hot market several years ago, sellers hate this market. Buyers, on the other hand, love it."

"What can we do? You know that my husband and I paid $425,000 for our house at the height of the boom market, and then spent $50,000 more remodeling it. We put it on the market in January at $495,000. Even though we dropped our asking price to $449,500 in March, we still haven't had even one offer."

"If you can't change what the house is or where it is, what's left to change, Jeannine?"

"Don't say the price, Ray. We're already losing money at $449,500."

"Property values in your neighborhood are nearly 20 percent lower today than they were three years ago when you bought the house, Jeannine. That's a hard, cold fact. Your chances of a break-even sale are no better than my chances of winning the Pulitzer Prize."

"All I can think about is the money we've lost."

"That's the problem, Jeannine. You're concentrating on money you've lost rather than money you still have."

"I don't understand."

"The money you lost when property values fell is gone. You can't get it back. Don't waste time thinking about it. Instead, focus on the money you've still got in the bank. Real money is money you haven't spent yet."

"What do you mean, Ray?"

"You told me how much money you'll save if you move to a community with less expensive housing and public schools to your liking."

"True."

"So every month the house doesn't sell means another raid on the real money in your savings account to pay high housing costs and private school expenses."

"Correct on both counts."

"That's real money you don't have to spend. You can't control the past. You can, however, control your future housing and school costs. Selling the house puts a tourniquet on the money bleeding out of your savings account. You know what you have to do to end this misery. The choice is yours."

Jeannine and her husband tried two more weeks to sell at $449,500, and then cut their asking price to $399,995. They accepted an offer of $395,000 within five days after the price reduction, and closed their sale 30 days later. They recovered the amount they lost as sellers by paying a lower price for their new home in a town with an outstanding public school system.

Part IV

The Brass Tacks of Getting Your House Sold

The 5th Wave   By Rich Tennant

"And I suppose you think this will attract prospective buyers?"

In this part . . .

Getting the word out about your wonderful house is key to making the sale. In this part, we highlight all the best marketing strategies and tactics for generating interest in your house, including a chapter devoted to how you can use the Internet to sell your house. Then, when the offers come rolling in (or trickling in, if your local real estate market is sick), we show you how to negotiate the best possible terms without driving away prospective buyers. Next, we cover all the small but important pieces that must fall into place for your house sale to officially close. Looking forward to that hefty check, aren't you? Finally, we take you through the state and federal tax filings required after your sale.

Chapter 12

Marketing Your House

In This Chapter
▶ Figuring out the advertising techniques that work to sell your house
▶ Using open houses to make a sale
▶ Knowing the house showing do's and don'ts

Curb appeal and staging are important aspects of showing your house off to its best advantage (see Chapter 9). But, by themselves, curb appeal and staging won't sell your house. Even adding the sophisticated pricing techniques from Chapters 10 and 11 to the package still won't do the trick. Regardless of how realistic your asking price may be, you lack one essential ingredient to make a sale.

Face it. Without a buyer, you're nothing more than the owner of a well-priced, bewitchingly staged property with loads of curb appeal. You need a buyer to convert you into a seller, and the best way to do so is to market your house. This chapter can help.

Advertising That Works

In a red-hot seller's market, just sticking a For Sale sign in your front yard produces all the buyers you need. When you have five buyers for every good property on the market, advertising isn't so critical.

Unfortunately for sellers, the market isn't always hot. In fact, it sometimes gets downright chilly. When your neighborhood is a forest of For Sale signs and buyers are few and exceedingly far between, merely getting a buyer's attention is a major victory. The key to selling your house for top dollar — even in a dismal market — is simple: Implement a broad-based advertising campaign to generate spirited buyer competition for your property.

Advertising isn't a cure-all. Glitzy advertising won't sell a house that's in terrible condition, poorly marketed, and overpriced to boot. Give buyers and agents credit for having a snippet of knowledge about property values and a smidgen of discernment. Think of advertising as the setting for an engagement ring. The world's most beautiful setting can't transform a cheap zircon into a priceless diamond. A stunning setting will, on the other hand, heighten the appeal of an appropriately exquisite diamond.

Whether you list your property with a real estate broker who handles all your advertising or you're selling on your own, the same rules apply. Certain types of advertising are *extremely* effective. Others, while popular, are big wastes of time and money. The following sections describe types of advertising that get our seal of approval.

For Sale sign

A humble, low-tech For Sale sign stuck in your front yard or nailed to your house is, without a doubt, one of the most effective ways to tell folks looking for a home in your area that your property is on the market.

Real estate brokers know that *sign calls* (people calling to get more information about a house after they see the For Sale sign) are far more likely to result in a sale than *ad calls* (people calling about property they read about in an ad). Why? When ad callers find out the location of the advertised property, the style of the house, the age of the house, or some other basic fact they'd already know if they'd actually seen the property from the street, they more often than not reject it. Sign callers, on the other hand, obviously like the neighborhood and at least the property's exterior, or they wouldn't have called; they have a higher probability of being serious buyers.

Good signs are simple and large enough for people to read easily. They include these elements:

- The words "For Sale"

- A phone number to call

- The phrase "shown by appointment only" (unless you want people dropping in on you unexpectedly at all hours of the day and night)

- Web site link (we cover using the computer to market your house in Chapter 13)

- The listing broker's company name (if you're using an agent)

This information is all that you need on a sign. To attract folks driving by your house, use a two-sided sign placed perpendicular to the road so that people can read it from either direction. If you have a corner lot, use two signs so both streets fronting your house have signs.

BEWARE

Ineffective advertising

More than 99 percent of all residential property sold in the United States is marketed using the advertising techniques that we describe in this chapter. True, you may need special marketing to sell highly unusual properties, such as a 250-year-old historic house in Olde Cape Cod or an authentic castle that was disassembled stone-by-stone in Ireland and painstakingly reassembled lock, stock, and drawbridge on the vast plains of Texas. However, ordinary advertising techniques work just fine for the rest of us.

It's flattering to hear agents say that your house is so special that only a fancy four-color brochure can do it justice. Furthermore, those same agents may say that to get top dollar your property must be advertised in their international affiliate's glitzy magazine that ends up on coffee tables in Paris, London, Rome, Rio, and other exotic spots around the world. And as soon as you sign on the dotted line to list your house with them, they'll be delighted to get started on the brochure and international advertising program.

You know what's happening (if not, we explain this gimmick in Chapter 10). The agents are trying to buy your listing. Before succumbing to their blandishments, ask yourself how often you see people from Paris, London, Rome, and Rio buying houses in your neighborhood. The world's best brochure coupled with a world-wide marketing effort won't sell overpriced property. Nor should you waste your time and money on deceptive marketing gimmicks. As noted in Chapter 11, essay contests don't work. Neither do bribes, such as trips to Tahiti or expensive cars for the buyers of your house or their agent. Stick to the basics; they work.

Be sure that your sign makes a good first impression. Recycling is fine, but don't let your agent reuse someone else's old, beaten-up For Sale sign on your wonderful property; get a spiffy new one. A worn, dented, faded sign makes your property look equally tired. Don't put up the sign before you're 100 percent ready to sell, because after the sign goes up, you *will* start receiving calls.

Classified ads

The classified section of your local newspaper is a cost-effective way to reach prospective buyers. Because most house hunters look at property on weekends, run an ad in your paper's Sunday real estate section or its weekend edition. If you're handling your own advertising, because you're selling your house without a broker, get some tips from the pros. Study real estate brokers' ads for ideas on phrasing your ad. People who work in the classified-ad department usually can help you draft an ad and suggest standard abbreviations — such as "br" for bedroom, "ba" for bathroom, and "fp" for fireplace — so you can save money without confusing readers.

Troublemakers to avoid when marketing your house

If you're writing your own ads because you aren't using an agent, don't put *everything* about your property in the ad. For one thing, running a big ad every week is expensive. In addition, describing your property in too much detail isn't smart; good ads always leave out one essential bit of information — such as the address or number of bedrooms — so that buyers have to call whoever placed the ad. Real estate agents use ad calls to make showing appointments. If you tell buyers *everything* in your ad, they won't have a reason to call, and you lose the opportunity to convince them to tour your wonderful property.

When you describe your house, failing to disclose information won't get you in trouble as long as you aren't withholding material facts that affect your property's value or desirability. What you do say, however, can turn out to be legally expensive if ever you cross the line between puffery and misrepresentation.

Puffery is the exorbitant use of high-sounding adjectives to extol the virtues of otherwise ordinary products. Everything from cars to cleaners is praised as being newer, bigger, faster, better, tastier, smoother, gentler, and, of course, brighter. Fine. Today's consumers are wise enough to make allowances for advertisers' excessive enthusiasm.

As bad as puffery is, misrepresentation is far worse. Folks can, after all, defend themselves against puffery because they can see reality with their own eyes. People know the difference between spacious and tiny no matter what the ad says.

Misrepresentation deals with factors that aren't readily apparent. For example, suppose that you're selling a house that appears to be in excellent shape. The buyer asks you if the roof leaks. If you say that it doesn't leak when you know for a fact that the roof *does* leak, that's out-and-out misrepresentation. If the buyers don't have the roof inspected because

they rely on your statement about the roof, they'll probably do two things after the first big rainstorm hits their new home — buy a new roof and sue you. *Never assume anything.* "I don't know" is a perfectly acceptable and absolutely safe response to any question you can't answer with complete certainty — *never, never guess.*

How can you protect yourself from inadvertent misrepresentation? Here are ten troublemakers to avoid when writing your ad:

✔ **All:** Comparable words such as *completely, totally, perfect, none, entirely,* and *fully* are equally naughty. They should be avoided because they leave no room for exceptions, errors, or discrepancies. "All hardwood floors," "completely remodeled," and "totally renovated" are phrases that can lead to a lawsuit if the buyer finds *one thing* that disproves your all-inclusive language. When that happens, your property isn't as advertised.

✔ **Custom-built:** The *American Heritage Dictionary* defines this as "built according to the specifications of the buyer." Was your house built to your specifications? This term doesn't apply to a home where the developer created a plan and reproduced it multiple times. Custom-built is only applicable to a made-to-order, one-of-a-kind home.

✔ **Fixed:** This term is used when an animal has been permanently neutered and can never reproduce. When used to describe corrective work done over the years, however, "fixed" leads many buyers to incorrectly believe a problem was *permanently* rectified. A leaky roof, for example, is never "fixed." Trust us, it *will* leak again sooner or later and when it does, the buyer will sue. Instead of saying the leak was fixed, say it was "repaired."

✔ **Never:** Just as dangerous as being too expansive is the tendency to deny that something can ever occur. "There has never been a problem with (fill in the blank)" has come back to haunt many a seller when the friendly next door neighbor tells the new owner about that one time there was a problem with the sewer overflowing, flooding, high winds, elephant stampedes, and so on.

✔ **New:** What's new? With cars, they technically stop being new the moment they're driven away from the car dealership. There isn't such a fine dividing line in real estate, but there's logic we can apply. After appliances have been used, they're no longer new. A roof is only new for a brief time after installation. Trying to be cute by saying "newer" begs the question "Newer than what?" It's best to truthfully state when appliances were installed or a repair took place. Rather than saying "new roof," use the phrase "new roof installed (date of installation)."

✔ **Panoramic:** Although views from a house may be great, they're seldom an unlimited view in all directions, which is the true definition of panoramic. Unless the house is located at the top of a hill with a 360 degree view of everything around it, this term should be avoided. Words like *breathtaking, sweeping, grand,* and *awesome* are preferable.

✔ **People:** Avoid describing the neighbors or the "ideal" future owner. Just because you get along wonderfully with your neighbors doesn't mean the next owner will. Your idea of the ideal future owner is subjective. Litigation lurks.

✔ **Quiet:** This seemingly innocuous word has triggered considerable litigation. In one case, the cul de sac in which a house was located was always quiet in the winter when the real estate agent saw the property. It was anything but quiet in the spring after escrow closed when the marching band began practicing in the football field behind the house. Quiet is subjective. For some people, hearing *any* noise at all means the area isn't quiet.

✔ **Safe:** Make no promise of safety or security. No matter how safe you think the neighborhood is or how secure the "child-safe pool cover" is supposed to be, bad things can and do happen. There's no guarantee of safety or security.

✔ **Square footage:** Three appraisers can measure a house and get three completely different square footages. Always preface any mention of square footage with a word such as *approximately, nearly, about,* or *around* to allow for error or lack of precision. Approximately 2,300 square feet is safer than 2,320 square feet. If you must use a precise number, cite the source of your information (per tax records, assessor's records, and so on.)

Kip Oxman, an attorney by trade and our brilliant technical reviewer, suggests using the following disclaimer when stating square footage: "If actual square footage is material to Buyer's decision to offer to purchase the subject property, Buyer should verify the square footage before making the offer. Although approximate square footage measurements according to tax records, or reported in previous appraisals, are sometimes available and are useful as informational guidelines, such numbers are frequently inaccurate. Seller can't guarantee the measurements of others."

The best ads are masterpieces of understatement. Ideally, you want to describe your property in such a way that it actually delivers more — not less — than the ads promise. No one ever complains about that.

Thanks to the ubiquitous Internet, you may get an even bigger bang for your classified advertising buck. Most newspapers now automatically put classified ads on their Web sites, so potential buyers from all around the world can look for a house with the click of a mouse. Check to see whether your local paper offers this benefit.

Multiple listing service (MLS)

A multiple listing service (MLS) is composed of and operated by local real estate brokers and agents who pool their listings so that information about property listed by any MLS member is immediately available to all participating members. Brokers and agents enter new listings into their computerized MLS database as soon as the listing contract is signed. Price changes and sales also are same-day entries. In most places, nonmembers (that is, the public) can't put property into an MLS.

If your property is listed with a real estate broker, insist that it be put into the MLS. An MLS listing gives your property wide exposure to a potent pool of market-educated buyers currently working with all other MLS members. If you're selling without an agent, consider paying a discount broker to put your property into the MLS. As we note in Chapter 8, you *must* offer a commission to a cooperating broker who procures a buyer for your property.

Listing statement

The *listing statement,* also called a *property statement,* is a data sheet and is given to people who tour your property on Sunday open houses or people who are shown through your house by appointment. Listing statements are effective point-of-purchase ads containing more information than you can put into a newspaper ad or an MLS listing (see Figure 12-1). This sheet offers you a chance to wax poetic about the special features of your property.

To satisfy buyers with short attention spans and too much to do, include an abstract to *briefly* give basic facts about your property. The headline, "Gardener's Delight" in the listing statement in Figure 12-1, emphasizes the property's hot button (see the sidebar "Hot buttons"). A good listing statement takes people through your house room-by-room pointing out special features they may not notice, such as the working fireplace with gas starter, the built-in curio cabinet, personal property such as fireplace tools included in the sale, garden plantings, and the intercom system. A few other tips to remember when writing your listing statement include the following:

✔ Don't use fancy 17-syllable words when simple ones will do.

✔ Avoid rhetorical overstatement, such as "world's most fantastic view" or "extraordinarily enormous living room."

✔ Keep the write-up short — one page maximum.

✔ *Always* include a disclaimer similar to the one we include at the bottom of our sample listing statement.

Figure 12-1: Here's what a good listing statement looks like.

ೞ **PIONEER REALTY** ಌ

One Main Street, Yourtown

Serving the area since 1776

Abstract: Lovingly maintained three bedroom, two bath home close to excellent schools, #4 bus line, shopping & just one block from Mountain Lake Park. Living room with fireplace, formal dining room, cook's kitchen, den, two car garage & garden. Built 1952.

Address: 1415 Poplar Lane

Lot Size: 25' X 120'

List Price: $149,500

Lot: 24 Block: 5724

Gardener's Delight

Spacious master bedroom with walk-in closet and adjoining master bath. Two smaller bedrooms have been recently painted. Bathrooms are older, in good shape & waiting for new owner's special touch.

Gracious living room has working fireplace with gas starter. Large formal dining room features a built-in curio cabinet & hardwood floors. Adjoining the dining room is a cheery den with windows that overlook the patio & garden.

Kitchen has a chef-efficient layout with ample cabinets and counterspace. Refrigerator, gas range & new dishwasher are included in the sale. Adjacent to the kitchen is a nook currently being used as a computer work space.

Directly outside the kitchen is an herb garden that leads to the meticulously maintained, fenced garden. Plantings include: oak & apple trees, roses, numerous perennial plantings, daffodil & tulip bulbs, which provide a riot of color in the spring & summer.

Full basement and insulated attic provide additional storage space. The two-car garage has overhead storage, bicycle & ski racks as well as a work bench & intercom to the kitchen.

To Show: By appointment with Listing Agent

Roland Jadryev   777. 777. 7777

ೞ E-Mail: Roland@wagontrain.net ಌ

The information contained herein has either been given to us by the owner of the property or obtained from sources that we deem reliable. We have no reason to doubt its accuracy, but we do not guarantee it. The prospective buyer should carefully verify all information contained herein. Taxes will be reassessed upon sale. Prospective purchasers are advised to review the "Real Estate Transfer Disclosure Statement" on file with this office prior to making an offer.

Hot buttons

If you want to be a successful seller, figure out exactly what you have to sell *before* you start advertising. People don't buy houses. They buy hot buttons and the house tags along.

Hot buttons vary from one house to the next. Gourmet kitchens, luxurious bathrooms, sensuous bedrooms, working fireplaces, panoramic views, and lovely gardens are turn-ons. So are huge, walk-in closets — no one ever has enough closet space. In densely populated metropolitan areas like New York, Boston, and San Francisco where parking spaces are slightly scarcer than Hope diamonds, garages can help sell houses. Location is a hot button if folks will buy a mediocre house to live in a superb neighborhood or to get their kids into a good school system.

Good agents see houses through the eyes of their owners. If you're working with an agent to sell your house, the agent will want to know about the property features that most appealed to you when you bought it. Whatever you liked when you first saw the house will most likely also be the next buyer's hot button.

For example, suppose that your favorite part of the house is the master bedroom with a charming little fireplace. You love watching the firelight dance on the walls and hearing the fire snap and pop as you nod off to sleep on cold winter nights. If that's your house's strongest feature, then guess which attribute is emphasized in the listing statement, in the MLS write-up, and in your weekly newspaper ads.

For Sunday open houses and broker tours, the master bedroom is filled with fresh flowers and a small fire crackles in the fireplace. Private showings of your house to prospective buyers always end, not by coincidence, in the master bedroom because that room has the greatest emotional impact on buyers. In fact, the master bedroom is the closing room where agents working with motivated buyers first suggest writing up an offer on the house.

This approach doesn't mean that the listing agent ignores the rest of your house. Everything is, of course, staged to show beautifully. But smart sellers and agents push the hot button because that feature is probably the reason the next owners will buy the property.

The best way to avoid getting sued because your house is smaller than you claimed it was is to avoid giving *any* square footages unless you're absolutely, positively, 100 percent certain about the measurements. If you're inadvertently a few square feet shy of the square footage you stated, you could end up being sued by a nit-picky buyer with a tape measure and too much spare time. Actual square footage is less important than your buyers' conclusion that your house is big enough based on *their* visual inspection.

Computers

In addition to the computerized MLS, many brokers now have Internet Web sites that they use to advertise their listings. As previously noted in the "Classified ads" section earlier in this chapter, most newspapers put classified ads on the Internet so computer users can access them without having to dirty their fingers with newsprint. We devote Chapter 13 to describing ways you can use a computer during your sale.

Word of mouth

Word-of-mouth advice sounds so darn primitive coming right after "Computers" in the preceding section, but networking is an extremely effective form of targeted advertising. Tell people you know — friends, business associates, folks who go to your church, club members, and especially your neighbors, that your house is for sale. Make a point of inviting your friends and neighbors to your first open house. Who knows? One of them may have a pal who'd love to buy your house. Stranger things happen every day.

Arranging Open Houses

If a picture is worth a 1,000 words, personally touring property must be worth at least a couple of encyclopedias. That's why, in a touchy-feely business like residential real estate sales, open houses are an invaluable sales tool.

You can hold two distinctly different types of open houses to sell your property. Even though each type of open house targets a different market segment, they share a common objective — to sell your property. This section focuses on your two options.

Brokers' opens

If you hire a broker to sell your house, one of the first things your listing agent does after you've signed the listing contract is tell the local brokerage community about your property. One extremely effective way to get the word out is scheduling a *brokers' open* — a special open house exclusively for local real estate agents.

Agents generally work with at least four or five *serious* buyers at any given time. After these buyers have, for one reason or another, seen and rejected all the houses of interest to them that currently are on the market, they go into a holding pattern waiting for a listing of just the right property. One primary mission of agents working with buyers is to scout out new property.

A brokers' open is amazingly targeted marketing. No guarantees, of course, but don't be surprised if the first brokers' open leads to a sale. After all, having 50 agents tour your house is the equivalent of showing it to 200 or 250 *motivated* buyers.

Although your house obviously won't appeal to every one of the agents' buyers, you can bet it'll press hot buttons for a few of them. Well-priced, attractive property almost always generates immediate showing requests. With the advent of cell phones, agents don't even have to wait until they get back to the office to call their clients about the fantastic property (yours, we hope) that they just saw on a brokers' tour.

Most areas designate one particular day each week as Brokers' Tour Day, the day on which agents and brokers tour newly listed properties. If many new listings enter the market the week of your first brokers' open, some agents won't see your property because of scheduling conflicts with brokers' opens on other houses. Even if only a few new listings are available when your property hits the market, some agents won't see your house because they're on vacation, have offers to present, have escrows to close, or are holding other houses open themselves. Whatever the reason, the way around scheduling conflicts is to be sure that your listing agent schedules at least two brokers' opens.

Weekend open houses

We start this section by noting that folks usually think of public open houses as *Sunday* open houses. That idea is prevalent because most houses are held open on Sundays. However, no law says that you can't hold a Saturday open house every now and then to scoop up people who can't come to a Sunday open house. Having planted that thought in your mind, we refer to all public open houses from now on as Sunday open houses for simplicity's sake.

Compared to brokers' opens (see the preceding section), you have lower odds of making a sale directly by holding a Sunday open house. But if you're trying to sell your house without an agent, you won't have access to brokers' opens.

After you open your house to the world at large, not everyone who walks through the front door is a legitimate buyer. You get Lookie Lou's trying to pick up some decorating hints and curious neighbors who always wanted to know how your house looks on the inside. You also get real buyers who were attracted by your open house sign, but need a home in a different size or price range. Unfortunately, other than an address, open house signs don't contain a wealth of specific information to help qualify prospective buyers.

The incidental traffic isn't necessarily bad for you. Unless your visitors are terribly antisocial, people who come to your Sunday open houses probably have friends or neighbors who want to buy in the neighborhood. Word of mouth *is* powerful advertising (see the section "Word of mouth" earlier in this chapter).

In a perfect world, nobody steals. Unfortunately, the world isn't perfect. Leaving small, easily portable valuables lying around during open houses is an open invitation to thieves. Either put expensive jewelry, precious coins, rare stamps, and your other small valuable items into a safe deposit box or figure out another place to put them so they are out of harm's way. If you expect a great many visitors, see if your listing agent can get another agent to help with your open house. One agent can show people through your house while the other stays at the front door to greet visitors, get names, answer basic questions, and, last but not least, watch for folks leaving the house with suspicious bulges.

Showing Your Property

No one will buy your property sight unseen. Luscious listing statements, appealing ads, and inviting photographs of your house's interior and exterior fan the flames of buyer curiosity. To satisfy the inquisitiveness that you arouse, you must let prospective buyers wander through your house.

If you list your house with a real estate agent, showings are an inconvenience rather than a problem because a good agent handles the actual buyer and broker showings for you. Your job is simple — make sure that the property is staged to show well and make yourself scarce while the property is being shown.

Preshowing preparations

If you don't know exactly how to generate property curb appeal and subtly stage your house, turn to Chapter 9 for the details. In this section, we cover a few final things you must do to maximize the showing process. These things include

✔ **Make showing your property easy for agents:** The easier your house is to show, the more often agents will show it, and, most likely, the more you'll get for your house and the faster it'll sell. If you force agents to get a house key from you before each showing, you'll have fewer showings because some agents are too busy to get the key, and others are too lazy. Instead of personally doling out your key each time there's a showing, you have two options:

- Give the listing agent a key if your house is only shown by appointment

- Have your agent put a house key in a lockbox that agents open by using a special lockbox key or electronically-coded lockbox card.

From an agent's perspective, nothing is more embarrassing or frustrating than trying to explain to an antsy buyer the reason she can't unlock the front door. Before you give the listing agent keys to your house, make sure that the keys actually unlock the door and that the lock works smoothly. (This is your chance to make a good first impression on the buyer.) Lastly, if the house has an alarm, make sure it's disarmed or that the showing agent knows how to turn the alarm off.

✔ **Make yourself scarce during showings:** If you have a listing agent, leave the property while your agent shows it. Some buyers are too polite to say so, but having you hover over them as they tour your house is *very* inhibiting. Serious buyers want to look into all your closets and cabinets, look under all your sinks, and explore every nook and cranny of the house — but they won't if you're hanging around.

By the same token, as long as you're around, buyers won't make derogatory comments. Sometimes, the most important information you get from a showing is the reason why someone *doesn't* like the property. Correcting a problem or overcoming an objection starts by finding out about the problem or objection. Your agent should follow up *every* showing by calling the buyer's agent to find out whether the buyer intends to make an offer and, if not, why not.

You can't vanish during open houses if you're selling without an agent. Try, however, to be as unobtrusive as possible when buyers tour your property. For example, don't walk them through the house pointing out the obvious: "This is the kitchen. Here's the bathroom. This bedroom is where the kids sleep." Instead, point out special things they may not notice, such as the high ceiling in your dining room or the fact that a hardwood floor is under the wall-to-wall carpet in the family room. Make your points selectively and remember that the quality of your guidance is more important than the quantity.

✔ **Get used to living in a fishbowl:** If you follow our sage advice, your house will sell quickly for top dollar. However, the sale probably won't *seem* quick. The best proof of the relativity of time is living in a house that's for sale and may be shown any time of the day or, within reasonable limits, night. You can't ever leave the bathtub dirty or dishes in the sink or clothes on the bedroom floor or cook liver and onions or lounge around in your bathrobe on Sunday morning or. . . . Be of good faith. This, too, shall pass.

The final showing

You may think that you've been put out of your misery after you accept an offer to purchase your property. "Goody," you say, "No more showings — I can have my life back."

Lockboxes versus shown-by-appointment arrangements

Depending on the location of your property, you may have to use a lockbox. If, for example, your property is 50 miles from the nearest town or located in a scenic but remote area, you may not have a viable alternative to a lockbox.

From the standpoint of making your property easy to show, lockboxes are great. Newer, electronic lockboxes contain a computer chip that maintains a record of which agent's lockbox card was used to open the box as well as the date and time the property was shown. Some lockboxes also have a lockout feature that limits key access to certain hours so that you can have some privacy every now and then. Super-sophisticated lockboxes can even be programmed with a call-before-showing code that forces agents to call the listing agent to get an additional code to enter the property.

But, the most sophisticated lockbox in the world still has drawbacks. Lockboxes can't straighten up your house before a showing, or tell you which agent let Duke, the wonder cat, out of the house, or point a finger at the agent who forgot to lock your front door after a showing, or, most important of all, help sell your house to buyers.

Houses can't speak for themselves. That's why, if humanly possible, your listing agent must be present every time your house is shown — to answer buyer questions, point out special features about your property and the neighborhood, and keep an eye on your pet and your valuables.

Not quite. Inspections by the buyer's property inspectors aside, one extremely important showing remains: the inspection an appraiser makes as a condition of your buyer's loan approval.

This final showing to the appraiser is *critically* important. If the buyer's loan isn't approved because the appraiser thinks that your property isn't worth the amount the buyer is willing to pay for it, your deal falls through, and you're back in the fishbowl again.

Take these two steps to prevent an appraiser from undervaluing your house:

✔ **Shower the appraiser with attention and comps.** Your agent (or you, if you're selling your house yourself) should be present during the appraiser's property inspection to "sell" your house one last time. In addition to pointing out to the appraiser each and every valuable feature of your house and the neighborhood, your agent can give the appraiser an *updated* copy of the comparable market analysis (see Chapter 10) originally used to establish your asking price. The appraiser can use the comparable sales data to justify the sale price.

✔ **Spiff your house up one more time.** Appraisers are *supposedly* above being influenced by a house's appearance. *Theoretically,* appraisers won't get a bad impression if your property looks lived in. Sure. No matter what appraisers say, they are human. Perfectly staging your house one last time almost certainly makes a favorable impression on the appraiser. And if you're going for a record sale price in your neighborhood, every little bit helps. One thing's for sure — it certainly can't hurt.

Chapter 13

Harnessing Your Computer for House Selling

In This Chapter

▶ Knowing what real-estate-related Web sites can and can't do for you

▶ Making the best and wisest use of software and the Internet to sell your house

*U*nlike the investment industry, which has numerous avenues for do-it-yourself investors to bypass securities brokers and their commissions, the residential real estate industry isn't easy for property sellers or buyers to bypass real estate agents and deal directly with one another. Through multiple listing services (MLS), in which local associations of Realtors pool their property listings and restrict access to only member Realtors, real estate agents retain a lock on about 80 percent of all property sales.

However, some say that the mushrooming use of computers and the Internet threatens to challenge agent dominance of the real estate world. In theory, at least, the Internet provides the public with a medium for direct and unfiltered exchange of real estate information. And, more and more home buyers and house sellers are turning to the Internet.

Real estate on the Internet has definitely changed and continues to change the industry. The multimedia aspects of the World Wide Web are now being better utilized in the selling process. Many house listings on the Web include color pictures and a video tour. More homebuyers are taking advantage of the Internet's potential for researching and the grassroots exchange of real estate information. This chapter includes our tips on the best ways to use (or not use) your computer in the house-selling process.

Knowing the Internet's Limitations: The Net Alone Can't Sell Your House

Many property sellers would love to sell their houses themselves to avoid paying those commissions (amounting to 5 or 6 percent of the sale price) that real estate agents collect. The Internet offers for-sale-by-owner (FSBO) house sellers a potentially powerful marketing medium. Don't think, however, that just throwing your house on the Web is enough to sell it for top dollar.

The Internet is one of many ways to market a house. And, as we discuss in Chapter 12, newspaper ads, For Sale signs, Sunday open houses, brokers' tours, listing statements, and listings in the local multiple listing service (MLS) are primary marketing vehicles. This section helps you identify what the Web can and can't do for you to help you sell your house.

Ensure good Web promo of your house

The Web can be a great way to promote your house, but you need to make sure that prospective buyers can see it and easily access it. Keep the following in mind to make sure your house listing gets ample hits on the Web:

- **If you're using a real estate agent to sell your house:** Be sure your agent has an Internet site through which you can list your house. Visit the site and see what you think of it. Are the properties for sale well presented? Is the site easy to use and visually appealing? Ask the agent if her company's Web site is an Internet Data Exchange (IDX) participant. This enables real estate brokers to share listings online among their various Web sites so that your property gets maximum online exposure. Please keep in mind, as we note in Chapter 7, that your selection of a good agent should be based on many important criteria, such as her experience and knowledge of the local real estate market and not simply their Web site.

- **If you're a FSBO seller:** Should you be going the FSBO route to sell your house, you're going to have to get your house online yourself. Some online options include

  - **PowerSites' Agency Logic (www.agencylogic.com):** For just $50, you get your own domain name (for example, www.yourstreet address.com) and hosting for one year ($25 for each additional year). You can post up to 100 photos (make sure they're good), unlimited property descriptions, and links to useful information, such as neighborhood info, school info, and so on.

    Having a dedicated Web site address can also save you money on print ads that you place for your house in newspapers and magazines. You can run shorter ads and put your Web address in the print ad for folks wanting more information. Agency Logic submits your Web site to all the major search engines, and for a $25 additional cost, gets your property listing, including the virtual tour feature, onto Realtor.com (discussed in the last section in this chapter).

- **ForSaleByOwner.com (`forsalebyowner.com`):** Enter your state and county, and this site, which sports the slogan, "No Commission. Lots of Help," walks you through preparing your online house-for-sale advertisement. The cost is $89.95 per month with up to six pictures or a one-time fee of $199.00 with up to six pictures. This site, moreover, sometimes directs users to affiliated For Sale By Owner magazines specific to states and other areas around the country.

- **The International Real Estate Digest (IRED) (`www.ired.com`):** An online listing service, IRED's "For Sale by Owner" category has a lengthy list of local FSBO listing services, such as the Madison Area for Sale by Owner Web service (`www.fsbomadison.com`). These local services often offer better coverage of a specific area than the national services.

- **SaleByOwnerRealty.com (`www.salebyownerrealty.com`):** This site not only helps you get your house-for-sale listing online, but it also gets you into the realtors' MLS for six months for a basic fee of $399.

- **Other sites:** Also tap into the popular real estate listing Web sites such as `www.craigslist.org` and `http://base.google.com` as well your local newspapers' classified ads and Web sites.

To understand what FSBO ads can and can't do for you, check out the next section for more info.

Knowing the truth about for-sale-by-owner (FSBO) sites

If you're attempting to sell your house yourself, the Internet can be useful as a supplementary marketing tool. You can either create your own Web site or list your property through one of the online FSBO listing services. Although creating your own site allows you to go crazy and take full advantage of the Web's multimedia capabilities (you can post color photos of your property, include a floor plan, offer a video tour, and so forth), consider using a good FSBO listing service, instead. Building your own site takes a great deal of time and money . . . and (sorry to say) you'll probably get as much traffic as a small North Dakota town in January.

Most FSBO online sites charge FSBO sellers a modest fee to list houses for sale. At Owners.com (`www.owners.com`), for example, for $80, you can list your house for sale along with unlimited photos and property descriptions, customized yard sign with a toll-free answering service, and a video. It also takes no time at all: Spend a few minutes filling out a simple online form, click "Enter Listing," and *presto!* You've just posted a national online For Sale sign.

The success rate for sellers using online listing sites is spotty. The owners.com site, for example, doesn't report the actual success rate of its customers (they do provide some testimonials).

These types of Web sites have relatively few listings and — compared to the overall number of houses on the market — aren't going to attract much traffic. Pat Low's experience was typical among online FSBO listers we know. She listed her house on a FSBO site and had few online inquiries. "The more serious inquiries came through more traditional channels, such as newspaper ads, lawn signs, and open houses," she said.

Before parting with any of your hard-earned money at a Web site, be clear about *why* you're going online. Remember that the Internet is only one of many marketing tools and rarely gets a house sold (see Chapter 12 for effective marketing tools). Also remember that most FSBO Web sites get little traffic. Finally, recognize that by placing ads in larger local newspapers, you'll probably be getting your ad online because most newspaper classifieds appear online now as well as in print.

Realize the limits of valuing your house online

Numerous Web sites, such as www.getmyhomesvalue.com, www.home pages.com, www.realestateabc.com, www.trulia.com, and www.zil low.com, offer "tools" that purportedly help you value your house online. Simply enter your street address, these sites say, and you'll be told what your house is worth. Before you spend any money or submit any personal information, understand that these sites can only do so much for you and most of them aren't worth your time or money.

In fact, the worst of these sites are frauds. They are nothing more than referral sources for real estate agents looking for new listings. After providing your address, phone number and all sorts of other personal information, one such site sends you an e-mail that says the following:

> "Thank you for telling us about yourself and your real estate needs. You may soon get a phone call from a number you don't recognize, if you fall within our service areas . . . Because instant, online valuation can be off by as much as 10 to 20 percent (we're talking tens of thousands of dollars here), we'll put you in direct contact with one qualified local real estate professional who will give you the most accurate information you can get."

View negative commentary by agents skeptically

If you're looking for online tips for selling your house yourself, be aware that real estate agents overparticipate in the exchanges and message-board postings on this topic. Consider, for example, the experience of a house seller who was trying to sell her house on her own and posted the following question on a message board supposedly devoted to FSBO issues:

> "I've run an ad for a week . . . a real estate friend says not to let the house get stale by letting it run in the paper for more than a week. Can a house get stale in a week?"

She asks a good question worthy of enlightened discussion. But that's not what she got. What she got was an earful on why she should get an agent to sell her house. Among the numerous responses by real estate agents, she received the following postings:

> " . . . Many, maybe most, FSBO sellers walk away with less money than a Realtor could have gotten them — even after paying the commission . . . we do a lot of work to earn our commissions."

> "As a top agent with a major company, I must let you know that it is extremely difficult to sell as a FSBO. There is so much available housing. Most serious buyers are working with real estate agents. Unless your home is unique or is in a special area where there is little availability of housing, I would say that you need the resources of a top agent with a major company . . . ."

If you want information about selling a house yourself, don't expect to find it online, especially from the many agents who populate online message boards. As we discuss in Chapter 6, selling your house yourself is far from impossible, especially if you have real estate experience, a good head on your shoulders, and the proper team assembled to help you. Reading a good book on house selling, such as the one you have in your hands, is essential, too!

This commentary is quite revealing in two respects. First, it demonstrates the true agenda for how these "free" online pseudo-valuation services make money — through referrals to real estate agents. Second, by their own admission, their accuracy isn't good.

Whether you're using a real estate agent or trying to sell your house on your own, don't determine your house's asking price in this way! Such methods won't work because

✔ **Web sites lack important property details.** When you type in your house's address into valuation Web sites, most sites know little more about your property than what you paid for it (and sometimes not even that) and perhaps how many bedrooms and bathrooms it has. Most sites don't know about the improvements you've made to the property, current square footage, yard size, and myriad other factors that affect your house's value.

✔ **Valuation methods generally are simplistic.** Because house valuation Web site tools have so little data on your property, most sites superficially value your house. For example, knowing that you bought your house three years ago, many sites simply add a percentage increase that the average home in your larger metropolitan area has enjoyed during that time period. For the reasons cited in the previous bullet, at best you're getting only a general assessment of what your house may now be worth. Home values don't all rise (or fall) by the same percentage in various towns and neighborhoods in a given metropolitan area. The price changes that Web sites use often are 6 to 12 months old, which in a rapidly changing real estate market can lead to large valuation differences.

We're not saying that Web site house valuation tools are totally worthless. Some of these sites enable you to find out what various properties in your area are selling for — information that's even more valuable if you've actually toured the insides of those houses. But please don't use these sites to value your house.

Relying on Software and the Web to Determine Whether to Sell

Whether you're trading up to a more costly property or looking to downsize and you need to figure out whether to sell your house, you need to review your overall personal financial situation, especially your budget. You can rely on financial software and the Web to help make the decision.

Chapter 2 details how to analyze a proposed house sale in the context of your overall finances. If you enjoy harnessing the power of your computer instead of using the old-fashioned tools of paper, pencil, and calculator, you can use software programs such as Quicken or Microsoft Money to assist with your budgeting and expense tracking. (If calculators are already considered old-fashioned, what does that make us?)

If you need to crunch some numbers to see where you stand in saving for your retirement, good software can be a godsend. Check out Vanguard's Web site (www.vanguard.com), or T. Rowe Price's workbooklets, which can be obtained by calling (800) 638-5660 or by using their online tools at www.t roweprice.com.

Using the Internet to buy your next home

Although this book is about selling your house, you probably need a new place to live after you sell your property. If you're in the market to buy a home, in addition to the International Real Estate Directory (IRED) at www.ired.com, you can also look at the following sources:

✔ **The National Association of Realtors:** The National Association of Realtors has a major online site (www.realtor.com) that links regional MLS systems all across the country and gives public access to more than 3 million listings in hundreds of metropolitan areas.

If a community that you're interested in is covered by the National Association of Realtors' Web site, you may be overwhelmed by the thousands, perhaps even tens of thousands, of houses for sale in that particular area. Fortunately, the site includes a handy-dandy search engine for screening homes based on dozens of criteria (such as property type, numbers of bedrooms and bathrooms, square footage, and whether the property offers a laundry room, swimming pool, or ocean view). From the National Association of Realtors' home page, use the "Find a Home" section to get started.

The Realtors aren't surrendering all their valuable information, partly for security reasons (for example, the site provides zip codes only, addresses are rarely given out). The site also doesn't reveal commission rates on listed houses. That disclosure might show the public that commission rates are, in fact, negotiable.

✔ **Local newspaper electronic classifieds:** Increasing numbers of local newspapers are putting their wares online, especially their classified advertising. Using one of the Internet search engines mentioned earlier in this chapter, simply enter the name of the town you're interested in along with the words "real estate." For example, type Chicago and real estate if you're in the market for a home in the windy city. Such a search ferrets out real estate newspaper classifieds as well as other online real-estate-related sites covering that market. Alternatively, if you know the name of the local newspaper, try doing a search using the newspaper's name.

If you're searching for a home in a small town, your search may come up empty. If so, try entering the names of large cities or towns nearby that delightful small town you want to move to.

Be skeptical of home-buying advice you find on real estate Web sites, especially recommendations about the mortgage amount you can afford when you're in the market as a buyer. Most mortgage calculators simplistically use your overall income figure and the current loan interest rate to calculate the mortgage amount you can "afford." Such calculators are really spitting out the maximum a bank will lend you based on your income. This figure has nothing to do with the amount you can really afford. These calculators don't ask, for example, how you're doing on saving for retirement, or how many kids you have to put through college.

Chapter 14

Negotiating Strategies for Sellers

· ·

· ·

*B*argaining isn't part of this country's mass-marketing culture. You'd be laughed out of your friendly neighborhood McDonald's if you tried haggling with the counterperson over the price of your Big Mac. Americans don't generally dicker to drive prices down. Instead, they comparison shop on the Internet or drive from shopping center to shopping center to find lower prices.

Face it. Whether you're aware of it or not, all the ads that you read in newspapers, hear on the radio, and see on TV through the years eventually take their toll. With most consumer products other than cars, we've been conditioned for generations to docilely pay the sticker price. (As we discuss in Chapter 11, smart sellers know how to use this conditioning to their advantage when pricing houses.)

Like it or not, you must sit at the bargaining table if you offer your house for sale to the public. Even if you're not the haggling sort, you certainly don't want to sell your house for less than it's really worth. And you have every right to be cautious regarding the advice of real estate agents and others involved in your transaction who stand to profit from a quick sale.

Knowing your house's worth, covered in Chapter 10, isn't enough. You must also be a good negotiator to minimize the chances of being forced into accepting a crummy offer and to maximize the proceeds from your house's sale.

We can't offer you a magical, one-size-fits-all, guaranteed *best* negotiating strategy that you can use in every situation, because no such strategy exists. Smart sellers adjust their negotiating strategies to accommodate such factors as whether they're dealing from a position of strength or weakness, how well-priced their houses are, how motivated the buyers are, and, of course, how motivated they, themselves, are.

Negotiation doesn't have to be complicated. On the contrary, good negotiation is based on a few simple concepts. Apply the concepts in this chapter to your negotiations to maximize the chances of getting precisely what you want when you sell your house.

Mastering Your Feelings

Unless you're an unquenchable emotional vampire, the massive pulses of intense feelings radiating from both sides of the bargaining table will quickly drain your energy. House sales are usually emotional roller coasters for everyone involved. You probably still bear the emotional scars from the turmoil you endured as a homebuyer.

Now, as a house seller, you're about to sit on the other side of the table. If you don't get enough from the sale, you may not be able to buy your next dream home. Buyers may accuse you of being greedy if you try to sell your house for a great deal more than you paid for it. Conversely, buyers won't shed any tears if you lose money when you sell; it's not *their* fault the local economy went as soft as a jelly doughnut.

Consider the powerful emotions acting on you when you sell your house:

- **Big needs:** Food, security, and shelter are the three most basic necessities of life. Like two bears fighting for a single cave, you and the buyers will do verbal battle over a place to live.

- **Big egos:** The house you're about to sell is your castle. If buyers or their agents attempt to justify a low offering price for your house by citing its real and imagined flaws, your blood may boil.

- **Big money:** Whether this house is the first you sell or the last, the money you have in it probably represents one of your largest investments. The amount of money you receive when you sell isn't the issue. When major sums of real money are at stake, the emotional intensity for you and the buyer is just as great, no matter whether your house sells for $150,000 or $1.5 million.

- **Big changes:** Selling a house would be stressful enough if you had to deal only with the impact of needs, egos, and money. Throw in a major life change, such as job relocation, marriage, divorce, birth, death, or retirement, and the result is an emotional minefield.

Putting emotions in their place

Suppose that you've been trying for months, without success, to sell your house in a profoundly depressed real estate market. In your dreams, you find buyers who fall so blindly in love with the property that they simply must have it and eagerly offer to pay your modestly inflated asking price. You conveniently ignore the glaring reality that property values in your area have plummeted since you bought the house several years ago — a fact that ought to dash any hope of selling the property for the amount you paid for it.

Allowing such wishful thinking to seep into a negotiation can cost you dearly, but what choice do you have? Unless your heart is a lump of coal, how can you *not* get emotionally involved when you sell something that you love and that holds many dear memories (not to mention most of your hard-earned money)?

Because you can never eliminate emotions from the process of selling your house, the next best option is to understand and manage them. Your choice is simple: Either you control your emotions, or your emotions control you. People can't upset you unless you let them. Folks who do the best job of controlling their emotions usually end up getting the best deals.

To control your emotions, try using the following time-tested tactics:

- **Keep your sale in perspective.** Which would you rather have fail — your house sale or your open-heart surgery? No matter how bad circumstances are with the sale, keep reminding yourself that this isn't a life-or-death situation. Tomorrow *is* another day. The sun *will* rise again, tulips *will* bloom again, and children *will* laugh again. Life goes on. If worse comes to worst, the deal will die — but you'll survive to find another buyer.

- **Make time your ally.** Even if you *must* sell because of some momentous life change — such as getting married or divorced, having a baby, or retiring — you probably have advance notice before the big event occurs. Don't put yourself under needless pressure by procrastinating. Give yourself enough time to sell your house. Allocate time properly, and it will be your friend and not your enemy.

- **Maintain an emotional arm's length.** Be prepared to walk away from a sale if you and the buyer can't reach a satisfactory agreement on price and terms. Mentally condition yourself to the possibility that the deal may fall through; keep other options open. Buyers are like buses — if you miss one, another one comes along in a little while.

- **Get the facts.** Use a comparable market analysis (CMA) to factually establish the fair market value (FMV) of your house (see Chapter 10). A good real estate agent can help in this area. If you're like most people, having someone to buffer you from your unavoidable emotional involvement helps. Make sure that you work with patient, not pushy, professionals who are committed to getting you the best deal.

> ✔ **Accept the unknown.** You always have more questions than answers at the beginning of a deal. Don't worry; you'll be fine as long as you know what you need to find out (and guess what — this book tells you), and you get answers in a timely manner during your transaction.

Gaining detachment through an agent

Unlike you and the buyers, good real estate agents don't take things personally. For example, your agent won't be offended if the buyers say that they hate the red-flocked wallpaper that you feel adds "just the right touch" to your den. On the contrary, your agent simply points out to the prospective buyers that they can easily customize the den with new wallpaper of their choosing. The buyers' agent, by the same token, won't be upset if your agent says that the buyers' offer for your exquisite house is ridiculously low.

Objectivity is easier for agents. After all, they're not the ones who spent three months looking for appropriate wallpaper to put in the den. Nor are their life's savings on the negotiating table. Good agents listen to what the market says that a house is worth. If they don't, the property doesn't sell, and they don't get paid. Agents don't allow distracting details (such as how much time and money you spent fixing up the house or how little the buyers can afford to pay for it) to confuse negotiations. As Chapter 10 explains, these need-based issues have nothing to do with a house's FMV.

Following Some Basic Rules

If you take the right steps, you end up in the right place. Your deal can practically take care of itself if you follow these basic negotiating guidelines:

> ✔ **Conduct all negotiations eyeball-to-eyeball.** Never, not ever, no way, no how let your agent or lawyer "save time" by using the phone to present a counteroffer or to negotiate important issues. It's too easy for people to say "no" over the phone. Even if the buyers agree with everything you want during a phone conversation, they may change their minds when it's time to actually sign on the dotted line.

> ✔ **Get everything in writing.** Written contracts evolved from the muck and mire of legal quicksand because people have lousy memories. If you want your deal to be enforceable in a court of law, put all the terms in writing. Make a habit of writing short, *dated MFRs* (Memos For Record) of important conversations (such as, "June 2 — buyers' agent said that they'll have loan approval by Friday," "June 12 — buyers asked to extend close of escrow one week," and so on).

✔ **Make sure that deadlines are met.** Real estate contracts are filled with deadlines for everything from contingency removals and deposit increases to the ultimate deadline, your close of escrow. Failure to meet each and every deadline can have dreadful consequences. Your deal may fall apart — you may even end up in a lawsuit. However, most deadlines are remarkably flexible. They can usually be lengthened or shortened by negotiation if the need for revision is properly explained and handled promptly with adequate lead time.

Surviving the Bargaining Process

Negotiation is like an escalator — both are a series of steps without a neatly defined beginning or end. Each step in the negotiating process begins by gathering information. Our goal for this book is to help you understand the procedure for selling a house. Your job is to translate this information into action that generates more information, which, in turn, leads to further action. And so it goes, until you sell your house.

You generally start the negotiating process by gathering information about real estate agents to select one to represent you. Next, you decide on an asking price for your house by gathering data on sale prices and asking prices of comparable houses. As you conduct this field research, you also prepare your house for sale by sprucing it up inside and out and by gathering information on its physical condition. This preliminary work sets the stage for the next action step in the negotiating process.

Receiving an offer to purchase

After your house goes on the market, you're ready to begin the formal part of the negotiating process — receiving an offer to purchase. Unfortunately, no standard, universally accepted real estate purchase contract is used throughout the country. On the contrary, purchase contracts vary in length and terms from state to state and, within a state, from one locality to another. The contract you get reflects what, generally, the buyer's agent or lawyer considers to be appropriate for your area.

In Appendix A, we include the California Association of Realtors' *Real Estate Purchase Contract,* so you can see what a well-written, comprehensive residential real estate contract looks like. California's contract is, legally speaking, well-tested and considered to be at the forefront of real estate purchase agreements. That fact is no surprise when you consider that, according to the California State Bar Association, one out of seven lawyers in the United States practices law in California.

A carelessly worded, poorly thought-out offer can turn a potentially productive negotiation into an adversarial struggle. Instead of working together to solve your common problem (that is, "I want to sell; you want to buy. How can *we* each get what *we* want?"), you and the buyer get sidetracked by issues that can't be resolved so early in the negotiating process.

Although selling a house can be a highly emotional experience, good offers defuse this potentially explosive situation by replacing emotion with facts. Buyers and sellers have feelings that can be hurt. Facts don't. That's why facts are the foundation of successful negotiations.

When you evaluate the offers that you receive, check for the following characteristics, because a *good* offer

> ✔ **Is based on the market value of your house as established by the sale of comparable property:** Smart buyers don't pull offering prices out of thin air. Instead, they base their offering price on properties comparable to your house in age, size, condition, and location that have *sold* within the past six months. As Chapter 10 explains, many house sellers' asking prices are sheer fantasy. Sale prices of comparable houses are facts.

Agent-negotiating warning signs

In Chapter 7, we advise you to select a real estate agent who's, among other things, a master negotiator. The fact that your agent has good negotiating skills, however, is no guarantee that he always uses them properly.

Good negotiators avoid making moral judgments. As long as a buyer's position isn't illegal, it's neither fair nor unfair. It's just a negotiating position. Of course, agents are human. Sometimes, even the best agents *temporarily* lose their objectivity in the heat of battle. You know that objectivity is flying out the window when your agent gets red in the face and starts accusing the other side of being unfair.

If your agent snaps out of the funk quickly, no problem. If, on the other hand, your agent can't calm down, you've lost your emotional buffer. Agents who lose their professional detachment are incapable of negotiating well on your behalf.

No matter how satisfying it may be to go on an emotional rampage with your agent about a buyer's utter lack of good taste, market knowledge, and common sense, getting angry won't sell your house. If your agent doesn't maintain a level head, you can ask your agent's broker (see Chapter 7) to step in to negotiate for you, or you can get another agent.

As we caution in Chapter 10, if your agent "bought the listing" by overstating your house's value so you'd list the property with him, you'll belatedly discover your property's real worth. After it goes on the market, your agent will misuse his negotiating skill by trying to persuade *you* to cut the asking price instead of diligently negotiating with buyers and agents to accept your price. *If you're in this position, dump the agent who betrayed your trust and find a new agent who tells you the truth.*

✔ **Has realistic loan terms:** The buyers' proposed mortgage interest rate, loan origination fee, and time allowed to obtain financing (which we explain in the upcoming section, "Dealing with contingencies — necessary uncertainty") should be based on current lending conditions in your area. Ideally, the buyers are also preapproved for a mortgage, indicating that they're ready, willing, and financially able to purchase your house (see the nearby sidebar, "Loan prequalification versus preapproval").

✔ **Doesn't ask for a blank check:** Unless property defects are glaringly obvious, or you already have inspection reports on your property, neither you nor the buyers know whether the house needs corrective work when the offer is submitted. Under these circumstances, consider using property-inspection clauses (which we explain in the next section) that allow you and the buyer to reopen negotiations for any necessary corrective work *after* the buyers get their inspection reports.

If you agree with the price and terms of the buyer's offer, all you have to do to indicate your approval is sign the offer. Your John Hancock turns the offer into a *ratified contract* (that is, a signed or accepted offer).

However, signing an offer does *not* mean that you've sold your house. Because of the various contingencies contained in most contracts, ratified offers remain highly conditional until all contingencies are removed.

Dealing with contingencies — necessary uncertainty

Any offer you receive may contain some buyer escape clauses known as contingencies. A *contingency* gives buyers the right to pull out of the deal if some specific future event, such as getting a mortgage, fails to happen within a certain period of time.

Contingencies create uncertainty for you as a seller. The more contingencies buyers put into a contract, the more ways they have either to get out of the deal or to reopen negotiations for better terms. Most offers contain contingencies, unless you have mobs of people falling all over themselves to buy your house. The two most common contingencies are

✔ **Property inspection contingencies:** Your house's physical condition greatly affects its value. Smart purchasers insist on finding out *exactly* what shape your house is in *before* they buy it. If they don't approve the inspection reports or can't reach an agreement with you about handling corrective work for problems uncovered during the inspections, these contingencies let buyers bail out of transactions.

✔ **Financing contingencies:** The buyers can withdraw from the contract if the mortgage specified in their contract isn't approved. That provision is usually fine. If the buyers can't get the loan they need to buy your house, why go any further — unless you're willing to risk personally offering them financing, a topic we discuss in Chapter 4.

Here's a typical loan contingency:

"Conditioned [the magic word] upon buyer getting a 30-year, fixed-rate mortgage secured by the property in the amount of 80 percent of the purchase price. Said loan's interest rate shall not exceed 7.5 percent. Loan fees/points shall not exceed 2 percent of loan amount. If buyer can't obtain such financing within 30 days from acceptance of this offer, buyer must notify seller in writing of buyer's election to cancel this contract and have buyer's deposits returned."

If you want to see a more detailed financing contingency, read paragraph 2 of the California Association of Realtors' (C.A.R.) purchase contract in Appendix A. Read paragraphs 4.A, 7, 9, and 14 of the C.A.R. agreement to see how most common kinds of property inspections are handled contractually.

Other common contingencies give buyers the right to review and approve your property's title report and, if you're selling a condominium, the condo's master deed, bylaws, and budget. Buyers can make their contracts contingent on other *reasonable* events, such as having their lawyers review and approve the contracts or having their parents inspect the house.

What good, you may wonder, is a ratified offer riddled with escape clauses so big you can drive a truck through them? We're glad you asked.

✔ **From the buyers' viewpoint, a contingency-filled ratified offer still shows your intention to sell them the property.** The buyers don't have to worry that you'll sell the house to someone else while they're spending time and money inspecting it.

✔ **From your perspective, a contingency-filled ratified offer ties up the buyers.** If the buyers deposit *earnest money* (money given by a buyer to a seller to bind a contract) into escrow to prove that they aren't toying with your affections and then spend hundreds of dollars more for inspections, they're serious buyers. (By the way, there isn't a standard earnest money deposit. The actual dollar amount varies from area to area, depending on local custom and practice.)

Making a counter offer

Counter offer forms are far less complicated than purchase offer forms. Take a look at the California Association of Realtors' Counter Offer in Figure 14-1, for example; it's only a one-page form.

Figure 14-1: A typical counteroffer form.

CALIFORNIA ASSOCIATION OF REALTORS®

COUNTER OFFER No. ________

For use by Seller or Buyer. May be used for Multiple Counter Offer.

(C.A.R. Form CO, Revised 10/04)

Date ______________________, at ____, California.
This is a counter offer to the: ☐ California Residential Purchase Agreement, ☐ Counter Offer, or ☐ Other __________________ ("Offer"), dated ______________________, on property known as ______________________________________ ("Property"), between ______________________________ ("Buyer") and ______________________________ ("Seller").

1. **TERMS:** The terms and conditions of the above referenced document are **accepted subject to the following:**
   A. **Paragraphs in the Offer that require initials by all parties, but are not initialed by all parties, are excluded from the final agreement unless specifically referenced for inclusion in paragraph 1C of this or another Counter Offer.**
   B. **Unless otherwise agreed in writing, down payment and loan amount(s) will be adjusted in the same proportion as in the original Offer.**
   C. ____
   D. **The following attached supplements are incorporated into this Counter Offer:** ☐ Addendum No. __________ ☐ __________ ☐ __________
2. **RIGHT TO ACCEPT OTHER OFFERS:** Seller has the right to continue to offer the Property for sale or for other transaction, and to accept any other offer at any time prior to notification of acceptance, as described in paragraph 3. If this is a Seller Counter Offer, Seller's acceptance of another offer prior to Buyer's acceptance and communication of notification of this Counter Offer, shall revoke this Counter Offer.
3. **EXPIRATION:** This Counter Offer shall be deemed revoked and the deposits, if any, shall be returned unless this Counter Offer is signed by the Buyer or Seller to whom it is sent and a Copy of the signed Counter Offer is personally received by the person making this Counter Offer or ______________________________, who is authorized to receive it, by 5:00PM on the third Day After this Counter Offer is made or, (if checked) by ☐ ______________ (date), at _______ AM/PM. This Counter Offer may be executed in counterparts.
4. ☐ **(If checked:) MULTIPLE COUNTER OFFER:** Seller is making a Counter Offer(s) to another prospective buyer(s) on terms that may or may not be the same as in this Counter Offer. Acceptance of this Counter Offer by Buyer shall **not** be binding unless and until it is subsequently re-Signed by Seller in paragraph 7 below and a Copy of the Counter Offer Signed in paragraph 7 is personally received by Buyer or by ______________________, who is authorized to receive it, by 5:00 PM on the third Day after this Counter Offer is made or, (if checked) by ☐ __________ (date), at _______ AM/PM. Prior to the completion of all of these events, Buyer and Seller shall have no duties or obligations for the purchase or sale of the Property.
5. **OFFER: BUYER OR SELLER MAKES THIS COUNTER OFFER ON THE TERMS ABOVE AND ACKNOWLEDGES RECEIPT OF A COPY.**
   ______________________ Date __________
   ______________________ Date __________
6. **ACCEPTANCE: I/WE** accept the above Counter Offer **(If checked ☐ SUBJECT TO THE ATTACHED COUNTER OFFER)** and acknowledge receipt of a Copy.
   ______________________ Date __________ Time ______ AM/PM
   ______________________ Date __________ Time ______ AM/PM
7. **MULTIPLE COUNTER OFFER SIGNATURE LINE: By signing below, Seller accepts this Multiple Counter Offer. NOTE TO SELLER: Do NOT sign in this box until after Buyer signs in paragraph 6. (Paragraph 7 applies only if paragraph 4 is checked.)**
   ______________________ **Date** __________ **Time** _____ **AM/PM**
   ______________________ **Date** __________ **Time** _____ **AM/PM**
8. (_____/_____) (Initials) **Confirmation of Acceptance:** A Copy of Signed Acceptance was personally received by the maker of the Counter Offer, or that person's authorized agent as specified in paragraph 3 (or, if this is a Multiple Counter Offer, the Buyer or Buyer's authorized agent as specified in paragraph 4) on (date) ______________, at ________ AM/PM. **A binding Agreement is created when a Copy of Signed Acceptance is personally received by the the maker of the Counter Offer, or that person's authorized agent (or, if this is a Multiple Counter Offer, the Buyer or Buyer's authorized agent) whether or not confirmed in this document. Completion of this confirmation is not legally required in order to create a binding Agreement; it is solely intended to evidence the date that Confirmation of Acceptance has occurred.**

The copyright laws of the United States (Title 17 U.S. Code) forbid the unauthorized reproduction of this form, or any portion thereof, by photocopy machine or any other means, including facsimile or computerized formats. Copyright © 1986-2004, CALIFORNIA ASSOCIATION OF REALTORS®, INC. ALL RIGHTS RESERVED.

THIS FORM HAS BEEN APPROVED BY THE CALIFORNIA ASSOCIATION OF REALTORS® (C.A.R.). NO REPRESENTATION IS MADE AS TO THE LEGAL VALIDITY OR ADEQUACY OF ANY PROVISION IN ANY SPECIFIC TRANSACTION. A REAL ESTATE BROKER IS THE PERSON QUALIFIED TO ADVISE ON REAL ESTATE TRANSACTIONS. IF YOU DESIRE LEGAL OR TAX ADVICE, CONSULT AN APPROPRIATE PROFESSIONAL.

This form is available for use by the entire real estate industry. It is not intended to identify the user as a REALTOR®. REALTOR® is a registered collective membership mark which may be used only by members of the NATIONAL ASSOCIATION OF REALTORS® who subscribe to its Code of Ethics.

SURE TRAC The System for Success®
Published and Distributed by:
REAL ESTATE BUSINESS SERVICES, INC.
a subsidiary of the California Association of REALTORS®
525 South Virgil Avenue, Los Angeles, California 90020

Reviewed by _______ Date _______

EQUAL HOUSING OPPORTUNITY

CO REVISED 10/04 (PAGE 1 OF 1) Print Date

COUNTER OFFER (CO PAGE 1 OF 1)

Reprinted with permission, CALIFORNIA ASSOCIATION OF REALTORS™. Endorsement not implied.

Counter offers are short because you use them to fine-tune the terms and conditions of offers that you get from prospective buyers. If an offer contains unreasonable contingencies, use a counter offer to propose that the buyer remove them.

Loan prequalification versus preapproval

Smart buyers get a lender's opinion of their creditworthiness *before* making an offer to purchase. They establish creditworthiness by going through two processes:

✔ **Prequalification:** An informal discussion between a prospective borrower and a lender. The lender provides an opinion of the loan amount a buyer can borrow based solely on information the buyer tells the lender. The lender doesn't verify anything the buyer says, nor is the lender bound to make a loan when the buyer is ready to purchase.

✔ **Preapproval:** A far more rigorous process. Loan preapproval is based on independently documented and verified information regarding a buyer's likelihood of continued employment, income, liabilities, and cash available to purchase a home. The only thing a lender can't preapprove is the property itself because, of course, the buyer hasn't found it yet.

If your prospective purchasers have taken the trouble to get preapproval for a loan, you know that you're dealing with serious buyers. A lender's preapproval letter is *considerably* stronger than a prequalification letter. In a multiple-offer situation when several different buyers simultaneously submit competing offers on your house, give purchasers who are preapproved for a loan much more consideration than buyers who aren't *proven* creditworthy.

For example, paragraph 1.C of your counter offer may say, "Buyers hereby agree to delete paragraph 40 of their purchase contract regarding Aunt Jane, the astronaut, inspecting the house when she returns from her trip to the moon." After all, who knows how long her mission may be delayed in space? What if Aunt Jane falls in love with the man in the moon and never returns? That contingency is too spacey.

Or suppose that the buyers offer $175,000 for your house and want you to close escrow 30 days after accepting their offer. Because you're asking $189,500, you think that their offering price is a smidge low. Furthermore, you need six weeks to relocate.

If everything else in the buyers' offer is fine with you, don't rewrite the entire offer. Instead, give the buyers a counter offer stating that you'll accept all the terms and conditions *except* that you want $185,000 for your house, and you need six weeks after the offer is accepted to close escrow.

Wham. The ball's back in the buyers' court. They review your counter offer and decide a six-week close of escrow is okay, but they won't pay more than $182,500. They zap you a *counter counter offer* to that effect. You sign it to ratify the offer.

Define time frames with counter offers

Reread the typical loan contingency near the beginning of this section. Note that it states that the buyers have 30 days after the offer is accepted to get approval for a mortgage. If the prospective buyers can't get a loan within 30 days, you have the choice of either giving them a few more days to get financing or putting the house back on the market. Either way, *you're* in control of the situation.

Good contingencies always have precisely defined time frames within which buyers must complete a specified action or drop out of the contract. Never accept an open-ended contingency. For example, if buyers want their parents to inspect your house but don't specify *when* that inspection will take place, counter them with "parental visit shall take place not more than 3 days after offer is accepted." Be realistic but brisk when you set time frames. As a rule, the faster you close buyer escape hatches, the better. You don't want your house off the market any longer than is absolutely necessary.

Think twice before accepting an offer that's subject to the buyers selling their present house before buying yours. This is the ultimate open-ended contingency. It stigmatizes your house by driving away other prospective purchasers who can't put their lives on indefinite hold while they wait to see whether the buyers sell their house.

If you accept a "subject to sale of buyer's property" contingency, counter it with a release clause giving you the right to accept a better offer if one comes along. This provision is called a *72-hour clause* because sellers generally specify that they can cancel a deal 72 hours after notifying the buyers that they've gotten another offer.

Why 72 hours? If the new offer comes in on Friday night, 72 hours gets the buyers through the weekend to the next business day in case they need to consult someone who's only available weekdays during normal business hours.

Pick your battles selectively

A counter offer is like a stick of dynamite. If you're not careful, it can blow your fledgling deal to smithereens.

Making counter offers is a great idea if you have a hot property. However, suppose that you get your first offer six weeks, three days, and four hours (but who's counting?) after putting your house on the market. You don't have bunches of buyers banging on your front door to get your attention. You need to sell your house and get on with your life. Under these conditions, you can't afford to squander your one and only live prospect.

If this scenario hits a little too close to home, follow these tips:

- ✔ **Don't counter small stuff.** Suppose that the price and terms are okay but the buyers want to include your 10-year-old washer and dryer in the sale. You want to take the washer and dryer with you to your new home, but what the heck. If they're 10 years old, the washer and dryer aren't worth much now. And, if you leave them for the next owner, you won't have to pay to move them to your new home. You can always buy a *brand new* washer and dryer if the house sells. Buyers often act emotionally and *then* find reasons to justify their actions. If you accept the buyers' offer, they'll think how smart they were to have made it. Conversely, countering the offer may give them a reason to kill the deal and find a more "cooperative" seller.

- ✔ **Don't kill the messenger.** If the offering price is *way* below your price, don't reflexively counter at full asking price. You (and your agent, if you're using one) may have overpriced the house initially, or market conditions may have worsened since you put the property up for sale. As we discuss later in this chapter, a low offering price from a prospective buyer may accurately reflect your property's current market value. Reanalyze your house's FMV by examining up-to-date asking prices and sales of comparable properties. Don't blow away a realistic buyer with an unrealistic counter offer.

- ✔ **Stay focused on your goals.** Suppose that you want to move into a new school district before school starts. Although you don't want to *give* your house away, ask yourself whether delaying the sale is worth protracted haggling over who's going to pay for a couple of hundred dollars in repairs. Set your priorities and don't take your eyes off your goals.

Backup offers

If you suspect that the deal on your house may fall through, you are wise to protect yourself by obtaining a backup offer. One situation that screams for a backup offer is any contract that contains a "subject to sale of buyer's property" contingency. A backup offer also is advisable if your buyer is obviously struggling to qualify for a loan or if you and the buyer hit a brick wall on some negotiable provision of the contract (such as the way to handle corrective work for problems discovered during property inspections).

A good backup offer clearly states that you've already accepted another offer on your property.

It also stipulates that the backup offer won't take effect until you give the backup buyers formal written notice that your prior contract is canceled. In other words, the backup offer is contingent on the deal in first position falling through.

Motivated buyers generally don't stay in backup position very long. They keep looking at other property after signing your backup offer. If something better comes on the market while you've got them on hold, they're gone in a flash. Backup buyers can usually bail out of a backup offer anytime they want before you advise them that the offer in first position is dead.

Negotiating from a Position of Strength

Hope springs eternal. So do motivated buyers and their agents — good market or bad. They gush from one new listing to another in high hopes that the next house they see will be that elusive "perfect home" for which they've been searching.

Hope is the reason that most new listings get so many showings. Hope also explains why, in a strong real estate market, new listings that are "priced to sell" generate multiple offers. Knowing that they're in a multiple offer situation puts buyers under tremendous pressure, which is wonderful for you, the seller.

In a *sellers' market,* competition forces buyers to take their best shot right off the bat. When the supply of ready, willing, and financially able buyers exceeds the inventory of houses available for sale, smart buyers follow the advice Civil War General Nathan Bedford Forrest gave his troops before they went into battle: "Get there firstest with the mostest."

If you're a seller in a buyers' market, don't give up. Even in a weak market, well-priced, well-marketed, attractive new listings can and do draw multiple offers. If you follow our advice in Chapter 9 on preparing your house for sale, and you use the smart pricing techniques we describe in Chapter 11, you can create your very own sellers' market — even when everybody around you is experiencing a buyers' market.

Death and taxes are sure things; multiple offers aren't. Your property won't generate the kind of excitement that produces multiple offers unless it really shines and is priced to sell.

Handling multiple offers

In quiet markets, or when a house is overpriced, offers slowly dribble in one-by-one, and agents or buyers present them to sellers as soon as possible. That's the customary way to handle offers throughout this great land.

Buyers and their agents are naturally paranoid. They suspect sneaky, dishonest behavior if sellers do *anything* that's the least little bit out of the ordinary. Postponing the presentation of an offer is generally considered unusual.

Suppose that you need 24 hours to respond to any offer you get because you must have your lawyer review it. Unless you explain the reason for your delay to the buyers, they'll think that you want to shop their offer. *Shopping an offer* means showing the offer to every other prospective buyer you and your agent can find, in an attempt to get someone to make a higher offer.

Shopping an offer isn't illegal, but it *is* considered unethical. Buyers have every right to expect that their negotiations will be handled discreetly. They don't want the terms and conditions of their confidential offer blabbed to the world anymore than you want everyone to know all your innermost financial secrets. Reputable sellers like you *never* shop offers.

Unfortunately, other folks don't know you as well as we do. Smart buyers try to prevent you from shopping their offers by putting short fuses on them. In such cases, shades of *Mission Impossible,* their offers may contain a clause saying that the offer expires if you don't either accept or counter it immediately upon presentation.

In multiple-offer situations, presentations often are delayed. If you anticipate receiving multiple offers, develop a strategy for handling them *before* putting your house on the market. If you don't, you'll probably end up trying to calm down an angry mob of buyers and their agents waving offers with short fuses. Events can move quickly after you set in motion the marketing process that we describe in Chapters 12 and 13.

Delaying presentation of offers

Why make buyers or their agents wait to submit offers? You want to be sure that your property gets sufficient exposure to prospective buyers so that you can generate multiple offers. Nothing is illegal or unethical about this technique. The key to success is alerting buyers and agents *well in advance* about the precise time you'll start accepting offers and the way you'll handle those offers when they come in.

How do you notify buyers and agents that you're requiring a waiting period before considering offers? Simple. In the Comments section of the multiple listing write-up and on your property's listing statement, your agent can note the time when you'll allow offers to be presented. Just to be safe, also instruct your agent to tell everyone who calls about the property that you're delaying the presentation of offers.

Timing is critical. If your property's market exposure is too short, you may accept an offer before a reasonable number of prospective buyers find out that your house is on the market. Conversely, if you make people wait too long while you try to expose the property to every possible purchaser in the universe, some motivated buyers may show their displeasure by withdrawing their offers or never making one in the first place.

No time frame is perfect — long enough to expose the house to every potential purchaser, yet short enough to avoid losing even one buyer. Some buyers won't get the word because they're out of town on vacations or business trips when your house hits the market. Others won't make an offer if they can't present it immediately. Some people may refuse to get into a multiple-offer situation because they fear they'll overpay for your house if they get into a bidding war.

To establish the waiting period before allowing presentation of multiple offers, try one of these two methods:

- ✔ **Ask your agent or lawyer whether your area has a commonly accepted protocol for handling multiple offers.** You can't go wrong doing business the same way most everyone else does. Don't go against local custom and practice unless you delight in provoking suspicion.

- ✔ **If no standard protocol exists for your area, complete the initial marketing sequence we describe in Chapters 12 and 13 before starting the presentation process.** As you expose the property to agents, they then schedule showings for their clients who may be interested in your house. To reach buyers who aren't working with agents, delay presentations until your classified ad appears once in the local paper, and you've had one Sunday open house.

Setting guidelines for an orderly presentation process

Unless you set firm ground rules early on, the presentation of offers may resemble the Oklahoma land rush. To ensure that presentations are handled fairly for each and every prospective buyer (and productively for you), you or your agent (if you're using one) should tell interested parties that the following guidelines are in effect:

- ✔ **Offers will be presented in the order in which you or your agent was notified that offers were pending.** As buyers or their agents announce that they have an offer to present, put their names on a list. What could be fairer than first come, first served? No one can accuse you of playing favorites.

- ✔ **Neither you nor your agent will accept offers before the designated formal presentation period.** No one can accuse you of shopping offers if you don't have any offers to shop!

- ✔ **Buyers or their agents can personally present offers directly to you and your agent.** This rule reassures buyers and agents that offers will be presented in the best possible way without any filtering or shading. This approach is also good for you because you can question buyers or their agents directly while evaluating the pros and cons of each offer that you receive.

Some sellers review multiple offers without permitting agent presentations. This approach speeds up the process because it keeps sellers from having to listen to endless twaddle about how wonderful buyers are, how much they love the house, how long they've been looking, and so on, gag, choke. Unfortunately, this practice enrages the losers because they all *know* they'd have won if only their offer had been presented properly. Upsetting potential buyers isn't wise. You may need them later if the offer you initially accept falls through.

✔ **Tell prospective buyers in advance that you'll either accept or counter the best offer you receive.** Getting multiple offers doesn't guarantee that any of the offers will be more than full asking price. However, if you announce *in advance* that you won't counter every offer, smart buyers make the best offer they can right off the bat. They know you don't intend to give them a second chance if they submit a tire-kicking, "let's leave room to negotiate" type of offer.

Selecting the best offer

By applying the astute marketing techniques and crafty pricing strategy we describe elsewhere in this book, you earn the right to dictate favorable terms and conditions of sale for yourself if you have multiple offers on your hands. Buyers know that you have a hot property. The pressure is on them to please you. No reasonable request you make will be refused. Your wish is their command.

Whether you have three offers or 33 lying on the kitchen table, you face the same dilemma: selecting the *best* one. Price isn't the sole criteria. The highest offer is far from best if it's riddled with dubious escape clauses, totally out of synch with your time frames, or made by someone who's a week or two away from declaring bankruptcy. What good is a high offer from a buyer who can't or won't perform?

Pitting buyers against each other is a double-edged sword. On the plus side, a bidding war can catapult the ultimate sale price above your asking price. You may, however, make a major mess of things if you're not careful. You may scare off all the buyers by making absurdly high counter offers. Worse yet, you may convert multiple offers into multiple lawsuits by inadvertently ratifying more than one offer.

As a seller in a sellers' market, avoid snatching defeat from the jaws of victory and follow these tips:

✔ **Think like a lender.** In a strong sellers' market, spirited buyer competition often pushes prices to new heights. Lenders usually support higher prices when they reflect an overall market trend and when the mortgage isn't an excessively high percentage of the purchase price. You determine that percentage, called the *loan-to-value ratio,* by dividing the loan amount by the purchase price.

Remember: From a lender's perspective, the higher the loan-to-value ratio, the greater the risk that a buyer will default on the loan. So, as a rule, the lower the loan-to-value ratio, the better the chances of getting loan approval.

Suppose that you get two offers: One offer is $200,000 with a $150,000 (75 percent loan-to-value) loan contingency. The other is $205,000 with a $184,500 loan (90 percent loan-to-value). If the highest previous comparable sale in your area is $190,000, you're smart to either accept or counter the $200,000 offer, as long as other terms and conditions of the two offers are about the same.

✔ **Don't issue more than one counter offer at a time.** When faced with multiple offers, you have four options — accept one, counter one, counter more than one, or reject all offers. If you counter several offers, you may inadvertently end up in contract to sell your house to more than one buyer. This dreadful situation is known as *double ratification.* The resulting debacle will devastate you financially and emotionally. The one sure way to avoid this dreadful scenario is to follow this rule.

If for some unfathomable, self-destructive reason you ignore our sage advice and issue multiple counter offers simultaneously, at least try to protect yourself from double ratification by using a clause similar to paragraph 4 of the C.A.R. Counter Offer shown in Figure 13-1. Be sure to specify that your counter offer must be resigned by you before it's fully ratified as noted in paragraph 7 of C.A.R.'s Counter Offer.

✔ **Qualify buyers carefully.** Commit the last section of this chapter (the one about real versus fake buyers) to memory. If you have a poor memory, put a bookmark in that section and keep this book by your side while evaluating prospective buyers. When you question agents about their buyers, scrutinize each purchaser's creditworthiness, motivation to purchase, and deadline for when the transaction *must* be complete.

If you have *any* doubts about buyers' financial qualifications, get their permission to contact the lenders directly to resolve your questions before accepting or countering their offers. A buyer who's been *preapproved* for a loan by a reputable lender has a *Good Borrower Seal of Approval* — as long as the mortgage that buyer needs to buy your house *doesn't exceed* the preapproved loan amount.

✔ **Pay as much attention to terms and conditions as you do price.** Sometimes, a lower price beats a higher one. For example, when you evaluate offers, seek terms that fatten your bottom line. If a buyer offers to purchase your house "as is," you won't have to worry about paying for corrective work or reducing your sale price because of a bad inspection report. If you need a quick sale, the best buyer is the one who can close fastest. Then again, the best buyer may be the one who'll let you rent your house back after the sale if you need a place to stay until the close of escrow on your new home. *Remember:* Price isn't everything if you have other, more compelling needs.

✔ **Avoid conflicts of interest resulting from dual agency.** *Dual agency* occurs when the same agent or real estate broker represents buyer and seller. If your listing agent also represents one of the people making an offer to buy your house, that agent has a conflict of interest, plain and simple. How can "your" agent get you the highest possible price and simultaneously help a buyer get the lowest possible price? Can "your" agent give you unbiased advice as you evaluate the other offers you receive? Read Chapter 7 for more information.

Most real estate firms have procedures to handle dual agency. If your listing agent also develops a buyer, the agent's sales manager or broker usually steps in to represent you during the presentation and evaluation of offers. This approach frees your agent to work with the buyer during this phase of the deal. However, if your listing agent is a sole practitioner, you may be wise to get a real estate lawyer or another outside expert to assist you.

Negotiating from a Position of Weakness

The opposite of multiple offers is no offers. Zero. Zip. None.

An absolute absence of offers may be caused by a horrendous real estate market plagued by a sagging economy, poor consumer confidence, and high mortgage rates. Like it or not, a divorce, job transfer, or some other major life change may compel you to sell in a rotten market. If it's any consolation, you'll probably recover the amount you lose as a seller by paying a proportionately lower price for your new home — unless you compound your misfortune by moving from a weak real estate market to a strong one.

However, suppose that the economy is booming, consumers are wildly optimistic, and houses around you sell faster than you can say, "We're outta here!" If you have a problem getting offers in such fertile ground, bunkie, something is seriously wrong either with your property or your asking price. Review Chapter 9 to make sure that you've done everything possible to spruce up your house, and Chapter 11 in case you inadvertently overpriced your property.

When either your price or property is flawed or your local market is stagnant, you may attract strange buyers bearing odd offers. The following sections offer tips to help you make the best of whatever comes your way.

Rejecting lowball offers

A *lowball* offer is one that's far below a property's true FMV. For example, if someone offers you $150,000 for your house when recent comparable sales data show that it's worth every penny of $300,000, that's a lowball offer.

Lowball offers are typically made by unmotivated buyers trying to get a deal, by sharks who hope that you're desperate and willing to negotiate, or by buyers who think that your property is overpriced. Serious, informed buyers know the difference between well-priced properties and overpriced turkeys. (See Chapter 10 for a brush-up on methods to determine your house's FMV.)

Dealing with lowball offers

Suppose that you just put your house up for sale. You priced it as close as humanly possible to its FMV. Two days after your house hits the market, you get an offer. Trembling with excitement, you open it. You don't read any further than the absurdly low purchase price.

Either the buyers haven't done their homework regarding comparable home sales, or they think that you don't know your house's real value and they're trying to exploit your ignorance, or they're trying to steal your house. As a seller, you can handle people who lowball your well-priced house in one of two ways:

- ✔ **Let the buyers know that their offer is totally unacceptable by having your agent return the offer unsigned.** Why waste time making a counteroffer to people who are either idiots or scoundrels?

- ✔ **Make a full-price counter offer.** Show your contempt by hardballing the buyers on each and every term and condition in their offer. Two can play this self-destructive game. If they waste your time, you waste theirs. (Although emotionally satisfying, this response is *lose-lose negotiating,* and we don't recommend this approach.)

People who lowball a well-priced property destroy any chance of developing the mutual trust and sense of fair play on which cooperative negotiation is based. Real buyers know the difference between an offering price that gives them room to negotiate and a preposterous lowball offer.

Recognizing lowball offers that aren't

An enormous difference exists between submitting an offer at the low end of a house's FMV and lowballing. For example, suppose that someone offers $240,000 for your house, which is listed at $249,500.

You based the asking price on the fact that comparable houses in your neighborhood recently sold in the $240,000 to $249,500 price range. You naturally opted to start at the high end of the range of FMVs. The buyer just as naturally began at the low end. Even though you and the buyer are $9,500 apart, each of you has a factual basis for your initial negotiating position.

As long as an offer is based on *actual* sales of *comparable* houses, it isn't insulting. The $9,500 gap sparks a lively debate as you and the buyer try to defend your respective prices. A buyer who comes in on the low side of a property's value is fine, as long as you have time to negotiate, and you believe that the buyer is motivated.

When you and a buyer come in on opposite ends of the fair market price range, the best defense is a good offense. You're most likely to prevail in the pricing debate if you have an encyclopedic CMA and your agent is a strong negotiator who's *personally* eyeballed all the comps. Follow our guidelines in Chapter 10.

Sometimes, a lowball offer is, in fact, a reality check. The offer isn't a lowball offer if it accurately reflects current market values. Ironically, some sellers provoke low offers by unwise pricing. These sellers insist on leaving *way* too much room for negotiation in their prices because they "know" that buyers never pay full asking price. Sound familiar?

Unfortunately, this practice becomes a self-fulfilling prophecy. When buyers who know property values make an offer on a grossly overpriced house, their initial offering price appears to be much lower than it really is. What goes around, comes around.

For example, suppose that your house's FMV is $200,000. You put it on the market at $240,000 to give yourself a 20-percent negotiating cushion. A buyer offers you $160,000 for the exact same reason. You and the buyer start out $80,000 apart. You must do a heap of negotiating to bridge a gap that enormous.

Real buyers don't play this game. They make an offer at the low end of your house's FMV and see how you respond. If you refuse to accept facts about recent comparable sales in your neighborhood, real buyers don't waste time trying to educate you. Instead, they take the path of least resistance and move on to find a real seller. If you keep receiving lowball offers, you probably have too much room to negotiate in your asking price.

Another possibility is that your asking price was close to FMV when you initially put the property on the market. However, in a weak market, prices keep declining. If your house has been for sale for months and the only offer you've gotten appears to be a lowball, have your agent review all recent *sale* prices of comparable houses before rejecting the offer. If prices are dropping like boulders, that "lowball" offer may be worth pursuing.

Considering other offers usually made in weak markets

When mortgage money is cheap and plentiful, deals are straightforward and simple. Buyers make cash down payments and get loans for the balance of the purchase price. Sellers use the proceeds from their sales to buy new homes.

However, when mortgage interest rates soared to more than 18 percent in the early 1980s, house sales activity plummeted. Buyers and sellers did some pretty unconventional maneuvering to transfer properties. Desperate times produce desperate measures.

When times get tough, unconventional purchasing techniques breed like bunnies. These next two offers don't come from *The Godfather.* If you need to sell your house pronto, you can (and should) refuse them. But, under certain circumstances, the offers in the next two sections may make sense for you.

Lease-options

A *lease-option* is exactly what the name implies: a rental agreement to *lease* your house but with an *option* to buy the house in the future. Lease-option offers are triggered by high mortgage rates or are made by folks who have good incomes but haven't managed to save enough cash yet to make a down payment.

If you must sell your house *quickly* to get the cash you need to buy a new home, read no further. A lease-option is too iffy. The house may or may not sell sometime during the lease's term, depending on whether the renter elects to exercise the option to purchase.

 Sometimes, however, a lease-option is the smart way to go. For example, suppose that high mortgage rates or a sluggish local real estate market make selling your house tough. If you don't need to sell right away and you must move soon, doing a lease-option helps you cover the house's monthly ownership expenses until mortgage rates or the local market improves enough for you to sell.

A lease-option is actually two contracts rolled into one. Here's how it works:

- ✔ **Lease:** The lease differs from a standard rental contract in several ways. First of all, the lease has an option giving the renter a right to purchase your house anytime during the lease's term. Second, the renter pays you a one-time fee called *consideration* in addition to the usual first and last month's rent plus security deposit. You get the consideration in return for providing an option to purchase. If the renter exercises the option, the consideration is credited toward the renter's down payment. Last, but not least, some of the rent usually is applied toward the down payment.

- ✔ **Purchase contract:** Attached to the lease is a contract that specifies the price and terms of sale if the renter opts to exercise the option to purchase. What's tricky about the purchase agreement is figuring out a purchase price that's fair for you *and* the buyer six months or a year down the road when the buyer may exercise the option.

A lease-option is more complex than a regular sale because in addition to negotiating the future purchase's price and terms, you also have to negotiate the following:

- ✔ **Option consideration:** No standard fee exists for option consideration. This fee is *totally* negotiable based on the amount you're willing to accept and the renter is willing to pay for an option to purchase your house.

- ✔ **Rent:** The house's rental value is usually easy to establish. If you and your agent don't know rental values, get help from an agent who specializes in rentals.

- ✔ **Amount of rent applied toward the down payment:** A lease-option's rent usually is higher than the market rental value of a house because lease-option rent also is used as a forced savings plan.

For example, suppose that your house's normal rental value is $750 a month, and the renter agrees to pay you a $5,000 consideration for the option to purchase. Your lease-option contract stipulates that the buyer pays a $1,000-per-month rent, $300 of which goes toward a down payment. If the renter exercises the option after 10 months, you credit the renter $8,000 ($5,000 option consideration plus $300 a month for 10 months) toward the down payment. However, if the renter allows the option to lapse without exercising it, you keep the option consideration money and all the rent money.

Before you agree to a lease-option contract, consider the reason that the renter is willing to leave $8,000 on the table by failing to exercise the option. Maybe mortgage rates remain high and the renter can't qualify for the loan needed to buy your house. Perhaps the renter can't save enough additional cash for the down payment. Or, perchance, property values have plummeted, and your house isn't worth the amount the renter would have to pay for it if the option is exercised. Under those circumstances, walking away from $8,000 is cheaper than paying what, with 20/20 hindsight, turns out to be a grossly inflated purchase price for your house.

Determining your house's value in six months, a year, or whenever the renter exercises the option is the trickiest part of the deal. House prices go down — *and up.* If property values skyrocket during the term of the lease, your house may end up being worth much more than the amount you'd receive under the terms of your lease-option contract. Unforeseen fluctuations in property value make lease-options tricky for sellers as well as buyers.

The longer the term of the option, the greater the risk of dramatic swings in property value.

Nothing down

Creative financing was born of dire necessity in the early 1980s, when interest rates were pushed to all-time highs by the Federal Reserve Board in an effort to stifle raging inflation. When mortgage rates hit 18 percent, only people who weren't borrowing much in relation to their incomes could qualify for conventional financing.

Ordinary mortals glued deals together by assuming the existing, lower-interest-rate loans on properties and using seller financing to bridge any gap between their down payments plus assumed loan amounts and the purchase prices. We cover seller financing in Chapter 4, if you're interested (pun intended).

The Frankenstein monster of creative financing is selling property to buyers who don't pay one red cent of down payment. Unfortunately, the nothing-down advocates didn't all go out of business when interest rates dropped back to normal. Some of these hucksters still peddle their seminars and how-to books to desperate buyers and vultures eager to learn new ways to fleece suckers.

Making nothing-down deals with unscrupulous, deadbeat "buyers" means they may live in your house rent-free for months while thumbing their noses at you as you go through the expensive, time-consuming foreclosure process. If well-intentioned but overextended nothing-down buyers fail to make their loan payments or pay the property taxes, you'll also be forced to foreclose. Buyers who have no financial stake in a property can walk away from it whenever they please and stick *you* with the mess. Nothing-down deals don't have an upside; they're financial suicide for sellers. *Do not, under any circumstances, get into a nothing-down deal!*

As we discuss in Chapter 4, you may consider helping to finance the sale of your property. But get a decent down payment from the buyer, in addition to checking him or her out thoroughly.

Negotiating credits in escrow

In a *really* rotten market, even putting a "let's sell it" price on your house may not be enough incentive to get the property sold. You may have to sweeten the deal by offering a buyer money in the form of seller-paid financial concessions. The two most common financial concessions are for nonrecurring closing costs and corrective work.

Nonrecurring closing costs

Nonrecurring closing costs are one-time charges that a buyer incurs for such expenses as the loan appraisal, loan points, credit report, title insurance, and property inspections. This amount can be major money. Closing costs can total 3 percent to 5 percent of the purchase price.

Some sellers come right out and tell buyers that they'll pay a portion or even all the nonrecurring closing costs to put a deal together. And, believe it or not, sometimes paying a buyer's nonrecurring closing costs is more effective than reducing your asking price by the exact same amount of money.

Even if you don't offer to pay their nonrecurring closing costs, some buyers may ask for this concession as one of the terms in their offers. Getting this request is highly unlikely in a sellers' market or if you're in a multiple-offer situation.

A credit to the buyer for nonrecurring closing costs works like this. Suppose that you recently ratified a contract to sell your house for $250,000. Your prospective buyer has $57,000 in cash for the purchase — enough, the buyer thought, to make a 20-percent down payment $50,000) plus $7,000 to cover the closing costs.

Much to the buyer's horror, the escrow officer says the nonrecurring closing costs total $10,000. Because only $7,000 was allocated for these fees, the buyer is $3,000 short of the total needed to buy your house.

About now, you may wonder, "What's the big deal? Why not just reduce the purchase price to $247,000 instead of giving the buyer a $3,000 credit?" After all, your net proceeds of sale are the same either way, and reducing the purchase price is much less complicated. Furthermore, if property taxes in your area are based on a percentage of the purchase price, lowering the purchase price cuts the buyers' annual tax bite.

Surprise. Assuming that your buyer is short of cash (as most buyers are) and has no rich relatives or pals to tap for a loan, a credit is *much* better for the buyer than a price reduction. Here's why.

Suppose that that you drop the house's price to $247,000. A 20-percent down payment at the new price comes to $49,400. But if closing costs are $10,000, the buyer has only $47,000 left for the down payment. Even with a $3,000 price reduction, the buyer is $2,400 short of the amount needed for a 20-percent down payment.

If the buyer puts less than 20 percent down, the monthly loan costs significantly increase because the buyer must pay a higher interest rate on the mortgage plus private mortgage insurance costs. Under these circumstances, prudent buyers may decide to kill the deal and buy a less-expensive house.

Contrast the price-reduction scenario with one where the buyer pays $250,000 for the house and gets a $3,000 credit from you at closing for the nonrecurring closing costs. After putting 20 percent $50,000) cash down to get the lowest interest rate loan, the buyer uses the remaining $7,000 plus your $3,000 credit to pay closing costs. Your credit makes the deal happen.

As an alternative to paying closing costs for your buyer, ask the buyer to check with the mortgage lender to see whether the lender will cut or eliminate the loan origination fee (points) if the buyer agrees to pay a slightly higher interest rate. This approach may reduce the buyer's total closing costs enough to eliminate the need for a credit from you for nonrecurring closing costs.

In many communities, the lower the purchase price is, the lower the annual property taxes are. For that reason, buyers with plenty of cash go for a price reduction instead of a credit. Some agents, however, may lobby for a credit because cutting the price also cuts their commissions. That kind of thinking is bad for your bottom line.

Corrective work

Typically, at the time the buyer submits an offer, neither you nor the buyer knows whether your property needs any corrective work. That uncertainty is why contracts usually have provisions for additional negotiations regarding credits for repairs *after* the necessary inspections are complete.

If property inspectors find that the property requires little or no corrective work, you and the buyer have little or nothing to negotiate. However, the inspectors may discover that your $200,000 house needs $20,000 of corrective work for termite and dry-rot damage plus major foundation repairs. *Big corrective work bills can be deal killers.*

Seeing is believing. We recommend that your agent (or you, if you're selling the property by yourself) be present during every property inspection so that you get firsthand reports about any damage that the inspector discovers. The buyer should also give you copies of any and all inspection reports for your review before you meet with them to negotiate a corrective work credit.

This is the moment of truth in most house sales. Buyers don't want to pay for corrective work; neither do sellers. Your deal will fall through if you and the buyer can't resolve this impasse.

Pricing your house is one time when knowing everything about comparable houses that have sold in your area is critically important. Determining who pays for corrective work is the other time when you *must* know comparable sales data. If you heed our advice in Chapter 7 and hire an agent who knows neighborhood property values, your agent can forcefully present facts regarding the physical condition and terms of sale of other, supposedly comparable, properties during corrective work negotiations with the buyer and his or her agent.

For example, suppose that your agent's property analysis establishes, beyond any shadow of a doubt, that houses comparable to yours with no termite or dry-rot damage and foundations that make the Rock of Gibraltar look like mush are selling for $200,000. Because your house needs $20,000 of corrective work, it's worth only $180,000 in its present condition.

At this point in the negotiations, it's critically important that you accept the fact that your house's value has just been slashed by the cost required to repair it. Don't go into denial. You must face the facts. ***Remember:*** Good negotiators are realistic.

You have other options for resolving the impasse. For example, you can refuse to pay for repairs found by the *buyer's* inspectors. You have the right to question the impartiality of the buyer's inspectors and the validity of inspection reports for which the buyer paid. If these issues concern you, consider getting your own inspections to refute those of the buyer. Realize, however, that a good inspection will probably set you back several hundred dollars, and your inspectors may end up verifying the buyer's inspector's results or, worse yet, discovering additional corrective work.

As a last resort, you can threaten to pull out of the deal if the buyer doesn't back off on the demands. In a strong market, this strategy may work. However, sellers who kill the messenger often regret their decisions. Buyers don't bring the damage with them, and, unfortunately for you, buyers won't take the damage with them when you kick them out of the deal. Like it or not, you're stuck with the damage.

As we point out in Chapter 8, even if you drive away buyers who discover damage to your house, you still may have a legal obligation to tell other buyers everything that you learn about the required corrective work. Any such disclosure will probably lower the price that a future buyer offers for your house. All things considered, working things out with the buyer who uncovers the damage is certainly much faster and probably no more expensive than waiting for another buyer.

Lenders also participate in corrective work problems. They get copies of inspection reports if borrowers tell them that a serious repair problem exists, if their appraisal indicates property obviously needs major repairs, or if the contract contains a credit for extensive repairs.

You can solve repair problems in a variety of ways:

- ✔ **Ideally, you leave money for repairs in escrow and instruct the escrow officer to pay contractors as they complete the work.** This approach offers several advantages. You avoid the dust and disruption of having work done while you're still living in the house. Plus, you don't incur liability for the workmanship. Let the buyer supervise the repairs to be sure that the work is done properly by contractors that *the buyer* chooses. Last, but not least, the lender knows that the property will be restored to pristine condition, which enhances its loan value.

- ✔ **Alternatively, the lender withholds a portion of the full loan amount in an interest-bearing savings account until the corrective work is complete.** In cases involving major corrective work, the lender may refuse to fund the entire loan amount until the problems are corrected.

- ✔ **You credit the buyers directly for corrective work at the close of escrow.** Lenders usually don't approve of this approach, because it raises uncertainties about whether the corrective work will actually be completed. If it isn't, the security of the lender's loan is impaired.

Join with your buyer in obtaining competitive bids on the repair work from several reputable licensed contractors. Use bids to establish the amount of the corrective work credit. This approach doesn't bother good buyers. They don't want to get rich from your misfortune. All they want is what they thought they were buying in the first place — a well-maintained house without termite or dry-rot problems and with a good foundation.

Distinguishing Real Buyers from Fakes

Fake buyers don't lie in wait like tigers itching to dig their claws into you for the thrill of killing your deal. The very thought that people would knowingly waste their time and money on an exercise in futility is ludicrous.

The key word is *knowingly*. All buyers start out thinking that they're sincere. As their quest for a house continues, however, circumstances ultimately prove that some are phony.

Fake buyers usually mimic genuine buyers very cleverly (so cleverly, in fact, they often fool themselves for quite some time). Like real buyers, counterfeit buyers may have agents, read ads about houses for sale, and go to Sunday open houses. They outwardly appear to be the real McCoy. If you (and your listing agent, if you're using one) don't know how to detect fake buyers, you end up wasting time, energy, and money fruitlessly negotiating to sell your house to less-than-genuine prospects.

Identifying bogus buyers is easy if you know how. The following sections include five tests that you can use to spot the fakes.

Are the buyers creditworthy?

Real buyers are ready, willing, and financially able to purchase. Having two out of three of these attributes isn't good enough. When so-called buyers don't satisfy all three criteria, they're phonies, regardless of whether they realize it. Genuine buyers want you to know that they're creditworthy. That's why they're willing to share important aspects of their financial situation at the time they present you with their offers, and perhaps even get preapproved or prequalified for a loan. In a strong local real estate market, smart, serious buyers seek preapproval or prequalification before making an offer.

People who make the offer to purchase your house subject to selling their present homes (which they haven't yet put on the market) are fakes — don't dignify their pseudo-offer with a response.

Are the buyers realistic?

Real buyers familiarize themselves with property values and market conditions *before* making an offer to purchase. They, and their agents, use sale prices of houses comparable to yours in price, age, size, condition, and location to establish the FMV of your house. They know the difference between fairly priced properties and overpriced turkeys.

Real buyers may offer less than your asking price because they expect to negotiate prices and terms of sale. However, legitimate buyers who are willing to pay you the amount your house is worth don't make a ludicrously low offer on your house if it's priced to sell. Genuine buyers understand the concept of FMV.

Are the buyers motivated?

People don't buy houses to generate commissions for real estate agents. Buyers often are motivated by a life change, such as wedding bells, a job transfer, family expansion, retirement, or a death in the family.

Lack of motivation almost always is a red flag. Establish the buyers' motivation when you receive an offer. When buyers tell you that they're just testing the market, run as fast as you can in the opposite direction.

Do the buyers have a time frame?

Buyer deadlines are established by such factors as when they have to begin new jobs in another city, when the twins are due, when school starts, when the escrow is due to close on the house that they're selling, and so on. Bona fide buyers almost always have a time frame within which they must act.

Time is a powerful negotiating tool. If you're under pressure to sell because you just got a promotion that forces you to move to another state next month and the buyer doesn't have a deadline to purchase, time is your enemy and the buyer's pal. Conversely, if the buyer sold a house in June, and desperately needs to settle into a new home before school starts in September, the watch is on the other wrist. Ideally, you know the buyer's deadline, but the buyer doesn't know yours. Most real negotiation occurs near the very end of a deadline.

If the buyer doesn't have a deadline, but discovers that you have one, the buyer can use your deadline to beat you to a pulp. Watch out for buyer procrastination. Don't let time bully you — and keep your deadlines to yourself.

Are the buyers cooperative?

Real buyers look for ways to make deals go smoothly. They work with you to solve problems instead of creating problems and finding excuses to make the transaction more difficult. Genuine buyers have a let's-make-it-happen attitude. They're deal makers, not deal breakers.

Inconsistent behavior is a red flag. When buyers suddenly start missing contract deadlines or become strangely uncooperative, they may have lost their motivation. Perhaps the blushing bride-to-be decided to call the wedding off, or the "sure-thing" promotion wasn't so certain. Whatever. People can and do switch from being real buyers to fakes in mid-transaction. Find out why buyers are acting strangely as soon as you notice changes, and you may be able to head off the problem. If you ignore danger signs, you'll never know what hit you if the sale blows up in your face.

Chapter 15

It Ain't Over 'til the Check Clears

In This Chapter

▶ Discovering the ins and outs of escrows

▶ Saying goodbye to your house

▶ Coping with seller's and buyer's remorse

*A*fter sprucing up the old place, sorting through hordes of prospects to find the most ready, willing, and able buyer, and haggling over price and terms, you finally signed a contract for the sale of your house. Are your troubles over? Have you sold your house at last? Nope. You've only *ratified* (signed) an offer. You can't start packing your bags yet. You have a lot of work to do before the sale is a done deal. This chapter can help.

Entering the Neutral Territory of an Escrow

You may be delighted to know that escrow has nothing to do with snails. *Escrow* refers to the holding of important documents and money related to the sale of your house.

After the offer is ratified, you need someone you can trust to hold the stakes while you and the buyer take care of unresolved contract details, such as arranging property inspections and getting financing for the purchase. On the first business day after you and the buyer sign the contract, either you or the buyer (or your agent or the buyer's agent, if agents are involved) open an escrow. This process happens by delivering all the funds and documents related to your sale to a neutral third party — the *escrow holder* (also called an *escrow officer*).

In accordance with instructions from you and the buyer, the escrow officer keeps these funds and documents in an escrow file created especially for your transaction. Depending on real estate practices in your area, your escrow may be handled by a lawyer, a firm that specializes in doing escrows, or a title company. Sellers and buyers usually select an escrow holder based on their agents' recommendations.

Based on your house's sale price, escrow fees can run from a couple of hundred dollars to several thousand dollars. Brokerage customs where the property is located usually dictate whether you or the buyer pay for the escrow, or you split the fee 50/50 with the buyer. Regardless of custom or practice, responsibility for the payment of escrow fees is a negotiable item. In a strong seller's market, for example, buyers may offer to pay for the escrow to sweeten their offers, even though local custom decrees that buyers and sellers usually split escrow costs.

Understanding the role of the escrow officer

Even though you went through the escrow process when you bought your house, you may not remember much about it. After a few years, the whole experience probably seems like nothing more than a big, expensive blur. But even if you purchased your house just last year, going through escrow is much different from the perspective of a seller. Rather than putting money into escrow to obtain title to the property, you're getting money out of escrow in return for relinquishing your ownership by transferring legal title to the new owner.

The escrow officer handles the nitty-gritty paperwork details so you can concentrate on the deal. To that end, here are some highlights from your escrow officer's to-do list:

✔ **Order a title search from the title company:** Soon after the escrow is opened, you and the buyers get copies of a preliminary report *(prelim)* showing who legally owns the property. The prelim also contains a list of items (such as loans secured by the property or public utility company easements to run power lines over the property) that affect the title or limit use of your property.

Look over the preliminary report carefully. Ask your agent, escrow officer, title company representative, or lawyer to explain *anything* in the report that you don't understand. Don't be shy — there's no such thing as a dumb question.

✔ **Request payoff information:** If you have a mortgage, home equity loan, or other liens on the property, your escrow officer contacts the lenders to get your current loan balances and instructions for paying off the various loans at close of escrow.

Defining encumbrances

Encumbrances are another person's or institution's rights to or interests in your property. Encumbrances either place limits on the use of your property or affect its legal title. Two kinds of encumbrances are possible — money and nonmoney.

Money encumbrances, called *liens,* use property as security for repayment of a debt. For example, when you obtained a mortgage to buy your house, you gave the lender the right to foreclose on your property if you failed to pay back the loan. Your lender made the lien a matter of public record by recording a document containing the lien information in your local County Recorder's office. Property tax liens, state and federal income tax liens, and court-imposed judgments or attachments are other examples of money encumbrances.

One type of nonmoney encumbrance is an easement. You've probably given an easement to your local public utility to string power lines over your land and another easement to the city to run water or sewer lines through your property. Condominium covenants, conditions, and restrictions (CC&Rs) are another example of nonmoney encumbrances.

Buyers have the right to review and approve the preliminary report. If your buyer *reasonably* objects to certain items shown on the prelim, the escrow officer works with you to remove the offending encumbrances prior to close of escrow. If you can't clear them from the property, your deal may fall through.

For example, asking you to pay off all debts secured by liens and judgments against the property is reasonable. If, however, you're selling a condo, asking you to remove the CC&Rs on your condo is unreasonable because CC&Rs are an integral part of the property. Should you have questions regarding the reasonableness of a request to remove an encumbrance, get a legal opinion on the issue from your attorney.

✔ **Prepare and record documents:** The escrow officer draws up a grant deed that you sign to formally transfer legal title to the buyer. The deed is recorded when escrow closes.

An escrow officer's job is to receive and follow your instructions. Be sure to instruct your escrow officer *not* to give the buyer the title to your property until you're completely satisfied that all terms and conditions of the contract are fulfilled.

✔ **Hold and disburse funds:** Easy come, easy go. At close of escrow, the escrow officer uses funds the buyers and their lender put into escrow to make payments required to close the escrow, such as paying off your old loans.

If you don't have a Social Security number and your property's gross sale price exceeds $300,000, your escrow officer may have to withhold up to 10 percent of the gross sale price to comply with the Foreign Investment In Real Property Tax Act (FIRPTA). This act is an IRS code requirement pertaining to potential capital gains tax liability. See a tax advisor if you need more details.

✔ **Prepare estimated and final closing statements:** These documents provide an accounting of all the money that comes into and goes out of your escrow.

Maximizing your escrow

If you want to eliminate escrow problems before they occur, call or visit your escrow officer as soon as possible to introduce yourself. See if the escrow officer needs any information from you to make the escrow go faster and smoother. In addition to finding out how to contact you during the day, the escrow officer may need the following:

✔ **A Statement of Information:** If you have a common name (such as Adams, Brown, Chan, Davis, Garcia, Jones, Lee, Miller, Nguyen, Smith, or Williams), you must complete a Statement of Information. Many title problems are caused by people with names similar (or identical) to yours. A Statement of Information helps to distinguish you from the scores of other folks with common names like yours.

What information is requested in a Statement of Information? You (and your spouse if you're married) must provide your full name, Social Security number, exact date of birth, birthplace, date and place of marriage (if applicable), previous marriages (if applicable), residence and employment information, and so on. Whatever is necessary to prove precisely who you are — and who you *aren't.*

✔ **Bills and documents:** You can speed up the information gathering process by giving your escrow officer copies of your most recent mortgage statement, property tax bill, and, if you're a condo or co-op owner, copies of the current homeowners' association dues and assessments.

Getting an estimated closing statement

During your initial contact with the escrow officer, request an estimated closing statement based strictly on your known closing costs at that time and assuming the escrow closes as scheduled. This statement obviously won't be precise. Factors such as whether you'll have to give the buyers a credit for repairs, and if so, how much, have yet to be determined. No matter. At least you have an approximation of your expenses of sale, and that helps you develop a rough idea about the amount of money you may have to spend on your next home.

Get the estimated closing statement updated a week before scheduled close of escrow. At that point, very few questions should remain. You're basically waiting for the clock to tick out. Check your second estimated closing statement extremely carefully, line by line from top to bottom, to be *absolutely certain* that it accurately reflects your credits and debits.

Escrow officers are human. They sometimes make mistakes. So do other parties in the transaction who may inadvertently give the escrow officer incorrect information. And when mistakes are found, whose favor do you think they are in? Probably not yours! *Your* money is on the table. Pay attention to details. Review the closing statement and question anything that isn't clear or correct.

Summing up your final closing statement

You may think that the most valuable piece of paper that you get when escrow closes is your check for the proceeds of sale. From an accounting standpoint, however, the most precious piece of paper is the final closing statement. If you think of the escrow as a checking account, the final closing statement is your checkbook. It records all the money related to your transaction either as credits or debits.

Any money that you receive in escrow is shown as a credit to your account. You won't have many credits; the biggie is always your credit for the amount of the sale price. You may get a credit from the buyers for the unused portion of property taxes that you prepaid. You get a check outside of escrow from your insurance company for any unused portion of your homeowners insurance premium. By the same token, if your lender collects extra money from you each month that goes into an impound account used to pay your property taxes and homeowners insurance premiums, any excess funds in the impound account are paid directly to you by the lender after the sale closes.

Debits are funds paid out of escrow on your behalf. Your biggest debit, as noted in Chapter 3, is usually the mortgage payoff. Other major closing costs listed as debits are the real estate commission, local transfer taxes, any corrective work credits that you give the buyer, and, depending on the date the sale closes, a credit to the buyer for your share of unpaid property taxes. The list also includes an assortment of small charges for notary fees, recording fees, document preparation fees, messenger fees, and so on.

The final closing statement is extremely important. Be sure to keep a copy for your files; you may need to refer to it when you prepare your income tax return. As Chapter 16 explains, some expenses of sale, such as the real estate commission, mortgage prepayment penalties, and property tax payments, are tax deductible. Furthermore, you may owe capital gains tax on a portion of your profit from selling the property.

Resolving disputes

Good escrow officers are worth their weight in gold in times of crisis when the shouting, tears, and threats of lawsuits begin. At moments like this, often only their incredible patience and crisis-mediation skills keep deals glued together. With luck, your escrow will be as smooth as silk from inception to close. But if an escrow officer gets conflicting instructions from the seller and the buyer, the escrow slams to a screeching halt until the parties resolve the problem.

What kind of conflicting instructions are possible? The conflict usually is a dispute between the seller and the buyer about whether some item of personal property (such as a refrigerator, fireplace screen, mirror, or light fixture) is included in the sale. Another classic point of contention is whether corrective work should be done before or after close of escrow.

A wise real estate attorney, Kip Oxman, has a saying that works miracles in dispute resolution situations: "When all else fails, RTC." You can find the answer to most disagreements if you *Read The Contract.* The real estate purchase contract included in Appendix A is an example of an extremely explicit contract intended to eliminate the ambiguity that creates disputes.

Avoiding the curse of December escrows

Escrows are perverse creatures under the best of circumstances. They're proof positive of Murphy's Law, which states that whatever can go wrong will — and *always* at the worst possible time. Experienced escrow officers are all too aware that nasty surprises can and often do rear their ugly heads whenever you least expect them.

What kind of surprises? The list is unpleasantly long — missed deadlines, title glitches, problems paying off existing loans, changes in the buyer's loan terms, insufficient funds to close escrow, and the like.

December escrows are notoriously perverse. Holiday partying saps people's strength and reduces their effectiveness. Folks forget to sign papers before going on vacation, and December 31 is an absolute deadline if you must close this year for tax purposes.

If you end up with a December escrow, make sure that you meet your deadline by following these tips:

✔ **Stay in touch with your escrow officer.** Don't let your file get buried in a pile of pending escrows on the corner of your escrow officer's desk. You or your agent should check with the escrow officer every few days to make sure that everything is going smoothly.

✔ **Order loan demands as soon as possible.** You must pay off any of your existing loans that are secured by the property before the buyer can have a new mortgage put on the property. Instruct your escrow officer to order payoff statements on all your existing loans *immediately.*

Lack of receipt of loan payoff statements is the single biggest cause of escrow delays.

✔ **If you're leaving town for the holidays, tell your agent and escrow officer well in advance of your departure.** Special arrangements can usually be made to close your escrow — no matter where you are — if people have advance warning and know how to reach you. The key to success is keeping everyone informed.

✔ **Check the calendar.** Many offices stay open only until noon on Christmas Eve and New Year's Eve. When Christmas and New Year's Day fall on Saturday or Sunday, office hours get extra crazy. Some businesses and public offices close the preceding Friday, others close the following Monday, and still others close Friday and Monday to give their employees a four-day holiday. Be sure to check the holiday office schedule of your agent, escrow officer, and other important people in your transaction. Don't let a holiday office-closing derail your deal.

✔ **Allow time between the date you want to close and the date you *must* close.** Give yourself maneuvering room to resolve last-minute problems that *inevitably* appear when you least expect them. Don't schedule your closing on the last business day of the year. You'll have no margin for error if you need to close by year's end.

Some deals fall through needlessly. These escrows could've been saved by applying a basic principle of winning golf — follow-through. Golf pros know that there's more to the game than simply making contact with the ball. Pros continue their swing "through the ball" after they hit it because they know that the last part of the stroke is as important as initial contact with the ball. If they don't follow through, the ball won't end up where they want it to go.

Your house isn't sold until your escrow closes. Follow-through is equally important in real estate deals. Buyers, sellers, and agents often carelessly say that a house has been *sold* as soon as the purchase contract is signed. That kind of foggy thinking can sink your transaction. You and the buyers have only ratified an offer at that point.

Letting Go of Your House

The day escrow closes is legally confusing. You still own your house when the day begins at 12:01 a.m., but you aren't the owner of record when the day ends at midnight. Sometime during the day, the escrow officer notifies the buyer that the deed has been recorded, officially announces that the buyer is now the proud owner of your house, and, of course, gives you the money you're owed from the sale proceeds. Your sale is a done deal. Congrats!

But in all the excitement, don't forget that you have to bid adieu to your house. This section helps you do that.

Moving daze

If you're one of the fortunate few, moving day won't be a problem because the place you're moving into will be vacated long before your escrow is scheduled to close. Lucky you. Life is sweet.

Moving day is considerably more treacherous if, like most sellers, you're involved in a daisy chain of concurrent transactions — selling your old house and *simultaneously* buying a new home from people who are also buying a new home for themselves, and so on like an endless hall of mirrors. In that case, your move's timing is just a tad less complex than the D-Day landings in Normandy during World War II. You may find yourself living on the street if you give up possession of the house you're selling before you can move into your next home. Don't worry. Millions of folks have coordinated sell-buy moves without a hitch. The secrets of success are *lead time* and *planning*.

The date the buyer actually takes possession of and moves into your house depends on the terms of your contract. Look at paragraph 3 of the sample purchase contract in Appendix A to see an example of a "Closing and Occupancy" clause that's used to specify date and time of possession and delivery of keys from seller to buyer. The next sections cover the usual options.

Buyer moves in the same day escrow closes

Same day move-in is fine if you're absolutely, utterly, positively, beyond-a-shadow-of-a-doubt certain of two factors:

- The escrow has closed on the house that you're selling.
- Your next home is vacant so you can move right into it — if you intend to move directly from your old house into the new home you're buying.

If the closing of your escrow is delayed or the seller of the house that you're buying can't vacate the place, you have a logistical problem. For two moving vans to occupy exactly the same driveway at exactly the same time borders on the impossible. Moving into a house while someone else is moving out is something you'll *never* attempt more than once. There are easier ways to go crazy.

If you can't move into your new home until the sellers vacate it, you must track three escrows: the escrow of the house you're selling, the escrow of the home you're buying, *and* the escrow of the new home for the people whose house you're buying. You need as much advance warning as possible from the sellers of your new home if they run into problems that can possibly delay the close of escrow on your new home. With adequate lead time, you can adjust the close of escrow on the house you're selling accordingly.

Buyer moves in the day after escrow closes

We recommend that the buyer move in the day after escrow closes because you can be certain that escrow closed. After all, you're still the owner until the title transfers. Moving day is stressful, even under the best of circumstances. Why create unnecessary stress for yourself by trying to move out while the buyer moves in? The sellers of your new home may use the day your mutual escrow closes to move out and then you can move in the following day.

Regardless of whether you move out of your house the day that escrow closes or the following day, make cancellation of your homeowners insurance, utilities, and phone service effective one day *after* your scheduled close of escrow and move. Carefully coordinate canceling your homeowners insurance policy with your insurance agent to avoid any gaps in your coverage.

Buyer moves in after a seller rent-back

Sellers sometimes stay in their houses several weeks after escrow closes while waiting to get into their new home. If this situation happens to you, you sign a separate rent-back agreement that becomes part of your purchase contract with the buyer. The rent-back agreement covers who pays for utilities and maintenance, what happens if property damage occurs after escrow closes, how much rent you must pay the buyers, and what penalties result if you don't vacate the house by the date specified in your agreement.

Sellers customarily pay rent equal to the amount the buyers must pay for *Principal and Interest* on their mortgage plus property *Taxes and Insurance,* so they break even on the cost of owning the house during the term of your rental. *PITI,* as this sum is known, is prorated on a per-day basis from close of escrow until you vacate the property.

For example, suppose that PITI is $50 per day, and you expect to be out three weeks after escrow closes. You and the buyer instruct the escrow officer to hold four weeks PITI in escrow so each of you has a cushion if you encounter an additional delay moving into your new home. When you move, you and the buyer jointly instruct the escrow officer to pay the buyer $50 per day for the actual rental period and to refund the unused portion of PITI funds held in escrow to you.

Don't let the buyers do any work on your house or, worse yet, move into the house prior to close of escrow. If you vacate your house prior to the close, the buyers may ask your permission to start fixing the house up before close of escrow. After all, painting or waxing floors, for example, is much easier and faster if the house is empty. Don't do it! The buyers may poke around and find a molehill that they turn into a mountain of trouble for you. If the deal falls through, you may get your house back in terrible condition. If the house catches fire, your insurance may not cover the losses. No matter how piteously they plead, be firm.

The final verification of condition

A smart buyer inspects the property a few days (ideally the day) before escrow closes. Why? To be sure that your property still is in the same general condition that it was in when the buyer signed the contract to buy it. That's why most residential real estate contracts contain a clause similar to Paragraph 15 of the C.A.R. purchase contract in Appendix A — the "Final Verification of Condition" clause.

If the buyer discovers that your living room picture window fractured during your going-away party, a giant sinkhole suddenly appeared last week in the middle of your driveway, and 200 fresh gopher holes emerged in what was a flawless carpet of velvety grass only yesterday, the buyer can instruct the escrow officer to stop the escrow until the problems are resolved. If you and the buyer can't work out a mutually satisfactory solution, the dispute can kill the deal.

Be sure to maintain your property inside and out until escrow closes and you move into your new dream home. Make sure that the movers don't damage the property when removing your belongings. Unless you and the buyer make other arrangements, your property should be left broom clean, which means to remove all garbage, trash, and litter, and then vacuum the carpets and sweep the floors.

Surviving Seller's Remorse or (Gasp) the Double Whammy

Most house sellers and homebuyers suffer, to greater or lesser degrees, the ravages of a peculiarly debilitating distress during their transactions and for up to six months after their deals close. This masochistic form of self-reproach has a name. Depending on which side of the contract you happen to be on, it's either called *seller's remorse* or *buyer's remorse*.

Seller's remorse is a stupendously strong conviction on your part that you're about to sell your house for way less than it's really worth. The fact that your sale price established a new high for the neighborhood is secondary to your perception that you're giving your house away. When you're in the cruel grip of seller's remorse, facts take a back seat to perceptions.

Don't feel like the Lone Ranger. You're not alone. The buyers of your house probably have an equally strong conviction that they're paying you *way* more than your house is worth. Their doubts began when they signed the purchase contract. Factually speaking, your house could be well worth every cent they're paying. That doesn't matter. Once again, the only thing that counts is their perception that they're overpaying.

If you're selling your old house and at the same time buying a new home, you are most likely being devastated by the dreaded *double whammy* — simultaneous buyer's and seller's remorse. In the worst-case remorse scenario, you suspect that you're getting financially creamed when you sell *and* when you purchase.

All too often these concerns are ignored or ridiculed by agents, friends, and family. You're patted on the head and told, "Don't worry. Everyone goes through this. Tough it out. Take two aspirin and get a good night's sleep. You'll be fine tomorrow." Not true. Unless you get remorse out in the open, it can tear you and your deals apart.

Confronting your fears

The first step in your recovery program is seeing seller's or buyer's remorse for what it is — plain, unadulterated fear. As a seller, you fear that you undervalued your property. As a buyer, you fear that you overpaid.

By scrutinizing these hidden fears in the bright light of day, you can counter them with facts. Maybe you *did* undervalue your house. Perhaps you *are* overpaying for your new dream home. Instead of just wringing your hands and gnashing your teeth until you worry yourself sick, get the facts about fair market value (see Chapter 10).

A seller's fear (giving the house away) is the flip side of a buyer's fear (overpaying). For that reason, sellers and buyers end up doing the same things to squelch their fears and factually establish the fair market value of the property they're selling or buying. Regardless of whether you're zapped by seller's remorse or buyer's remorse, after signing the contract you can

✔ **Discuss your deal with friends, neighbors, business associates, and folks standing in front of you in the checkout line at the supermarket.** You ask anyone and everyone you can grab if they think that you're getting a good deal. This exercise is only good for venting your fears.

Precisely 99.9999 percent of the people that you talk to won't have the faintest idea about fair market value of the property in question.

✔ **Read classified ads in the real estate section of your newspaper even more intently than you did before you signed the contract.** As a seller, you circle all the ads for houses that aren't as nice as yours that have higher asking prices. As a buyer, you circle ads for houses that sound similar to or nicer than the one you're buying but that have lower asking prices.

Keep in mind as you brood over real estate ads that most houses don't sell for the asking price. Conversely, most houses read much better than they eyeball when you tour them.

✔ **Spend Saturday and Sunday touring open houses.** The streets are filled with remorseful buyers looking for better deals and remorseful sellers searching for less-nice properties with higher asking prices. Seeing, after all, *is believing.* Touring property is the best way to determine whether your fears are valid (which is highly unlikely if you follow the advice in this book) or groundless.

Facing the ultimate test

The faster you get your fears out in the open and confront them with facts, the less you suffer. Accept the fact that property can have more than one correct price. Pricing and negotiation are arts, not precise sciences. If you have the time, energy, and skill to search long enough and negotiate hard enough, you *may* find a buyer who'll pay a *little* more for the house you're selling or, conversely, a seller who's willing to accept a *slightly* lower price for the next home that you purchase.

Don't beat yourself up with *asking* prices. Asking prices are fantasies that remind us of an old saying: "If pigs had wings, they could fly." You don't see many flocks of pigs in the sky, do you?

Sale prices are facts. You can sleep soundly if the price you received as a seller or the price you paid as a buyer is in line with the *sale* prices of comparable properties.

Knowledge is power. If you follow the principles we cover in this book, you have nothing to fear. Your knowledge makes you extremely powerful. Get on with your life and remember — your home is an excellent *long-term* investment.

Chapter 16

Income Tax Filings after the Sale

*Y*ou've successfully sold your old house and moved into your new dream home. "At last," you think to yourself, "I can get on with my life and stop spending so much of my leisure time on housing decisions, transactions, and paperwork."

If the idea sounds too good to be true, it is. Unfortunately, the Internal Revenue Service (IRS) and most state tax agencies may want to know all about the sale of your house because you may owe income tax on profits that you receive from the sale. This chapter helps you square away any tax-related issues you may encounter when selling your house.

Profits from a House Sale

If you sell your house for a profit, you can legally avoid paying income tax on that profit as long as you meet certain requirements. Wanna know how? Check out this section.

Defining profits

Most people sell their houses for more money than they originally paid to purchase them. The difference between the price you pay to buy a home and the amount you receive when you sell it is generated by some combination of two factors:

- ✔ Increases in value that have nothing to do with you (the rising tide of real estate prices)

- ✔ Improvements that you put into the place

Fortunately, the IRS only defines the first factor as potentially taxable *profit*.

Suppose that you buy a house for $225,000 and sell it ten years later for $325,000. While you owned the place, you spent $20,000 remodeling the kitchen and bathroom. According to the IRS, your profit on the sale is $80,000.

Later in the chapter, we get into more of the nitty-gritty details about all the items that the IRS requires you to consider in calculating your house sale profits.

Excluding house sale profits from tax

So, you've made a profit of $80,000 on the sale of your home (from the preceding section). How much federal income tax do you owe on it? Probably none.

In fact, thanks to the Taxpayer Relief Act passed in 1997, single taxpayers can realize up to $250,000 and married couples up to $500,000 of profit on a house sale without having to pay any federal income tax on it. Most people's house sale profits fit well under these limits.

As long as the house that you're selling has been your principal residence for at least two of the previous five years, you can take the tax exclusion at any age and for as many times in your life as you want (but not more than once every two years). There are no restrictions on what you must do with the profits; you can trade up, trade down, dump it all in the stock market, stuff it all under the mattress . . . it's up to you.

The old rules were much more restrictive: Before, if you were under age 55, you couldn't exclude any gain from federal income taxation; you could only *defer* it by purchasing a replacement residence that cost at least as much as the one you sold. If you were older than 55, you could take an exclusion, but it was only for $125,000 and only a once-in-a-lifetime deal.

Here are some other important rules and insights regarding this terrific tax break:

✔ For a married couple to qualify for the $500,000 exclusion, both spouses must individually meet the qualifications. That is, each spouse must have lived in the house for two of the previous five years, and *neither* spouse can have taken an exclusion on another house sale during the previous two years. If only one spouse qualifies, then the couple is allowed only a $250,000 exclusion.

✔ If you fail to meet the two-year requirements because of an unexpected move relating to your job, your health, and so on, you're still entitled to a prorated amount of the exclusion based on how much time of the two-year requirement you were able to meet. For example, if you're forced to sell after only one year and you meet the other requirements of this tax break, you're entitled to 50 percent of the capital gains exclusion ($125,000 for a single person and $250,000 for a married couple filing jointly).

✔ How you hold title to the property affects your capital gain when the owner dies. If you hold title to your house as a joint tenant with another person, you get a *stepped-up basis* for tax purposes on half of the property when the other joint tenant dies. If the title to the house is held as community property, both halves of the house get a stepped-up basis when one spouse dies. See the glossary and a good tax/legal advisor for more details.

Tax Filings Required after the Sale

After you sell your house, you don't need to immediately report the sale to the IRS. Rest assured, however, that the IRS knows of the sale because the firm that handles the closing (typically an escrow company) reports the financial details of the sale on Form 1099-S, *Proceeds From Real Estate Transaction* (see Figure 16-1), if required. You should receive a copy of this form, as well. Form 1099-S must be filed to report the sale of real estate unless the sale price is less than or equal to $250,000 ($500,000 or less for married couples) and all the sellers provide written certification that the full gain on the sale isn't subject to taxation.

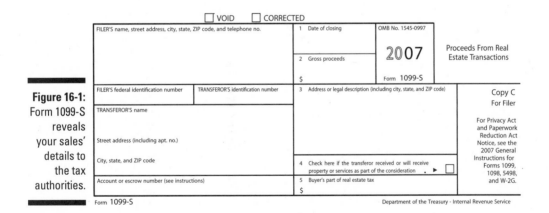

Figure 16-1:
Form 1099-S reveals your sales' details to the tax authorities.

Schedule D: Capital Gains and Losses

When the time comes to file your annual IRS Form 1040, you may need to complete *Schedule D: Capital Gains and Losses* (see Figure 16-2) if you sold your house. Use Schedule D to report to the IRS that you've sold your house and determine if you owe federal income tax on the profit.

SCHEDULE D	**Capital Gains and Losses**		OMB No. 1545-0074
(Form 1040)			**2006**
Department of the Treasury	▶ Attach to Form 1040 or Form 1040NR. ▶ See Instructions for Schedule D (Form 1040).		
Internal Revenue Service (99)	▶ Use Schedule D-1 to list additional transactions for lines 1 and 8.		Attachment Sequence No. **12**
Name(s) shown on return			Your social security number

Part I   **Short-Term Capital Gains and Losses—Assets Held One Year or Less**

(a) Description of property (Example: 100 sh. XYZ Co.)	(b) Date acquired (Mo., day, yr.)	(c) Date sold (Mo., day, yr.)	(d) Sales price (see page D-6 of the instructions)	(e) Cost or other basis (see page D-7 of the instructions)	(f) Gain or (loss) Subtract (e) from (d)
1					

2 Enter your short-term totals, if any, from Schedule D-1, line 2	**2**		
3 **Total short-term sales price amounts.** Add lines 1 and 2 in column (d)	**3**		
4 Short-term gain from Form 6252 and short-term gain or (loss) from Forms 4684, 6781, and 8824		**4**	
5 Net short-term gain or (loss) from partnerships, S corporations, estates, and trusts from Schedule(s) K-1		**5**	
6 Short-term capital loss carryover. Enter the amount, if any, from line 10 of your **Capital Loss Carryover Worksheet** on page D-7 of the instructions		**6** (	)
7 **Net short-term capital gain or (loss).** Combine lines 1 through 6 in column (f)		**7**	

Part II   **Long-Term Capital Gains and Losses—Assets Held More Than One Year**

(a) Description of property (Example: 100 sh. XYZ Co.)	(b) Date acquired (Mo., day, yr.)	(c) Date sold (Mo., day, yr.)	(d) Sales price (see page D-6 of the instructions)	(e) Cost or other basis (see page D-7 of the instructions)	(f) Gain or (loss) Subtract (e) from (d)
8					

9 Enter your long-term totals, if any, from Schedule D-1, line 9	**9**		
10 **Total long-term sales price amounts.** Add lines 8 and 9 in column (d)	**10**		
11 Gain from Form 4797, Part I; long-term gain from Forms 2439 and 6252; and long-term gain or (loss) from Forms 4684, 6781, and 8824		**11**	
12 Net long-term gain or (loss) from partnerships, S corporations, estates, and trusts from Schedule(s) K-1		**12**	
13 Capital gain distributions. See page D-2 of the instructions		**13**	
14 Long-term capital loss carryover. Enter the amount, if any, from line 15 of your **Capital Loss Carryover Worksheet** on page D-7 of the instructions		**14** (	)
15 **Net long-term capital gain or (loss).** Combine lines 8 through 14 in column (f). Then go to Part III on the back		**15**	

Figure 16-2a: The Schedule D: Capital Gains and Losses Form.

For Paperwork Reduction Act Notice, see Form 1040 or Form 1040NR instructions.   Cat. No. 11338H   Schedule D (Form 1040) 2006

Schedule D (Form 1040) 2006   Page **2**

Part III   **Summary**

16	Combine lines 7 and 15 and enter the result. If line 16 is a loss, skip lines 17 through 20, and go to line 21. If a gain, enter the gain on Form 1040, line 13, or Form 1040NR, line 14. Then go to line 17 below	**16**
17	Are lines 15 and 16 **both** gains? ☐ **Yes.** Go to line 18. ☐ **No.** Skip lines 18 through 21, and go to line 22.	
18	Enter the amount, if any, from line 7 of the **28% Rate Gain Worksheet** on page D-8 of the instructions . . . . ▶	**18**
19	Enter the amount, if any, from line 18 of the **Unrecaptured Section 1250 Gain Worksheet** on page D-9 of the instructions . . . . ▶	**19**
20	Are lines 18 and 19 **both** zero or blank? ☐ **Yes.** Complete Form 1040 through line 43, or Form 1040NR through line 40. Then complete the **Qualified Dividends and Capital Gain Tax Worksheet** on page 38 of the Instructions for Form 1040 (or in the Instructions for Form 1040NR). **Do not** complete lines 21 and 22 below. ☐ **No.** Complete Form 1040 through line 43, or Form 1040NR through line 40. Then complete the **Schedule D Tax Worksheet** on page D-10 of the instructions. **Do not** complete lines 21 and 22 below.	
21	If line 16 is a loss, enter here and on Form 1040, line 13, or Form 1040NR, line 14, the **smaller** of: • The loss on line 16 or • ($3,000), or if married filing separately, ($1,500) } . . . . **Note.** When figuring which amount is smaller, treat both amounts as positive numbers.	**21** ( )
22	Do you have qualified dividends on Form 1040, line 9b, or Form 1040NR, line 10b? ☐ **Yes.** Complete Form 1040 through line 43, or Form 1040NR through line 40. Then complete the **Qualified Dividends and Capital Gain Tax Worksheet** on page 38 of the Instructions for Form 1040 (or in the Instructions for Form 1040NR). ☐ **No.** Complete the rest of Form 1040 or Form 1040NR.	

Schedule D (Form 1040) 2006

Figure 16-2b: The Schedule D: Capital Gains and Losses Form continued.

After you've calculated your profit on the sale, figuring out how much, if any, of that gain is taxable is quite simple, thanks to the capital gains rules for all houses selling after May 6, 1997. As long as the property has been used and owned as the sellers' principal residence for at least two of the five years before the sale, married couples are allowed to exclude up to $500,000 of profits from tax and single taxpayers up to $250,000. If your profits are less than your allowable exclusion, you owe no federal income tax on the sale.

The following sections walk you through relevant information on the form.

Figuring your taxable gain on sale

The first parts of the calculations are the more difficult. You need to tally the expenses involved in selling your house, and you need to determine the amount that the IRS calls the *cost basis* of the house. Determining the cost basis gives many a house seller a headache, because that figure reflects not only the amount you originally paid for the house but also the money spent on improvements while you owned the property.

Calculating your gain on the sale, you need to determine two important numbers: the *expenses of sale* and the *adjusted cost basis* of the house that you sold:

✔ **Expenses of sale:** After selling your house, the IRS allows you to deduct from the selling price certain expenses incurred in the transaction, such as

- Real estate agent commissions

- Attorney fees

- Title and escrow fees

- Recording fees

- Advertising expenses

- Buyer's loan fees

Unfortunately, paying off your outstanding mortgage does *not* count as an expense of sale.

✔ **Adjusted cost basis:** For tax purposes, the cost basis of your house starts with the price you originally paid for it, including certain closing or escrow costs, which the IRS allows you to add to the purchase price of the house. During the time you own the house, however, that basis can change. Home improvements increase your cost basis by the dollar amount you spend on them.

In the eyes of the IRS, an improvement is anything that increases your home's value or prolongs its useful life, such as landscaping, installing a new roof, adding rooms, installing a new heating or air conditioning system, and so on. On the other hand, repairs that simply maintain your home's condition — fixing a leaking pipe, repainting, replacing a broken window, spackling holes in walls and baseboards — aren't considered improvements.

Another factor that may affect your cost basis is depreciation taken for rental or business use of a portion of your property over the years. For example, if you convert your two-car garage into a tattoo parlor or if you're renting a spare room, you can take depreciation on the portion of the property devoted to business or rental purposes. Depreciation reduces your property's cost basis. (***Note:*** The portion of your property devoted to business or rental purposes isn't eligible for the tax deferral under the primary residence tax deferral rules. See Chapter 18 for more details.)

Here's a simple example to show how the IRS wants you to calculate the gain on your house sale. Suppose that you bought your house for $100,000. Through years of ownership, you spent the following on improvements:

✔ $6,000 on a new roof

✔ $2,500 on landscaping

✔ $1,500 on new electrical wiring

Thus, you raise your cost basis in the property to $110,000.

You sell the house for $200,000. However, after paying real estate commissions and other expenses of sale, you only receive $180,000. Thus, your *profit* as defined by the IRS comes to $180,000 – $110,000 = $70,000.

Understanding exclusion and taxable gain

Taken from the example in the preceding section, a $70,000 profit incurs no federal income tax, regardless of whether you were single or married. If your profits are greater than your allowable exclusion, then you pay capital gains tax on whatever amount exceeds the limit. Say you're married and the profit on your house sale is $540,000. You owe tax on $40,000.

The actual rate that you pay on this amount depends on your tax bracket and how long you owned the house. However, if you owned the house longer than 12 months, you pay no higher than 20 percent, which is the maximum long-term capital gains rate.

State income taxes on housing profits

As most of us are aware, the federal government isn't the only government entity that assesses and collects taxes on income (which includes capital gains) — the vast majority of states do as well. Most states simply use the same capital gains exclusion rules that the federal government uses. Thus, if you don't owe federal income tax on the sale of your house, you probably won't owe state income tax either. Check with your state income tax entity or a local tax advisor for more details.

Part V
The Part of Tens

In this part . . .

Ah . . . the Part of Tens. If you don't enjoy reading long chapters, but you want to enhance your house-selling knowledge, this part is for you! In each of the following chapters, we tackle topics that just didn't fit elsewhere in this book. Do you want to know what steps to take after you sell your house, what special issues come into play when selling rental real estate, or what questions you may encounter from potential buyers and how to answer them? Well then, read on.

Chapter 17

Ten Things to Do After You Sell

In This Chapter
- ▶ Tying up odds and ends
- ▶ Organizing your sale and tax documents
- ▶ Thinking ahead to your next home purchase

Selling real estate is stressful. After the ink has dried on the deed and you've dropped your house keys into the hands of the new owners, the thought of refocusing on your job and other life responsibilities may seem like a tropical vacation. The last thing you want to do is worry about another real-estate-related to-do list.

Here's a carrot to keep you reading: The ten items in this chapter can save you big money and preserve your peace of mind. So, if you're looking for an incentive to get you through some of these loose-end-tying tasks, think about more cash.

Keep Copies of the Closing and Settlement Papers

At the closing for your property's sale, you're going to be buried in an avalanche of paperwork. After you dig yourself out, you may just want to run away from it all. Avoid this temptation! You have to keep copies of all those papers for the good ol' IRS. Next time you file your taxes, you may need documentation for the expenses and proceeds of the sale (see Chapter 16 for details). And even if you don't have to file any additional forms with your tax return, hold onto this paperwork in case you're ever audited.

Keep Proof of Improvements and Prior Purchases

Whether they help you or hurt you, tax laws all have one thing in common: They're a headache. A perfect example is the law that allows you to add the cost of improvements to your home's cost basis (see Chapter 16) during your years of ownership — a potentially nice tax break, if you have a sizable capital gain.

The problem is, to be able to take advantage of this tax break, you need to save receipts for every dollar you spend on home improvements. And, for as long as you're a homeowner (which can be decades) and continue to defer paying tax on your profits, you have to hang onto these receipts. As if you don't already have enough clutter in your life!

We realize that saving all these receipts can seem like an exercise in futility. If you're never audited, your receipts may never see the light of day. In fact, if your house-sale profits fall under the exclusion limits, your adjusted cost basis for tax purposes is a moot point. But the point of keeping documentation for tax purposes is to anticipate the unexpected; think of it as insurance. Someday, you may sell your house and owe tax on your profits. And, because you never know when one of those dreaded IRS audit letters will land in your mailbox, keep those receipts!

Stash Your Cash in a Good Money Market Fund

If you sell your house and don't immediately buy another one, you need to find a safe place to park your proceeds. You don't want to put that money somewhere volatile, such as the stock market, where a market crash on any given day, week, month, or year can delay the purchase of your new home for a long, long time. On the other hand, you also don't want tens of thousands of dollars languishing in a low- or no-interest checking or savings bank account.

Money market mutual funds offer you the best of both worlds — safety and reasonable rates of return. Although money market funds aren't insured by the Federal Deposit Insurance Corporation (FDIC), no money market fund has ever lost retail shareholder principal in the history of the fund business. Currently, money market funds are yielding about 5 percent.

Like bank savings accounts, but unlike certificates of deposit (CDs), money market funds offer daily access to your money without penalty. Most money market funds also offer free check-writing privileges, usually with the stipulation that the checks are for at least $250 or $500.

Among the major mutual fund companies with good money market funds, consider Vanguard (800-662-7447), Fidelity Spartan (800-544-8888), and USAA (800-531-8181). If you're in a high tax bracket, consider a tax-free money market fund that may end up netting you a higher effective return than a taxable money market fund on whose dividends you must pay federal and state income taxes. For more details on money market and other types of mutual funds, pick up a copy of the latest edition of *Mutual Funds For Dummies* (Wiley) by Eric Tyson.

Double-check the Tax Rules for Excluding Tax on Profits

As we discuss in Chapters 2 and 16, a tax law passed in 1997 enables you to exclude from taxation a significant portion of the profits from the sale of your primary residence. Congress can't ever seem to leave things alone, though, so keep your eyes and ears open for possible changes to the real estate tax laws. If you base important decisions on outdated rules, you risk losing loads of money.

Cast a Broad Net When You Consider Your Next Home

Selling your house and buying another takes a great deal of your time and money. The more often you move, the more these costs compound. So, when you choose your next home, choose carefully.

Before setting your mind on living in one specific area or type of property, check out a variety of different areas and housing options that address your needs. As a variation of the famous Socrates' quote, "The unexamined life is not worth living," we say, "You'll probably be less happy in your next home and want to move soon if you haven't explored alternatives before buying."

Remember That Renting Can Be a Fine Strategy

Don't feel pressured to rush into purchasing your next home, especially if you're having doubts about the location and the type of home you want. Renting isn't "throwing money away," especially in the short-term. Buying a home you soon have to sell because it doesn't meet your needs or wants *is* throwing money away — the transaction costs of buying and selling real estate can dwarf the short-term costs of renting.

If you're unsure about where you want to buy, try renting in the area you love most. If the neighborhood turns out to be everything you dreamed (or at least good enough), then you're in position to move fast when homes in that area become available. On the other hand, if you find that the neighborhood has too many warts, you can pat yourself on the back for not rushing into a purchase and use the rental as a base for investigating other options.

If you do rent after selling your house — because you no longer have those tax-deductible mortgage interest and property tax payments — be sure to increase your income tax withholding or estimated quarterly payments. Your employer's benefit department can provide you with Form W-4 for adjusting your withholding. If you're self-employed, adjust your quarterly tax payments using the "Estimated Tax Worksheet" that comes with Form 1040-ES.

Reevaluate Your Personal Finances When Things Change

While you're waiting to purchase another home, your situation can change, of course. Perhaps you get a big promotion at work or inherit money. Or maybe you have twins instead of one baby, and your expenses increase while your income decreases.

No matter the change, be sure to revisit your ability to make future housing payments and accomplish your other financial and personal goals before signing any real estate contracts. When you do buy another home, be sure to adjust your income tax payments by using the forms we mention in the preceding section.

Don't Simply Rehire Your Listing Agent When You Repurchase

The agent who just sold your house may have done a terrific job. And you may be tempted to simplify the selection process for finding an agent for your repurchase by asking that same agent to help you with buying.

You're possibly making a mistake if you rehire the listing agent when you repurchase. Here's why:

- Buying and selling require different skills.

- Moving from one geographic area to another requires knowledge of two local real estate markets that may have quite different issues and property values.

- Different agents specialize in different price ranges and types of properties, and you're probably not moving to a property of the same type and in the same price range.

If you believe that your listing agent also has the skills needed to be a good buying agent, and you're moving within the community into a similar type of property, then interview that agent as one of the three agents you're considering hiring. Make clear to the agent who sold your house that, although you appreciate his or her efforts for you as a seller, the agent who best meets your needs as a buyer is a separate issue.

Think through Your Next Down Payment

After you sell your house, you may well have some choices about the size of the down payment on your next home purchase. At a minimum, we recommend that you make a down payment of at least 20 percent of the purchase price of your next home. Why? Because that's the percentage that generally qualifies you for the best mortgage programs available.

What if you can make more than a 20-percent down payment? In that case, the real question is whether you can earn a high enough return investing that extra money in mutual funds, stocks, bonds, and so on to beat the cost of borrowing money on your mortgage.

Suppose that you get a quote for a fixed-rate mortgage that charges 7 percent in annual interest. Ask yourself whether you think that you can invest your extra cash and earn more than a 7 percent return (ignore the tax write-offs of mortgage interest because those are offset by the tax you'll owe on your investment profits). Investing in bank accounts, money market funds, or quality bonds surely won't do the trick. To have the potential to earn a return that high, you must consider growth-oriented and riskier investments, such as stocks, investment real estate, or small business investments.

Younger homebuyers willing to take on more investment risk should lean toward a 20-percent down payment. Older homebuyers who tend to invest less aggressively should opt for larger down payments.

Remember to Send Change of Address Notices

Although you may want those to whom you owe money to think that you've fallen off the face of the earth, you don't want to rack up late payment fees, interest charges, and damage your credit report because your bills can't find you. Don't forget to change your address with the following folks:

- ✔ Billing companies (credit and charge cards, cell phones, loans, and so on)
- ✔ Investment accounts
- ✔ Places of employment
- ✔ Family and friends

Don't delay informing all parties you know of your change of address! Visit or call your local post office and request a Mover's Guide, which includes a permanent Change of Address Order Card (or do everything online at www.moversguide.com). The Postal Service recommends that you complete and mail your Change of Address Order Card or Internet form 30 days before you move to ensure timely forwarding of mail after the date of the move.

Chapter 18

Ten Tips for Selling Rental Real Estate

. . . .

In This Chapter

▶ Understanding the tax issues involved with selling rental real estate

▶ Knowing the pros and cons of dealing in rental/investment real estate

▶ Getting the proper investment property advice

. . . .

*I*f you own your own home, you may also own property that you rent out and may someday sell. Or perhaps you've rented your house or a portion of it for a time and are interested in selling.

No matter, this chapter highlights some critical issues for you to consider before trying to sell your rental real estate. And, because the profitability (that is, your rental income less expenses) of your rental property has an enormous impact on the property's worth, we also provide you with tips for boosting your property's profitability well in advance of selling.

Don't Inadvertently Convert Your House into Income Property

Suppose that you list your house for sale and it sits and sits for months on end without any offers. (Clearly, you haven't yet read this book and heeded its advice!) You need to move, and because you're not Bill Gates, you can't afford to leave the house vacant while you're making your mortgage payments, paying property tax and insurance payments, and simultaneously shouldering the cost of renting or buying another home. So, you decide to rent out your difficult-to-sell house for a number of months while still on the market.

The advantages of rental real estate

Suppose that you made a killing when you sold your house, or you're simply a good saver, or you're the beneficiary of a nice inheritance. If you have some extra cash burning a hole in your pocket, consider investing in some rental real estate.

Real estate is a good long-term investment. Historically, real estate investors have enjoyed average annual rates of return (in the range of 9 percent to 10 percent) comparable to stock market investors' returns.

Part of the reason for those healthy real estate returns comes from the fact that land is in limited supply, so the price of land — and the property on it — generally faces upward price pressure as the economy and population expands. And, because you can borrow upward of 80 percent of the purchase price of a property, you leverage your invested capital to work harder for you; you earn returns not only on your down payment but also on the borrowed money.

Looking ahead to your golden retirement years, rental real estate not only should appreciate in value but also should provide you with rental income for living expenses. And, when you eventually decide to sell your rental real estate to tap into the equity in your property, under current tax laws, the maximum federal income tax rate that you pay on your long-term capital gain (assets held more than one year) is just 15 percent, which may be less than the tax rate that you pay on your employment or investment income.

And, last but not least, if you have a great deal of your retirement nest egg stashed in the stock market, rental real estate can help you diversify your investment portfolio. Of course, when you consider how diversified your investments are (or aren't), don't forget all the money that you may have "invested" in real estate by virtue of owning your home.

If you cease seriously trying to sell your house while renting, the IRS deems that you've converted your home into rental property, and you owe capital gains tax unless you buy a replacement rental property. If you have any doubts about running afoul of the tax laws, please consult with a good tax advisor.

Exercise Extra Care When You Sell Rental Property

The IRS makes a distinction between property that a taxpayer lives in and property that he rents out to others, even if both are within the same building. You need to understand this distinction and its tax implications.

For example, suppose that you've owned and lived in a home for a number of years. Your house has an attached rental unit that you rent out. You've claimed depreciation deductions for the rental portion of your property on your annual income tax return. Suppose further that the rental unit accounts for about 25 percent of the total living space of the building. When you sell the property, the IRS treats the sale as two separate transactions — the sale of your primary residence (the 75 percent portion of the property) and the sale of a rental property (the other 25 percent portion of the property). Therefore, 75 percent of your profits are subject to the primary residence capital gains exclusion rules explained in Chapter 16.

As for the profits on the rental portion of the property, you owe capital gains tax on those profits unless you buy another building with a rental unit that meets the particular requirements that we discuss in the next section.

Know How to Defer Your Investment Property Profits

Taxable profits on the sale of an investment property often are much greater than on a comparable residential property. The difference is that the IRS allows you to depreciate investment property while you own it and deduct the depreciation amount from your income taxes every year. The tax break is nice, but the IRS always is careful not to give people too much of a good thing. Therefore, when you sell the property, you must factor the depreciation you took on the property into the property's adjusted cost basis (see Chapter 16).

Suppose that you buy an investment property for $200,000, and many years later you sell it for $350,000. During your years of owning the property, you claim a total of $50,000 in depreciation on your tax returns. The amount of depreciation reduces your cost basis from the original $200,000 purchase price to $150,000, thus making your "taxable profit" that much larger. You owe capital gains tax on $200,000 — the difference between the sale price of $350,000 and the adjusted cost basis of $150,000.

Fortunately, you can defer taxes on these gains by rolling over your profits into another investment property. If you simultaneously sell an investment property and buy another, that one exchange is called a *1031 exchange* (1031 refers to the section of the tax laws that allows these exchanges). If the exchange isn't simultaneous — that is, if you delay your purchase of the second property — you must meet some specific requirements (called the *Starker rules,* after a famous tax case).

If you're going to do a Starker or a 1031 exchange, be sure to enlist the help of an attorney or tax advisor who's an expert at these transactions to ensure that you do it right. You need an experienced professional to help you jump the many legal hoops (such as filling out special tax forms like Form 8824, which tells the IRS that you bought a "like kind" investment property). See Chapter 7 for advice on finding good advisors.

Understand Your Local Market to Time Your Sale

If you own property that you hold solely for rental/investment purposes, you probably have a great deal of discretion about when you sell the property. As with other investments, you may wonder when a good time to sell is.

Surely you have some sense from watching real estate prices and rental vacancy rates whether your local market is strong, weak, or somewhere in between. Although we don't believe that we — or you — can predict future real estate prices in a given community, to help you better determine whether now is a good time to be cashing in your chips, examine the following factors:

- **Economic health:** The vitality of the local employment market is crucial to a healthy local real estate market. What's the unemployment rate in your local area and how does that rate compare with prior months and years?

- **New construction:** If real estate prices have been on the rise, the number of new building projects may be on the increase, which can be a sign that now is a good time to sell. As more properties come onto the market and prices spiral higher and higher, eventually the increase in construction acts like water on a fire, extinguishing future strength.

- **Available land:** Housing units must be built on land; the less land that remains available for development, the more upward pressure is exerted on housing prices.

- **Housing for sale:** All things being equal, the fewer properties for sale, the better the environment in which to be selling. In a strong real estate market, housing sells relatively quickly and the inventory of property for sale is in relatively short supply.

- **Rental real estate market health:** Although being a renter is tough when vacancy rates are low and falling and rental rates are escalating, being the owner of rental/investment real estate is great. Rental real estate is worth more when the local rental market is strong.

You need to spend some time and energy tracking down useful information. Try these suggestions:

- ✔ Your local Association of Realtors should be able to provide you with some historic house sales data.
- ✔ The local Chamber of Commerce can steer you in the direction of job market data.
- ✔ The U.S. Bureau of Labor Statistics also compiles employment data.
- ✔ Apartment and other rental property owners also have local associations that can provide you with rental data on the local market.

Understand Opportunities for Adding Value

Before you bought your property, you should've taken the time to research and understand the effects of zoning or possible rezoning on your property's use. A surprising number of real estate buyers, however, neglect this important step. Even if you did understand the zoning of the property before you bought, the mood of your local planning department, which interprets zoning laws and approves building projects, may have changed in the meantime.

So, before you consider listing your property for sale, be sure that you know how you can improve its use and value. Even if you don't want to do significant renovation or contracting work, you need to at least understand how you can further develop the property so that you can sell for a higher price by promoting the opportunity to add value.

Maximize Your Property's Income

The income and resulting cash flow (income less expenses) that a property can generate drive the amount a rental property is worth. Suppose that you can purchase a four-unit building in a rural area or you can buy a similar four-unit building in an upscale suburban community just a half-hour's commute from an economically robust city.

If each unit in the rural building rented for just $350 per month whereas those near the city rented for $1,000 per month, which building do you think would be worth more money? Or, looking at it another way, which building would you prefer to buy if both buildings were for sale for the same price? Higher rents translate into a much higher property sale price.

Suppose that property like yours typically sells for 10 times the property's gross annual income. For example, each unit rents for $1,000 per month × 4 units × 12 months = $48,000. And $48,000 × 10 (gross multiplier) = $480,000 market value.

Suppose that, through property improvements, you can increase the unit rents by 10 percent. Now the building is worth $1,100 per month × 4 units × 12 months = $52,800. And $52,800 × 10 = $528,000 market value. Thus, a mere $100 per month per unit increase results in a $48,000 increase in the building's value.

Plan for the sale of your rental property as far in advance as possible so your rental income is maximized. If any units are coming vacant, examine what upgrades can be done to boost the rent you can charge. Also consider what enhancements you can make to the building and survey the local rental marketplace to ensure that you're not underpricing units.

Minimize Your Property's Expenses

In addition to maximizing income, you can also increase a property's cash flow by minimizing its expenses. Planning at least a couple of years in advance for the sale of your building should give you enough time to make your property more cost efficient to operate and therefore more profitable and appealing to the next buyer.

For example, although you have to shell out some money upfront, investing in energy efficiency by insulating your property and installing modern appliances can really slash your operating costs. If you haven't evaluated your insurance for at least a couple of years, shop around to be sure that you're getting the best insurance value that you can.

Reducing the operating costs of your property increases its cash flow and, hence, its value.

Utilize Agents with Investment Property Experience

In Chapter 7, we provide a great deal of sound and practical advice for locating an extraordinary real estate agent. The tips and techniques apply equally well to landing a great agent for the sale of an investment property.

However — and this is a big however — be sure to hire an agent who specializes in selling your type of investment property in your area. An agent lacking experience with selling investment real estate similar to yours may misprice your property or lack the special skills necessary to market and successfully sell it — or both! Be sure to ask agents you're interviewing for activity lists detailing each property they listed and sold during the past year. Check out Chapter 7 for more info.

Visit Comparables and Review the Valuation Analysis

Especially if you've owned investment real estate for a number of years, your property may be very valuable. But if you overprice your property, it may sit unsold for many months and end up fetching less than it otherwise could in the real estate marketplace. Underprice your property and you may leave money on the table.

If you're going to hire a real estate agent to help sell the property, interview at least three agents who specialize in selling such property in your area. Each agent should prepare a comparable market analysis (CMA) to evaluate your property's worth. See Chapter 10 for more on CMAs.

By digging into the details of each CMA the agents provide you, you can better determine your property's real worth. And as you continue finding out more about your local market and visiting properties, you can determine which agent did the best job with her analysis.

For properties that have sold recently, there's no substitute for actually seeing the property. You may be surprised at how many property owners are willing to show you their properties. Remember, though, you won't get to see any unless you ask.

Some rental buildings simply are a pain in the posterior to find comparable sales for. Perhaps no similar buildings have sold for a long time in the area or no similar properties exist.

Don't be penny-wise and pound-foolish. If you have doubts about the value of your property, even after having real estate agents prepare a CMA, spring for the fee of several hundred dollars to hire a good real estate appraiser who has experience with rental properties like yours in the area.

Work with Rental-Property-Experienced Tax and Legal Advisors

If you're dealing with rental real estate, expect complicated and unclear tax and legal issues to get in your way. If you choose to hire advisors to help you navigate the morass, be sure that you're getting your money's worth in good advice.

Working in residential real estate isn't sufficient experience for advisors to whom you're paying high fees for advice about your rental property. Tax and other laws pertaining to rental property sometimes differ tremendously from laws regulating owner-occupied housing. Hire advisors who specialize in dealing with rental property.

Chapter 19

Ten Questions Home Buyers May Ask and How to Answer 'Em

In This Chapter

▶ Preparing to answer awkward questions

▶ Placing yourself in the buyer's shoes

As a house seller, you should anticipate tough questions smart home buyers (or their agents) may ask you. Most sellers and their agents are quick to praise property *features* such as a remodeled kitchen, new roof, and swimming pool. That's great, but what home buyers really want to know about are *benefits* — how house features translate into advantages for them. For example, that fancy kitchen may inspire more family meals and a swimming pool becomes an entertainment center for healthy outdoor family activities during the lazy, hazy days of summer. Other types of benefits buyers may be looking for include quality schools, a low crime rate for safety and security, convenient nearby shopping, hospitable neighborhood, and favorable fair market value (FMV) appreciation (showing the home is likely to be a profitable investment).

You need to make sure you're prepared to answer these potential questions in a manner that honestly represents your house without jeopardizing a potential sale. The best defense is a good offense. Sellers (and their listing agents) who are prepared should have nothing to fear from buyers who ask these questions. This chapter includes ten challenging questions you may be asked and some advice on how to handle them.

What Do You Like Best and Least about Living Here?

When someone asks you what you like the most and the least about living in your house, you don't want to look like the proverbial deer in the headlights. Do your homework. Make a list of items you like about your house. Do another list of things you don't like. On your "like" list, put things like waking up with the sun on your face, watching the moon rise while sitting on the back porch, family dinners in the kitchen, and playing board games by the fireplace — whatever you truly enjoy about your house.

The "dislike" list is more difficult. On one hand, you don't want to scare away buyers. Conversely, every property has flaws, and you want to be honest. Ray once owned a house he loved except when he had to do battle with poison oak. Maybe you don't like navigating the driveway when it snows. Perhaps you hate the long central hallway or small kitchen or hot attic. Just because you dislike something about the property doesn't mean the next buyer will.

Folks in the market for a condo usually ask this question. They're curious about the issues that don't apply to a single-family detached home, such as a dictatorial condo homeowner's association board of directors or a president who refuses to listen to condo owner opinions.

Veteran real estate writer and syndicated columnist Robert Bruss, who contributed much of the material for this chapter, shares the following story about a second-home condo he owns:

> "Several months ago, a prospective buyer was waiting in the entrance foyer for her realty agent to show her a unit which was for sale. As I was picking up my mail, she asked me if there was anything I didn't like about the 63-unit condo complex. Thinking fast, I explained my condo unit has been in my family for 29 years, so we must like the building. Then I pointed out she should check the soundproofing of the unit she's considering for purchase because poor soundproofing is the number one complaint of condominium buyers. Other than occasionally hearing my neighbors, I said, I thought the condo building's benefits far outweighed any disadvantages. I hope that condo buyer asked the same question of other current owners, especially her prospective adjacent neighbors."

Why Are You Selling This Lovely House?

When buyers ask you the reason why you're selling your house, they have a hidden agenda. They're either probing your motivation for selling to see if they can exploit a weakness, or they're looking for property flaws.

If the buyer knows you're under severe pressure to sell your property as soon as possible, negotiating can be difficult. (A few examples of deadline situations are things like buying a new home before you sell the old one (see Chapter 6), being transferred to a new job in another city, getting a divorce, and property foreclosure.) If you have a deadline and the buyers don't, they may use that deadline against you. Therefore, never divulge your deadline. See Chapter 14 for more information about time and negotiations.

If you have a nice, unstressed reason for selling, candidly answer the question. "We're selling because the house has gotten too big for us since the kids moved out to start their own families" or "We'd like a bigger place because the kids need rooms of their own" are examples of answers that won't get you in trouble. If, however, you're going through the divorce from hell or are about to depart for Timbuktu tomorrow, just say, "My housing needs have changed" and change the topic.

How Much Did You Pay for This House?

Some buyers may want to know the amount you paid for your house in order to discover how much room you have to negotiate on price and terms. In most states, the seller's purchase price is recorded in the public records. But even in the few states which don't record price information, the buyer's agent can find out what you paid through the local Multiple Listing Service (MLS) or by other methods.

A related question buyers may ask you or your listing agent is "What is the current mortgage balance and are there any other liens, such as a second mortgage, a home equity loan, or a mechanics' lien? The answer shows prospective buyers how much cash you need to pay off those secured obligations.

As Chapter 10 points out, cost and fair market value are wildly different things. Cost is a measure of past expenditure. Fair market value is what a buyer will pay and a seller will accept for something given the item has had proper exposure to the market and neither the buyer not the seller is under duress.

Smart buyers know that what you paid for the house when you bought it has no bearing on its value today. You may have made extensive renovations. Certainly internal and external market factors have changed since you acquired the property. Talking about what you paid for your house is as productive as discussing the price of tea in China.

But if those persistent buyers do ask the question, tell 'em what Bob Bruss tells his buyers: "I got a bargain price when this was a run-down shack so my purchase price is irrelevant in today's market." He has fun with buyers and lets them or their agents work to discover how much he paid.

How Did You Establish the Asking Price?

Some prospective home buyers may ask how you determined your asking price. When someone asks this question, reference the information in Chapter 10.

Smart sellers base their asking price on *facts* established by a written comparable market analysis (CMA). You or your agent can respond to this question by telling buyers about other properties comparable to yours in size, age, location, and condition (comps) that are either currently on the market or have sold within the past six months. Comps are the best, most powerful indicators of FMV.

Have You Received Inspection Reports?

Buyers may ask you when or if your house was inspected, and this question should be an easy one to answer. As noted in Chapter 7, we recommend that you obtain customary inspections *before* putting your property on the market. That step gives you time to decide if you want to do the recommended repairs before you put your house on the market or sell the property "as is" and let the buyer make the repairs (often in return for a credit in escrow for the buyers).

Always fully divulge any and all corrective work you've done recently. Check out Chapter 12 for a list of adjectives you should avoid when describing your house.

Customary local inspections vary. Local realty agents can tell you which inspections are required or recommended in your area, such as for termites, radon, energy efficiency, building code compliance, and so on. Either you or your agent should have any recent inspection reports easily available for serious buyers to inspect. This process saves time and removes the fear some prospective buyers may have that you're trying to hide something.

May I See Your Written Defect Disclosure Statement?

If a prospective buyer asks to see your written defect disclosure statement, you should say, "Sure, here it is." Sellers who don't prepare a written disclosure form for serious prospective buyers to review prior to making a written purchase offer are waving a "red flag" that warns buyers that you don't have a savvy listing agent who insists on such defect disclosures at the time of signing the listing agreement. Smart buyers understand that some sellers may lie or "forget" to disclose a known property defect. If you have to ask whether to disclose something about your property or the immediate neighborhood, you've probably answered your own question. When in doubt, disclose. (Check out Chapter 8 for more information on seller disclosure statements.)

Most states now have laws or precedent court decisions requiring some form of written home defect disclosures. This requirement began in California after the famous 1984 court decision in *Easton v. Strassburger*. This wise change quickly spread to other states. In this important case, the seller and the real estate agent were held liable to the home buyer for damages resulting from failure to disclose that there had been a recent hill slide adjacent to the house. A second hill slide after the buyer's purchase caused more damage than the house was worth.

Even in the few states where there aren't disclosure requirements, smart agents recommend that their sellers provide written house defect disclosures to prevent future lawsuits. Most agents now also recommend that home buyers obtain their own professional home inspection reports even if the seller already has provided one.

Are There Any Neighborhood Changes that May Affect the Home's Desirability?

House sellers almost always know if any significant civic changes are under discussion, such as street widening, construction of a new nearby noisy freeway, or a planned special assessment for civic improvements such as new sewers or streets. However, smart buyers will verify any planned improvements affecting the property at the local city hall or other government agency.

Any of these changes would materially affect the property values. Therefore, you should disclose all changes in writing to prospective buyers. This info includes plans your neighbors may have to improve their property if such improvements affect your house's views or your access to adjoining public areas.

How Many Times in the Last Year Have You Called the Police and Why?

When potential buyers ask about police calls and possible neighborhood nuisances, they're trying to determine how safe and secure your house is. Answering this question is easy if you don't have any problems of this nature. If, however, you do, you must disclose any and all such problems.

This open-end question covers many potential problems, which can affect a home's desirability. These problems include barking dogs, noisy late night parties, and troublesome neighbors. If the situation is continuing, make sure you disclose all issues to prospective buyers to prevent a future lawsuit for nondisclosure of a serious defect.

The leading court decision on this issue is *Shapiro v. Sutherland* where the sellers phoned the local police many times about their noisy neighbors. But the sellers "forgot" to disclose this problem to the buyer. The noise from the neighbors was so bad the buyer moved out almost immediately. He then sued the seller for rescission of the sale to get a refund of the purchase price. The court ordered rescission for the seller's failure to disclose the very noisy neighbors.

A visit to the local police station can reveal local crime statistics for the neighborhood. Also, this is usually the place to search public records for any registered child sex predators living nearby (called Megan's law; www. parentsformeganslaw.org). But home buyers shouldn't expect sellers to know the neighborhood crime statistics, nor to know if a registered sex offender lives nearby.

What Problems Have You Had with the House?

This open-ended question is intended to bring out past problems, which may have been solved. This question has one major thing in common with many of the other questions in this chapter — a variation of queries about property inspection reports and defect disclosure forms. Buyers have many ways of probing for property defects. Answer this question by giving the buyer a copy of your written disclosure statement. (This issue is covered in detail in Chapter 8).

What Are the Local Public Schools Like?

If prospective buyers have school-age children, they may have asked this question first. Even if buyers don't have children, the quality of the public schools has a strong effect on whether families with children want to move to your area, thus affecting buyer demand and future appreciation in market value.

Presuming that your school system's test scores are good, you can provide the data yourself. Contact your local district if your agent doesn't have the data already. Just be careful not to imply that your house is within a particular boundary area for a particular school unless you're 100 percent certain that you're correct!

Part VI
Appendixes

"My suggestion would be to cover it with a bush and hope no one notices."

In this part . . .

Appendixes are usually parts of books that readers never read and publishers add to bulk up emaciated books. However, we've added vital documents to our appendix! When you're selling your house, you should know what a good real estate contract and premarketing inspection report look like. We provide real examples of each. We also include a handy-dandy glossary to define all the jargon that so often gets thrown around in the real estate field.

Appendix A

Sample Real Estate Purchase Contract

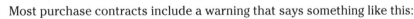

*L*ife would be simple, indeed, if everyone in the United States used the same real estate purchase contract. Unfortunately, that's not how the house-selling game is played. On the contrary, purchase contracts vary widely in both length and content from state to state and, within a state, from one locality to another.

Depending on where you live, the contract you actually receive from the buyer's agent or lawyer may range from a relatively short, simple form to a complicated, multipage document chock-full of legalese.

This appendix includes a copy of the California Association of Realtors' real estate purchase contract. We chose California's contract not just because we live here, but also because it's one of the most comprehensive residential real estate contracts used anywhere in the country.

Most purchase contracts include a warning that says something like this:

> "This is more than a receipt for money. It is intended to be a legally binding contract. Read it carefully."

Heed the warning!

Read the contract you receive extremely carefully before signing it. Don't sign the purchase contract until you understand each and every one of the terms and conditions of sale. If you have any questions about the legality of your contract, consult a lawyer.

CALIFORNIA ASSOCIATION OF REALTORS®

CALIFORNIA RESIDENTIAL PURCHASE AGREEMENT AND JOINT ESCROW INSTRUCTIONS

For Use With Single Family Residential Property — Attached or Detached

(C.A.R. Form RPA-CA, Revised 1/06)

Date _____, at _____, California.

1. **OFFER:**
   A. **THIS IS AN OFFER FROM** _____ ("Buyer").
   B. **THE REAL PROPERTY TO BE ACQUIRED** is described as _____
      _____, Assessor's Parcel No. _____, situated in
      _____, County of _____, California, ("Property").
   C. **THE PURCHASE PRICE** offered is _____
      _____ Dollars $ _____
   D. **CLOSE OF ESCROW** shall occur on _____ (date)(or ☐ _____ **Days** After Acceptance).

2. **FINANCE TERMS:** Obtaining the loans below **is a contingency** of this Agreement unless: **(i)** either 2K or 2L is checked below; or **(ii)** otherwise agreed in writing. Buyer shall act diligently and in good faith to obtain the designated loans. Obtaining deposit, down payment and closing costs **is not a contingency.** Buyer represents that funds will be good when deposited with Escrow Holder.
   A. **INITIAL DEPOSIT:** Buyer has given a deposit in the amount of . . . . $ _____
      to the agent submitting the offer (or to ☐ _____), by personal check
      (or ☐ _____), made payable to _____
      which shall be held uncashed until Acceptance and then deposited within **3** business days after
      Acceptance (or ☐ _____), with
      Escrow Holder, (or ☐ into Broker's trust account).
   B. **INCREASED DEPOSIT:** Buyer shall deposit with Escrow Holder an increased deposit in the amount of . . . . $ _____
      within _____ **Days** After Acceptance, or ☐ _____.
   C. **FIRST LOAN IN THE AMOUNT OF** . . . . $ _____
      (1) NEW First Deed of Trust in favor of lender, encumbering the Property, securing a note payable at
      maximum interest of _____% fixed rate, or _____% initial adjustable rate with a maximum
      interest rate of _____%, balance due in _____ years, amortized over _____ years. Buyer
      shall pay loan fees/points not to exceed _____. (These terms apply whether the designated loan
      is conventional, FHA or VA.)
      (2) ☐ FHA ☐ VA: (The following terms only apply to the FHA or VA loan that is checked.)
      Seller shall pay _____% discount points. Seller shall pay other fees not allowed to be paid by Buyer,
      ☐ not to exceed $_____. Seller shall pay the cost of lender required Repairs (including
      those for wood destroying pest) not otherwise provided for in this Agreement, ☐ not to exceed $
      _____. (Actual loan amount may increase if mortgage insurance premiums, funding fees or
      closing costs are financed.)
   D. **ADDITIONAL FINANCING TERMS:** ☐ Seller financing, (C.A.R. Form SFA); ☐ secondary financing, ... $ _____
      (C.A.R. Form PAA, paragraph 4A); ☐ assumed financing (C.A.R. Form PAA, paragraph 4B)
      _____
      _____
   E. **BALANCE OF PURCHASE PRICE** (not including costs of obtaining loans and other closing costs) in the amount of . . . $ _____
      to be deposited with Escrow Holder within sufficient time to close escrow.
   F. **PURCHASE PRICE (TOTAL):** . . . . $ _____
   G. **LOAN APPLICATIONS:** Within **7 (or ☐** _____**) Days** After Acceptance, Buyer shall provide Seller a letter from lender or mortgage loan broker stating that, based on a review of Buyer's written application and credit report, Buyer is prequalified or preapproved for the NEW loan specified in 2C above.
   H. **VERIFICATION OF DOWN PAYMENT AND CLOSING COSTS:** Buyer (or Buyer's lender or loan broker pursuant to 2G) shall, within **7 (or ☐** _____**) Days** After Acceptance, provide Seller written verification of Buyer's down payment and closing costs.
   I. **LOAN CONTINGENCY REMOVAL: (i)** Within **17 (or ☐** _____**) Days** After Acceptance, Buyer shall, as specified in paragraph 14, remove the loan contingency or cancel this Agreement; **OR (ii)** (if checked) ☐ the loan contingency shall remain in effect until the designated loans are funded.
   J. **APPRAISAL CONTINGENCY AND REMOVAL:** This Agreement is (**OR**, if checked, ☐ is NOT) contingent upon the Property appraising at no less than the specified purchase price. If there is a loan contingency, at the time the loan contingency is removed (or, if checked, ☐ within **17 (or _____) Days** After Acceptance), Buyer shall, as specified in paragraph 14B(3), remove the appraisal contingency or cancel this Agreement. If there is no loan contingency, Buyer shall, as specified in paragraph 14B(3), remove the appraisal contingency within **17 (or _____) Days** After Acceptance.
   K. ☐ **NO LOAN CONTINGENCY** (If checked): Obtaining any loan in paragraphs 2C, 2D or elsewhere in this Agreement is NOT a contingency of this Agreement. If Buyer does not obtain the loan and as a result Buyer does not purchase the Property, Seller may be entitled to Buyer's deposit or other legal remedies.
   L. ☐ **ALL CASH OFFER** (If checked): No loan is needed to purchase the Property. Buyer shall, within **7 (or ☐** _____**) Days** After Acceptance, provide Seller written verification of sufficient funds to close this transaction.

3. **CLOSING AND OCCUPANCY:**
   A. Buyer intends (or ☐ does not intend) to occupy the Property as Buyer's primary residence.
   B. **Seller-occupied or vacant property:** Occupancy shall be delivered to Buyer at _____ AM/PM, ☐ on the date of Close Of Escrow; ☐ on _____; or ☐ no later than _____ **Days** After Close Of Escrow. (C.A.R. Form PAA, paragraph 2.) If transfer of title and occupancy do not occur at the same time, Buyer and Seller are advised to: **(i)** enter into a written occupancy agreement; and **(ii)** consult with their insurance and legal advisors.

RPA-CA REVISED 1/06 (PAGE 1 OF 8) Print Date

Buyer's Initials (_____)(_____)
Broker's Initials (_____)(_____)
Seller's Initials (_____)(_____)
Reviewed by _____ Date _____

EQUAL HOUSING OPPORTUNITY

CALIFORNIA RESIDENTIAL PURCHASE AGREEMENT (RPA-CA PAGE 1 OF 8)

Reprinted with permission, CALIFORNIA ASSOCIATION OF REALTORS™. Endorsement not implied.

Property Address: _____ Date: _____

    C. **Tenant-occupied property: (i) Property shall be vacant** at least **5 (or** ☐ _____ **) Days** Prior to Close Of Escrow, unless otherwise agreed in writing. **Note to Seller: If you are unable to deliver Property vacant in accordance with rent control and other applicable Law, you may be in breach of this Agreement.**
    OR (ii) (if checked) ☐ **Tenant to remain in possession.** The attached addendum is incorporated into this Agreement (C.A.R. Form PAA, paragraph 3.);
    OR (iii) (if checked) ☐ **This Agreement is contingent** upon Buyer and Seller entering into a written agreement regarding occupancy of the Property within the time specified in paragraph 14B(1). If no written agreement is reached within this time, either Buyer or Seller may cancel this Agreement in writing.
    D. At Close Of Escrow, Seller assigns to Buyer any assignable warranty rights for items included in the sale and shall provide any available Copies of such warranties. Brokers cannot and will not determine the assignability of any warranties.
    E. At Close Of Escrow, unless otherwise agreed in writing, Seller shall provide keys and/or means to operate all locks, mailboxes, security systems, alarms and garage door openers. If Property is a condominium or located in a common interest subdivision, Buyer may be required to pay a deposit to the Homeowners' Association ("HOA") to obtain keys to accessible HOA facilities.

4. **ALLOCATION OF COSTS** (If checked): Unless otherwise specified here, this paragraph only determines who is to pay for the report, inspection, test or service mentioned. If not specified here or elsewhere in this Agreement, the determination of who is to pay for any work recommended or identified by any such report, inspection, test or service shall be by the method specified in paragraph 14B(2).
    A. **WOOD DESTROYING PEST INSPECTION:**
        (1) ☐ Buyer ☐ Seller shall pay for an inspection and report for wood destroying pests and organisms ("Report") which shall be prepared by _____, a registered structural pest control company. The Report shall cover the accessible areas of the main building and attached structures and, if checked: ☐ detached garages and carports, ☐ detached decks, ☐ the following other structures or areas _____. The Report shall not include roof coverings. If Property is a condominium or located in a common interest subdivision, the Report shall include only the separate interest and any exclusive-use areas being transferred and shall not include common areas, unless otherwise agreed. Water tests of shower pans on upper level units may not be performed without consent of the owners of property below the shower.
    OR (2) ☐ **(If checked)** The attached addendum (C.A.R. Form WPA) regarding wood destroying pest inspection and allocation of cost is incorporated into this Agreement.
    B. **OTHER INSPECTIONS AND REPORTS:**
        (1) ☐ Buyer ☐ Seller shall pay to have septic or private sewage disposal systems inspected _____.
        (2) ☐ Buyer ☐ Seller shall pay to have domestic wells tested for water potability and productivity _____.
        (3) ☐ Buyer ☐ Seller shall pay for a natural hazard zone disclosure report prepared by _____.
        (4) ☐ Buyer ☐ Seller shall pay for the following inspection or report _____.
        (5) ☐ Buyer ☐ Seller shall pay for the following inspection or report _____.
    C. **GOVERNMENT REQUIREMENTS AND RETROFIT:**
        (1) ☐ Buyer ☐ Seller shall pay for smoke detector installation and/or water heater bracing, if required by Law. Prior to Close Of Escrow, Seller shall provide Buyer a written statement of compliance in accordance with state and local Law, unless exempt.
        (2) ☐ Buyer ☐ Seller shall pay the cost of compliance with any other minimum mandatory government retrofit standards, inspections and reports if required as a condition of closing escrow under any Law. _____.
    D. **ESCROW AND TITLE:**
        (1) ☐ Buyer ☐ Seller shall pay escrow fee _____.
        Escrow Holder shall be _____.
        (2) ☐ Buyer ☐ Seller shall pay for **owner's** title insurance policy specified in paragraph 12E _____.
        Owner's title policy to be issued by _____.
        (Buyer shall pay for any title insurance policy insuring Buyer's **lender**, unless otherwise agreed in writing.)
    E. **OTHER COSTS:**
        (1) ☐ Buyer ☐ Seller shall pay County transfer tax or transfer fee _____.
        (2) ☐ Buyer ☐ Seller shall pay City transfer tax or transfer fee _____.
        (3) ☐ Buyer ☐ Seller shall pay HOA transfer fee _____.
        (4) ☐ Buyer ☐ Seller shall pay HOA document preparation fees _____.
        (5) ☐ Buyer ☐ Seller shall pay the cost, not to exceed $ _____, of a one-year home warranty plan, issued by _____,
        with the following optional coverage: _____.
        (6) ☐ Buyer ☐ Seller shall pay for _____.
        (7) ☐ Buyer ☐ Seller shall pay for _____.

5. **STATUTORY DISCLOSURES (INCLUDING LEAD-BASED PAINT HAZARD DISCLOSURES) AND CANCELLATION RIGHTS:**
    A. **(1)** Seller shall, within the time specified in paragraph 14A, deliver to Buyer, if required by Law: **(i)** Federal Lead-Based Paint Disclosures and pamphlet ("Lead Disclosures"); and **(ii)** disclosures or notices required by sections 1102 et. seq. and 1103 et. seq. of the California Civil Code ("Statutory Disclosures"). Statutory Disclosures include, but are not limited to, a Real Estate Transfer Disclosure Statement ("TDS"), Natural Hazard Disclosure Statement ("NHD"), notice or actual knowledge of release of illegal controlled substance, notice of special tax and/or assessments (or, if allowed, substantially equivalent notice regarding the Mello-Roos Community Facilities Act and Improvement Bond Act of 1915) and, if Seller has actual knowledge, of industrial use and military ordinance location disclosure (C.A.R. Form SSD).
        (2) Buyer shall, within the time specified in paragraph 14B(1), return Signed Copies of the Statutory and Lead Disclosures to Seller.
        (3) In the event Seller, prior to Close Of Escrow, becomes aware of adverse conditions materially affecting the Property, or any material inaccuracy in disclosures, information or representations previously provided to Buyer of which Buyer is otherwise unaware, Seller shall promptly provide a subsequent or amended disclosure or notice, in writing, covering those items. **However, a subsequent or amended disclosure shall not be required for conditions and material inaccuracies disclosed in reports ordered and paid for by Buyer.**

Buyer's Initials (_____)(_____)
Seller's Initials (_____)(_____)

RPA-CA REVISED 1/06 (PAGE 2 OF 8)

Reviewed by _____ Date _____

EQUAL HOUSING OPPORTUNITY

CALIFORNIA RESIDENTIAL PURCHASE AGREEMENT (RPA-CA PAGE 2 OF 8)

Property Address: _____   Date: _____

(4) If any disclosure or notice specified in 5A(1), or subsequent or amended disclosure or notice is delivered to Buyer after the offer is Signed, Buyer shall have the right to cancel this Agreement within **3 Days** After delivery in person, or **5 Days** After delivery by deposit in the mail, by giving written notice of cancellation to Seller or Seller's agent. (Lead Disclosures sent by mail must be sent certified mail or better.)

(5) Note to Buyer and Seller: Waiver of Statutory and Lead Disclosures is prohibited by Law.

B. **NATURAL AND ENVIRONMENTAL HAZARDS:** Within the time specified in paragraph 14A, Seller shall, if required by Law: **(i)** deliver to Buyer earthquake guides (and questionnaire) and environmental hazards booklet; **(ii)** even if exempt from the obligation to provide a NHD, disclose if the Property is located in a Special Flood Hazard Area; Potential Flooding (Inundation) Area; Very High Fire Hazard Zone; State Fire Responsibility Area; Earthquake Fault Zone; Seismic Hazard Zone; and **(iii)** disclose any other zone as required by Law and provide any other information required for those zones.

C. **DATA BASE DISCLOSURE:** Notice: Pursuant to Section 290.46 of the Penal Code, information about specified registered sex offenders is made available to the public via an Internet Web site maintained by the Department of Justice at www.meganslaw.ca.gov. Depending on an offender's criminal history, this information will include either the address at which the offender resides or the community of residence and ZIP Code in which he or she resides. (Neither Seller nor Brokers are required to check this website. If Buyer wants further information, Broker recommends that Buyer obtain information from this website during Buyer's inspection contingency period. Brokers do not have expertise in this area.)

6. **CONDOMINIUM/PLANNED UNIT DEVELOPMENT DISCLOSURES:**

A. **SELLER HAS: 7 (or ☐ _____) Days** After Acceptance to disclose to Buyer whether the Property is a condominium, or is located in a planned unit development or other common interest subdivision (C.A.R. Form SSD).

B. If the Property is a condominium or is located in a planned unit development or other common interest subdivision, Seller has **3 (or ☐ _____) Days** After Acceptance to request from the HOA (C.A.R. Form HOA): **(i)** Copies of any documents required by Law; **(ii)** disclosure of any pending or anticipated claim or litigation by or against the HOA; **(iii)** a statement containing the location and number of designated parking and storage spaces; **(iv)** Copies of the most recent 12 months of HOA minutes for regular and special meetings; and **(v)** the names and contact information of all HOAs governing the Property (collectively, "CI Disclosures"). Seller shall itemize and deliver to Buyer all CI Disclosures received from the HOA and any CI Disclosures in Seller's possession. Buyer's approval of CI Disclosures is a contingency of this Agreement as specified in paragraph 14B(3).

7. **CONDITIONS AFFECTING PROPERTY:**

A. Unless otherwise agreed: **(i) the Property is sold (a) in its PRESENT physical condition as of the date of Acceptance and (b) subject to Buyer's Investigation rights; (ii)** the Property, including pool, spa, landscaping and grounds, is to be maintained in substantially the same condition as on the date of Acceptance; and **(iii)** all debris and personal property not included in the sale shall be removed by Close Of Escrow.

B. **SELLER SHALL, within the time specified in paragraph 14A, DISCLOSE KNOWN MATERIAL FACTS AND DEFECTS affecting the Property, including known insurance claims within the past five years, AND MAKE OTHER DISCLOSURES REQUIRED BY LAW (C.A.R. Form SSD).**

C. **NOTE TO BUYER: You are strongly advised to conduct investigations of the entire Property in order to determine its present condition since Seller may not be aware of all defects affecting the Property or other factors that you consider important. Property improvements may not be built according to code, in compliance with current Law, or have had permits issued.**

D. **NOTE TO SELLER: Buyer has the right to inspect the Property and, as specified in paragraph 14B, based upon information discovered in those inspections: (i)** cancel this Agreement; or **(ii)** request that you make Repairs or take other action.

8. **ITEMS INCLUDED AND EXCLUDED:**

A. **NOTE TO BUYER AND SELLER**: Items listed as included or excluded in the MLS, flyers or marketing materials are **not** included in the purchase price or excluded from the sale unless specified in 8B or C.

B. **ITEMS INCLUDED IN SALE:**

(1) All EXISTING fixtures and fittings that are attached to the Property;

(2) Existing electrical, mechanical, lighting, plumbing and heating fixtures, ceiling fans, fireplace inserts, gas logs and grates, solar systems, built-in appliances, window and door screens, awnings, shutters, window coverings, attached floor coverings, television antennas, satellite dishes, private integrated telephone systems, air coolers/conditioners, pool/spa equipment, garage door openers/remote controls, mailbox, in-ground landscaping, trees/shrubs, water softeners, water purifiers, security systems/alarms; and

(3) The following items: _____
_____.

(4) Seller represents that all items included in the purchase price, unless otherwise specified, are owned by Seller.

(5) All items included shall be transferred free of liens and without Seller warranty.

C. **ITEMS EXCLUDED FROM SALE:** _____
_____.

9. **BUYER'S INVESTIGATION OF PROPERTY AND MATTERS AFFECTING PROPERTY:**

A. Buyer's acceptance of the condition of, and any other matter affecting the Property, is a contingency of this Agreement as specified in this paragraph and paragraph 14B. Within the time specified in paragraph 14B(1), Buyer shall have the right, at Buyer's expense unless otherwise agreed, to conduct inspections, investigations, tests, surveys and other studies ("Buyer Investigations"), including, but not limited to, the right to: **(i)** inspect for lead-based paint and other lead-based paint hazards; **(ii)** inspect for wood destroying pests and organisms; **(iii)** review the registered sex offender database; **(iv)** confirm the insurability of Buyer and the Property; and **(v)** satisfy Buyer as to any matter specified in the attached Buyer's Inspection Advisory (C.A.R. Form BIA). Without Seller's prior written consent, Buyer shall neither make nor cause to be made: **(i)** invasive or destructive Buyer Investigations; or **(ii)** inspections by any governmental building or zoning inspector or government employee, unless required by Law.

B. Buyer shall complete Buyer Investigations and, as specified in paragraph 14B, remove the contingency or cancel this Agreement. Buyer shall give Seller, at no cost, complete Copies of all Buyer Investigation reports obtained by Buyer. Seller shall make the Property available for all Buyer Investigations. Seller shall have water, gas, electricity and all operable pilot lights on for Buyer's Investigations and through the date possession is made available to Buyer.

Buyer's Initials (_____)(_____)
Seller's Initials (_____)(_____)

Reviewed by _____ Date _____

RPA-CA REVISED 1/06 (PAGE 3 OF 8)

CALIFORNIA RESIDENTIAL PURCHASE AGREEMENT (RPA-CA PAGE 3 OF 8)

Property Address: _____ Date: _____

10. **REPAIRS:** Repairs shall be completed prior to final verification of condition unless otherwise agreed in writing. Repairs to be performed at Seller's expense may be performed by Seller or through others, provided that the work complies with applicable Law, including governmental permit, inspection and approval requirements. Repairs shall be performed in a good, skillful manner with materials of quality and appearance comparable to existing materials. It is understood that exact restoration of appearance or cosmetic items following all Repairs may not be possible. Seller shall: **(i)** obtain receipts for Repairs performed by others; **(ii)** prepare a written statement indicating the Repairs performed by Seller and the date of such Repairs; and **(iii)** provide Copies of receipts and statements to Buyer prior to final verification of condition.

11. **BUYER INDEMNITY AND SELLER PROTECTION FOR ENTRY UPON PROPERTY:** Buyer shall: **(i)** keep the Property free and clear of liens; **(ii)** Repair all damage arising from Buyer Investigations; and **(iii)** indemnify and hold Seller harmless from all resulting liability, claims, demands, damages and costs. Buyer shall carry, or Buyer shall require anyone acting on Buyer's behalf to carry, policies of liability, workers' compensation and other applicable insurance, defending and protecting Seller from liability for any injuries to persons or property occurring during any Buyer Investigations or work done on the Property at Buyer's direction prior to Close Of Escrow. Seller is advised that certain protections may be afforded Seller by recording a "Notice of Non-responsibility" (C.A.R. Form NNR) for Buyer Investigations and work done on the Property at Buyer's direction. Buyer's obligations under this paragraph shall survive the termination of this Agreement.

12. **TITLE AND VESTING:**
    A. Within the time specified in paragraph 14, Buyer shall be provided a current preliminary (title) report, which is only an offer by the title insurer to issue a policy of title insurance and may not contain every item affecting title. Buyer's review of the preliminary report and any other matters which may affect title are a contingency of this Agreement as specified in paragraph 14B.
    B. Title is taken in its present condition subject to all encumbrances, easements, covenants, conditions, restrictions, rights and other matters, whether of record or not, as of the date of Acceptance except: **(i)** monetary liens of record unless Buyer is assuming those obligations or taking the Property subject to those obligations; and **(ii)** those matters which Seller has agreed to remove in writing.
    C. Within the time specified in paragraph 14A, Seller has a duty to disclose to Buyer all matters known to Seller affecting title, whether of record or not.
    D. At Close Of Escrow, Buyer shall receive a grant deed conveying title (or, for stock cooperative or long-term lease, an assignment of stock certificate or of Seller's leasehold interest), including oil, mineral and water rights if currently owned by Seller. Title shall vest as designated in Buyer's supplemental escrow instructions. THE MANNER OF TAKING TITLE MAY HAVE SIGNIFICANT LEGAL AND TAX CONSEQUENCES. CONSULT AN APPROPRIATE PROFESSIONAL.
    E. Buyer shall receive a CLTA/ALTA Homeowner's Policy of Title Insurance. A title company, at Buyer's request, can provide information about the availability, desirability, coverage, and cost of various title insurance coverages and endorsements. If Buyer desires title coverage other than that required by this paragraph, Buyer shall instruct Escrow Holder in writing and pay any increase in cost.

13. **SALE OF BUYER'S PROPERTY:**
    A. This Agreement is NOT contingent upon the sale of any property owned by Buyer.
    OR B. ☐ (If checked): The attached addendum (C.A.R. Form COP) regarding the contingency for the sale of property owned by Buyer is incorporated into this Agreement.

14. **TIME PERIODS; REMOVAL OF CONTINGENCIES; CANCELLATION RIGHTS: The following time periods may only be extended, altered, modified or changed by mutual written agreement. Any removal of contingencies or cancellation under this paragraph must be in writing (C.A.R. Form CR).**
    A. **SELLER HAS: 7 (or ☐ _____) Days** After Acceptance to deliver to Buyer all reports, disclosures and information for which Seller is responsible under paragraphs 4, 5A and B, 6A, 7B and 12.
    B. **(1) BUYER HAS: 17 (or ☐ _____) Days** After Acceptance, unless otherwise agreed in writing, to:
        (i) complete all Buyer Investigations; approve all disclosures, reports and other applicable information, which Buyer receives from Seller; and approve all matters affecting the Property (including lead-based paint and lead-based paint hazards as well as other information specified in paragraph 5 and insurability of Buyer and the Property); and
        (ii) return to Seller Signed Copies of Statutory and Lead Disclosures delivered by Seller in accordance with paragraph 5A.
        (2) Within the time specified in 14B(1), Buyer may request that Seller make repairs or take any other action regarding the Property (C.A.R. Form RR). Seller has no obligation to agree to or respond to Buyer's requests.
        (3) By the end of the time specified in 14B(1) (or 2I for loan contingency or 2J for appraisal contingency), Buyer shall, in writing, remove the applicable contingency (C.A.R. Form CR) or cancel this Agreement. However, if **(i)** government-mandated inspections/ reports required as a condition of closing; or **(ii)** Common Interest Disclosures pursuant to paragraph 6B are not made within the time specified in 14A, then Buyer has **5 (or ☐ _____) Days** After receipt of any such items, or the time specified in 14B(1), whichever is later, to remove the applicable contingency or cancel this Agreement in writing.
    C. **CONTINUATION OF CONTINGENCY OR CONTRACTUAL OBLIGATION; SELLER RIGHT TO CANCEL:**
        (1) Seller right to Cancel; Buyer Contingencies: Seller, after first giving Buyer a Notice to Buyer to Perform (as specified below), may cancel this Agreement in writing and authorize return of Buyer's deposit if, by the time specified in this Agreement, Buyer does not remove in writing the applicable contingency or cancel this Agreement. Once all contingencies have been removed, failure of either Buyer or Seller to close escrow on time may be a breach of this Agreement.
        (2) Continuation of Contingency: Even after the expiration of the time specified in 14B, Buyer retains the right to make requests to Seller, remove in writing the applicable contingency or cancel this Agreement until Seller cancels pursuant to 14C(1). Once Seller receives Buyer's written removal of all contingencies, Seller may not cancel this Agreement pursuant to 14C(1).
        (3) Seller right to Cancel; Buyer Contract Obligations: Seller, after first giving Buyer a Notice to Buyer to Perform (as specified below), may cancel this Agreement in writing and authorize return of Buyer's deposit for any of the following reasons: **(i)** if Buyer fails to deposit funds as required by 2A or 2B; **(ii)** if the funds deposited pursuant to 2A or 2B are not good when deposited; **(iii)** if Buyer fails to provide a letter as required by 2G; **(iv)** if Buyer fails to provide verification as required by 2H or 2L; **(v)** if Seller reasonably disapproves of the verification provided by 2H or 2L; **(vi)** if Buyer fails to return Statutory and Lead Disclosures as required by paragraph 5A(2); or **(vii)** if Buyer fails to sign or initial a separate liquidated damage form for an increased deposit as required by paragraph 16. **Seller is not required to give Buyer a Notice to Perform regarding Close of Escrow.**
        (4) Notice To Buyer To Perform: The Notice to Buyer to Perform (C.A.R. Form NBP) shall: **(i)** be in writing; **(ii)** be signed by Seller; and **(iii)** give Buyer at least **24 (or ☐ _____)** hours (or until the time specified in the applicable paragraph, whichever occurs last) to take the applicable action. A Notice to Buyer to Perform may not be given any earlier than **2 Days** Prior to the expiration of the applicable time for Buyer to remove a contingency or cancel this Agreement or meet a 14C(3) obligation.

Buyer's Initials (_____)(_____)
Seller's Initials (_____)(_____)

RPA-CA REVISED 1/06 (PAGE 4 OF 8)

Reviewed by _____ Date _____

CALIFORNIA RESIDENTIAL PURCHASE AGREEMENT (RPA-CA PAGE 4 OF 8)

Property Address: _____ Date: _____

D. EFFECT OF BUYER'S REMOVAL OF CONTINGENCIES : If Buyer removes, in writing, any contingency or cancellation rights, unless otherwise specified in a separate written agreement between Buyer and Seller, Buyer shall conclusively be deemed to have: **(i)** completed all Buyer Investigations, and review of reports and other applicable information and disclosures pertaining to that contingency or cancellation right; **(ii)** elected to proceed with the transaction; and **(iii)** assumed all liability, responsibility and expense for Repairs or corrections pertaining to that contingency or cancellation right, or for inability to obtain financing.

E. EFFECT OF CANCELLATION ON DEPOSITS: If Buyer or Seller gives written notice of cancellation pursuant to rights duly exercised under the terms of this Agreement, Buyer and Seller agree to Sign mutual instructions to cancel the sale and escrow and release deposits to the party entitled to the funds, less fees and costs incurred by that party. Fees and costs may be payable to service providers and vendors for services and products provided during escrow. **Release of funds will require mutual Signed release instructions from Buyer and Seller, judicial decision or arbitration award. A party may be subject to a civil penalty of up to $1,000 for refusal to sign such instructions if no good faith dispute exists as to who is entitled to the deposited funds (Civil Code §1057.3).**

15. FINAL VERIFICATION OF CONDITION: Buyer shall have the right to make a final inspection of the Property within **5 (or _____) Days** Prior to Close Of Escrow, NOT AS A CONTINGENCY OF THE SALE, but solely to confirm: **(i)** the Property is maintained pursuant to paragraph 7A; **(ii)** Repairs have been completed as agreed; and **(iii)** Seller has complied with Seller's other obligations under this Agreement.

16. LIQUIDATED DAMAGES: If Buyer fails to complete this purchase because of Buyer's default, Seller shall retain, as liquidated damages, the deposit actually paid. If the Property is a dwelling with no more than four units, one of which Buyer intends to occupy, then the amount retained shall be no more than 3% of the purchase price. Any excess shall be returned to Buyer. Release of funds will require mutual, Signed release instructions from both Buyer and Seller, judicial decision or arbitration award.

BUYER AND SELLER SHALL SIGN A SEPARATE LIQUIDATED DAMAGES PROVISION FOR ANY INCREASED DEPOSIT. (C.A.R. FORM RID)

Buyer's Initials _____ / _____	Seller's Initials _____ / _____

17. DISPUTE RESOLUTION:

A. MEDIATION: Buyer and Seller agree to mediate any dispute or claim arising between them out of this Agreement, or any resulting transaction, before resorting to arbitration or court action. Paragraphs 17B(2) and (3) below apply to mediation whether or not the Arbitration provision is initialed. Mediation fees, if any, shall be divided equally among the parties involved. If, for any dispute or claim to which this paragraph applies, any party commences an action without first attempting to resolve the matter through mediation, or refuses to mediate after a request has been made, then that party shall not be entitled to recover attorney fees, even if they would otherwise be available to that party in any such action. THIS MEDIATION PROVISION APPLIES WHETHER OR NOT THE ARBITRATION PROVISION IS INITIALED.

B. ARBITRATION OF DISPUTES: (1) Buyer and Seller agree that any dispute or claim in Law or equity arising between them out of this Agreement or any resulting transaction, which is not settled through mediation, shall be decided by neutral, binding arbitration, including and subject to paragraphs 17B(2) and (3) below. The arbitrator shall be a retired judge or justice, or an attorney with at least 5 years of residential real estate Law experience, unless the parties mutually agree to a different arbitrator, who shall render an award in accordance with substantive California Law. The parties shall have the right to discovery in accordance with California Code of Civil Procedure §1283.05. In all other respects, the arbitration shall be conducted in accordance with Title 9 of Part III of the California Code of Civil Procedure. Judgment upon the award of the arbitrator(s) may be entered into any court having jurisdiction. Interpretation of this agreement to arbitrate shall be governed by the Federal Arbitration Act.

(2) EXCLUSIONS FROM MEDIATION AND ARBITRATION: The following matters are excluded from mediation and arbitration: (i) a judicial or non-judicial foreclosure or other action or proceeding to enforce a deed of trust, mortgage or installment land sale contract as defined in California Civil Code §2985; (ii) an unlawful detainer action; (iii) the filing or enforcement of a mechanic's lien; and (iv) any matter that is within the jurisdiction of a probate, small claims or bankruptcy court. The filing of a court action to enable the recording of a notice of pending action, for order of attachment, receivership, injunction, or other provisional remedies, shall not constitute a waiver of the mediation and arbitration provisions.

(3) BROKERS: Buyer and Seller agree to mediate and arbitrate disputes or claims involving either or both Brokers, consistent with 17A and B, provided either or both Brokers shall have agreed to such mediation or arbitration prior to, or within a reasonable time after, the dispute or claim is presented to Brokers. Any election by either or both Brokers to participate in mediation or arbitration shall not result in Brokers being deemed parties to the Agreement.

"NOTICE: BY INITIALING IN THE SPACE BELOW YOU ARE AGREEING TO HAVE ANY DISPUTE ARISING OUT OF THE MATTERS INCLUDED IN THE 'ARBITRATION OF DISPUTES' PROVISION DECIDED BY NEUTRAL ARBITRATION AS PROVIDED BY CALIFORNIA LAW AND YOU ARE GIVING UP ANY RIGHTS YOU MIGHT POSSESS TO HAVE THE DISPUTE LITIGATED IN A COURT OR JURY TRIAL. BY INITIALING IN THE SPACE BELOW YOU ARE GIVING UP YOUR JUDICIAL RIGHTS TO DISCOVERY AND APPEAL, UNLESS THOSE RIGHTS ARE SPECIFICALLY INCLUDED IN THE 'ARBITRATION OF DISPUTES' PROVISION. IF YOU REFUSE TO SUBMIT TO ARBITRATION AFTER AGREEING TO THIS PROVISION, YOU MAY BE COMPELLED TO ARBITRATE UNDER THE AUTHORITY OF THE CALIFORNIA CODE OF CIVIL PROCEDURE. YOUR AGREEMENT TO THIS ARBITRATION PROVISION IS VOLUNTARY."

"WE HAVE READ AND UNDERSTAND THE FOREGOING AND AGREE TO SUBMIT DISPUTES ARISING OUT OF THE MATTERS INCLUDED IN THE 'ARBITRATION OF DISPUTES' PROVISION TO NEUTRAL ARBITRATION."

Buyer's Initials _____ / _____	Seller's Initials _____ / _____

Buyer's Initials (_____)(_____)
Seller's Initials (_____)(_____)

Reviewed by _____ Date _____

CALIFORNIA RESIDENTIAL PURCHASE AGREEMENT (RPA-CA PAGE 5 OF 8)

Property Address: _____ Date: _____

18. **PRORATIONS OF PROPERTY TAXES AND OTHER ITEMS:** Unless otherwise agreed in writing, the following items shall be PAID CURRENT and prorated between Buyer and Seller as of Close Of Escrow: real property taxes and assessments, interest, rents, HOA regular, special, and emergency dues and assessments imposed prior to Close Of Escrow, premiums on insurance assumed by Buyer, payments on bonds and assessments assumed by Buyer, and payments on Mello-Roos and other Special Assessment District bonds and assessments that are now a lien. The following items shall be assumed by Buyer WITHOUT CREDIT toward the purchase price: prorated payments on Mello-Roos and other Special Assessment District bonds and assessments and HOA special assessments that are now a lien but not yet due. Property will be reassessed upon change of ownership. Any supplemental tax bills shall be paid as follows: **(i)** for periods after Close Of Escrow, by Buyer; and **(ii)** for periods prior to Close Of Escrow, by Seller. TAX BILLS ISSUED AFTER CLOSE OF ESCROW SHALL BE HANDLED DIRECTLY BETWEEN BUYER AND SELLER. Prorations shall be made based on a 30-day month.
19. **WITHHOLDING TAXES:** Seller and Buyer agree to execute any instrument, affidavit, statement or instruction reasonably necessary to comply with federal (FIRPTA) and California withholding Law, if required (C.A.R. Forms AS and AB).
20. **MULTIPLE LISTING SERVICE ("MLS"):** Brokers are authorized to report to the MLS a pending sale and, upon Close Of Escrow, the terms of this transaction to be published and disseminated to persons and entities authorized to use the information on terms approved by the MLS.
21. **EQUAL HOUSING OPPORTUNITY:** The Property is sold in compliance with federal, state and local anti-discrimination Laws.
22. **ATTORNEY FEES:** In any action, proceeding, or arbitration between Buyer and Seller arising out of this Agreement, the prevailing Buyer or Seller shall be entitled to reasonable attorney fees and costs from the non-prevailing Buyer or Seller, except as provided in paragraph 17A.
23. **SELECTION OF SERVICE PROVIDERS:** If Brokers refer Buyer or Seller to persons, vendors, or service or product providers ("Providers"), Brokers do not guarantee the performance of any Providers. Buyer and Seller may select ANY Providers of their own choosing.
24. **TIME OF ESSENCE; ENTIRE CONTRACT; CHANGES:** Time is of the essence. All understandings between the parties are incorporated in this Agreement. Its terms are intended by the parties as a final, complete and exclusive expression of their Agreement with respect to its subject matter, and may not be contradicted by evidence of any prior agreement or contemporaneous oral agreement. If any provision of this Agreement is held to be ineffective or invalid, the remaining provisions will nevertheless be given full force and effect. **Neither this Agreement nor any provision in it may be extended, amended, modified, altered or changed, except in writing Signed by Buyer and Seller.**
25. **OTHER TERMS AND CONDITIONS,** including attached supplements:
    A. ☑ Buyer's Inspection Advisory (C.A.R. Form BIA)
    B. ☐ Purchase Agreement Addendum (C.A.R. Form PAA paragraph numbers: _____)
    C. ☐ Statewide Buyer and Seller Advisory (C.A.R. Form SBSA)
    D. _____
26. **DEFINITIONS:** As used in this Agreement:
    A. **"Acceptance"** means the time the offer or final counter offer is accepted in writing by a party and is delivered to and personally received by the other party or that party's authorized agent in accordance with the terms of this offer or a final counter offer.
    B. **"Agreement"** means the terms and conditions of this accepted California Residential Purchase Agreement and any accepted counter offers and addenda.
    C. **"C.A.R. Form"** means the specific form referenced or another comparable form agreed to by the parties.
    D. **"Close Of Escrow"** means the date the grant deed, or other evidence of transfer of title, is recorded. If the scheduled close of escrow falls on a Saturday, Sunday or legal holiday, then close of escrow shall be the next business day after the scheduled close of escrow date.
    E. **"Copy"** means copy by any means including photocopy, NCR, facsimile and electronic.
    F. **"Days"** means calendar days, unless otherwise required by Law.
    G. **"Days After"** means the specified number of calendar days after the occurrence of the event specified, not counting the calendar date on which the specified event occurs, and ending at 11:59PM on the final day.
    H. **"Days Prior"** means the specified number of calendar days before the occurrence of the event specified, not counting the calendar date on which the specified event is scheduled to occur.
    I. **"Electronic Copy" or "Electronic Signature"** means, as applicable, an electronic copy or signature complying with California Law. Buyer and Seller agree that electronic means will not be used by either party to modify or alter the content or integrity of this Agreement without the knowledge and consent of the other.
    J. **"Law"** means any law, code, statute, ordinance, regulation, rule or order, which is adopted by a controlling city, county, state or federal legislative, judicial or executive body or agency.
    K. **"Notice to Buyer to Perform"** means a document (C.A.R. Form NBP), which shall be in writing and Signed by Seller and shall give Buyer at least 24 hours **(or as otherwise specified in paragraph 14C(4))** to remove a contingency or perform as applicable.
    L. **"Repairs"** means any repairs (including pest control), alterations, replacements, modifications or retrofitting of the Property provided for under this Agreement.
    M. **"Signed"** means either a handwritten or electronic signature on an original document, Copy or any counterpart.
    N. **Singular and Plural** terms each include the other, when appropriate.

Buyer's Initials (_____)(_____)
Seller's Initials (_____)(_____)

Reviewed by _____ Date _____

EQUAL HOUSING OPPORTUNITY

CALIFORNIA RESIDENTIAL PURCHASE AGREEMENT (RPA-CA PAGE 6 OF 8)

Property Address: _____ Date: _____

27. AGENCY:

A. DISCLOSURE: Buyer and Seller each acknowledge prior receipt of C.A.R. Form AD "Disclosure Regarding Real Estate Agency Relationships."

B. POTENTIALLY COMPETING BUYERS AND SELLERS: Buyer and Seller each acknowledge receipt of a disclosure of the possibility of multiple representation by the Broker representing that principal. This disclosure may be part of a listing agreement, buyer-broker agreement or separate document (C.A.R. Form DA). Buyer understands that Broker representing Buyer may also represent other potential buyers, who may consider, make offers on or ultimately acquire the Property. Seller understands that Broker representing Seller may also represent other sellers with competing properties of interest to this Buyer.

C. CONFIRMATION: The following agency relationships are hereby confirmed for this transaction:
Listing Agent _____ (Print Firm Name) is the agent of (check one): ☐ the Seller exclusively; or ☐ both the Buyer and Seller.
Selling Agent _____ (Print Firm Name) (if not same as Listing Agent) is the agent of (check one): ☐ the Buyer exclusively; or ☐ the Seller exclusively; or ☐ both the Buyer and Seller. Real Estate Brokers are not parties to the Agreement between Buyer and Seller.

28. JOINT ESCROW INSTRUCTIONS TO ESCROW HOLDER:

A. The following paragraphs, or applicable portions thereof, of this Agreement constitute the joint escrow instructions of Buyer and Seller to Escrow Holder, which Escrow Holder is to use along with any related counter offers and addenda, and any additional mutual instructions to close the escrow: 1, 2, 4, 12, 13B, 14E, 18, 19, 24, 25B and 25D, 26, 28, 29, 32A, 33 and paragraph D of the section titled Real Estate Brokers on page 8. If a Copy of the separate compensation agreement(s) provided for in paragraph 29 or 32A, or paragraph D of the section titled Real Estate Brokers on page 8 is deposited with Escrow Holder by Broker, Escrow Holder shall accept such agreement(s) and pay out from Buyer's or Seller's funds, or both, as applicable, the Broker's compensation provided for in such agreement(s). The terms and conditions of this Agreement not set forth in the specified paragraphs are additional matters for the information of Escrow Holder, but about which Escrow Holder need not be concerned. Buyer and Seller will receive Escrow Holder's general provisions directly from Escrow Holder and will execute such provisions upon Escrow Holder's request. To the extent the general provisions are inconsistent or conflict with this Agreement, the general provisions will control as to the duties and obligations of Escrow Holder only. Buyer and Seller will execute additional instructions, documents and forms provided by Escrow Holder that are reasonably necessary to close the escrow.

B. A Copy of this Agreement shall be delivered to Escrow Holder within **3** business days after Acceptance (or ☐ _____). Buyer and Seller authorize Escrow Holder to accept and rely on Copies and Signatures as defined in this Agreement as originals, to open escrow and for other purposes of escrow. The validity of this Agreement as between Buyer and Seller is not affected by whether or when Escrow Holder Signs this Agreement.

C. Brokers are a party to the escrow for the sole purpose of compensation pursuant to paragraphs 29, 32A and paragraph D of the section titled Real Estate Brokers on page 8. Buyer and Seller irrevocably assign to Brokers compensation specified in paragraphs 29 and 32A, respectively, and irrevocably instruct Escrow Holder to disburse those funds to Brokers at Close Of Escrow or pursuant to any other mutually executed cancellation agreement. Compensation instructions can be amended or revoked only with the written consent of Brokers. Escrow Holder shall immediately notify Brokers: **(I)** if Buyer's initial or any additional deposit is not made pursuant to this Agreement, or is not good at time of deposit with Escrow Holder; or **(ii)** if Buyer and Seller instruct Escrow Holder to cancel escrow.

D. A Copy of any amendment that affects any paragraph of this Agreement for which Escrow Holder is responsible shall be delivered to Escrow Holder within **2** business days after mutual execution of the amendment.

29. BROKER COMPENSATION FROM BUYER: If applicable, upon Close Of Escrow, **Buyer** agrees to pay compensation to Broker as specified in a separate written agreement between Buyer and Broker.

30. TERMS AND CONDITIONS OF OFFER:

This is an offer to purchase the Property on the above terms and conditions. All paragraphs with spaces for initials by Buyer and Seller are incorporated in this Agreement only if initialed by all parties. If at least one but not all parties initial, a counter offer is required until agreement is reached. Seller has the right to continue to offer the Property for sale and to accept any other offer at any time prior to notification of Acceptance. Buyer has read and acknowledges receipt of a Copy of the offer and agrees to the above confirmation of agency relationships. If this offer is accepted and Buyer subsequently defaults, Buyer may be responsible for payment of Brokers' compensation. This Agreement and any supplement, addendum or modification, including any Copy, may be Signed in two or more counterparts, all of which shall constitute one and the same writing.

RPA-CA REVISED 1/06 (PAGE 7 OF 8)

Buyer's Initials (_____)(_____)
Seller's Initials (_____)(_____)

| Reviewed by _____ Date _____ |

EQUAL HOUSING OPPORTUNITY

CALIFORNIA RESIDENTIAL PURCHASE AGREEMENT (RPA-CA PAGE 7 OF 8)

Property Address: _____ Date: _____

31. **EXPIRATION OF OFFER:** This offer shall be deemed revoked and the deposit shall be returned unless the offer is Signed by Seller and a Copy of the Signed offer is personally received by Buyer, or by _____, who is authorized to receive it by 5:00 PM on the third Day after this offer is signed by Buyer (or, if checked, ☐ by _____ (date), at _____ AM/PM).

Date _____ Date _____
BUYER _____ BUYER _____
_____ _____
(Print name) **(Print name)**
_____
(Address)

32. **BROKER COMPENSATION FROM SELLER:**
    A. Upon Close Of Escrow, **Seller** agrees to pay compensation to Broker as specified in a separate written agreement between Seller and Broker.
    B. If escrow does not close, compensation is payable as specified in that separate written agreement.
33. **ACCEPTANCE OF OFFER:** Seller warrants that Seller is the owner of the Property, or has the authority to execute this Agreement. Seller accepts the above offer, agrees to sell the Property on the above terms and conditions, and agrees to the above confirmation of agency relationships. Seller has read and acknowledges receipt of a Copy of this Agreement, and authorizes Broker to deliver a Signed Copy to Buyer.
    ☐ (If checked) **SUBJECT TO ATTACHED COUNTER OFFER, DATED** _____.

Date _____ Date _____
SELLER _____ SELLER _____
_____ _____
(Print name) **(Print name)**
_____
(Address)

(___/___) **CONFIRMATION OF ACCEPTANCE:** A Copy of Signed Acceptance was personally received by Buyer or Buyer's authorized
(Initials) agent on (date) _____ at _____ AM/PM. **A binding Agreement is created when a Copy of Signed Acceptance is personally received by Buyer or Buyer's authorized agent whether or not confirmed in this document. Completion of this confirmation is not legally required in order to create a binding Agreement; it is solely intended to evidence the date that Confirmation of Acceptance has occurred.**

REAL ESTATE BROKERS:
A. **Real Estate Brokers are not parties to the Agreement between Buyer and Seller.**
B. **Agency relationships are confirmed as stated in paragraph 27.**
C. If specified in paragraph 2A, Agent who submitted the offer for Buyer acknowledges receipt of deposit.
D. **COOPERATING BROKER COMPENSATION:** Listing Broker agrees to pay Cooperating Broker **(Selling Firm)** and Cooperating Broker agrees to accept, out of Listing Broker's proceeds in escrow: **(i)** the amount specified in the MLS, provided Cooperating Broker is a Participant of the MLS in which the Property is offered for sale or a reciprocal MLS; or **(ii)** ☐ (if checked) the amount specified in a separate written agreement (C.A.R. Form CBC) between Listing Broker and Cooperating Broker.
Real Estate Broker (Selling Firm) _____ DRE Lic. # _____
By _____ DRE Lic. # _____ Date _____
Address _____ City _____ State _____ Zip _____
Telephone _____ Fax _____ E-mail _____

Real Estate Broker (Listing Firm) _____ DRE Lic. # _____
By _____ DRE Lic. # _____ Date _____
Address _____ City _____ State _____ Zip _____
Telephone _____ Fax _____ E-mail _____

ESCROW HOLDER ACKNOWLEDGMENT:
Escrow Holder acknowledges receipt of a Copy of this Agreement, (if checked, ☐ a deposit in the amount of $ _____),
counter offer numbers _____ and _____,
_____, and agrees to act as Escrow Holder subject to paragraph 28 of this Agreement, any supplemental escrow instructions and the terms of Escrow Holder's general provisions.

Escrow Holder is advised that the date of Confirmation of Acceptance of the Agreement as between Buyer and Seller is _____

Escrow Holder _____ Escrow # _____
By _____ Date _____
Address _____
Phone/Fax/E-mail _____
Escrow Holder is licensed by the California Department of ☐ Corporations, ☐ Insurance, ☐ Real Estate. License # _____

(___/___) **REJECTION OF OFFER:** No counter offer is being made. This offer was reviewed and rejected by Seller on
(Seller's Initials) _____ (Date)

Reviewed by _____ Date _____

RPA-CA REVISED 1/06 (PAGE 8 OF 8)
CALIFORNIA RESIDENTIAL PURCHASE AGREEMENT (RPA-CA PAGE 8 OF 8)

Appendix B

Example of a Good Inspection Report

. . . .

*T*he physical condition of your house greatly affects its value. Prudent purchasers always have a property *thoroughly* inspected before they buy it. No matter how beautifully you dress it up, buyers won't pay top dollar for a house that needs extensive, expensive repairs.

Don't let corrective-work problems sabotage your sale. Arrange your own inspection before you put your house on the market. In Chapter 7, we discuss four compelling reasons why getting a premarketing inspection is a good idea. We also explain how to choose a qualified inspector.

Be sure that the premarketing inspection covers all your house's major structural and mechanical systems, inside and out, from foundation to roof. Anything less is unacceptable. Thoroughly inspecting a house or condo of average size usually takes three to four hours.

Reading the best report ever written is no substitute for seeing defects with your own eyes. That's why we strongly recommend that you (and your agent, if you're using one) tag along when your inspector does the premarketing inspection. Use this opportunity to question the inspector about a defect's ramifications and explore corrective work alternatives.

Warren Camp Inspection Services

P.O. Box 986, Arnold, CA 95223

(209) 795-7661

- **Inspection Date:** _____ xx, xxxx
- **Date of Report:** _____ xx, xxxx

- **Report Number:** xx- _____
- **Inspector:** Warren Camp, ASHI® Certified Member, #732

- **Report:** "Premarketing" Inspection at: x x x x _____ Street, San Francisco
- **Dwelling Description:** Single-family dwelling
- **Present During Inspection:**
  Property Owner: Red. Tooselle
  Owner's Agent: Ken B. Elpful; Izzy Elpful and Associates Realtors
  Others: Bugzie O. Bliterate; Sooner-Is-Safer Pest Control Company

- **Weather:** No rain within 10 days

- **The inspected unit was fully furnished.**

- **A Structural / Pest-Control Inspection Report was not yet provided.**

- **The Seller's Disclosure Statement was not yet prepared or provided.**

As requested, this report is being prepared for the exclusive use of the property owner. In no way is it to be used by, nor are we obligated to review it with, any third parties. Because Warren Camp Inspection Services (WCIS) has not personally described the extent and nature of its findings to anyone but those present for the inspection, WCIS strongly discourages third parties from using this report. Interested parties should arrange with WCIS for an inspection that meets their more individualized needs.

This report provides a professional opinion of general features and major deficiencies of the building and its systems at inspection. It does not necessarily analyze or report on adjacent properties, nor does it cover environmental/neighborhood concerns. It summarizes observations on components inspected in accordance with customary property-inspection standards. The scope of our inspection is limited only to items discussed. It is not technically exhaustive. And, because certain findings are variable (cracking lengths throughout the structure that increase in time, erosion and corrosion levels that do not remain static, and so on), no one should rely on any reported findings for more than one year.

This is not a code compliance report; a home, product, or system guarantee of any kind; nor is it an evaluation of the property's salability. It includes only those items accessible to visual inspection; no furniture relocation, dismantling, demolition, or other manual handling, would have occurred in the preparation of this report. This report does not fulfill the requirements set forth in California Civil Code Section 1102 as to the required disclosures of a transferor of real property.

The WCIS inspector explained to the owner the two types of reports WCIS prepares. Rather than selecting the in-depth, narrative report with extensive recommendations, the client selected the highlighted, standard narrative report. Findings and recommendations that would normally have been included in an in-depth report have been excluded from this report.

Please call WCIS with your questions.

TABLE OF CONTENTS

Warren Camp Inspection Services

• Sample "Premarketing" Inspection Report — A single-family dwelling
xxxx_____Street, San Francisco, California _____ xx, xxxx

INTRODUCTION

The inspected property was a single-family dwelling with most of its interior spaces furnished and filled with personal belongings. Low-voltage wiring, heat exchangers, gardens, fences, retaining walls, underground piping and storage tanks, and sprinklers are not included in the scope of WCIS inspection reports, which are designed to meet or exceed current "Standards of Practice" established by the American Society of Home Inspectors (ASHI) of which the WCIS inspector is a certified member-inspector. A copy of the Standards is available upon request.

For the most part, the building was a three-level, framed structure with an attic and a partially accessible crawl space. The built-in garage was constructed partially below grade, with construction upgrades therein performed over the years. Built around 1915, this wood-framed building typically does not comply with today's building standards, although it has maintained its stature remarkably well, given its age. Because WCIS is not a structural engineering firm, it is restricted from evaluating structural integrity of buildings. However, a number of important structural features were inspected. See the STRUCTURAL section for a description of our findings.

Although structurally the building was generally in satisfactory condition, some components had not been maintained and have begun to fail. There were also a number of safety concerns and a few items need repair or replacement.

The building interior and exterior were well maintained. But of course, all buildings have flaws. We'll discuss some of these flaws but we cannot discover and report on every one. This premarketing inspection and report are not technically exhaustive. With only a few hours in which to inspect the entire property, WCIS provides, at best, a professional opinion based upon experience. WCIS does not provide a thorough or fully detailed analysis of problem areas.

Clients should not assume that items not discussed in this report are, by their omission, sound and operational. WCIS can imply no warranty or guarantee for any component or system. And, because building code and zoning conformity inspections are made only building departments having such jurisdiction, no code conformity evaluation can be made herein. Neither does WCIS suggest or provide any assurances that the property, in its current or corrected condition, will easily sell.

All the main point of this report were fully discussed with Red E. Tooselle and his agent, Ken B. Elpful, at inspection. The following sections describe the findings discussed. Please call with questions.

Repairs, corrections, and other follow-up items to consider, prior to marketing your building for sale. (Note: Check-marked concerns are merely highlights of the inspector's findings. Read the entire report to fully appreciate this effort. Where you have interest, follow these and the following recommendations and have specialists address those items excluded from this inspection and report.)

 ✓ Check with the building inspection department about permits and inspections for building alterations and additions.

Warren Camp Inspection Services

- Sample "Premarketing" Inspection Report — A single-family dwelling
xxxx_____ Street, San Francisco, California   _____ xx, xxxx

EXTERIOR
Building Exterior
This building, stuccoed on the façade, and with horizontal-wood siding on the rear wall, was, for the most part, adequately painted and maintained. Routinely, all exterior joints should be caulked and painted.

Left- and right-side walls were blocked by adjacent buildings. When references are made to the front, rear, left, and right, they are made facing the building from_____Street.

At the front wall, soil was close to the top of the foundation. This condition can cause wood decay and deterioration, but, because WCIS is not a structural/pest control inspector, our client should discuss this condition with the structural/pest control inspector performing such inspection.

The recently-installed electrical conduit, the rear door, and metal gutters and downspouts were not yet painted or weathersealed.

Aluminum windows on the façade were new. Wooden windows elsewhere were old but generally in satisfactory condition. Exterior window sashes, sills, and trim, especially on the rear wall, need caulking and weathersealing.

The garage entry door was a sectional type with open-vent screens in place to protect against accidental suffocation from auto exhaust and other fumes and aid in evaporative ventilation. Unfortunately, each was covered over with cardboard that should be removed.

Garage access was benefited by an electric opener that was operated. When testing for a functional contact-reversing safety feature on this electric opener, it was either not programmed into the opener or simply was not functioning at inspection.

Supported by concrete, the left alley stairs were in acceptable condition but lacked a much-needed handrail.

A wooden stairway at the rear was in satisfactory condition. The handgrip for its stairway handrail, however, was wider than today's industry practices suggest. Handrails can be easily made safe! Modify them.

Pavement and Drainage
The front walkway had concrete settlement and cracking. The garden patio and pathway was unlighted, and changes in the height of pavement and steps could prove hazardous.

Adequate soil drainage for Bay Area homes is imperative since soil types in this area swell when saturated and may damage a building's foundation. Grade at the front of the building was sloped likely ensuring adequate drainage away from the foundation during rainstorms. A drainage pattern at the rear patio was not as easy to predict. Water entry appears probably possibly because pavement was not adequately sloped away from the building and the surface drain was clogged. Red E. Tooselle should unclog this drain and keep all drains, patios, and walkways clean and well maintained.

Underground Piping
WCIS detected no outward signs of presently existing or previously placed underground fuel storage tanks (USTs) within the inspected areas. There were no fill spout, vent pipe, supply tubing and return line, or a fuse box — typical indicators of USTs. Interested parties may wish

Warren Camp Inspection Services

• Sample "Premarketing" Inspection Report — A single-family dwelling
xxxx_____ Street, San Francisco, California _____ xx, xxxx

to explore further since such exploration is not within the scope of ASHI standard inspection practices.
  ✓ Refer to a current Structural / Pest-Control Inspection Report for findings and corrective recommendations.
  ✓ Prime and paint the raw materials exposed to the elements.
  ✓ Caulk and weatherseal exterior window sashes, sills, and trim.
  ✓ Uncover the garage door's two open-vent screens.
  ✓ Provide or program the contact-reversing mechanism for the automatic garage door opener.
  ✓ Provide and modify handrails.
  ✓ For safety's sake, improve lighting at the front and rear.
  ✓ Unclog the patio's surface drain.

FOUNDATION

Only portions of the foundation were visible at inspection. Many areas were blocked by finished walls and an extensive amount of personal belongings.

A cementlike soil covering, called ratproofing, was in place in the crawl space. The membrane appeared intact, with two small openings in the center that could be easily patched.

Visible foundation stem walls in the garage and crawl space appear to have been installed according to customarily practiced standards. Foundation legs were made of continuous concrete, which is often reinforced with internally placed steel bars. However, the existence, extent, or condition of any such bars could not be verified.

There was hairline or minor cracking on the right-longitudinal leg. Such cracking in a building of this type and age is not uncommon and should be routinely monitored. Minimal levels of plateau variations (uneven surface levels at cracks) were detected. Looking for any direct and current transference of foundation movement to adjacent finished walls, ceilings, and floors to rooms above, no outward sign was detectable. It was not possible to determine if this cracking was a current condition. If more information is needed, a qualified structural engineer, experienced in similar structures, should be contacted to fully inspect and evaluate findings on these and any other structural concerns.

The rear-latitudinal leg was water-stained and had efflorescence on its base. This appeared related to the lack of fresh-air ventilation in the subarea, failure of the patio's reversed-slope grade, and the clogged surface drain, all of which should be corrected.

Because many garage and basement walls were closed to view, WCIS could not inspect for anchor bolting and other concealed fasteners.

  ✓ Clear the subarea of personal belongings to facilitate buyers' upcoming pre-purchase inspections.
  ✓ Patch the ratproofing openings.
  ✓ Routinely monitor the foundation.
  ✓ Ventilate the subarea.

Warren Camp Inspection Services

• Sample "Premarketing" Inspection Report — A single-family dwelling
xxxx_____ Street, San Francisco, California   _____ xx, xxxx

STRUCTURAL FRAMING
Substructure
Visual access to structural framing was limited. Many of the structural members within the basement and garage were blocked or covered by drywall, an extensive amount of personal belongings, building materials, appliances, an automobile, and thermal insulation. Remove such blockage in preparation for upcoming prepurchase inspections.

Wood posts in the garage were in satisfactory condition. Most were straight and vertical. For the most part, the tops and bottoms of the posts have been customarily connected. It appeared, however, that one post toward the front of the garage, which originally supported the overhead girder, had been removed several years ago. No related structural movement was visible. Contact a structural engineer if further evaluation is desired.

Three or four garage joists were some cause for concern, apparently damaged by questionable performance when previous trades inappropriately notched the bottoms of these structural members for pipe installations. Framing can easily be supplemented with new supporting members.

Most of the structural posts, beams, plates, and studs had not yet been retrofitted for earthquake preparedness. Prior to or after sale, these measures should be taken, Corrective recommendations should come from a qualified, licensed, structural engineer.

Moisture staining was found on the garage walls and ceiling. These areas were dry to the touch and, when tested with a biprobe electric moisture meter, were absolutely dry.

The subarea should have additional cross-ventilation (screen and louvered) installed to reduce damp wood deterioration, control moisture and condensation, and aid in the complete combustion of gas-fueled appliances in these areas. Remember, Red, to uncover the garage door vents.

Main Structure
No evidence of current structural movement was noted during inspection of samplings of doors, windows, floors, walls, and ceilings. The tops of some doors were taper-cut to allow for wall shifting over the years. Any separations on walls, molding, or ceilings, or sagging or sloping for floors, appeared to be the result of ordinary shifting and/or expansion within framing and supporting soils. In WCIS's opinion, the findings do not represent significant, current movement.

Attic Area
An attic access door was in the garage loft ceiling. It was painted shut, preventing inspection. Make access available for the upcoming "buyer's inspections" and fully determine conditions therein.

✓ Make the subarea accessible for upcoming prepurchase inspections.
✓ Add supplemental members to the notched joists.
✓ Seismically retrofit some or all structural posts, beams, plates, and studs for earthquake preparedness.
✓ Improve ventilation throughout the subarea.
✓ Free the attic access door for subsequent inspections.

Warren Camp Inspection Services

• Sample "Premarketing" Inspection Report — A single-family dwelling
xxxx_____ Street, San Francisco, California   _____ xx, xxxx

SECURITY AND FIRE SAFETY

WCIS has some fire-safety concerns about this property. Subarea wall and ceiling surfaces in mechanical rooms (housing the furnace and water heater) adjacent to habitable rooms were not completely fire-resistant. Neither was the door from the garage to habitable spaces upstairs. Fully separate the mechanical rooms from habitable ones (e.g., by patching all openings with drywall, plaster, sheet metal, and so on or undertaking appropriate fire-resistant construction). Line the door's inside face with fire-resistive drywall and install a tightly sealed automatic door closer.

WCIS was unable to locate any smoke detectors or sprinklers in this area. A monitored alarm system with adequate smoke and heat detectors could be installed.

Smoke detectors were on each level's hallway ceilings, however, each was without its require battery. Because state and local codes change frequently, consult the building department for direction on optimal number, type, and location of units when selling a property.

The building's front, side, and rear doors were each equipped with a lock and deadbolt. Unfortunately, the front entry deadbolt was a "double-keyed" type - a key for the inside as well as the outside of the lock is required. If these keys are no easily accessible, emergency egress could be impossible, and bear serious safety consequences. Conversion to single-keyed bolts is easy, affordable, and should be considered before showing the property to buyers. Contact a locksmith.

Glass in the sliding glass doors had glazing labels. Front door glazing did not appear to have a glazing label certifying specification (e.g., tempered, safety, etc.). Door and window panes without safety glazing can be hazardous when broken, so current building code requires safety-labeled glass to minimize possible injury. Replacement of this glazing may not now be required; however, install decals and exercise caution and common sense in this area to prevent accidental breakage and possible bodily injury.

Means of egress from the basement bedroom was of concern. Two windows had iron bars installed across them that prevent emergency egress. These should be removed prior to showing.

Supplement interior and exterior lighting for overall security and safety.
  ✓ Provide and install needed fire-protection devices or systems.
  ✓ Immediately provide the smoke detectors with fresh batteries.
  ✓ Improve door-lock safety.
  ✓ Remove the permanently installed iron-bar window coverings.
  ✓ Add lighting for overall security and safety.

PLUMBING

Water Supply

The shutoff valve for the main water-service line was on a garage front wall. It was operable; no leakage was detected.

A 1-inch galvanized iron water line joined the building from the street. Domestic hot- and cold-water-supply lines were mostly made of iron. WCIS found a combination of iron and copper water lines next to the garage stairway. Its plumbing connection was inappropriate,

Warren Camp Inspection Services

• Sample "Premarketing" Inspection Report — A single-family dwelling
xxxx_____ Street, San Francisco, California   _____ xx, xxxx

likely contributing to galvanic corrosion within these lines. It would be easy to install a di-electric fitting between iron and copper to separate these dissimilar metals.

Measured at the side of the garage, static pressure on the water line was 108 pounds per square inch (PSI), which is excessive. Prescribed water-pressure-ratings are set at 55 to 65 PSI to prevent leakage from excessive pressures. A water-pressure regulator and pressure gauge on the incoming water line recommended.

The garage hose Bibb leaked when tested; washer replacement may be all that is needed.

Part of the hot-water piping in the water heater area had no thermal insulation. Full insulation would reduce energy consumption and improve the hot-response time for each water fixture.

Inspecting and test drip-irrigation, sprinkler, or low-voltage systems is not included in ASHI(r) inspection practices.

Vents, Drains, and Traps
Throughout much of this structure, visible waste and vent piping were made of iron as well as copper. There was no evidence of leakage in visibly accessible waste lines.

A number of drains were inspected and maintaining an effective trap-seal with water.

Gas Supply
The main gas-shutoff valve, located on the front wall, was operable.

  ✓ Add a di-electric fitting to separate iron and copper piping.
  ✓ Install a water-pressure regulator and pressure gauge on the incoming water line.
  ✓ Replace the washer on the leaking garage hosebibb.

Water Heater
The hot water heater, gas-fueled and located in the garage, was operating during inspection. It had no thermal insulation jacket which would be easy to add before showing the property to buyers.

The water heater also lacked adequate cross-strapping and restraining blocks designed to resist movement during an intense earthquake. (See the accompanying pamphlet on water heater bracing.)

It was apparently a recently installed model. With a fiberglass tank, an identification plate indicated that this A.O. Smith appliance had a 40-gallon capacity, a setting of 38,000 BTUs, and a 40.4-gallon-per-hour recovery rating.

Its tank bottom was slightly rusty. No leaks were evident.

A safety valve on water heater tops, referred to as a "temperature and pressure relief valve," is necessary to the operation of these appliances. The T&PR valve was properly located. A water overflow tube was installed according to accepted trade practices.

The shutoff valve on the cold-water supply piping was operational and no leakage was evident.

Hot-water piping immediately above the water heater had some thermal wrapping, however, an "energy inspection" is not within the scope of our inspections.

Warren Camp Inspection Services

• Sample "Premarketing" Inspection Report — A single-family dwelling
xxxx_____ Street, San Francisco, California _____ xx, xxxx

A drain valve at the base of the heater tank, when opened, showed minimal sludge deposits.

As a standard earthquake-preparedness consideration before transferring title, some or all of the following installations could be undertaken:
a. Flexible water-supply piping to water heaters
b. Fully functional seismic cross-strapping (see enclosed WCIS brochure), and
c. Flexible gas-supply piping to heaters and all gas-fueled appliances.

✓ Install a thermal insulation jacket.
✓ Provide and install bracing and strapping.

LAUNDRY

Laundry equipment was in the unfinished basement. The washer and dryer were the side-by-side type. Testing appliances is outside the scope of ASHI(r) inspections.

Water supply hoses to the washer were holding pressure and not leaking.

The washer's drain hose was simply hung over the ledge of the laundry sink and, under pressure, could fall off. Secure the hose with tape or wire.

The dryer was fueled by natural gas. Its lint-exhaust hose was connected well to an exterior vent cowl.

✓ Tape or wire the drain hose securely.

ELECTRICAL

Service and the Main Disconnect

Electrical wiring for this building was fed from underground and provided approximately 240 volts to the meter. The main disconnect switch and panel, located on the right side of the building, had a 125-amp circuit breaker as the overcurrent device for the building, protecting #2-guage copper conductors.

Ampacity (the service entrance capacity) was adequate, based on the building's current load-demands.

Subpanel Distribution

The building's main disconnect device was combined in a panel with other circuits. There was also a subpanel on a garage side wall.

Protected by circuit breakers, the combined main-disconnect-and-distribution panel had the following circuitry distribution:

4   @ 120-volt circuits at 15 amps
14 @ 120-volt circuits at 20 amps
3   @ 240-volt circuits at 20 amps
2   @ 240-volt circuits at 30 amps
1   @ 240-volt circuits at 70 amps

Warren Camp Inspection Services

- Sample "Premarketing" Inspection Report — A single-family dwelling

xxxx_____ Street, San Francisco, California   _____ xx, xxxx

The subpanel also contained circuit breakers for branch circuitry. Its distribution was:

> 6   @ 120-volt circuits at 15 amps
> 2   @ 120-volt circuits at 20 amps

Inspected circuitry in each panel was adequately wired for current electrical demands. Neither subpanel was fully circuit-labeled but they should be before showing the property.
   Both panels were benefited by closed-front protection covers.

Grounding and Polarity

Of course, all electrical systems should be safely and properly grounded. An appropriately driven grounding rod was not easily located, however, the system ground wire provided at least minimal grounding levels where sample-tested. A number of convenience receptacles in the kitchen, bathrooms, laundry, basement, and garage provided grounding protection.

Wiring

Much of the basement's exposed writing has been piped into conduit. The following is only a sampling of wiring concerns and is not intended to take the place of an electrical contractor's findings:

   a. In a random sampling of receptacles, "reverse polarity" was found to the right of the kitchen sink. This condition, hazardous in certain instances, can be easily corrected and should be.
   b. Sample testing receptacles and switches revealed a loose installation in the master bedroom. Because outlet movement permits disconnection of power and grounding protection, a licensed electrician should examine and service all loose installations to provide the maximum amount of safety.
   c. The powder room's 3-slot receptacle was not grounded and should be to provide full protection.
   d. Detection or evaluation of electromagnetic fields (EMFs) is not a part of our industry's Standards of Practice and is not included.

All of the above wiring and grounding items should be remedied immediately to prevent accidental injury.
   Warren Camp always recommends the installation of ground-fault and circuit-interruption-type receptacles in kitchens, bathrooms, and other wet locations as an added safety measure. None were as yet installed.

> ✓ Provide panels with complete circuit identification.
> ✓ Remedy immediately the wiring problems.
> ✓ Install ground-fault circuit-interruption-type receptacles in all wet locations.

HEATING

Heat Source Types and Condition

The living room was equipped with a gas-fueled wall heater, operational at inspection and

Warren Camp Inspection Services

• Sample "Premarketing" Inspection Report — A single-family dwelling
xxxx_____ Street, San Francisco, California   _____ xx, xxxx

installed several years ago. Its control chamber and flue diverter were extremely dirty and should be vacuumed as soon as possible.

As expected, a heater of this age would have no pilot-light safety device to stop the pilot's gas flow if the flame accidentally blew out.

Vent and Flue Piping
The flue was encased within the wall. Inaccessible portions of flue piping were not inspected. There was nothing on the wall to suggest inadequacy.

Heat Exchanger
This heater's gas burners appeared to be out of balance with unusual flame characteristics. Unevenness is difficult for anyone but a heating contractor or utility company technician to analyze. Such a check-up should be made.

The firebox (heat exchanger) of this heater separates and redirects hot air from ambient air, which it also warms and circulates. A full inspection of a heat exchanger is not possible without dismantling a heater which was not done. There was also no access for an inspection mirror. The local utility or a heating contractor should conduct a standard safety check of this and all gas appliances, supply lines, and flues at every change of occupancy.

> ✓ Vacuum the control chamber thoroughly as well as the flue diverter.
> ✓ Ask the local utility or a heating contractor to conduct a standard test and safety check of all gas-fueled appliances, supply lines, and flues.

INTERIOR
Interior spaces were fully furnished at inspection, some areas were inaccessible and not inspected. Generally, walls, ceilings, and floors were well maintained. The inspection industry does not report on cosmetic details.

There were water stains in a few locations. Two window walls of the attic loft and one living room bay window wall were noticeably stained, indicating possible leakage or condensation. However, when tested with an electric biprobe moisture meter, it was determined conclusively that there was no moisture retention and this staining was historic.

Much of the upper-level flooring was carpeted. Uncovered hardwood flooring on the first level was adequately maintained.

Wood-framed windows on the rear wall should be repaired. Some window locks and hardware need adjustment while some double-hung sashes had broken wires. Generally, any broken, deteriorated, and/or missing door and window locks and components, even though not specifically called out in this report, should be replaced or repaired.

> ✓ Repair windows, doors, and hardware as needed.

KITCHEN
The kitchen was well maintained. The sink, faucet, trap and drain, and shutoff valves were working when tested. Water pressure was adequate.

Warren Camp Inspection Services

- Sample "Premarketing" Inspection Report — A single-family dwelling

xxxx_____ Street, San Francisco, California   _____ xx, xxxx

The dishwasher did have an anti-siphoning device and was well secured to the underside of the counter. An anti-siphoning device, installed above the sink rim, prevents backflow of waste products into the clean dishwasher appliance if the sewer system is blocked.

Stained-wood cabinets were in satisfactory condition; however, only a sampling of doors, drawers, and connections was made.

Plastic-laminate counters were also in satisfactory condition. Two miter joints were slightly open and should be fully sealed with a good quality caulking.

A ducted exhaust fan on the ceiling was operational but the fan motor drew air weakly and may be grease-bound. For an efficient exchange of air, clean, repair, or replace components as needed.

Not recently installed, the ceramic tile floor was well maintained.

✓ Seal the countertop's miter joints with a good quality caulking.
✓ Clean, repair, or replace exhaust fan components.

BATHROOM

This building had two bathrooms, a powder room, and vanity closet. All of the rooms were well maintained. Sinks, faucets, traps and drains, and angle stops worked well when tested.

The angle stop (shutoff valve) for the master bathroom washbasin was dripping slowly and requires adjustment and/or washer replacement.

Water pressure was adequate at each fixture, however, measurement is only a relative comparison rating.

No evidence of significant or unusual deterioration was evident on visible drain lines and trap piping. Tested drains ran freely.

Toilets in each bathroom were well secured to the floor. Support screws inside the guest bathroom's wall-mounted toilet tank were extremely rusted and should be replaced immediately.

Grout or caulking was missing around bathroom tub-to-tile connections and should be caulked.

✓ Correct the leaking valve.
✓ Replace the deteriorated toilet tank's mounting screws immediately.
✓ Apply caulking where needed.

ROOFING

Accessibility and Warranty

The shingle roof was very steep, and the inspector did not walk on it. Inspection was strictly visual, made through nearby attic windows, and from the adjacent deck and street levels in the neighborhood. Only the general condition of visible roofing surfaces was observed. This report does not provide an opinion on, or a warranty against, past present, or future leakage.

Membrane Types and Condition

Asphalt-composition-type shingling was recently installed. No distinct failures were

Warren Camp Inspection Services

- Sample "Premarketing" Inspection Report — A single-family dwelling
xxxx_____ Street, San Francisco, California _____ xx, xxxx

detectable to visual inspection. There was little or no evidence of unusual or significant roof deterioration.

Chimneys, Gutters, and Flashing
Two metal chimneys at the right property line were elevated well above the roof line, lacking adequate seismic strapping or bracing. Chimney guy wires or bracing were missing but could easily be added.

Debris in the right-hand Dutch gutter (the common roof gutter between adjacent properties) must be immediately removed. Gutter outlets at the tops of downspouts should have mesh screening installed to prevent clogging.

The downspout system was, for the most part, customarily installed. One downspout at the front wall likely dumps water directly onto the foundation and garden area below, which can cause erosion. A splash block should be set at the downspout base to divert this collected water away from the building.

The following additional items were also observed:

    a. A metal antenna that was considerably rusted was loosely connected to the chimney and should be removed and discarded.
    b. The front firewall had separations and needs to be sealed.
    c. Vent and perimeter flashing which is unsealed needs the immediate attention of a roofer.

Roofs are seldom, if ever, regularly inspected. Regardless of whether a WCIS roof inspection was made, roofing problems are often subtle and difficult to evaluate. Because property inspectors don't often have the hands-on training and accessibility roofers have, whenever questions of adequacy of roofing arise, a licensed roofing contractor could be asked to provide a thorough inspection and evaluation.

    ✓ Add chimney guy wires or bracing.
    ✓ Clean the debris from the right-hand Dutch gutter and insert outlet screens.
    ✓ Place a splash block at the base of the front downspout.
    ✓ Remove and dispose of the metal antenna.
    ✓ Reseal the firewall sections and flashing

SEISMIC MAP EVALUATION NOTATIONS (an optional evaluation that was ordered by Red E. Tooselle)

    Map #1 — Intensity of Ground Shaking During a Major Earthquake (having a Richter rating of 8.0 or higher): From "A" to "E," this property's location is rated "E" (Fortunately, this location the least intense shaking rating the city.)
    Map #2 — Potential Landslide Location: This building is within such location. It's approximately three blocks from an active slide area.

The contents of this report have been prepared for the exclusive use of Red E. Tooselle. Reliance by other is prohibited.
Warren Camp Inspection Services

Warren Camp Inspection Services

- *Sample* "Premarketing" Inspection Report — A single-family dwelling
xxxx_____Street, San Francisco, California _____xx, xxxx

Map #3 — Estimated Building Damage from a Major Quake: Seismologists anticipate minimal damage to this building and from adjacent structures.
Map #4 — Potential Reservoir Failure: This building is outside such location.
Map #5 — Geological Makeup Beneath This Building: This building sits on unsheared Franciscan rock (designated KJU by geologists), which has the highest stability rating in the city.
Map #6 — Liquefaction Potential: This building is outside such location.
Map #7 — Subsidence Potential: This building is outside such location.
Map #8 — Tsunami Potential: This building is outside such location.

Thank you for calling Warren Camp, your ASHI-certified-member property inspector.

Additional articles/pamphlets provided:
All-Points Bulletin (a home remodeling and repair newsletter): a PG&E utilities pamphlet regarding electromagnetic fields; published articles by Warren Camp about smoke detectors, asbestos, water intrusion and GFCI electrical receptacles; and his year-round home-maintenance checklist.

Copies to:	delivery	mail	pick-up	fax	email
Owner:	[ ]	[x]	[ ]	[ ]	[ ]
Owner's agent:	[ ]	[ ]	[x]	[ ]	[ ]

Warren Camp Inspection Services

Appendix C

Glossary

··

Terms appearing in *italic type* within the definitions are defined elsewhere in the glossary.

acceleration clause: In a mortgage contract, this provision gives the lender the right to demand payment of the entire outstanding balance if a homeowner misses a monthly payment, sells the property, or otherwise fails to perform as promised under the terms of the mortgage. (See also *due-on-sale clause*.)

adjustable-rate mortgage (ARM): An ARM is a mortgage whose *interest rate* and monthly payments vary throughout its life. Usually, the ARM's interest rate is tied to an *index,* which measures the overall market level of interest rates. If the overall level of interest rates rises, the interest rate of an ARM generally follows suit. Similarly, if interest rates fall, so does the mortgage's interest rate and monthly payment. The amount that the interest rate can fluctuate is limited by *caps* (see also *periodic caps* and *lifetime caps*). Before you agree to an adjustable-rate mortgage, be sure that you can afford the highest payments that would result if the interest rate on your mortgage increased to the maximum allowed. For specifics on how an ARM's interest rate is calculated, see *formula* and *teaser rate.*

adjusted cost basis: The adjusted cost basis is important when you sell your house because this amount allows you to determine your profit or loss for tax purposes. You can arrive at the adjusted cost basis by adding the cost of the capital improvements that you've made to the home to the price that you originally paid for the home. Capital improvements, such as adding rooms or remodeling a bathroom, increase your property's value and its life expectancy. Repairs that merely maintain the value of your home, such as fixing a leaky pipe, aren't considered capital improvements.

adjusted sale price: An adjusted sale price is the actual selling price of a house less the expenses of sale, such as real estate agents' commissions, legal fees, and so on.

adjustment period or adjustment frequency: This term refers to how often the *interest rate* for an *adjustable-rate mortgage* changes. Some adjustable-rate mortgages change every month, but one or two adjustments per year is more typical. The less frequently your loan rate shifts, the less financial uncertainty you face. But less frequent adjustments in your mortgage rate mean that you will probably have a higher *teaser* or initial interest rate. (The initial interest rate is also called the "start rate.")

annual percentage rate (APR): The APR measures the total cost of a mortgage, assuming that the borrower holds it for its entire life. It's expressed as an annualized rate of all interest charges — which includes not only the base *interest rate* reflected in the monthly mortgage payments but also the *points* and any other add-on, upfront loan fees — spread out over the life of the loan. The APR is thus invariably higher than the rate of interest that the lender quotes for the mortgage, but it gives a more accurate picture of the likely cost of the mortgage. Keep in mind, however, that most mortgages aren't held for their full 15- or 30-year terms, so the effective annual percentage rate is higher than the quoted APR because the upfront fees are spread out over fewer years.

appraisal: Mortgage lenders require an appraiser to give an opinion of the *market value* of a house a homeowner wants to sell or refinance. This professional opinion helps to protect the lender from lending money on a house that's worth less than the amount the buyers have agreed to pay for it or that the seller wishes to obtain when refinancing the existing loan. For typical houses, the appraisal fee is several hundred dollars and is usually paid for by the borrower.

appreciation/depreciation: Appreciation refers to the increase of a property's value. Depreciation (the reverse of appreciation) is when a property's value decreases.

arbitration (of disputes): This method of solving real estate contract disputes is generally less costly and faster than having lawyers duke it out in a court of law. In arbitration, the dissenting sides each present their perspectives to a neutral arbitrator who, after hearing the evidence, makes a decision that resolves the disagreement. The arbitrator's decision is final and may be enforced as if it were a court judgment. Consult a real estate lawyer if you're ever a party in an arbitration. (See also *mediation*.)

"as is": If you're selling a property "as is," you aren't providing any guarantees or warranties to the buyer as to the condition of the property and won't make further allowances, credits, or price reductions for any problems with your property.

assessed value: The assessed value is the value of a property for the purpose of determining *property taxes.* This figure depends on the methodology used by the local tax assessor and, thus, may differ from the *appraised* or *market value* of the property.

assumable mortgage: Some mortgages don't require a borrower to pay off the outstanding balance after the house sells. Instead, the new owner can simply take over the remaining loan balance and continue making payments under the loan's original terms. This arrangement benefits the buyers if the assumable mortgage has a lower interest rate than the current going interest rate for new loans. Most assumables are adjustable-rate mortgages. Fixed-rate, assumable mortgages are nearly extinct these days because lenders realize that they lose money on such mortgages when interest rates soar.

balloon loan: This kind of loan requires level payments just as a 15- or 30-year *fixed-rate mortgage* does. However, well before the loan's maturity date — the date when it would normally be paid off if the borrower kept making those fixed, monthly payments (typically three to ten years after its start date) — the full remaining balance of a balloon loan becomes due and payable. Although balloon loans can save you money because they charge a lower rate of interest relative to fixed-rate loans, balloon loans are dangerous. If you don't have a big chunk of cash sitting around somewhere to pay off the outstanding balance, you'll be forced to *refinance* the loan. Refinancing a loan is never a sure thing because your employment and financial situation may change, and interest rates may fluctuate. Beware of balloon loans!

bridge loan: If you find yourself in the inadvisable situation of having closed on the purchase of another home before you sell your current one, you may need a bridge loan. Such a loan enables you to borrow against the *equity* that is tied up in your old house until it sells. The bridge loan is aptly named because such a loan may keep home buyers financially above water during this period when they own two houses. Bridge loans are expensive compared to other alternatives, such as

tapping into savings, borrowing from family or friends, or using the proceeds from the sale of the current house. In most cases, home buyers need the bridge loan for only a few months in order to tide them over until they sell their house. Thus, the loan fees can represent a high cost (about 10 percent of the loan amount) for such a short-term loan.

broker: A real estate broker is one level higher on the real estate professional totem pole than the *real estate agent* (or salesperson). Real estate agents can't legally work on their own; a broker must supervise them. To become a broker in most states, a real estate salesperson must have a number of years of full-time real estate experience, meet special educational requirements, and pass a state-licensing exam. See also *real estate agent* and *Realtor.*

buydown: In a buydown, the builder or house seller agrees to pay part of the home buyer's mortgage for the first few years. The term also refers to the practice of a seller paying a mortgage lender a predetermined amount of money to reduce his or her mortgage interest rate, thereby creating more attractive financing for a potential buyer. Veterans with low or modest incomes may be able to get buydowns through a *Veterans Administration loan* plan that's available in some new housing developments.

buyer's broker: Historically, real estate *brokers* and *agents* worked only for sellers. A buyer's broker, on the other hand, only owes allegiance to the buyer and doesn't have an agent relationship with the seller.

Buyer's brokers, however, are generally paid on a *commission basis,* so they still have the same conflict of interest other commissioned real estate agents have — the higher the price of your next home, the more money the buyer's broker makes because a broker's commission is based on a percentage of the purchase price of the home you buy.

capital gain: A capital gain is the profit, as defined for tax purposes, that a home-owner makes when he sells a house. For example, if you buy a house for $200,000 and then sell the house years later for $240,000, your capital gain is $40,000. See *capital gains exclusion.*

capital gains exclusion: Normally, a *capital gain* generated by selling an asset is taxable. Thanks to the Taxpayer Relief Act of 1997, however, subject to meeting particular requirements, a significant portion of your gain on the sale of a primary residence is excludable from tax: up to $250,000 for single taxpayers and $500,000 for married couples filing jointly.

caps: *Adjustable-rate mortgages* (ARMs) specify two different types of caps or limits on how much the interest rate of an ARM can move up or down. The *life cap* limits the highest or lowest *interest rate* that's allowed over the entire life of a mortgage. The *periodic cap* limits the amount that an interest rate can change in one *adjustment period.* A one-year *ARM,* for example, may have a start rate of 6.5 percent with a plus or minus 2-percent periodic adjustment cap and a 6-percent life cap. In a worst-case scenario, the loan's *interest rate* would be 8.5 percent in the second year, 10.5 percent in the third year, and 12.5 percent (6.5 percent start rate plus the 6-percent life cap) every year after that. If you were that unlucky, though, we'd recommend seeing an astrologer.

cash reserve: Most mortgage lenders require that home buyers have sufficient cash left over after closing on their home purchase to make the first two mortgage payments or to cover a financial emergency. As a seller, if you're providing financing to the buyers, you should insist on this requirement, too.

closing costs: Closing costs generally total about 2 to 5 percent of the home's purchase price and include the loan origination fee or *points, appraisal* fee, *credit report* fee, mortgage interest for the period between the closing date and the first mortgage payment, *homeowners insurance* premium, *title insurance,* pro-rated *property taxes,* and recording and transferring charges. Despite the fact that a buyer needs a down payment to close on a home purchase, closing costs, technically speaking, don't include the cash down payment, which is considered to be a separate item. Don't neglect to consider these costs when weighing the purchase of your next dream home.

commission: Commission is the percentage of the selling price of a house that's paid to the *real estate agents* and *brokers.* For a house seller, the fact that the more the house fetches, the more agents get paid is good — this arrangement incites agents to go for the highest possible sale price for a house (unless selling at a lower price may result in a quicker sale). Remember that commissions are always negotiable.

common areas: Common areas are the shared ownership portions of a *condominium* complex (such as the lobby, recreational areas, parking lot, underlying land on which buildings are located, and so on).

community property: Community property is a way that married couples may take title to real estate. Community property offers two major advantages over *joint tenancy* and *tenancy-in-common*. First, community property ownership allows either spouse to transfer interests, by last will and testament or otherwise, to whomever he or she wishes. Second, if one spouse dies, the *cost basis* of the entire house is "stepped up" (increased) to equal its current *market value* for the surviving spouse. Assuming that the house has appreciated in value since it was originally purchased, this "stepped-up basis" reduces the taxable profit owed when the house is sold.

comparable market analysis (CMA): A written analysis of comparable houses currently being offered for sale and comparable houses that sold in the past six months is called a comparable market analysis (CMA). In order to price your house appropriately, you need to know how much houses like yours are selling for. Identify houses "comparable" to yours that sold within the last six months, are in the immediate vicinity of your house, and are as similar as possible to your house in terms of size, age, and condition. By analyzing the asking prices of houses comparable to yours that are currently on the market, you can see whether prices are rising, flat, or declining.

condominium: Condominiums are housing units within a larger development area in which you own your own unit, plus a proportionate share of the development's *common areas:* the lobby, elevator, parking lot, and so on. Condominiums are a less-expensive form of housing than single-family homes. However, condominiums generally don't increase in value as rapidly as single-family houses do because the demand for condos is lower than the demand for houses. And because condominiums are far easier for builders to develop than single-family homes are, the supply of condominiums often exceeds

the demand for them. (Cool cats call condominiums "condos.")

contingency: Contingencies are conditions contained in almost all home purchase offers. The seller or buyer must meet or waive all contingencies before the deal can be closed. These conditions relate to such factors as the buyer's review and approval of property inspections or the buyer's ability to get the mortgage financing that's specified in the contract. Sellers may include contingencies as well, such as making the sale of their house contingent on their successful purchase of another home. If a contingency can't be met, the party for whom it was established may legitimately withdraw from a contract.

convertible adjustable-rate mortgage: Unlike a conventional *adjustable-rate mortgage,* a convertible adjustable-rate mortgage gives borrowers the option to convert to a *fixed-rate mortgage,* usually between the 13th and 60th month of the loan. For this privilege, convertible adjustable-rate mortgage loans have a higher rate of interest than conventional adjustable-rate mortgages, and a conversion fee is charged (the fee can range from a few hundred dollars to one percent or so of the remaining balance). Additionally, if borrowers choose to convert to a fixed-rate mortgage, they pay a slightly higher rate than they can get by shopping around for the best fixed rates available at the time they convert.

cooperative (co-op): These buildings aren't to be confused with "communes," which are places in Oregon where hippies hang out together. Cooperatives are apartment buildings where residents own a share of a corporation whose main asset is the building that the residents live in. In high-cost housing areas, cooperatives (like their cousins, *condominiums* and *townhouses*) are cheaper alternatives to buying single-family houses. Unfortunately, cooperatives also resemble their cousins in that they generally lag behind single-family homes in terms of *appreciation.* Co-ops are also, as a rule, harder to sell and obtain loans for than condominiums.

cosigner: If you have a checkered past in the credit world, you may need help securing a mortgage, even though you're financially stable. A friend or relative can come to your rescue by cosigning, which literally means being indebted for, a mortgage. A cosigner can't improve your *credit report* but can improve your chances of getting a mortgage. Cosigners should be aware, however, that cosigning for your loan adversely affects their future credit-worthiness because your loan becomes what's known as a contingent liability against their borrowing power.

cost basis: See *adjusted cost basis.*

covenants, conditions, and restrictions (CC&Rs): CC&Rs establish a condominium by creating a homeowners association, by stipulating how the condominium's maintenance and repairs are handled, and by regulating what can and can't be done to individual units and the condominium's common areas. These restrictions may apply to lawn maintenance, window curtain colors, pet ownership, and whether residents can hang wet underwear on their decks.

credit report: A credit report is the main report that a lender uses to determine an applicant's creditworthiness. Applicants must pay for a lender to obtain this report, which the lender uses to determine the applicant's ability to handle all forms of credit and to pay off loans in a timely fashion. If you provide financing to the buyer of your property, be sure to first run a credit report on the buyer/borrower.

debt-to-income ratio: Before you trade up to a more expensive home, determine your price range. Lenders generally figure that you shouldn't spend more than about 33 to 40 percent of your monthly income for your housing costs. The debt-to-income ratio measures your future monthly housing expenses, which include your proposed mortgage payment (debt), property tax, and insurance, in relation to your monthly income.

deed: A deed is the document that transfers title to real property. Before you can give a buyer the deed to your property, you must show that you hold clear and legal title to the property. Also, the escrow holder must receive the mortgage company's payment and the buyer's payments for the down payment and closing costs.

default: You default if you violate the terms of your mortgage agreement. In most cases, missing two or more monthly mortgage payments triggers default. Defaulting can lead to foreclosure on your house.

delinquency: Delinquency occurs when a monthly mortgage payment isn't received by the due date. At first borrowers are delinquent; then they're in default.

depreciation: See *appreciation.*

disclosure statement: See *transfer disclosure statement.*

down payment: The down payment is the part of the purchase price that the buyer pays in cash, up front, and doesn't finance with a mortgage. Generally, the larger the down payment, the better the deal that the buyer can get on a mortgage. In most cases, a down payment equal to 20 percent of the property's purchase price qualifies a buyer for the best available mortgage programs.

due-on-sale clause: A due-on-sale clause contained in the mortgage entitles the lender to demand full payment of all money due on a loan secured by the property when a borrower sells or transfers title to the property.

earnest money: Earnest money is a home buyer's "good faith" deposit that accompanies a written purchase offer.

earthquake insurance: Californians aren't the only people who have to worry about the ground shaking; other areas in the United States are also prone to earthquakes. The dwelling coverage of most homeowners insurance policies doesn't cover damage caused by an earthquake, so homeowners must purchase an earthquake insurance rider to their homeowners policy or a separate earthquake policy to protect them from this risk.

encumbrance: An encumbrance is a right or interest someone else holds in a homeowner's property that affects its title or limits its use. A mortgage, for example, is a money encumbrance that affects a property's title by making it security for repayment of the loan. A right-of-way for someone to pass over land or an easement granted to the local utility company to run sewer lines under a property are examples of non-money encumbrances.

equity: Equity is the difference between the market value of a house and the amount the homeowner owes on it. For example, if your house is worth $230,000 and you have an outstanding mortgage of $160,000, your equity is $70,000.

escrow: Escrow is the holding — by a neutral third party called, naturally, an escrow officer — of important documents and money related to the sale of a house. After a seller accepts a buyer's offer to purchase property, the buyer doesn't immedi- ately move in. A period follows when contingencies have to be met or waived. During this period, the escrow service holds the buyer's down payment and documents pertaining to the sale. "Closing escrow" means that the deal is completed. Among other duties, the escrow officer makes sure that all the players in the transaction — mortgage companies, real estate agents, and, of course, the seller — are paid the amount that's due them.

exclusive agency listing: An exclusive agency listing is a listing contract between property owners and a real estate broker that's very similar to an exclusive right to sell listing except that the property owners specifically reserve the right to sell the house themselves without compensating the listing broker if they find the buyer. (See also *listing contract.*)

exclusive right-to-sell: An exclusive right-to-sell listing is a listing contract between a property owner and a real estate broker in which the property owner agrees to compensate the listing broker if anyone, including the property owner, sells the house during the listing period. (See also *listing contract.*)

fair market value (FMV): FMV is the price a market-educated buyer will pay and a market-savvy seller will accept for property given that neither the seller nor the buyer is under duress caused by a divorce, an unanticipated job transfer, or some other circumstance that puts either party under pressure to perform quickly.

Fannie Mae: See *Federal National Mortgage Association.*

Federal Home Loan Mortgage Corporation (FHLMC): The FHLMC (or Freddie Mac) is one of the best-known institutions in the secondary mortgage market. *Freddie Mac* buys mortgages from banks and other mortgage-lending institutions and, in turn, sells these mortgages to investors. These loan investments are considered safe because Freddie Mac buys mortgages only from companies that conform to its stringent mortgage regulations, and Freddie Mac guarantees the repayment of *principal* and interest on the mortgages that it sells.

Federal Housing Administration (FHA) mortgage: FHA mortgages are marketed to people with modest means. The main advantage of these mortgages is that they require a small down payment (usually between 3 and 5 percent of a home's purchase price). FHA mortgages also offer competitive interest rates — typically 0.5 to 1 percent below the interest rates on other mortgages. The downside of an FHA mortgage is that the buyer must purchase mortgage default insurance (see *private mortgage insurance*).

Federal National Mortgage Association (FNMA): The FNMA (or Fannie Mae) is one of the best-known institutions in the secondary mortgage market. *Fannie Mae* buys mortgages from banks and other mortgage-lending institutions and, in turn, sells them to investors. These loan investments are considered safe because Fannie Mae buys mortgages only from companies that conform to its stringent mortgage regulations, and Fannie Mae guarantees the repayment of principal and interest on the loans that it sells.

fixed-rate mortgage: A fixed-rate mortgage lets you lock into an interest rate (for example, 7.5 percent) that never changes during the entire life (term) of a 15- or 30-year mortgage. The mortgage payment is the same amount each and every month. Compare fixed-rate mortgages with *adjustable-rate mortgages.*

flood insurance: If you suspect even a remote chance that your area may flood, having flood insurance is prudent. In federally designated flood areas, flood insurance is required in order to obtain conventional mortgage financing.

foreclosure: Foreclosure is the legal process by which a mortgage lender takes possession of and sells property to attempt to satisfy indebtedness. If you default on your loan and the lender deems that you're incapable of making payments, you may lose your home to foreclosure. Being in default, however, doesn't always lead to foreclosure. Some lenders are lenient and help you work out a solution if they see that your financial problems are temporary.

formula: Formula is jargon for the method used to calculate the revised interest rate on an adjustable-rate mortgage. Add the margin to the index to get the adjusted interest rate (margin + index = interest rate).

Freddie Mac: See *Federal Home Loan Mortgage Corporation.*

For Sale By Owner (FSBO): A FSBO property isn't listed for sale through a real estate broker. Instead the homeowner tries to sell the home on his own.

graduated-payment mortgage: With a graduated-payment mortgage, monthly payments are increased by a predetermined amount and schedule. For example, your monthly payment increases 5 percent annually for seven years. Thereafter, your payments stay constant for the rest of your loan's term.

home-equity loan: A home-equity loan is technical jargon for what used to be called a second mortgage. With this type of loan, a homeowner borrows against the equity in her house. If used wisely, a home-equity loan can pay off consumer debt, which is usually at a higher interest rate than a home-equity loan and isn't tax-deductible. Homeowners can also use home-equity loans for other short-term needs, such as for payments on a remodeling project.

homeowners insurance: This type of insurance is required and necessary — period. A homeowners insurance policy protects what's likely your most valuable asset — your home. The most fundamental component of the policy is the "dwelling coverage" that covers the cost to repair or rebuild your house in the event of fire, storm, or other insured real property damage. The liability insurance portion of this policy protects you against accidents that occur on your property. Another essential piece is the personal property coverage that pays to replace your lost worldly possessions and usually totals 50 to 75 percent of the dwelling coverage. Finally, get *flood* or *earthquake insurance* if you're in an area susceptible to these natural disasters. As with other types of insurance, get the highest deductibles with which you are comfortable.

home warranty plan: A home warranty plan is a type of insurance that covers repairs to specific parts of a house for a predetermined time period. Because home warranty plans typically cover small-potato items, such plans generally aren't worth buying. Instead, spend your money on a good *house inspection* before you buy the house in order to identify any major problems, such as trouble with electrical or plumbing systems.

house inspection: Like *homeowners insurance,* we think that a house inspection is a necessity when you're buying and a smart thing to do when you're selling. The following items should be inspected: overall condition of the property, inside and out; electrical, heating, and plumbing systems;

foundation; roof; pest control and dry rot; and seismic, slide risk. A good premarketing house inspection can save you money and negotiate hassles by helping you find corrective work problems prior to putting your house on the market so you have lead time to either make the necessary repairs or develop a plan for dealing with them.

hybrid loan: A hybrid loan combines the features of *fixed-rate* and *adjustable-rate mortgages.* The initial *interest rate* for a hybrid loan may be fixed for the first three to ten years of the loan (as opposed to only six to twelve months for a standard adjustable-rate mortgage), and then adjusted biannually or annually. The longer the initial interest rate remains the same, the higher the interest rate is. These hybrid loans are best for people who plan to own their house for a short time (less than ten years) and who don't like the volatility of a typical adjustable-rate mortgage.

index: An index measures the current level of market interest rates. Adding the index to the margin is the formula for determining the specific interest rate on an adjustable-rate mortgage. One index used on some mortgages is the six-month treasury bill. If the going rate for these treasury bills is 6 percent and the margin on your loan is 2.25 percent, your interest rate is 8.25 percent. Other common indexes used are certificates of deposit index, the 11th District Cost of Funds index, and the LIBOR index.

interest rate: Interest is what lenders charge borrowers to use their money. The greater the risk of not getting the money back, the more a lender charges to use it. In general, interest charges are accrued as a percentage of the amount borrowed; that percentage is known as the interest rate.

joint tenancy: Joint tenancy is a form of co-ownership that gives each tenant equal interest and rights in the property, including the right of survivorship. At the death of one joint tenant, ownership automatically transfers to the surviving joint tenant. This form of ownership is most appropriate for unmarried people. Some of the limitations of joint tenancy are (first) that each person must own an equal share of the house and (second) that the right of survivorship is terminated if one person transfers his or her interest in the property by deed to a third party.

lease-option: A property that tenants can lease with an option to purchase at a later date has a lease-option contract. These contracts generally require an upfront payment (called "option consideration") to secure the purchase option. The consideration is usually credited toward the down payment when the tenant exercises his or her option to buy the home. An important factor in a lease-option agreement is what portion of the monthly rent payments (typically one-third) is applied toward the purchase price if the tenant buys. Rent is usually slightly higher because of the lease-option privilege.

leverage: Remember playing with levers in high school physics? Using leverage, you could exert a great deal of force with little effort. Your flimsy-looking cash can also function like a crowbar when you borrow money to help you make an investment. For example, suppose that you make a 20 percent down payment on a $200,000 house and borrow the $160,000 difference. If you consider the fact that you control a $160,000 property with only a $40,000 investment, you can already see leverage at work. But the potential power of that leverage comes into play if the house appreciates — let's say to $240,000. Now you've made a $40,000 profit on a $40,000 investment — a 100-percent return, thanks to leveraging. However, if you find that your house has

declined in value since you bought it, you're painfully aware that leverage cuts both ways. (See also *return on investment.*)

lien: A misspelling of the word "line" (just kidding). In real estate, a lien is a legal claim or encumbrance on a property that's used as security for repayment of an outstanding debt such as a mortgage, unpaid taxes, money owed to a contractor, and so on. Liens must be paid off before a property can be sold or title transferred to a subsequent buyer. The liens that are a matter of public record appear on a property's preliminary report.

life cap: The total amount that an *adjustable-rate mortgage* interest rate and monthly payment can fluctuate up or down during the duration of the loan is determined by the life cap. The life cap is different from the *periodic cap* that limits the extent to which an interest rate can change up or down in any one *adjustment period.*

liquidated damages: In many real estate contracts, buyers and sellers, at the beginning of the transaction, agree on the liquidated damages — how much money will be awarded to one party if the other party violates the terms of the contract without good cause. Buyers, for example, generally limit their losses to the amount of their deposit. Discuss the advisability of using the liquidated damages provision with a lawyer or real estate agent.

listing broker: The real estate broker who lists a property for sale and who, if the terms of the listing contract are satisfied, will be compensated, typically in the form of a commission on the selling price of the house, when the property sells.

listing contract: This term is an employment contract between a property seller and a real estate broker. Under the terms of a listing contract, the property seller agrees to compensate the broker for procuring a ready, willing, and able buyer for the property.

listing presentation: A proposal by a real estate broker or agent outlining how a property would be marketed and recommending an asking price based on a *comparable market analysis*.

lock-in: A lock-in is a mortgage lender's written commitment to a specified interest rate to the home buyer, provided that the loan is closed within a set period of time. The lock-in also usually specifies the number of points to be paid at closing. Most lenders don't lock-in unless the home buyer has made an offer on the property, and the property has been appraised. For the privilege of locking in the rate in advance of the closing of a loan, home buyers may pay a slight interest rate premium.

margin: The margin is the amount that's added to the *index* in order to calculate the *interest rate* for an *adjustable-rate mortgage*. Most loans have margins around 2.5 percent. Unlike the *index* (which constantly moves up and down), the margin never changes during the life of the loan. See *formula*.

market value: See *fair market value*.

marketable title: A title to property that's free and clear of objectionable liens and encumbrances and thus acceptable to buyers and mortgage lenders.

mechanic's lien: An encumbrance filed on title to a property by contractors or workmen who claim that the owner still owes them money for labor or materials expended to improve the property.

mediation of disputes: Because mediation is faster and less expensive than arbitration or litigation in a court of law, mediation is often the first formal step taken to resolve simple contract disputes. In mediation, buyers and sellers present their differences to a neutral mediator who doesn't have the power to impose a settlement on either party. Instead, the mediator helps buyers and sellers work together to reach a mutually acceptable solution of their differences. Statistically speaking, over 80 percent of the cases that go through mediation are resolved at that level. Parties who seek mediation spare themselves the additional time and money required to pursue their differences in arbitration or a court of law. (See also *arbitration*.)

mortgage broker: A mortgage broker buys mortgages wholesale from lenders, marks the mortgages up (typically from 0.5 to 1 percent), and then sells them to buyers. A good mortgage broker is most helpful for people who don't shop around on their own for a mortgage or for people who have blemishes on their credit reports.

mortgage life insurance: Mortgage life insurance guarantees that the lender will get the loan money back in the sad event that the borrower meets an untimely demise. If you need life insurance, buy low-cost, high-quality term life insurance instead of mortgage life insurance, which is basically overpriced term insurance. We don't recommend the purchase of mortgage life insurance.

multiple listing service (MLS): An MLS is a cooperative arrangement among real estate brokers in a particular area to share their property listings with each other. Usually a computer-based service, an MLS allows member brokers and agents to track all property listed for sale with cooperating brokers who participate in the MLS.

negative amortization: Although it sounds like it, this term isn't from science fiction. Still, you can say that it describes a kind of black hole. Negative amortization occurs when an outstanding mortgage balance increases despite the fact that the borrower is making the required monthly payments. Usually this condition only happens with adjustable-rate mortgages that cap the increase in the monthly payment but do not cap the interest rate. Therefore, if the interest rate rises high enough, the monthly payments won't cover all the interest that the borrower actually owes. If you've ever watched your credit card balance snowball as you made only the minimum monthly payment, then you already have experience with this phenomenon. Avoid negative amortization loans!

open listing: An open listing is a non-exclusive listing contract that may be given to any number of real estate brokers. A seller is obligated to compensate the first broker who either secures a buyer ready, willing, and able to meet the terms of the listing contract or procures an acceptable offer. If the seller finds the buyer, he or she doesn't have to pay any of the brokers a commission.

origination fee: See *points.*

partnership: A partnership is a way for unmarried people to take title of a property together. Partnerships most often occur among people who have a business relationship and who buy the property as either a business asset or for investment purposes. If you intend to buy property with partners, have a real estate lawyer prepare a written partnership agreement for all the partners to sign before making an offer to purchase.

periodic cap: This cap limits the amount that the interest rate of an *adjustable-rate*

mortgage can change up or down in one adjustment period. See also *caps.*

points: Also known as the loan's origination fee, points are interest charges paid upfront when a borrower closes on a loan. The charges are calculated as a percentage of the total loan amount — one point is equal to 1 percent of the loan amount. For a $100,000 loan, one point costs $1,000. Generally speaking, the more points that a loan has, the lower its interest rate should be. All the points that you pay on a purchase mortgage are deductible in the year that you pay them. If you refinance your mortgage, however, the points that you pay at the time that you refinance must be amortized over the life of the loan. If you get a 30-year mortgage when you refinance, for example, you can deduct only one-thirtieth of the points on your taxes each year.

prepayment penalty: One advantage of most mortgages is that borrowers can make additional payments to pay the loan off faster if they have the inclination and the money to do so. A prepayment penalty discourages borrowers from doing this by penalizing them for early payments. Some states prohibit lenders from penalizing people who prepay their loans. Avoid mortgages that penalize prepayment!

principal: The principal is the original amount that a person borrows for a loan. If a home buyer borrows $180,000, the principal is $180,000. Each monthly mortgage payment consists of a portion of principal that must be repaid plus the interest that the lender is charging for the use of the money. During the early years of a mortgage, the loan payment is primarily interest. Gradually, over time, more and more of the monthly payments go toward principal and less toward interest.

private mortgage insurance (PMI): If the down payment is less than 20 percent of a home's purchase price, the borrower will probably need to purchase PMI (also known as "mortgage default insurance"). Lenders feel that homeowners who can only come up with small down payments are more likely to default on their loans. Therefore, lenders make these homeowners buy PMI, which reimburses them the loan amount in case the borrower does default. Private mortgage insurance can add hundreds of dollars per year to loan costs. After the equity in the property increases to 20 percent, borrowers no longer need the insurance. Don't confuse this insurance with *mortgage life insurance*.

probate sale: A probate sale is the sale of a home that occurs when a homeowner dies and the property is to be divided among inheritors or sold to pay debts. The executor of the estate organizes the probate sale, and a probate court judge oversees the process. The highest bidder receives the property.

property tax: You have to pay a property tax on the home you own. Annually, property tax averages 1 to 2 percent of a home's value, but property tax rates vary widely throughout this great land. As one of the conditions of selling a house, property taxes are prorated (see *prorations*) and must be paid up to the date of sale.

prorations: Certain items (such as property taxes and homeowners association dues) are continuing expenses that must be prorated (distributed) between the buyers and sellers at close of escrow. If the buyers, for example, owe the seller money for property taxes that the seller paid in advance, the prorated amount of money due the seller at the close of escrow appears as a credit to the seller from the buyers.

real estate agent: Real estate agents are the worker bees of real estate sales. Also called "salespeople," agents are supervised by a real estate *broker*. Agents are licensed by the state; typically their pay is from commissions generated by selling property.

Realtor: A Realtor is a real estate *broker* or agent who belongs to the National Association of Realtors, a trade association whose members agree to its ways of doing business and code of ethics. The National Association of Realtors offers its members seminars and courses that deal with real estate topics.

redlining: Redlining is the discriminatory refusal to provide mortgage loans or homeowners insurance policies in certain neighborhoods due to a higher rate of problems with loans and insurance policies in such areas. Redlining is illegal!

refinance: Refinance, or "refi," is a fancy word for taking out a new mortgage loan (usually at a lower interest rate) to pay off an existing mortgage (generally at a higher interest rate). Although this step can be lucrative in the long run, refinancing can be an expensive hassle in the short run. Carefully weigh the costs and benefits of refinancing.

return on investment (ROI): The return on investment is the percentage of profit that an investor makes on an investment. If, for example, you put $1,000 into an investment and a year later sell the investment for $1,100, you make $100. You calculate ROI by dividing the profit ($100) by your original investment ($1,000), which equals a 10 percent return. (See also *leverage.*)

reverse mortgage: A reverse mortgage is a way for elderly homeowners, especially those who are low on cash, to tap into their home's equity without selling their home or moving from it. Specifically, a lending institution makes a check out to a homeowner each month, and the home-owner can use the check as he or she wants. This money is really a loan against the value of the home. Because it's a loan, the money is income tax-free when the homeowner receives it. The downside of these loans is that they deplete the equity in the estate, the fees and interest rates tend to be on the high side, and some require repayment within a certain number of years.

second mortgage: A second mortgage is a mortgage that ranks after a first mortgage in priority of recording. In the event of a foreclosure, the proceeds from the sale of the house are used to pay off the loans in the order in which they were recorded. Homeowners can have a third (or even a fourth) mortgage, but the further down the trough the mortgage is, the greater the risk that no leftovers will be available to feed it — hence, the higher interest rate that homeowners pay on junior mort-gages. (See also *home-equity loan.*)

the 72-hour clause: The 72-hour clause is commonly inserted into real estate pur-chase offers when the purchase of a home is contingent on the sale of the buyer's current house. The seller accepts the buyer's offer but reserves the right to accept a better offer if one should happen to come along. However, the seller can't do this arbitrarily. If the seller receives an offer that he wants to accept, he must notify the buyer of that fact in writing. The buyer then has 72 hours (though the allotted amount of time can vary) from the seller's notification to remove the contingency-of-sale clause and move on with the purchase; otherwise, the buyer's offer is wiped out.

subagents: Many commonly used listing contracts permit the listing broker to delegate the work of procuring a buyer for the property to his or her salespeople as well as to cooperating brokers. All these people are classified as subagents. The listing broker is, however, liable for any work delegated to or performed by these subagents.

subprime loan: The term applied to loans offered to borrowers viewed as riskier. Lenders charge higher rates on such loans.

tax deductible: Tax deductible refers to payments that people may deduct against federal and state taxable income. The interest portion of mortgage payments, loan points, and property taxes are tax deductible. Taxpayers can use tax deductible items to shelter some employ-ment income, which is not!

teaser rate: Otherwise known as the initial interest rate, the teaser rate is the attractively low interest rate that most adjustable-rate mortgages start with. Don't be sucked into a mortgage because it has a low teaser rate. Look at the mort-gage's formula (index+ margin = interest rate) for a more reliable indication of the loan's future interest rate — the interest rate that will apply after the loan is "fully indexed."

tenancy-in-common: Tenancy-in-common is probably the best way for unmarried co-owners to take title to a home (except for those unmarried co-owners who are involved in close, long-term relationships — see joint tenancy). Tenancy-in-common doesn't require co-owners to own equal shares of the property. Tenancy-in-common also doesn't provide for the right of survivor-ship that automatically passes the deceased partner's ownership to the survivor without probate. The deceased's share of the property involved in a tenancy-in-common passes to the person named to receive that share of the property in the deceased's will or living trust.

title insurance: Title insurance covers the legal fees and expenses necessary to defend a property's title against claims that may be made against the ownership of the property. The extent of the coverage depends on whether the homeowner has an owner's standard coverage or extended-coverage title insurance policy. To get a mortgage, homeowners also have to buy a lender's title insurance policy to protect the lender against title risks.

top producer: A top producer is a real estate agent who sells a great deal of real estate. Just because someone is a top producer, however, doesn't guarantee that she's your best choice as a listing agent. Make sure that the agent has enough time to serve you properly, that the agent knows property values in your area, and that the agent has been successful selling properties like yours.

townhouses: These homes are a row or attached home. Townhouses are cheaper than single-family homes because they use common walls and roofs, and they save land. In terms of investment appreciation potential, townhouses lie somewhere between single-family homes and condominiums.

transfer disclosure statement (TDS): Some states require that sellers give prospective buyers a written disclosure regarding all known property defects and all known material facts that may affect the property's value or desirability. So if you know for a fact that the world's largest garbage dump will be built directly behind your house next year, 'fess up.

VA (Department of Veterans Affairs) loans: Congress passed the Serviceman's Readjustment Act, commonly known as the GI Bill of Rights, in 1944. One of its provisions enables the VA to help eligible people on active duty and veterans obtain mortgages on favorable terms (generally 0.5 to 1 percent below the rate currently being charged on conventional loans) to buy primary residences. Like the *FHA*, the VA has no money of its own. It guarantees loans granted by conventional lending institutions that participate in VA mortgage programs.

zoning: Certain city and county government bodies have the power to regulate the use of land and buildings. For example, the neighborhood where your house is located is probably zoned for residential use. It most likely also has zoning codes or ordinances to regulate building heights, yard sizes, and the percentage of lot coverage by buildings. Thanks to zoning codes, you don't have to worry about an auto wrecking shop being built next door to your house.

Index

Notes

Notes

Notes

Notes

BUSINESS, CAREERS & PERSONAL FINANCE

0-7645-9847-3

0-7645-2431-3

Also available:
- Business Plans Kit For Dummies
  0-7645-9794-9
- Economics For Dummies
  0-7645-5726-2
- Grant Writing For Dummies
  0-7645-8416-2
- Home Buying For Dummies
  0-7645-5331-3
- Managing For Dummies
  0-7645-1771-6
- Marketing For Dummies
  0-7645-5600-2

- Personal Finance For Dummies
  0-7645-2590-5*
- Resumes For Dummies
  0-7645-5471-9
- Selling For Dummies
  0-7645-5363-1
- Six Sigma For Dummies
  0-7645-6798-5
- Small Business Kit For Dummies
  0-7645-5984-2
- Starting an eBay Business For Dummies
  0-7645-6924-4
- Your Dream Career For Dummies
  0-7645-9795-7

HOME & BUSINESS COMPUTER BASICS

0-470-05432-8

0-471-75421-8

Also available:
- Cleaning Windows Vista For Dummies
  0-471-78293-9
- Excel 2007 For Dummies
  0-470-03737-7
- Mac OS X Tiger For Dummies
  0-7645-7675-5
- MacBook For Dummies
  0-470-04859-X
- Macs For Dummies
  0-470-04849-2
- Office 2007 For Dummies
  0-470-00923-3

- Outlook 2007 For Dummies
  0-470-03830-6
- PCs For Dummies
  0-7645-8958-X
- Salesforce.com For Dummies
  0-470-04893-X
- Upgrading & Fixing Laptops For Dummies
  0-7645-8959-8
- Word 2007 For Dummies
  0-470-03658-3
- Quicken 2007 For Dummies
  0-470-04600-7

FOOD, HOME, GARDEN, HOBBIES, MUSIC & PETS

0-7645-8404-9

0-7645-9904-6

Also available:
- Candy Making For Dummies
  0-7645-9734-5
- Card Games For Dummies
  0-7645-9910-0
- Crocheting For Dummies
  0-7645-4151-X
- Dog Training For Dummies
  0-7645-8418-9
- Healthy Carb Cookbook For Dummies
  0-7645-8476-6
- Home Maintenance For Dummies
  0-7645-5215-5

- Horses For Dummies
  0-7645-9797-3
- Jewelry Making & Beading For Dummies
  0-7645-2571-9
- Orchids For Dummies
  0-7645-6759-4
- Puppies For Dummies
  0-7645-5255-4
- Rock Guitar For Dummies
  0-7645-5356-9
- Sewing For Dummies
  0-7645-6847-7
- Singing For Dummies
  0-7645-2475-5

INTERNET & DIGITAL MEDIA

0-470-04529-9

0-470-04894-8

Also available:
- Blogging For Dummies
  0-471-77084-1
- Digital Photography For Dummies
  0-7645-9802-3
- Digital Photography All-in-One Desk Reference For Dummies
  0-470-03743-1
- Digital SLR Cameras and Photography For Dummies
  0-7645-9803-1
- eBay Business All-in-One Desk Reference For Dummies
  0-7645-8438-3
- HDTV For Dummies
  0-470-09673-X

- Home Entertainment PCs For Dummies
  0-470-05523-5
- MySpace For Dummies
  0-470-09529-6
- Search Engine Optimization For Dummies
  0-471-97998-8
- Skype For Dummies
  0-470-04891-3
- The Internet For Dummies
  0-7645-8996-2
- Wiring Your Digital Home For Dummies
  0-471-91830-X

* Separate Canadian edition also available

† Separate U.K. edition also available

Available wherever books are sold. For more information or to order direct: U.S. customers visit www.dummies.com or call 1-877-762-2974. U.K. customers visit www.wileyeurope.com or call 0800 243407. Canadian customers visit www.wiley.ca or call 1-800-567-4797.

SPORTS, FITNESS, PARENTING, RELIGION & SPIRITUALITY

0-471-76871-5

0-7645-7841-3

Also available:
- Catholicism For Dummies
  0-7645-5391-7
- Exercise Balls For Dummies
  0-7645-5623-1
- Fitness For Dummies
  0-7645-7851-0
- Football For Dummies
  0-7645-3936-1
- Judaism For Dummies
  0-7645-5299-6
- Potty Training For Dummies
  0-7645-5417-4
- Buddhism For Dummies
  0-7645-5359-3

- Pregnancy For Dummies
  0-7645-4483-7 †
- Ten Minute Tone-Ups For Dummies
  0-7645-7207-5
- NASCAR For Dummies
  0-7645-7681-X
- Religion For Dummies
  0-7645-5264-3
- Soccer For Dummies
  0-7645-5229-5
- Women in the Bible For Dummies
  0-7645-8475-8

TRAVEL

0-7645-7749-2

0-7645-6945-7

Also available:
- Alaska For Dummies
  0-7645-7746-8
- Cruise Vacations For Dummies
  0-7645-6941-4
- England For Dummies
  0-7645-4276-1
- Europe For Dummies
  0-7645-7529-5
- Germany For Dummies
  0-7645-7823-5
- Hawaii For Dummies
  0-7645-7402-7

- Italy For Dummies
  0-7645-7386-1
- Las Vegas For Dummies
  0-7645-7382-9
- London For Dummies
  0-7645-4277-X
- Paris For Dummies
  0-7645-7630-5
- RV Vacations For Dummies
  0-7645-4442-X
- Walt Disney World & Orlando
  For Dummies
  0-7645-9660-8

GRAPHICS, DESIGN & WEB DEVELOPMENT

0-7645-8815-X

0-7645-9571-7

Also available:
- 3D Game Animation For Dummies
  0-7645-8789-7
- AutoCAD 2006 For Dummies
  0-7645-8925-3
- Building a Web Site For Dummies
  0-7645-7144-3
- Creating Web Pages For Dummies
  0-470-08030-2
- Creating Web Pages All-in-One Desk
  Reference For Dummies
  0-7645-4345-8
- Dreamweaver 8 For Dummies
  0-7645-9649-7

- InDesign CS2 For Dummies
  0-7645-9572-5
- Macromedia Flash 8 For Dummies
  0-7645-9691-8
- Photoshop CS2 and Digital
  Photography For Dummies
  0-7645-9580-6
- Photoshop Elements 4 For Dummies
  0-471-77483-9
- Syndicating Web Sites with RSS Feeds
  For Dummies
  0-7645-8848-6
- Yahoo! SiteBuilder For Dummies
  0-7645-9800-7

NETWORKING, SECURITY, PROGRAMMING & DATABASES

0-7645-7728-X

0-471-74940-0

Also available:
- Access 2007 For Dummies
  0-470-04612-0
- ASP.NET 2 For Dummies
  0-7645-7907-X
- C# 2005 For Dummies
  0-7645-9704-3
- Hacking For Dummies
  0-470-05235-X
- Hacking Wireless Networks
  For Dummies
  0-7645-9730-2
- Java For Dummies
  0-470-08716-1

- Microsoft SQL Server 2005 For Dummies
  0-7645-7755-7
- Networking All-in-One Desk Reference
  For Dummies
  0-7645-9939-9
- Preventing Identity Theft For Dummies
  0-7645-7336-5
- Telecom For Dummies
  0-471-77085-X
- Visual Studio 2005 All-in-One Desk
  Reference For Dummies
  0-7645-9775-2
- XML For Dummies
  0-7645-8845-1

HEALTH & SELF-HELP

0-7645-8450-2   0-7645-4149-8

Also available:
- Bipolar Disorder For Dummies
  0-7645-8451-0
- Chemotherapy and Radiation
  For Dummies
  0-7645-7832-4
- Controlling Cholesterol For Dummies
  0-7645-5440-9
- Diabetes For Dummies
  0-7645-6820-5* †
- Divorce For Dummies
  0-7645-8417-0 †

- Fibromyalgia For Dummies
  0-7645-5441-7
- Low-Calorie Dieting For Dummies
  0-7645-9905-4
- Meditation For Dummies
  0-471-77774-9
- Osteoporosis For Dummies
  0-7645-7621-6
- Overcoming Anxiety For Dummies
  0-7645-5447-6
- Reiki For Dummies
  0-7645-9907-0
- Stress Management For Dummies
  0-7645-5144-2

EDUCATION, HISTORY, REFERENCE & TEST PREPARATION

0-7645-8381-6   0-7645-9554-7

Also available:
- The ACT For Dummies
  0-7645-9652-7
- Algebra For Dummies
  0-7645-5325-9
- Algebra Workbook For Dummies
  0-7645-8467-7
- Astronomy For Dummies
  0-7645-8465-0
- Calculus For Dummies
  0-7645-2498-4
- Chemistry For Dummies
  0-7645-5430-1
- Forensics For Dummies
  0-7645-5580-4

- Freemasons For Dummies
  0-7645-9796-5
- French For Dummies
  0-7645-5193-0
- Geometry For Dummies
  0-7645-5324-0
- Organic Chemistry I For Dummies
  0-7645-6902-3
- The SAT I For Dummies
  0-7645-7193-1
- Spanish For Dummies
  0-7645-5194-9
- Statistics For Dummies
  0-7645-5423-9

Get smart @ dummies.com®

- **Find a full list of Dummies titles**
- **Look into loads of FREE on-site articles**
- **Sign up for FREE eTips e-mailed to you weekly**
- **See what other products carry the Dummies name**
- **Shop directly from the Dummies bookstore**
- **Enter to win new prizes every month!**

* Separate Canadian edition also available
† Separate U.K. edition also available

Available wherever books are sold. For more information or to order direct: U.S. customers visit www.dummies.com or call 1-877-762-2974.
U.K. customers visit www.wileyeurope.com or call 0800 243407. Canadian customers visit www.wiley.ca or call 1-800-567-4797.